SOCIALIST REGISTER 2 0 0 8

THE SOCIALIST REGISTER
Founded in 1964

Visit our website at:
http://www.socialistregister.com
for a detailed list of all our issues, order forms and an online selection of
past prefaces and essays, and to find out how to join our listserv.

..

SOCIALIST REGISTER 2008

GLOBAL FLASHPOINTS
Reactions to Imperialism and Neoliberalism

Edited by LEO PANITCH and COLIN LEYS

THE MERLIN PRESS, LONDON
MONTHLY REVIEW PRESS, NEW YORK
FERNWOOD PUBLISHING, HALIFAX

First published in 2007
by The Merlin Press Ltd.
96 Monnow Street
Monmouth
NP25 3EQ
Wales

www.merlinpress.co.uk

British Library Cataloguing in Publication Data is available from the British
Library

Library and Archives Canada Cataloguing in Publication
Socialist register 2008 : global flashpoints : reactions to
imperialism and neoliberalism / Leo Panitch and Colin Leys, editors.
Includes bibliographical references and index.
1. World politics--21st century. 2. Socialism. 3. Social movements.
4. Neoliberalism. 5. Imperialism. I. Panitch, Leo, 1945- II. Leys, Colin, 1931-
HX44.5.S623 2007   909.83   C2007-903887-5

ISSN. 0081-0606

Published in the UK by The Merlin Press
ISBN. 9780850365870 Paperback
ISBN.9780850365863 Hardback

Published in the USA by Monthly Review Press
ISBN. 9781583671672 Paperback

Published in Canada by Fernwood Publishing
ISBN. 9781552662540 Paperback

Printed in the UK by Cromwell Press, Trowbridge, Wiltshire

CONTENTS

CONTRIBUTORS

Bashir Abu-Manneh teaches in the Department of English, Barnard College, New York.

Gilbert Achcar is professor of Development Studies and International Relations at the School of Oriental and African Studies (SOAS), London.

Aijaz Ahmad is a senior editorial consultant at Frontline Magazine, Chennai.

Gregory Albo is professor in the Department of Political Science, York University, Toronto.

Sabah Alnasseri teaches in the Department of Political Science, York University, Toronto.

Elmar Altvater is at the Otto Suhr Institute for Political Science, Free University, Berlin.

Edur Velasco Arregui is an Economics professor at the Universidad Autonoma Metropolitana (UAM) in Mexico City and a leading trade union dissident.

Yildiz Atasoy teaches at the Department of Sociology and Anthropology at Simon Fraser University, Vancouver.

Asef Bayat is Academic Director of the International Institute for the Study of Islam in the Modern World (ISIM), Leiden.

Atilio Boron is professor of Political Science at the University of Buenos Aires and Director of the Latin American Program of Distance Education in the Social Sciences (PLED) at Centro Cultural de la Cooperación, Buenos Aires.

Emilia Castorina is a doctoral candidate at the York University Department of Political Science, Toronto.

Ana Esther Ceceña is at the Institute for Economic Research at the Universidad Nacional Autónoma de Mexico (UNAM), Mexico City.

Wes Enzinna is an award winning investigative journalist and a graduate student in Latin American Studies at University of California, Berkeley.

Marta Harnecker has been an active participant in Venezuela's Bolivarian revolution and an adviser to that country's president, Hugo Chavez.

Raghu Krishnan is a translator and interpreter in Toronto. He spent a number of years in France in the 1990s.

Margarita López Maya is a historian at the Center for Development Studies at the Central University of Venezuela, Caracas.

Kim Moody was a co-founder of Labor Notes and is a senior research fellow at the Centre for Research in Employment Studies at the University of Hertfordshire.

William I. Robinson is professor of Sociology at the University of California, Santa Barbara.

Richard Roman teaches in the Department of Political Science at York University, Toronto.

Alfredo Saad-Filho is currently Head of the Department of Development Studies at the School of Oriental and African Studies (SOAS), London.

João Pedro Stédile is a member of the national board of the Movimento dos Trabalhadores Rurais Sem Terra (MST) and of Via Campesina-Brasil.

G.M. Tamás is a former member of the Hungarian parliament and currently deputy chair of ATTAC Hungary.

Adrien Thomas is a doctoral candidate in political science at University Paris I – Panthéon Sorbonne.

PREFACE

For some twenty years after the Socialist Register was founded in 1964 – until it was decided in the 1980s to give each volume a specific theme – the cover always described it as 'a survey of movements and ideas'. The communist and socialist parties and labour movements, the emerging new social movements, and the national liberation and left nationalist forces in the Third World, constituted the political topography to which the survey could be presumed to refer. Today this topography has radically changed, making any attempt to map today's movements and ideas from a socialist perspective a difficult challenge. Nonetheless, thirty years after the inauguration of the neoliberal counter-revolution, and a decade after the open reassertion of US imperialism, the challenge needs to be taken up, and this, the 44th volume of the Register, is an attempt to do so.

The current conjuncture is defined by the accumulating contradictions that now face both neoliberalism and imperialism, as it becomes increasingly evident that not only can the tide of capitalist globalization not raise all boats, but that the American empire cannot impose its military might at will. The exhaustion of the confident bravura with which both the neoliberal project and the imperial Project for a New American Century were launched is now apparent, and reflects significant cracks in the edifice of capitalist political and economic power. Neoliberalism's economic momentum continues, and the foundations of the US empire remain strong, but resistance and challenges, both reactionary and progressive, and in some cases even potentially socialist, have become more and more widespread and strong.

Astonishingly enough, in face of the appalling suffering and loss to which this resistance and these challenges are a response, there are people in high places, sustained by a good number of intellectuals, who try to paint imperialism and neoliberalism as benevolent and beneficent – as a latter-day version of the old colonial mission to bring civilization to the heathen, which is itself accordingly being rehabilitated. Gordon Brown, for example, now Prime Minister of the United Kingdom, declared in 2005 that 'the days of Britain having to apologize for its colonial history are over… we should talk, and rightly so, about British values… tolerance, liberty, civic duty, that grew in Britain and influenced the rest of the world'. And indeed, the recent celebrations that marked the 200th anniversary of the banning of the slave trade mostly focused on the benevolent work of William Wilborforce and the British state, and overlooked the role of Africans who revolted against slavery, as in Haiti, and who asserted their humanity in the face of European slave traders and slave-owners in the colonial states. As a minimum, the courageous struggles being waged against contemporary colonialism and neocolonialism give the lie to such shameful falsifications of history, past and present.

Our aim in this volume, however, is to offer careful and sober analyses of the political forces that have produced today's 'flashpoints' of reaction to imperialism and neoliberalism, focusing particularly, but not exclusively, on the Middle East and Latin America. Of these two major regions where such 'flashpoints' are concentrated, one is at the forefront of the contradictions of empire, the other of the contradictions of neoliberalism, although the contradictions of imperial power and of neoliberal globalization – and the reactions to them – are, of course, linked in both cases. Our goal has been to offer probing examinations of not only the potential but also the limitations of the politics that underlie these reactions.

As the first essay in the volume forcefully reminds us, to represent the confrontation in the Middle East – and now, thanks to Bush's declaration of 'war on terror', everywhere – in terms of 'Islamism' (or even 'Islam') versus 'the West', is to let ideology triumph over history and reason. The role of western interests and states in creating the conditions for the rise of radical Islamism, and the destruction of radical secular forces in Muslim countries from Palestine to Indonesia, is forgotten, and the diversity, humanity and natural rights of whole populations, and the secular and progressive forces among them, are buried under the blanket label of 'Muslim'. The political role of religion is never 'natural', but the product of both internal and external historical forces, as is amply demonstrated by our two essays which examine the role of religion in the Middle East.

The fact remains that anti-imperialism now increasingly finds expression through Islamist political forces – the essay here on the transformation of the resistance to the Israeli siege in Palestine also shows this – and the implications of this from a socialist and feminist perspective must be honestly confronted in any serious analysis of the conjuncture from the Left. It needs to be recognized as well that among the many versions of political Islam present on the scene today there are some with affinities to neoliberalism, exemplified by the new Islamic capitalists described in our essay on Turkey.

In Iraq the US empire has already suffered the greatest set-back in its history – greater than Vietnam. Unlike Vietnam, Iraq was not an exercise in mopping up after an old imperial power, and containing the spread of

Communism. On the contrary, Iraq was supposed to be the first instalment of the Project for a New American Century; the aim in occupying it was no less ambitious than in the occupation of Germany and Japan after World War Two, the goal being to remake the country and incorporate it into the American empire. The importance of the defeat of this project can hardly be overstated, yet even here the incongruous nature of Islamic anti-imperialism (as one of our essays puts it) needs to be carefully and soberly addressed. Our essay on Iraq insists that the conflict there cannot be understood as a civil war between Islamic sects; rather it reflects the way the correlation of political power and economic interest between the Bush administration and the Iraqi ruling and governing classes is playing itself out in the face of the resistance.

If it is the Middle East that has revealed most clearly the reality, as well as some of the limits, of the imperialism of our time, it is Latin America which has in the past decade revealed most clearly the nature and limitations of neoliberalism. The political forces that have come to the fore in one Latin American country after another have demonstrated once again that subordinate classes can still make history; they have put their needs and desires for a better world on the political agenda, and even brought their leaders to state power. As an essay in this volume which surveys the transformative possibilities of Latin America's 'pink tide' puts it, 'the current round of social and political struggle in Latin America highlights the changing relation between social movements of the left, the state, and global capitalism'. Yet the political forces involved represent very different political projects, and the limits of each of them, as well as their promise and potentiality, also require careful and sober analysis from a socialist perspective.

Attention focuses naturally on President Chavèz's project for a 'socialism of the 21st century' in Venezuela and his dramatic defeat of successive US-supported attempts to thwart it, the subject of two essays from sympathetic but differing perspectives; and on Brazil, the largest country in Latin America, represented here by an extended interview with the leader of the powerful Landless People's Movement, João Pedro Stédile – which also affords, indirectly, a critical commentary on the Workers' Party government of President Lula da Silva. The government of President Evo Morales' Movement for Socialism in Bolivia is also critically examined by an essay here in light of the experience of that country's Landless Peasant Movement; while another essay analyses the way 'democratic' neoliberalism under Kirschner in Argentina has proved able to substantially co-opt the protest 'from below' of the piqueteros. Two more essays focus on aspects of Latin American resistance that have had a strong impact in Mexico, especially: one addresses the powerful 'native' moment of this resistance (represented most famously by Chiapas's Zapatistas), while the other examines the extraordinary experience of the Oaxaca Commune which arose in 2006 out of a grassroots working-class rebellion in support of the Teachers' Union. Insofar as the latter offered an alternative model (albeit a precarious one, because of its local/regional character) not only to the electoralism of the left reformist parties, but also to the abstentionism of the Zapatistas, with their opposition to 'taking power', it is noteworthy that the essay here on Oaxaca concludes that 'it is mistaken to see the strategic choice as being between aspiring to manage the existing capitalist state apparatus, or ignoring it. This is a false dichotomy. The strategic task is to transform the nature of power through popular insurgency and organizational forms of control from below. This is the only way the people can rule and transform themselves as they transform society'.

While the Middle East and Latin America are the most obvious areas of resistance, they are not uniquely so. The unprecedented mobilization of six million Latino workers in the US itself on May Day 2006 can be seen as a 'harvest of empire' – the result, as our essay on this shows, of a wide variety of forms of organization, some of them novel, in face of the denial of basic rights to immigrant workers. Two further essays draw attention to significant reactions also taking place in Eastern and Western Europe. One, starting out from the riots that erupted in Budapest in 2006 after the exposure of the centre-left government's systematic practice of lying, followed by its imposition of radical austerity measures, goes on to show that the 'xenophobic, anti-Semitic, anti-Western, anti-immigrant agitation' that characterized these riots, reflected the complex and often perversely reactionary ways in which the populations of Eastern Europe generally have responded to the depredations of neoliberalism on their living standards and sense of self-worth. The other essay examines the very different and far more promising character of the three major episodes of resistance to neoliberalism in France in 2005-6 (the No vote to the European Constitution, the riots of immigrant youth in the French *banlieues*, and the student-led movement against labour-law reform), and puts them in perspective in relation to the earlier gradual demise of the 'French social model', on the one hand, and the factors that led to Sarkozy's victory in the 2007 election, on the other.

The volume concludes with a symposium on neoliberalism, which began as contributions to a workshop at the Historical Materialism/Socialist Register conference in London in December 2006, on 'What is the difference between a Keynesian and a Marxian critique of neoliberalism?' Taken together these essays make clear the coherence and power of the neoliberal project, which effective resistance must reckon with. At the same time they bring out its contradictions and costs – growing imbalances of world trade, the counterproductive character of military occupations, increasingly un-bearable inequalities, the inefficiencies of privatized monopolies, incapacity to avert the global ecological crisis, etc. But they also throw into relief the limitations of Left analyses as well as the struggles so far mobilized against all this.

These struggles have developed in the vacuum created by the exhaustion, or repression, of the old socialist and communist parties and politics, and many of them deserve admiration not only for their vision and courage, but also for being determined to avoid repeating past mistakes and adopting outworn forms of organization. On the other hand, what is needed is to find new and better ways to do some of the things the old parties set out to do – to educate the electorate, take power nationally, transform the state, develop popular capacities for both self-government and for making representatives accountable – without which resistance remains just resistance, and the task of transcending capitalism remains to be undertaken.

We thank all our contributors very warmly, while noting, as we always do, that neither they nor we necessarily agree with everything in the volume. We also want to thank several people who have played important parts in making this volume the success we believe it is, in spite of the many difficulties involved: our editorial assistant, Alan Zuege, our cover designer, Louis Mackay; and our colleagues at the Merlin Press, Adrian Howe and Tony Zurbrugg (not least for his contribution to preparing this preface). Above all, we owe thanks to our friend and editor for Latin America, Atilio Borón, for his major contribution in conducting the interview with João Pedro Stédile, for securing the translation services of Barbara Schijman, and for helping us in many other ways in putting together the Latin American part of the volume.

Finally we wish to report an important development concerning the future of the Register itself: the appointment of three associate editors who have agreed to start sharing the editing task with a view to reinforcing our presence among younger generations of socialists in several continents: Greg Albo in Toronto, Vivek Chibber in New York and Alfredo Saad-Filho in London. We are delighted that they have accepted, and are confident that their involvement will assure the Register's high quality and vigorous development in the coming years. And we are also sure they will be able to count on, as we once again did in planning this volume, the continuing support of the entire collective of contributing and corresponding editors.

LP
CL
July 2007

ISLAM, ISLAMISMS AND THE WEST

AIJAZ AHMAD

Identity politics in the widest sense is now quite the norm, and it comes to us in many guises, in the actual conduct of politics as well as in political theories and analyses, from the right, the left, the liberal centre. Culturalism, or the view that culture is the primary and determining instance of social existence, is a by-product of this identitarianism, and wherever politics and religion come to inflame each other, religion itself becomes synonymous with culture, and culture with religion, so that, for example, a constitutive difference between Islam and Christianity, as regards the scope for egalitarian politics in their respective zones, can be posited from the left, while the most hard-nosed geopolitical prescriptions can come to us from the right, in the guise of a discourse on religion, culture and civilization.

Countries where Muslims were the majority and which were therefore designated as 'Muslim countries' until just a decade or so ago, in a sort of shorthand, are now called 'Islamic countries', shifting the nomenclature from the softer matter of plain demography to the harder, narrower matter of religious belief. Among Muslims themselves, the two terms are held to be distinct. For most, being a Muslim mainly signifies the fact of birth in a Muslim family, at best a Muslim sub-culture within a wider national culture (Egyptian, Nigerian, Lebanese or whatever); while religion, even when observed, is lived as one of the many ingredients in one's complex social identity, which is always specific, and hence deeply tied to language, region, custom, class, and so on; religious observance, if any, remains largely local and personal. This subcultural Muslimness itself is contextual, deeply shaped by history, geography, politics, the larger multi-religious milieu, myriad rhythms of material life. To be a Bengali-speaking Muslim in the Indian state of West Bengal is not the same thing as being a Bengali-speaking Muslim in neighbouring Bangladesh; the immediate surroundings impinge decisively. The religious dimension of this Muslim subcultural existence may itself be refracted through sectarian and ideological particularity: Shia and Sunni, for instance, or various sub-sects among the Shia, the more puritanical sub-sects among the Sunnis such as the Wahhabi or the Ahl-e-Hadith, those others who may be inclined toward some transgressive tendency Sufic tradition, or still others who are inclined toward secular nationalism, communism, agnosticism, atheism, etc., and yet feel, existentially, part of a Muslim (but not Islamic) subculture.

Indonesia is the largest Muslim country, and for the vast majority the culture of daily life bears notable imprints of Hinduism, in particular, and, in some places, even Buddhism. India has the second largest population of Muslims in the world, and the extensive research volumes published by the Anthropological Survey of India demonstrate that Muslims living in any particular region of the country (e.g. Kerala in the South, West Bengal in the East, Uttar Pradesh in the North) share well over 80 per cent of their daily cultural practices with their Hindu neighbours in the same region, and very little with Muslims of distant regions within the country; with their distant co-religionists they share some protocols of prayer and a common fear of the Hindu majoritarian communalism which has engulfed the country in the political domain.

Bangladesh, the third largest Muslim country, was *born*, less than forty years ago, out of a secular nationalism which rejected the idea that a common religion was sufficient basis for the making of a nation-state (the 'idea' of Pakistan). The creation of Bangladesh was *opposed* by the Islamicists, as was the creation of Pakistan by the majority of the clergy, for a variety of reasons, in 1947. The emergence of a terrifying Bangladeshi Islamicist movement there is a recent phenomenon, and in considerable degree a part of the globalization of the armed Islamicist militancy which was first spawned by the Carter administration for the anti-communist jihad in Afghanistan. This example illustrates how politically motivated, historically contingent and ideologically fictive the making and unmaking of such religious and cultural identities can be.

The ecumenical popular Islam of Indonesia; the varieties of the lived Muslim subcultures in secular, multi-religious India; the vagaries of the 'Muslim nationalism' which provided the ideological justification for the creation of Pakistan; the incoherence of the linguistic nationalism of the East Pakistanis, which led to the creation of Bangladesh as a secular nation – all these indicate how misleading it is to ascribe to some inherent Islamic-ness of the polity or the culture as such. To refer to all these people as 'Islamic' is to occlude the specificity and novelty of Islamism in general, to posit hyper-Islamicity of Muslim peoples, and to succumb to the idea, propagated by the religious right as well as the Orientalists, that religion is the constitutive element of a culture, and hence also of its social existence and political destiny.

MAKING SOCIETIES ISLAMIC:
FROM AFGHANISTAN TO IRAQ

The charge of Islamic fundamentalists is, precisely, that these countries are *not* Islamic because their legal structures, social norms, the predominant educational systems, popular cultures, etc., are manifestly un-Islamic. Hence the projects of *Islamization*; they are Muslim but they are to be *made* Islamic. For the Sunni fundamentalist, Iran is un-Islamic for the simple reason that it is predominantly Shia. For the neo-Wahhabi opposition, out of which so many Saudi members of al-Qaeda have arisen, neither the ruling House of Saud nor the clerical establishment which legitimates it, can be called Islamic; Saudi Arabia itself has to be recaptured for *true* Islam. I shall return to the historical origins of these phenomena. Suffice it to say here that the distinguishing feature of the various Islamicist groupings which started becoming so prominent in diverse countries from mid-1970s onwards was that virtually every one of them, unconnected with others, grew within its national milieu and sought to transform their own nation-state. (The major exception here would be the Ikhwan al-Muslimun, the Muslim Brotherhood, which started in the 1920s as a specifically Egyptian phenomenon but was then patronized by some Gulf regimes after it was suppressed under Nasser during the 1950s and gradually became a pan-Arab phenomenon, with branches in various countries.) This was equally true of the neo-Wahhabi group in Saudi Arabia which created a world-wide media sensation when it captured the Mecca mosque in November 1979; of the several Islamicist groups in Egypt which came collectively to be known as Jamaa'at el-Islamiyya and whose most spectacular act in that period was the assassination of Sadat; and of General Zia ul Haq, the military dictator who initiated the state-led process of Islamization in Pakistan. The United States had of course been a staunch supporter of the Saudi regime despite its Wahhabi autocracy but it had also been systematically supporting the Islamicists, in a variety of countries, in opposition to communism and radical secular nationalism since the very inception of the Truman doctrine.

The singular achievement of the Carter administration was to bring together personnel from many of these groups – from countries as diverse as Indonesia and Algeria, the Philippines and the Sudan, not to speak of Egypt and Saudi Arabia itself – and organize them into a single, well-trained, well-financed, well-equipped force to fight communism in Afghanistan, well before any direct Soviet intervention and indeed – we have it directly from Brzezinski, Carter's National Security Advisor – to *entice* the Soviet Union into the conflict.[1] Most of what is now called 'Islamic terrorism' and even

'Islamo-fascism', though not all of it, is a consequence of it. The Islamic Republic of Iran was born roughly at the same time, quite independently, but then got drawn into the wider regional configuration owing to a variety of pressures: Saddam's invasion of Iran, Israeli invasion of Lebanon, the influx of Afghan refugees into Iran, etc. Hezbollah in Lebanon was and continues to be independent of the 'Afghani Arabs' (as CIA-recruited Arab jihadis in Afghanistan came to be called); infiltration of such elements into some Palestinian camps in Lebanon is a recent phenomenon and Hezbollah is opposed to them. The Islamicist parties in Pakistan have far older origins but the Afghan jihad, conducted from Pakistani soil, catapulted them from their marginal positions in Pakistani society to the very centre, with immense material and organizational resources at their disposal; they played the key role in the ideological formation of what later became the Taliban.

Even as the Afghan jihad was unfolding, some of these personnel were also infiltrating other regions, such as Kashmir, the then Soviet and predominantly Muslim republics of Central Asia, Chechnya, Bosnia and so on. The long-term consequence of this US strategy was not only that when these seasoned cadres were de-commissioned at the conclusion of the Afghan jihad they were free to create mayhem in their respective countries while maintaining that loose network of connections which is now called al-Qaeda. The origins of the term 'al-Qaeda' are obscure. It is said to have originally referred to the register/ledger which was kept during the anticommunist Afghan jihad for entering the names, allowances, etc., of the contingent of jihadis that had been assembled from numerous foreign countries. Osama bin Laden was by no means a central leader of this vast group and no one can plausibly suggest that it remained a cohesive, centrally-led group after its various members and sub-groups had been dispersed when that jihad ended. Afghanistan itself went through bloody internecine fighting among the mujahideen groups that the US had installed in power, and these groups were collectively overthrown by the new force of the Taliban. The country could not have remained a consistent central locus for directing so amorphous a globally dispersed phenomenon, the Taliban's hosting of Osama notwithstanding. Indeed, the Taliban were preoccupied with stabilizing their own rule rather than waging a global jihad. What now gets called al-Qaeda is at best a loose network of affinity groups with very weak mutual linkages, even though the invasions of Afghanistan and Iraq have certainly contributed to a great expansion of such groups as well as to the numbers of freelance, self-styled martyrs.

The immense publicity that the US-led mass media gave them as 'freedom-fighters' bestowed upon them a global legitimacy and aura. One forgets now that the force of Islamic jihadis which the US assembled in Afghanistan was called 'the mujahideen' (those who conduct jihad), and that when their leaders visited the Oval Office President Reagan introduced them as 'moral equivalents of our Founding Fathers'. The other two major contributions have come from the current Bush administration. The first was to treat the hideous events of 11 September 2001 not as an international crime for which the surviving criminals bore individual as well as group responsibility, but as an act of 'war' against which a global war was declared in retaliation: Afghanistan and Iraq – whose governments had nothing to do with that crime – were invaded, other countries of the region were coerced and threatened, and Israel was given a free hand in the Occupied Territories. As criminals on the run, sought not just by the US but by every law enforcement agency of the world, they would have been annihilated or forced to languish in obscurity. As partners in a globalized civilizational war, their aura was enhanced immensely; few people in the world had heard of Osama until then, and only some lunatic fringes in some Muslim countries celebrated the fireballing of the World Trade Centre; there were street demonstrations in Tehran in solidarity with the American people, and leaders like Arafat sent messages of sympathy and condolence, while the Taliban themselves denounced the act. It is the scale of aggression in the American response, coupled with ritual incantations of Osama's name as the mastermind, and the televising of the latter's defiant statements by outlets like al-Jazeera, which turned him into a household legend and even a hero for many. As some Muslim countries were invaded and others threatened with invasion, any number of footloose Muslim youth, ranging all the way from products of the Islamic medressas to LSE graduates, now wanted to join the new jihad. It needs to be reiterated that joining the jihad had been made fashionable by the US itself; the fashion now continued, against the US itself.

Second, after occupying Iraq, the US moved swiftly to communalize it as well, re-making it along sectarian lines, relying first on the exile luminaries and technocrats who had been re-imported from California and London, then shifting briefly to the CIA asset, Iyad Allawi, and eventually settling on outright fundamentalist Shiite organizations such as al-Da'wa and the Supreme Council for the Islamic Revolution in Iraq (SCIRI), which had long been nurtured, paradoxically enough, by the clerical regime in Iran. The exact date for the founding of al-Da'wa is unclear but it certainly was there from the 1960s onwards as a small, ineffectual Shia sectarian organization. Much of this organization shifted to Iran after the Islamic Revolution and the onset of the Iraq-Iran War, with a sizeable militia being confected for it by the Iranian Revolutionary Guards. SCIRI was established later, on Iranian soil, reputedly on the express instruction of Ayatollah Khomeini himself. Its militia was nurtured by the Iranians with special care. Muqtada al-Sadr, the young firebrand cleric who joined neither organization, was also patronized intermittently, as was the Kurdish leader, Jalal Talabani, not a Shia but a foe of Saddam. When the US also turned against Saddam, especially after the first Gulf War, Iran facilitated amicable contacts between those two organizations and the US. When, in the pre-invasion days, US leaders claimed that Shias would welcome them, they weren't talking pure nonsense. They had been assured that these organizations and the higher clergy would keep the Shia masses out of the anti-imperialist militancy.

Meanwhile, the Sunni fundamentalist groups, inspired by and converging with the pan-Arab Ikhwan al-Muslimun (the Muslim Brotherhood), which had been fighting Saddam Hussein, now shifted to fighting the Americans and were quickly joined by the demobilized Baathists as well. These came to be called, successively, 'Saddam loyalists', 'Baathist remnants', and finally 'Sunni insurgency'. This was greatly complicated by two further factors. Under the new constitutional arrangements that were being devised, power and patronage systems were to be forged along sectarian and ethnic lines, which led to a competition of all against all, by all means fair or foul, to gain as much advantage as possible during this period of dire uncertainty. Second, and most crucially, the methodical dismantling of the Iraqi state – the disbanding of the entire Iraqi army and security forces, and the dismantling of civilian institutions under the rubric of 'de-Baathification' – led to complete social breakdown in a time of great adversity. Cumulatively, over the period of the pre-invasion 'sanctions' and during the occupation, close to a tenth of the Iraqi population is estimated to have died; an even larger number have become refugees, either inside the country or outside; by some calculations, unemployment runs to roughly 70 per cent; health and educational facilities have been reduced to a minimum; weapons are everywhere, and criminal gangs are let loose, often posing as militias. The scale of the ensuing sectarian strife – now a horrific bloodbath all around – has no precedent in Iraqi history.

The current US Secretary of State, Condoleezza Rice, described the Israeli invasion of Lebanon approvingly as just a 'teething problem' in the birth of a New Middle East. The US can likewise pretend that the communal holocaust it has unleashed in Iraq is also a 'teething problem', that Shia-Sunni conflict was always there in Iraq, from time immemorial, and that it has now come to the fore because America's destruction of the Saddam regime has blown the lid off the seething emotions that had been kept under a tight lid by the Ottomans, the British mandate authorities, the Hashemite king, and the various 'Sunni' dictatorships afterwards. This is dangerous nonsense.

Saddam's rule was a ferocious autocracy. The most fundamental require-ment was personal loyalty, and he was prone to eliminating even his trusted advisors – including his close relatives – if he suspected them of disloy-alty. His clansmen, from Tikrit, were given powerful positions because they could be trusted more than others. Then there was the party and one-party Baathist rule, at times in coalition with mainly emasculated 'allies'. The far-ther away you were from centres of power the less power you had, and certainly none if you were not a Baathist, but Tariq Aziz, a devout Baathist and personally loyal to Saddam, could be a key member of the cabinet and the inner circle; that he was a Christian meant nothing. The Shia clergy never approved of Saddam, nor did the Sunni fundamentalists; he suppressed both with equal relish and brutality. The Shia clergy commanded far greater institutional power, which made them and their followers, along with the public rituals which were staged to demonstrate their strength, the greater target of repression. Meanwhile, Karbala in southern Iraq remained the great pilgrimage centre for Shias of the world, and Najaf the chief seminary town, where Ayatollah Khoi, the senior cleric before al-Sistani, commanded prob-ably far greater influence among the Shia, globally, than did any Iranian cleric until after Khomeini's rise to great earthly power after the revolution. Khomeini himself had lived all the years of his exile peacefully in Najaf un-der the Baathists, on Iraqi soil, until the very last few months when Saddam bowed to pressure from the Shah of Iran and requested Khomeini to leave. He left for France and, a few months later, returned to Iran as the hero of the revolution.

Only then did Saddam invade Iran, with the express purpose of top-pling Khomeini, because he did not want an Islamic regime so close to his borders and on the soil of a country both powerful and traditionally in conflict, including even territorial conflict, with Iraq. Saddam's army was led by Baathist officers who tended to be of Sunni origin but the rank and file was composed of Shias as much as Sunnis and everyone fought; there is little history of Iraqi Shias refusing to fight Shia Iran, and the war was fought in regions with majority Shia populations. We might recall also that, for all its horrendous crimes, Saddam's treatment of the Kurds was not notably worse than that of the European, modern, democratic Turks. The point is not to exonerate the dead dictator but to keep things in perspective.

This perspective is all the more essential because the tendency now, even among some leftists, is to adopt a standpoint that converges alarmingly with the hyper-Islamicized version of recent Iraqi history that has been confected by the Shia communal elite and the US-based Islamic Studies industry. During the Saddam period, Shia-Sunni intermarriages were common; as the Shia-Kurdish alliance took power under American tutelage, such couples were told at gunpoint to divorce each other, and when about a hundred such families formed an association for the defence of their collective rights several of them were shot and the association was disbanded. When hundreds of thousands of Shias streamed into southeastern Baghdad – later to be called Sadr City – during the Saddam period hardly any communal tensions ensued; after the US occupied the city, the first big anti-occupation demonstration began at a Sunni mosque with members of both sects participating and Shia clergy in the lead; four years later, every neighbourhood is being subjected to ethnic cleansing. Yet the characterization of the Saddam autocracy as a 'Sunni regime' has taken hold, even in some circles of the left. Saddam ruled Iraq for close to a quarter century, and readers of this essay may well ask themselves just when, how recently, did they come to hear of it as a 'Sunni regime'.

As the invasion of Iraq was being prepared, some intellectuals who had been prominent on the left put forth a remarkable argument: since Saddam was a ferocious dictator, a latter-day Hitler of sorts, and since the West was manifestly liberal-democratic, the latter had the right to make war in order to overthrow the former and to liberate Iraq for liberal democracy; the analogy was with the Second World War when liberal-democratic states had fought a war to defeat the Nazi-fascist alliance. In this argument, there was no room for all the historical evidence that the United States had *never* invaded any Third World country in pursuit of peace and justice but *always* for the opposite reason. Nor did it matter that this argument, presented from the left, converged alarmingly with the kind of quasi-philosophical claptrap about 'just wars' that we were getting from the likes of Walzer and Ignatieff, both defenders of the imperium. Now, after the actual experience, there still appear to be people on the left who contrive to believe that elections held under the guns of the occupation army, on the basis of sectarian and ethnic electoral lists, under a constitution written by the Americans, are an advance toward democracy, and that the government that has ensued is a legitimate government. We can set aside the question of Marxism for the moment, as well as the Geneva Conventions which this kind of exercise specifically violates. Even by ordinary liberal democratic standards, an electoral design based on sectarian and ethnic divisions, which gives the sectarian majority an automatic plurality of seats in parliament, would be considered an instrument meant to perpetuate sectarian divisions and obstruct the emergence of liberal, secular democracy. One should have thought that the experience of Lebanon, where the French bequeathed the country just such a constitution as a power-sharing mechanism for the respective confessional elite and where civil wars have been endemic as these intra-elite arrangements break down, would be a lesson against following that precedent elsewhere. It turns out, instead, that this Lebanization of politics elsewhere is to be supported as a step toward greater democracy. How could this possibly be argued?

One would then have to argue several things: the Saddam regime was so fascistic that *anything* would be better than that – foreign occupation for a while, engineered elections, parliaments based on sect and ethnicity, whatever; so long as that 'fascism' is buried for good. One would also have to argue that Iraqi society as a whole – and other societies in the region: Syrian, Egyptian, Iranian – have been so brutalized by dictatorships that they really are not able to handle democracy of the kind the West has. They need a period of transition, and of tutelage; they have to learn to handle democracy. In this process, so the argument must go, you have to begin with their existing reality which is, above all, religious. The Shia majority in Iraq has lived for a long, long time under Sunni rule – under the Ottomans, during the Mandate period which imposed the Hashemite monarchy, under successive post-monarchical regimes which only extended this Sunni dominance, culminating in Saddam's 'Sunni' regime – and so Iraq needs a period in which the Shia can taste the power that is rightfully owed to them as the most numerous of the sectarian and ethnic groups. Negotiations among sectoral blocs within a framework of some constitutional safeguards will, one would have to believe, teach all of them the fine art of negotiations which is at the heart of democratic rule. The contrary example of India, which has more Muslims in it than most Arab countries put together (minus Egypt), and which institutionalized universal suffrage and secular democracy at the very moment of decolonization, with much lower levels of literacy and per capita income, really doesn't matter, because the vast majority in India is Hindu and Hindus are just civilizationally different. Muslim-majority countries don't have that kind of a civilizational ethos. There is nothing in their religion or their early history which prepares them for egalitarian outlooks and their intellectual life is in any case still dominated by a medievalist clergy. And so on.

Ungrounded in historical knowledge, such arguments present themselves as high-minded and fearless but partake, willy-nilly, in eschatologies of primordialism and cultural differentialism. Whole peoples get essentialized in terms of their religious particularity; the distribution of political power along religious/sectarian lines is declared to be the essence of democratic multicultural/multidenominational societies; and religion itself, thinly understood, becomes the explanation for why certain Islamic extremist groups, of the fascistic kind, become prominent in politics in particular historical conditions. The conjunctural fact can then be seen as a local expression of a permanent, primordial reality about Islam as such. This kind of commitment to the idea of intractable civilizational difference – and, implicitly in this case yet again, the hallowed idea of the intrinsic superiority of Christianity over Islam – ignores any number of utopian socio-political formations within the histories of early and medieval Islam, as well as any number of modern Muslim divines and believing Muslims who have held that Islam and Marxism are compatible and that the institution of private property is un-Islamic. The idea that Christianity is somehow more egalitarian, more a religion of the poor, dies hard, however. The depressing contemporary fact in any case is that even as many parts of Latin America are today convulsed by insurrectionary currents, what is spreading among the slum-dwellers of the great Latin American cities is not so much liberation theology as Evangelical Protestantism and the Pentecostal Church.

'MUSLIMNESS' AND THE WEST

We live at a time when governments of key capitalist countries, the mass media and much of the academic world, including some on the left, would have us believe in precisely that Islamic exceptionalism, that hyper-religiosity among the Muslims, that civilizational *difference* of Islam which the Islamic revivalists, fundamentalists and would-be martyrs would have us believe in. The secular intelligentsia in the Western countries are caught between these two extremes, all the more so because their guilty liberal conscience is bewildered by the brand new kinds of 'Islamic' communities formed in their own midst, thanks to the stresses of migration into racially-biased societies (race too becomes religion/culture in these postmodern climes) which then becomes an object of race relations management (e.g. in Britain) or multiculturalist management (e.g. in Canada), offering openings to entrepreneurs (social, political, academic, religious entrepreneurs) to pose as 'community leaders', simply because managing the multitudes that suffer discriminations of all sorts is easier through 'dialogue' with 'community leaders'. The word 'community' (another word for 'identity') becomes sacrosanct, palpable and administratively manageable in the perspectives of a multiculturalist communitarianism that comes to us in the mutually comforting guises of government policy and postmodern rhetoric, while a diverse immigrant social mass comprised – for instance – of Somalis and Bangladeshis, urban Indians and rural Pakistanis, Iranian teachers and restaurateurs as well as Arab workers and kiosk-owners can all be jettisoned into 'the Muslim community' and can then Islamicize themselves as such – by invitation as well as by the circumstantial need to re-Orientalize themselves; because having lost their original national identities, they cannot find in the race-ridden country of their adoption an identity at par with the identity of their white compatriots.

These diverse immigrant strata must therefore *forge* a *fictive* collective identity – an identity that gathers to itself all the performative density of a stage-managed refusal: dress code as visible sign, the mosque as designated site for the ingathering of males of the tribe, purification of food and beverage, excessive ritualization of private belief, and brand new social bondings across diverse origins which have no common roots in prior civil histories, but become necessities of immigrant life. Similar processes are afoot among Hindu immigrant communities in various Western countries, with all the stigmata of religious identity – dress, rituals, temple-building, getting virginal and traditional wives for the boys from the home country, etc. – and sections of this diaspora contribute substantial funds to extremist, fascistoid Hindu organizations in India, defend those organizations against criticism in the West, and open branches for them in what is called 'the Hindu diaspora'. However, this Hinduized political extremism draws no ire from governmental agencies or media pundits, because the post-89 neoliberal state in India has opened up India's vast markets to Western capital while the country is not only a key strategic ally of the United States but also the biggest buyer of Israeli arms. In turn, Indian rulers have their own ways of ignoring Hindu terrorism and focusing on the Islamic variety, which suits the US perfectly.

Just a couple of decades ago, when race itself was a permissible primary category of identification, these very different groups might have collectively represented themselves in racial categories ('people of colour', 'non-white', even the currently fashionable but nonetheless offensive term in liberal/multiculturalist Canada: 'visible minorities'). Now, 'culture' has increasingly displaced 'race' in rhetorics of public representation and self-representation – while in relation to people of Muslim backgrounds culture itself has been made synonymous with religion – those same people are making claims as Muslim/Islamic, which is all the more convenient because a lot of Muslims just aren't terribly dark-skinned but suffer from that other kind of anti-Semitism which is today directed not at Jews but at Arabs (in this symbolic configuration Iranians and other light-skinned Muslims become surrogate Arabs because they are all Muslims in any case).[2] These positionings required by immigrant life are, of course, greatly re-enforced by governmental/mediatic representations of their countries as 'Islamic' (we must have been *that*; I saw it on TV), and by the power and publicity that Islamicist establishments in their countries of origin have gathered unto themselves in this period of the decline of the left. Islamism is *the* big news: how long has it been since

Western TV audiences saw anything about Pakistan which was not connected with 'Islam', 'dictatorship', and General/President Musharraf's double
game with Islam and dictatorship? Are there workers in Pakistan? Peasants in
Pakistan? The work of foregrounding and occluding is almost magical.

Again, a forceful Islamism that is recent and conjunctural is lifted – even
in the self-consciousness of these newly-branded 'communities' – into
something of a perennial marker of a transnational civilization. Diverse people migrating into a new, threatening environment imagine for themselves
a permanent, shared past that never was. They are branded and stigmatized anyway, and stigmatized even in phrases of patronising neglect ('not *all*
Muslims are terrorists', as if a substantial number, possibly a majority, are).
This daily stigmatizing strengthens, in turn, their rage, resolve and sense of
civilizational difference. The hardened Islamic identity then serves as a vehicle for exiting proudly what they had once desired and no longer hope to
become: just normal Westerners (British, Canadian, American, French) like
their white neighbours or classmates, which is what their new citizenship
papers had promised. In the process, those great numbers of secular individuals of Muslim extraction within Western countries who do not adopt an
Islamic identity and do not participate in multiculturalist community claims
get sidelined and occluded. They just don't make enough trouble to deserve
much attention or publicity; they are not *real Muslims*, either for the Islamicists or for their adversaries – the governmental agencies and the media – or
even for their friends in the Western, secular, postmodernist, multiculturalist milieu; they represent only themselves, not a 'culture', a 'civilization',
a threat. Some of them begin drifting into the Islamicist ranks, for a sense
of belonging which the racialized character of Western liberal democracy
denies them.

Like any other people who feel they are under siege, all varieties of Islamicists and would-be Islamicists, from the most benign to the most violent, pay a great deal of attention to what their enemies, real and/or imagined, are saying about them, about themselves, about the basis of differences
and animosities between 'us' and 'them'. That has always been the case,
but with limited literacy at home and the relatively undeveloped means of
transcontinental communication during the colonial period, the means for
gathering such knowledge were limited, and only the highly educated were
to any degree conversant with discourses prevailing in the West. No longer.
The postcolonial period has witnessed immense strides in literacy and general education in the rest of the world, and one of the effects of the immense growth and globalization of the electronic media is that many of the
visible aspects of American power have entered their living quarters, even

when this does not take the shape of outright war and coercion; they read and see, on their TV screens, the West's representations of its own power, its identity, its civilizational difference and superiority. They don't know of the *Socialist Register*; Bush and Rumsfeld, Powell and Rice, Huntington and Wolfowitz are people they see and hear, and they know how the various participants in the wars of West Asia, including themselves, are portrayed in the US media. Many of them know of the power of the religious right in America and some may have even watched the evangelical preachers on TV. These images do not convince them of any essential secularity or benign Christianity in the West.

Remarkably large numbers of even the extremist Islamicists have had college education and they all come from countries that were colonized or otherwise dominated by European powers, some of which are now under occupation by the US; they see a continuity. They get to know what people who now have military, political, religious, or academic power in the aggressor countries are saying, and they see a connection between word and deed. Civilizational discourse becomes a two-way street, each begetting the other. Sophisticated Islamicists may be aware of the entire complexity of Western traditions and societies (the current speaker of Iranian parliament is also a translator of Kant), and secular intellectuals within the Muslim milieus may even understand that civilizations are not real entities but discursive and performative categories, with immense plasticity, so that the politically-motivated civilizational discourses of our time are essentially acts of bad faith. But the Islamicist militant is, above all, a simplifier and a literalist, with a unique mode of interpreting what he sees. From his exposure to the electronic media, this militant gets essentially two pictures of American society: one comes through the entertainment industry, and his puritanical imagination interprets all that as sheer corruption and degradation; the other is a picture of relentless war-mongering and word-mongering in favour of war, against Islam and the Muslims. The West becomes in their overheated imaginations a crusading Christendom in its religious life and an abode of sin in its secular life. The psychological reflex is that of revulsion, fear and fury. A call to arms ensues.

In the Arab world at least (and in Iran under the Shah), they have seen their rulers mortgaging their national resources to the West; squandering their rentier wealth on luxury for themselves and their ilk; and on building armies that may fight each other but never the invader and the occupier; and they have seen the armies of their secular nationalist leaders losing war after war against the US-Israeli juggernaut. They find no credible armies to join. They must make one of their own, stateless, in deep secrecy, loosely organized, not for pitched battles, for which their arms and numbers are much too inferior, but for spectacular action: propaganda of the deed. Power is so asymmetrical that their methods must reflect that lack of symmetry. And they have seen so many countless civilians getting killed by the Americans and the Israelis that they do not deem their own killing of civilians as terrorism, or even comparable to what their own people have suffered. If anything, they would consider themselves *counter*-terrorists.

They are entirely devoted to Islam but those who live and die on the extremist fringe tend to know little of its theology. Some of that theology makes them uncomfortable, since killing of civilians as well as suicide (and hence suicide bombings) are forbidden. So they make up new theological doctrines on the run, to justify preaching and doing in the name of Islam what is forbidden in Islam. In this sense, many of them simply do not qualify as fundamentalist or revivalist in any accurate sense. They are innovators, but the products of their innovation remind one not so much of some other period or incident in Muslim history as of some elite groupings of revolutionary terrorists in Czarist Russia, just as the horrendously punitive and arcane regime that the Taliban imposed on war-ravaged Afghanistan in the name of 'the true Islam of the Prophet' resembled nothing on earth as much as it resembled the regime of Pol Pot in an equally war-ravaged Cambodia. Invocations of Islam here, of communism there. In both cases, the US imperial aggressions had much to do with the ravages of the respective wars, the traumatization of entire national collectivities and with the utter destruction of social fabrics as well as the even minimally secure material means of daily life, that paved the way for the Pol Pots and the Mullah Omars of this world. One now fears a similar fate for Iraq.

At this point, though, I want to suspend the discussion of wars and their consequences, so as to return to the issue of the high-minded civilizational discourses which are also monitored in the Muslim world – by all sections, from the most secular to the most religiously inclined, and even by the some of the armed militants. The plain fact here is that ideas of civilizational difference are rooted in certain notions not only about the 'Islamic East' but also about its discursive opposite, 'the West'. The more sophisticated among the civilization-mongers hold certain views in relation to capitalism, the Enlightenment, the rationalist secularization of Christianity: sufficient capitalism in the West, versus insufficient capitalism among Muslims; the inherently egalitarian and rationalist kernel within Christianity, and the thoroughgoing secularization of Christian societies by Enlightenment thinkers, the French Revolution, etc. – all of which would then be contrasted with the lack of all these things in Muslim societies, as well as the unbridgeable gulf that is said to separate Islam from secular Reason. The less sophisticated might speak of tradition versus modernization; still others, the postmodern ones, in terms of the authenticity, multiplicity and impermeability of cultures; for the hard right-wing, it is still culture, but cast in terms of the way biologically-defined racism has always functioned: this is *how* they are because of *who* they are. Cultural differentialism, which now animates so many of the epistemologies of matters social and political, is the ground on which several of these tendencies can intersect, even as they pull away from each other in other respects.

GEOPOLITICS: THE POPE, THE PRESIDENT AND THE PROFESSOR

There is a very benign idea which surfaces in many forms across the spectrum from the right to the left that the West is, despite all deviations from its own norm, and certainly in its present formation, essentially secular, liberal democratic and Judeo-Christian; the far right may be upset by the secularism and excessive liberalism, the left may find the West not sufficiently liberal or democratic, but there is a broad agreement on this characterization (the term 'Judeo-Christian' for 'the West' appears even in the work of as rigorous a cultural theorist as Fredric Jameson). Now, if the West is all these things (and peculiarly the West, because if others too were all that, there would be no reason to single out the West as a bearer of these virtues), it would require a relatively short step to start arguing that these various virtues are inter-connected parts of an integral whole, and that there is something in the very origins of the West which makes possible this integrative wholeness.

My own sense is that in all those areas where culture, religion and politics intersect, the 'Christian' West began describing itself as 'Judeo-Christian' so pervasively only in recent decades, essentially to accommodate Israel and, especially after the devastating Israeli victory of 1967, partly to compensate for its sense of guilt regarding the Holocaust and partly to identify with someone else's military victory at a time when the US was facing defeat in Vietnam; before that, anti-Semitism rather than some pride in Judeo-Christian identity was much more the norm. Furthermore, one would have to forget most of the pre-Second World War history of Europe to think of liberal democracy as a relatively uniform Western political practice ('value' is the preferred term in our culturalist times; democracy is a *value* to which the West is said to subscribe, eternally, practices of racism, fascism and Nazism, etc., notwithstanding). And, there is the interesting idea that you can be secular and Judeo-Christian simultaneously. Would it be possible to say that you are secular and Islamic at the same time?

Now, only an *a priori* assumption that Judaism and Christianity are wholly compatible with modern-day secularism and liberalism, while Islam intrinsically is not, could possibly sustain the idea that the West's self-description as Judeo-Christian can seamlessly fuse with its secular and liberal-democratic claims; whereas Muslim-majority societies owning up to the Islamic component of their heritage within their contemporary identity are manifestly not secular and cannot be. In this context, then, it is also very striking that Israel, an admired outpost of Western civilization in the geographical heart of West Asia, can constitutionally and emotively describe itself as a 'Jewish state' while a third of its citizenry is non-Jewish and subject to certain ethno-religiously defined restrictions, and still be regarded as a model of secular, liberal, Western-style democracy in a sea of autocracies and fundamentalisms.

One need pay no more attention to pronouncements of the American religious right, in the current context, than one does to those of Osama bin Laden (even though many of the pronouncements of bin Laden are more astute and even acceptable); one may refer, however, to a recent lecture by the present Pope to see how firmly and diligently these connections between the West, Christianity and Reason itself can be drawn, partly to demarcate the rational/Christian West from the world of Islam. This is particularly interesting because the Pope (formerly famous as Cardinal Ratzinger – or 'Cardinal Rat' in leftwing Catholic humour) enjoys an immense reputation for erudition among those sections of the Catholic Church who supported him all the way up to his august office.

The Pope delivered this much-publicized lecture at the University of Regensburg in Germany on 12 September 2006, and there are surely different ways of reading it. One could read the text in the context of the extreme religious sentimentalism that is now so pervasive among Muslims who claim to have been offended by the brief and obscure quotation that the Pope used in his lecture; and those expressions of anger, leading even to the burning down of some churches by Muslim vigilante groups in Turkey or Palestine, can then be cited as evidence of intolerance among Muslim communities generally, and in the Islamic faith as such. Or, one can read the speech, as the Pope himself urges us to do, as a politically neutral theological reflection upon the constitutive difference between Christianity and Islam on the one hand, and a profound identity between Christianity and Europe on the other. I would prefer to read the whole thing historically and in a variety of contexts within which the lecture makes its mark, from one of the most esteemed pulpits in 'the West'.

Let us begin with the offending quotation itself: 'Show me what Mohammed brought that was new, and there you will find things only evil and in-human, such as his command to spread by the sword the faith he preached'.[3] That particular observation in the 14th century had a specific context: the Byzantine Emperor was embroiled in a war with the Turks, from a position of inferior armed might, and was petitioning various powers in Europe to come to his aid, to organize yet another crusade, and so on; and, in turn, he was promising to unite the Western and the Eastern Churches. Nothing came of it, and Constantinople fell to the Turkish armies soon after the death of the said Emperor. The point nevertheless is that the words were penned at a time of military combat, and vilification of Islam served that precise purpose. One rightly wonders, therefore, why this obscure passage is being dredged up today – by yet another Pope, and a Roman one at that – in the midst of yet another global war that calls upon the democratic, Judeo-Christian West to unite against the global terror unleashed by what is now being called 'Islamo-fascism'. A secular war on religious terrain, so to speak.

The quotation appears in the course of a generally theological exposition of a fundamental, religious, civilizational difference between Christianity and Islam, in so far as, according to the Pope, the Christian faith has always been embedded, from its very beginning, in Greek conceptions of the Logos, so that an identity of faith and reason is fundamental to it; whereas Islam posits a transcendent God who has no integral relationship with Reason and is, in fact, so Absolute that He can – presumably, often does – issue injunctions which can in no way be justified in terms of the 'reasonableness of faith' which, the Pope said, is fundamental to Christianity. The purported injunction to spread Islam by the sword would then be an instance of the radical unreasonableness of the Islamic faith. To be sure, the Pope recognized in his speech that the Qu'ran at one point reads: 'There is no compulsion in religion'; but he explained this as related to 'the early period' when 'Mohammed was still powerless and under threat', while speaking throughout as if Christianity itself had no history of Inquisitions and violence of all sorts.[4]

The theological dispute between Islam and Christianity is not our concern here, though it is worth remarking that just as the Turkish prime minister criticized the Pope for his observations, the German Chancellor and several of her colleagues came forcefully to the Pope's defence. One therefore wonders whether the Turkish and German heads of states represent religions and civilizations, as Huntington might claim, or do they represent nation-states and therefore act under political compulsions arising in their respective states – coloured as the compulsions may be by religious considerations. In context, then, it is useful to recall that before taking up the mantle of the Papacy, Cardinal Ratzinger was a chief theologian of the Vatican and in that capacity told *Le Figaro*, the French newspaper, that Turkey, since it was a Muslim nation, should not be admitted to the European Union: 'In the course of history, Turkey has always represented a different continent, in permanent contrast to Europe... [Turkey] could try to set up a cultural continent with neighbouring Arab countries and become the leading figure of a culture with its own identity'.[5] Again a deep, unbridgeable civilizational difference – and remarks such as these, bearing upon Turkey's attempt to join the EU, might well explain why the Turkish prime minister was constrained to take such exception to the Pope's most recent innuendo about Islam as such. All this seems to sit rather comfortably with a Westocentric discourse in which academics such as Samuel P. Huntington can posit a fundamental 'clash of civilizations', and the Pope himself can speak of a theologico-civilizational incommensurability between the Islamic East and the Christian West.

Other features of that speech are actually just as striking. The Pope says that its intrinsically Hellenistic character is absolutely central to Christianity and gives to it – and to Europe – a distinctive identity. He goes on to name quite a few pernicious attempts to de-Hellenise Christianity, starting with the Reformation and coming right up to the current ideas of pluralism and multiculturalism which would exempt other cultures from the obligation to Hellenize themselves. He goes on to observe:

> This inner rapprochement between Biblical faith and Greek philo-
> sophical inquiry was an event of decisive importance... Given this
> convergence, it is not surprising that Christianity, despite its origins
> and some significant developments in the East, finally took on its
> historically decisive character only in Europe. We can also express
> this the other way around; this convergence, with the subsequent
> addition of the Roman heritage, created Europe and remains the
> foundation of what can rightly be called Europe.[6]

Now any number of literate Muslims (and not only Muslims) of course believe that medieval Muslim philosophical rationalism was an indispensable source for transmitting Greek thought to Western Europe; Islamic neo-Platonism predates European Humanism and the Renaissance. That, however, is not my point here. What I am suggesting is that the particular quotation which has given such offence to Islamic religious sentimentalism needs it-self to be read not just in the larger contexts of Islamophobia and wars of purported Islamo-fascism, but also in the context of the Pope's own views on the Reformation, on pluralism and multiculturalism, on the identity of Europe and Christianity, on the inferiority of not only Islam but also Eastern

Christianity, on Turkey as a country civilizationally unworthy of full membership in the European Union, not to speak of an earlier characterization of liberation theology as a 'deviation' from true Christianity. As he put it during his tenure as Vatican's chief theologian, liberation theology's 'challenge to the Church' had to avoided at all costs: 'It is the sacramental and hierarchical structure of the church willed by the Lord himself that is challenged. This position means that ministers take their origin from the people, and every affirmation of faith is ultimately subordinated to a political criterion'.[7] He who is illiberal within his own Church can hardly be expected to be tolerant toward other religions.

However, we cannot ignore this simply as the fulminations of a particularly illiberal personnage. Whether or not Turkey is civilizationally suitable for membership in the EU – whether Europe can accommodate so many Muslim citizens within its borders without losing its unique cultural character, whether it is prudent for Europe to admit a country with so large and powerful a Muslim military establishment – is a matter of open anxiety all over the EU, at all levels. What the Pope says is not only his personal opinion but a very large part of the European common sense. Similarly, the main body of Western scholarship would entirely endorse the Pope's proposition that the tie between Judeo-Christian religious heritage and Greek Reason and political thought is at the very foundation of Europe, its unique attribute, and that which has given to Western democratic and secular traditions their unique character. Even the matter of liberation theology, which does not surface in this lecture but which was a major preoccupation of the Pope when he was Cardinal and chief theologian, was by no means a matter internal to the Church; and the warnings against it by men like him were very much taken to heart by rulers of the United States.

In May 1980, as US presidential elections neared, with Ronald Reagan as the Republican candidate, a group of experts working for the party prepared a document that was to become a basic political 'primer' for Reagan, the famous Santa Fe Document. In the second part, entitled 'Internal Subversion', proposal No. 3 states:

> United States' foreign policy must begin to confront (and not only react a posteriori to) liberation theology. In Latin America the Church's role is vital for the concept of political liberty. Unfortunately Marxist-Leninist forces have used the Church as a political weapon against private property and the capitalist system of production, infiltrating the religious community with ideas that are more communist than Christian.

If Afghanistan was the site for a confrontation between capitalism and communism, which was to be won with the aid of 'Islamo-fascism', Central America became the ground for a contest between North American hegemony and Latin American revolutionary insurgency, in which liberation theology was identified as a source of strength and sustenance for the revolutionaries, and against which, therefore, a different kind of Christianity – the US religious right, in all its shadings – was to be mobilized, funded, even armed if necessary, with the blessing of the Vatican no doubt, overt or implied.

The quotation about Muhammad was by no means germane to the argument of the Pope's lecture. A shrewd and highly political man, he went out of his way to include it in the knowledge that what was purported to be at stake in the contemporary wars against 'Islamo-fascism' was the very idea of 'the West' – the Hellenized, rational, Christian West – which is what he was defining in the first place. A civilizational war, if there ever was one.

His high status in the spiritual economy of the Church requires that the Pope must not spell out the policy implications of his theological discourse directly. There are no such compunctions for an academic with influence in Washington, such as Samuel P. Huntington whose famous book, *The Clash of Civilizations and the Remaking of the World Order*, was published in 1996 with laudatory blurbs by Brzezinski and Kissinger, indicating a rare bipartisan enthusiasm for the author's strategic vision. One brings this up here not for the book's profundity but for its reach and influence. From an academic standpoint, it is a shoddy performance. Huntington chastises the Enlightenment thinkers for spawning the illusion that there would eventually be universal civilization and predicts that the 21st century shall be riven with wars between cultures (he uses 'culture' and 'civilization' interchangeably), but he is not sure how many civilizations there really are: seven or eight, he says.

At the heart of his argument, Huntington identifies Western civilization with *Western* Christianity, Catholicism and Protestantism, so as to distinguish it sharply not only from the world of Islam but also of the Orthodox Church because that would bring in Russia, Serbia, Levantine Christianity and so on. Latin America poses a problem for him, however, since Latin America too is overwhelmingly Catholic and Protestant. Huntington goes through all kinds of contortions to argue that Latin America is in some fundamental ways different and should be regarded either as an autonomous civilization or an auxiliary of the Western one; he seems unsure. His two paragraphs on Africa begin with the word *perhaps*, in parentheses, followed by the observation that '[m]ost major scholars of civilization except Braudel do not recognize a distinct African civilization'. His subsequent sentence suggests that there may *perhaps* be such a civilization but, if so, that exists only in the southern half of the continent; the upper half plus a thin strip on the eastern coast are parts of the Islamic civilization, not African. In his cartography, African Christians seem to belong to no civilization at all. India is said to be squarely a Hindu civilization despite the fact that some 200 million Indian citizens subscribe to other religions and the country prides itself on its secular constitution; at the time of this writing, India has a Muslim president and a Sikh prime minister while a Roman Catholic woman of Italian origin is politically the most powerful person in the country. As regards the Orthodox Church, Huntington laments as something anomalous the fact that Greeks, who subscribe to an Orthodox Church of their own, are also members of NATO, which Huntington regards as an indispensable security alliance of the Western civilization, as well as to the European Union which, according to Huntington, should include only those who subscribe to Western Christianity. He goes so far as to say that there is so much dissent against US policies and the role of NATO in Greece only because Greeks, in their religious affiliation, do not really belong to the West. He insists that religion is the marker of each civilization and therefore feels constrained to treat Confucianism too as if it were, for all practical purposes, a religion.

Huntington's categorizations are incoherent but the policy recommendation is sharp:

> The West's universalist pretensions increasingly bring it into conflict with other civilizations, most seriously with Islam and China... The survival of the West depends on Americans reaffirming their western identity and westerners accepting their civilization as unique not universal and uniting to renew and preserve it against challenges from non-western societies... In the post-Cold War world, the most important distinctions among peoples are not ideological, political, or economic. They are cultural... We know who we are only when we know who we are not and often only when we know who we are against...[8]

What is being staged here is actually a geopolitical scenario of permanent conflict in the name of a civilizational discourse, with a virtually Schmittean distinction between friend and foe, us and them: we know ourselves only when we know who our enemies are. The main enemies of the West are Islam and China, but there are some lesser complications as well. While for Huntington the West includes Europe and North America, plus far flung cousins in 'settler countries' like Australia and New Zealand, there is actually a 'central dividing line' in Europe itself. This line, shifted eastward with the fall of the Iron Curtain, is now also religious: 'It is now the line separating the peoples of Western Christianity on the one hand, from Muslim and Orthodox peoples on the other...'.[9] In the clash between Christianity versus Islam, the Orthodox Church and China, America must lead and the West must unite to defend itself. The problem with the West has been that it has had universalist pretensions. Repudiation of universalism thus yields, in Huntington's vision, not mutual accommodation or respect among diverse cultures but a state of permanent warfare. No postmodern, benign relativism here! Invert Huntington and you get Osama bin Laden.

VARIETIES OF ISLAM: ATTENDING TO HISTORY

We have so far reviewed various discourses which present issues involving Islam in terms of 'civilization', but we cannot avoid also discussing the issue of terror, or violence, which a select group of Islamists have adopted as their chosen mode of confrontation. This focus on terror or violence, which has been forced upon us by the discourses, right and left, dominant in the West today, is especially unfortunate because it leads to a concentration on tendencies which were until recently marginal elements in their own societies, and continue to remain so in most places. This focus of Western discourses is rooted in a rampant Occidentalism which divides the world of Muslims into a simplistic binary of secularists and Islamicists, and looks at all Islamicists as belonging to the same conceptual and ideological universe – which not only exonerates all secularists as at least the lesser evil, however corrupt or dictatorial they may be, but also treats all Islamicists as being at least potentially terroristic. Here, I cannot review the historical evidence which proves that in the past fifty years or so the vast majority of politically active Islamicists have been pro-Western, and that it is only the extreme aggressivity of Western-Israeli policies that has driven so many of them into the anti-Western camp; increasingly since the Western-backed Israeli victory of 1967, and especially since the unfolding of Western wars on what is now called 'Islamo-fascism'. I just wish to address the issue of the uses, and abuses, of 'Islamism' (or 'fundamentalism') as a convenient all-purpose category.

Like any political movement of any ideological complexity that commands a substantial mass base, Islamism has everywhere comprised various currents. By and large, the currents that have sought to use political and electoral processes to achieve their objectives have been dominant within Islamicist politics, while those who reject such processes and wish to impose Islam through the gun – and in the case of some of them, only through the gun – have been very much in the minority. Among the Shia, Khomeinism was a stunning innovation, with its doctrine of the *Vilayat-e-Faqih*, which held that the clerical order should itself take hold of worldly government and that armed insurrection was a legitimate means for bringing this about. The dominant view among the Shia had been that while the Twelfth Imam was in hiding, all government was basically illegitimate and the collectivity could do little else than wait for him to re-appear and set things right (the quasi-messianic doctrines of Occultation and *Intezar*, which in English-language scholarship have gone under the heading of 'Quietism'); in the interim the task of the clergy was to refrain from the exercise of political power and guide the community of believers in their religious, social and cultural life as best as it could. In modernist terms, one could say that this doctrine effectively restricted the direct power of the religious institution to the domain of civil society and allowed the construction of secular power in the political domain, with the hope that the legal structures of the political state would be as close as possible to the basic principles of Islamic justice.

It is possible to argue, in the opinion of this author, that it was the peculiar combination of (1) the suppression of the leftist and secular anti-imperialist forces in Iran by the CIA-sponsored coup of 1953, and by the regime that followed it, (2) the extreme autocracy of the Shah, and (3) the extremely close ties of the Shah's regime with the US, which account for the success of the Khomeini'ite forces in Iran, other possibilities having been foreclosed by the successful elimination of the secular opposition to the monarchy. Those other traditions, which are not Khomeini'ite, and which continue to believe in much milder versions of the relation between Islam and modern politics, are still alive wherever there are sizeable Shia populations, but they are very much on the retreat as they are no longer faced with free choice and rational dialogue but with extreme forms of Western aggression. This same distinction, and shifts from one viewpoint to another, prevail in countries with Sunni-majority populations.

In Algeria, which has recently witnessed a vicious war between the Islamicists and the state, the vast majority of Islamicists participated in national elections, won the first round, and were poised to form government by winning later rounds, when the state called off the electoral process altogether, with loud support from Europe and the United States, which then helped the substantial jihadi elements in becoming dominant within Algerian Islamism. In the case of Egypt, some of the most famous of the gun-toting Islamicist militants and organizations have arisen there but to this day the parliamentary party of the Muslim Brotherhood has an incomparably greater following. Mubarak, one of the great darlings of the US in the Arab world, rigged the recent elections, jailed leaders of the Brotherhood, and is in the process of passing laws that would make it at least very difficult for Islamicists of any stripe to participate in elections. With the electoral route barred to them by a government which fears that they are likely to win the elections, will the bulk of the Egyptian Muslim Brothers go the way of their Algerian counterparts? Only time will tell.

In Palestine, Hamas rejected the Oslo Accords because they were deemed capitulationist, a position that was adopted by even as sober and large-hearted a secular intellectual as Edward Said, but the entire political program of Hamas is premised on the idea that a two-state solution is entirely possible if Israel vacated the Palestinian territories that it occupied in 1967 and accepted that the borders it had before that occupation were indeed its final borders. This perspective on what can be a final solution reflects the aspirations of the vast majority of Palestinians, who have also come to believe, after forty years of occupation and the dismal failure of Oslo, that Israel will never agree to it without pressure from an armed Palestinian resistance. Furthermore, the sheer corruption and incompetence of the Palestine Authority (PA), led by Fatah, made the general Palestinian population look for an alternative, which Hamas provided by organizing the social services which PA was unwilling to offer, and through a leadership that lived among the masses of Gaza and whose frugal life and incorruptibility was transparent. The masses of the Occupied Territories voted overwhelmingly for Hamas but when this entirely legitimate government was formed, the West decided to strangle economically the Palestinian electorate which had voted out the West's favourites, President Abbas and his notorious security chief Dahlan; and pressed Abbas and Dahlan to destroy the popularly elected government by any means, fair or foul, while Israel went ahead with its policy of so-called 'targeted killings' – in plain language, assassinations – of any Palestinian leadership which did not accept the Israeli diktat. Any number of Hamas' parliamentarians and ministers were jailed by the Israelis, and the prime minister's own home was bombed. How much longer can the Hamas leadership go on impressing upon its mass base that politics of the electoral field should be its main form of expression, while the business of armed struggle is left to its militia?

In Lebanon, Hezbollah has gone through many transformations. The least one can say is that since Nasrallah firmed up his grip on the organization there has been a clear policy: selective and restrained armed struggle against Israel so long as the latter holds on to any sliver of Lebanese territory and holds large number of Lebanese citizens in its prisons, but strictly electoral and political means – including, at times, mass demonstrations and street actions to gain its political objectives – within Lebanese society, with a complex set of alliances with other political forces, Muslim and non-Muslim alike. The declared US policy of not seeing it as a legitimate political party in Lebanese politics, and categorizing it as simply a 'terrorist' organization – a policy, moreover, that is backed by major European players such as France, as well as by powerful US-allied Arab regimes such as that of Saudi Arabia – is again strengthening the tendency within Hezbollah which argues that the West (including Israel) has no respect for electoral processes in Muslim countries, and so the gun is the only viable means of struggle.

We can point to similar developments in other countries as well, such as Somalia or Sudan or Pakistan. The precise developments which are causing this rapid shift within Islamicist movements, from moderate electorally-inclined Islamism, to armed extremist Islamism, are undoubtedly specific to each situation. There is, however, a nefarious combination of domestic, anti-left, and mostly autocratic right-wing regimes on the one hand and, on the other, determined imperialist-Zionist policies, which are creating the objective conditions within which 'moderate', democratic Islamism is itself giving way, in so many places, to the extremist, millenarian variety. The West thus has to account for three successive sins over a period of roughly half a century. First, it helped Islamism flourish by recruiting it as a force against 'communism', which encompassed not only the broadly-based communist movements that had arisen among the Muslim peoples but also any regime which subscribed to economic nationalism against Western corporate capital. The Western left typically underestimates all that history as a minor episode in what it too calls 'the Cold War', a term it has borrowed from the imperialist vocabulary. Second, by ensuring the overthrow of those secular regimes that were not communist (most of them were actually anti-communist) but which either tolerated communists (the Sukarno regime in Indonesia), or refused to align with the West (Sukarno again, but also Nasser in Egypt), or were even mildly nationalist in the economic domain (Mossadegh in Iran) – the West ensured the narrowing of the space for secular politics and therefore the emergence of varieties of Islamism, moderate as well as militant: Sadat, who succeeded Nasser and brought Egypt into the US-led camp, patronized the moderate wing of the Muslim Brothers but was gunned down by the armed ones who had broken with their parent organization, precisely on the question of Sadat's alliance with the US and what they regarded as a capitulation on the question of Israel. Third, when Islamism became a powerful tendency in so many of those countries, the West played a cynical game of extreme pragmatism: continued support for regimes like the Saudi one; the organization of the jihad against Afghan communism, as if what developed there was just a 'Soviet invasion', with no domestic basis; support for the most autocratic regimes, such as that of Mubarak in Egypt, against the Islamicists, adding to their claim to be 'anti-imperialist'; displaying nothing but contempt for those Islamicists who had actively demonstrated their belief in electoral politics (in Algeria, in the Occupied Territories of Palestine, in Lebanon) and treating them as just 'terrorists'.

All this is then connected, in very condensed ways, with the question of Israel, its long-lasting occupation of Palestinian territories; its treatment of the subject populations; its turning of Gaza into a vast prison; its carving up of even the West Bank in such a way that roughly 40 per cent of the Occupied Territories are already annexed in one form or another; American support for and European collaboration in Israel's policies; and the Western-Israeli attempts to prop up their own friends in the Palestine Authority using brutal means, in opposition to a popular electoral mandate by the Palestinians in favour of Hamas. The wound is deep. A settler state was established, through what the Israeli scholar Ilan Pappe describes as a full blown ethnic cleansing, at precisely the time when much of Asia and Africa were being decolonized. This has been crowned by an occupation that has lasted for forty years and has involved not just a regime of periodic atrocities against the population under occupation, but also the flagrant flouting of international law. Islamicists just don't believe that Western law – the very law that the Western discourse regards as the very foundation of civilized existence – will ever give them justice.

In this context, then, the rest of us have to undertake a dialectical analysis so complex as to be almost impossible: to take the full measure of the histories that have produced such points of view, make distinctions between one tendency and another, not succumb to any of their various modes of comprehension or their conclusions or their favoured lines of action, and yet attempt to see those histories through their eyes, with at least some degree of empathy, so that, at the very least, they do not appear to us as just so many primitives that need to be contained, disciplined, perhaps even annihilated, selectively, in 'just wars' waged by us, the civilized. If they can be seen as particular kinds of human beings who have been produced not by civilizations or religious frenzies and fatalities but by histories, then one can at least begin to attend to these histories.

It is very difficult, however, to say much that can apply to the various Islamist currents generally. Far from being various expressions of some essential feature of Islam (or a lack in it, as some would argue), each has been formed in distinctive ways by the history which has given rise to it. This applies even to the contentious notion of 'fundamentalism' itself. Even if we were to grant, for arguments' sake, that the term 'fundamentalist' applies to

them all, which is doubtful, one would still have to radically distinguish between one fundamentalism and another. This is where the elementary tasks
of a comparative sociology of Islamisms – not of religions, but of various
Islamisms – begins. I shall again proceed not with generalizations but with
just one contrast, which should illustrate the whole point: the 'fundamentalisms' of Afghanistan and Iran respectively, two adjacent countries which
experienced revolutions (communist in one case, and Islamicist in the other)
at roughly the same time.

Islam in 20th century Afghanistan, after it had been sundered from its
historical linkages with what is now Pakistan (thanks to British colonialism)
and Central Asia (thanks to Czarist expansionism), grew in a geographical
environment of largely arid mountain fastnesses and plateaus, with scant agricultural resources, hardly any industrial development, largely tribal social
solidarities and hierarchies, and small clusters of the modern middle class in
the main cities. This was all held together by a mildly Muslim monarchy
in Kabul with limited direct control over the outlying regions which made
up the bulk of the country and were dominated by regional satraps. At the
time of the communist coup in 1978, there was one mullah for every 60
people, an overall nine per cent literacy rate (one per cent among women),
and a general rural populace that was often tied to their overlords both by
debt bondage as well as by primordial loyalties of tribe and sect, especially
in the Pashtun areas. As most of the overlords and the urban elite fled after
the coup, primarily to Pakistan (the case of the refugees in Iran is again different), inciting the dependent peasants to flee with them, the Islamism that
grew in exile – in luxurious bungalows for the rich, in miserable camps for
the poor – had all the features of a society in which tribal custom was taken
to be the authentic Islamic practice; the clientelist relationship survived in its
tribal form, as did the mullah-laity relation. Indeed, the lack of a centralized
state and the conditions of exile in a foreign country, Pakistan, where they
eked out their meagre existence, served to intensify relations of overlord-
ship and dependence among the poor refugees. Such were the conditions
in which the actual Afghan nucleus for the anti-communist jihad was assembled (as distinguished from the tens of thousands of the foreign jihadi
mercenaries who were assembled by the CIA and associated agencies).

A population of hundreds of thousands who were poor, lacking in modern education, prey to feudal and clerical domination, and frightened by the
fact of exile and the misery of refugee camps, was thus the social mass that
was mobilized by the American decision to launch an Islamic jihad against
the godless communists who had taken over that country – and against the
Soviet Union which subsequently intervened militarily; and by the deci-

sion of the Pakistani Islamicist parties, which until then had been fringe elements in their own country, to create the ideological apparatuses for this jihad. That was the first edition of Afghan Islamism which came to fruition with the withdrawal of Soviet troops, the defeat of the communists, and the creation of the government of the mujahideen, the first Islamist government in the history of Afghanistan – an Islamism of warlords and the urban elite, who now went about making money in all sorts of ways, ranging from poppy cultivation to the sale of US-supplied weapons in the regional and global arms bazaars.

The second edition of Islamism came in the form of the Taliban. The word means 'students' and they had indeed been students in the rudimentary Islamic seminaries (medressas) which had been funded by the Americans, the Saudi and other Gulf rulers, NGOs, etc., and were effectively run by the Pakistani Islamicist parties, for children of the destitute Afghan refugees – children who had never known any settled life, but were products of their tribalist ancestry and their war-torn present: the mudhouses that were their homes, their continuing semi-literacy, their indoctrination into the most rabid kinds of fanaticism, their utter ignorance of Islamic theology or jurisprudence or hermeneutics, their gun-toting adolescence that was devoted to training as soldiers in an eternal jihad. In the midst of it all they grew up into young men and came eventually to be joined by some other fractions that were less illiterate and somewhat more urbanized and worldly. As the US-foisted government of the warlord mujahideen collapsed in cesspools of corruption, orgies of rape and murder and mutual elimination, the Pakistan government, overseen by the Americans, decided to organize these former students (now history's timeless 'Taliban') into an intervention force. They swept into Afghanistan with the force of a hurricane (although it is said that most of the fighting was done by the Pakistan army, on their behalf) and swiftly occupied it.

They created the only kind of Islamic regime their own lives had prepared them for: puritanical, illiterate, rigid, medievalist. Their predecessors had raped tens of thousands of women; Taliban did nothing of the kind but turned the whole of Afghanistan into a vast prison of pure domesticity for the country's women, with no rights to public life, and in conditions of mass destitution and starvation. As they fell from America's grace, their social severities against women became legend, but the mass rapes of Afghan women that were perpetrated by men of the Northern Alliance went unmentioned because the rapists of that Alliance had been part of the ruling coalition that the US foisted upon the country after the communist defeat, and again part of the coalition that emerged after the US invasion and the anointing of the

Karzai government. Taliban rule was hideous but it was also the only time in post-communist Afghanistan when no women were raped by the ruling elite, no rulers took bribes, no poppy was grown or heroin manufactured.

Compare, then, these brands of 'fundamentalism' with the Iranian variant. Rich in all kinds of natural resources including water and fertility of soil, home to a splendid pre-Islamic civilization, home also to one of the great Muslim cultures for many centuries, Iran has been for the cultural complexes of southwest Asia, in the majesty of its literary and artistic achievements, what Italy has been to Europe. Of the two poets generally regarded the greatest in Farsi literature, Rumi (literally, Roman) is buried in Konea, a small pilgrimage town in eastern Anatolia, and has followers in countless Sufi Tariqas (guilds) across the Muslim world; the other, Hafiz, was once invited, in his old age, to grace with his presence the provincial court in Bengal.

Modernist reform first came to Iran in the first quarter of the 20th century, almost a century later than in Ottoman Turkey, and that left a mark in the lesser development and density in its bourgeois culture. The monarchical form was retained when the Pahlevis took over in the 1920s (just when monarchy was getting abolished in Turkey by a secular-nationalist, statist republic) and in due course was greatly intensified. No bourgeoisie could grow that was not connected to the throne, a phenomenon for which Ervand Abrahimian, a superb historian of modern Iran, has invented the apt term 'monarcho-bourgeoisie', a corporate class comprised of roughly two thousand families, assimilated into the monarchical system and detached from the rest of society.[10] The rentier state and its beneficiaries, grown excessively rich from the influx of oil income, were politically aligned with and dependent on Western powers (mainly the US, which after the Second World War had eliminated Britain as the main power in the region), and were excessively Westernized in what they took to be their culture. Unlike the upstart sheikhdoms of the Gulf, however, Iran was not just oil. Earlier forms of accumulation had also given rise to a much older, remarkably powerful traditional bourgeoisie of the bazaars, much less wealthy than the monarcho-bourgeoisie, wider in its social base, resentful of the monarcho-bourgeoisie's claims and connections, including its dependent economic and cultural connections with the West. Post-Second World War Iran also had a substantial professional, urban middle class, a vibrant literary intelligentsia and a growing working class. The lack of organic correlation between the rentier state and civil society also left for the clerical establishment a vast arena in which much of it could distance itself from the court and its associates and yet have vast influence among the populace through a very elaborate marriage network which associated it with the mercantile and landowning

elites and connected it with the general populace through the well organized, hierarchical religious institutions. Communist, secular nationalist and
even mildly Islamicist oppositions to the monarchical regime also grew in
this milieu, in an intricate web of competitions and collaborations.

The first post-war opposition gathered around communists and secular
nationalists, formed a government headed by the National Front, and led
to the first oil nationalization in Middle Eastern history, under Mossadegh,
a patrician prime minister who had nothing to do with the left as such but
was heading a coalition which wished to restrict foreign control over its key
natural resource and, inter alia, also pave the way for bringing the monarchy
more under parliamentary control, more or less on the British model. The
US reacted with a CIA-executed coup, restored the Shah to his throne, and
set about erecting for the monarchy the most ferocious intelligence service
in the region, the SAVAK, which also served essentially as a paramilitary
police. The extreme repression of the leftists and secular nationalists which
the SAVAK conducted after the coup created a situation in which the widespread anti-monarchical and anti-American sentiment remained in place and
was greatly strengthened, but no secular institution in civil society was left
intact – or, at least, strong enough – to give expression to that sentiment,
while the religious elite was left almost wholly untouched. The Shah, his
supporters, even his foreign sponsors were misled by the powerfully secular history of 20th century Iran into greatly underestimating the expanding
power of the clergy in this situation where it no longer faced any substantial
rivals; no one believed that a movement led by the mullahs could overthrow
the monarchy.

This is not the place to rehearse details of that revolution. The main point
here is that there were substantial secular and leftist forces involved in the
making of that revolution, and it was only after Khomeini had consolidated
his power that those forces were methodically eliminated, often by very
violent means. Furthermore, the Islamicist forces were themselves by no
means uniform. Aside from the dominant clerical element, there were also
Islamicists drawn from the professional middle class or the more traditional
bourgeoisie of the bazaar who were socially conservative but by no means
inclined toward extreme forms of Islamization; younger people who were
drawn from the student movements of the modern universities; powerful
intellectuals who had been disenchanted by leftist movements but were also
deeply influenced by leftist ideas. Even the higher echelons of the clergy
were deeply divided along ideologico-theological lines; aside from Khomeini, there were other Ayatollahs powerful in their own right, such as Ayatollah Taleqani whose version of the political economy of Islam was closer to

that of the left wing of modern social democracy; or Shariatmadari, who had a great following of his own, and whose views were much more patriarchal and traditionalist but who also did not subscribe to Khomeini's version of things. The first government was headed by Mehdi Bazargan and Beni Sadr, neither of whom was a member of the clergy. The parliament was deeply divided over the extent of the radicalism of the projected land reforms, and the ensuing vision of the economic structure resembled the Nasserist model where heights of the economy were to remain in the public sector.

There were compromises all along the line. Iran was to be Islamic but also a republic armed with a constitution: the Islamic Republic of Iran, even though nothing in the history of early or medieval Islam could possibly yield a *republican* constitution. Only individuals approved by the clerical Supreme Council could run for elections but the elections themselves were to be free and fair. The most senior clerics are known to have been unhappy with the candidacy of Ahmadinejad, the current prime minister, but he won a clear vote and no one tried to prevent him from winning those elections – the Iranian clerics thus displaying rather more respect for constitutional and electoral processes than the secular FLN in Algeria. Western social and philosophical sciences are now taught in the seminaries of Qom, where libraries are organized and computerized on perfectly modern lines, and no one blinks when a new translation of Kant or Hegel appears. Islamic feminists trained in California have excellent chances of getting positions in government, even as the moral police punish other women for allowing strands of their hair to be seen in public, from under the hijab. Indeed, women of the popular classes have made much greater strides in higher education and the professions under the Islamic regime than was conceivable for their mothers during the secular and Westernizing rule of the Shah in pre-revolutionary Iran. The whole political fabric is a peculiar mix of democracy and theology, authoritarianism and populism, developmentalism and extreme social conservatism. One could also plausibly argue that internal forces struggling for democratization and secularization would have far greater chances of success if the West and Israel did not constantly allow the most extreme factions within the regime to cite the palpable threat from the West so as to unite the populace behind the national government and ward off criticism.

The point, again, is not to defend the Iranian clerics but to simply illustrate the difference in the respective contexts in which the 'fundamentalisms' of Afghanistan and Iran have grown. One could go further and cite the case of contemporary Turkey, where the ruling Islamicist party which governs with a comfortable majority initially grew in the milieu of small capitalists of the regional towns, especially towns on the eastern coast, who were angry with the dominance of Istanbul-based capital but are now strong enough even in Istanbul itself to challenge that earlier hegemony most profoundly; in the process, their Islamism has come to be quite comparable to the Christianity of the German Christian Democrats.

THE DESTRUCTION OF SECULARISM EAST AND WEST

Any careful examination of the map of Muslim-majority countries during the years immediately after the Second World War – between 1945 and 1965, let us say – will show that most Muslim societies, from Indonesia to Algeria, with notable exceptions such as Saudi Arabia and the Gulf sheikh-doms – were extraordinarily hospitable to communist, Marxist and more generally secular ideas. Between the mid-60s (the coup in Indonesia; the fatal destruction of secular Arab armies in 1967, and so on) and the late 1970s (the Islamic Revolution in Iran in 1978, the beginning of Afghan jihad in 1979-80), that earlier world of predominant secularity and leftwing offen-sives entered into deep crisis, while that whole state system came to be under siege from the competing fundamentalisms of Iran and Saudi Arabia. The dramatic shift in Iran, from three quarters of a century of modernizing, secu-larizing anti-monarchical movements of the communist left and the secular nationalists, to a fully clerical revolutionary elite, was in reality perhaps less dramatic than the march of Saudi Arabia from a precarious existence on the margins of Arab history, under siege by modernist impulses across the Arab world, to the commanding centre of that world. When Israel destroyed Nasser's forces in 1967, it also defeated Nasserism as the dominant secular-nationalist, authoritarian-socialist current in the Arab world, and thereby changed drastically the balance of forces between a defeated, traumatized Egypt – at the centre of urbane, Mediterranean Islam – and the oil-rich, monarchical, Wahhabi-puritanical, desert kingdom of Saudi Arabia. For the first time in perhaps a millennium, the Islam of the desert and the oases came to dominate the cosmopolitan Islam of the great cities (Cairo, Damascus, Baghdad, Beirut, Aleppo, and the cities of Occupied Palestine as well), the coasts, and the fertile valleys (the Nile, Tigris and the Euphrates).

By 1990 (the withdrawal of the Soviet Union from Afghanistan and its systemic collapse; the collapse of the communist government in Kabul, and the advent of the first Islamicist regime in the modern history of that coun-try, under American tutelage) that same map of the Muslim-majority coun-tries was to be gripped overwhelmingly by what Bernard Lewis was to call 'the resurgence of Islam', and what Huntington portrays as a civilizational clash between Islam and the Judeo-Christian West. It may be helpful to clarify all this – the historic and fatal shift from the great secular-leftist offensives to the rapid rise of Islamism as the dominating force – with quick reference to particular events.

- In 1948, the British Resident in Tehran writes to the Foreign Office in a secret communication that the Tudeh need make no revolution because it is poised to come to power through peaceful means. Now, Tudeh was, for all its much broader trappings, the communist party of Iran; in the over-heated imagination of the British Resident, it was about to take power. In the event, it was the secular, liberal National Front, led by Mossadegh, which formed the government, sought to nationalize oil and clashed with the monarchy on the issue. The point here is that as of the early 1950s the political field in Iran was dominated entirely by the communists and liberal/secular democrats who opposed each other on many issues but were united in a certain kind of radical economic nationalism. The coup that the CIA engineered in 1953 to defeat that economic nationalism restored the monarchy and created the bloodthirsty internal security force of the SAVAK. The communists and the liberal democrats were eliminated, creating the wide political vacuum within which the clerical opposition came to dominate. The clergy – itself comprised of such 'left-wingers' as Ayatollah Taleghani and 'rightwingers' as Ayatollah Shariatmadari, but also backed by such 'radical' voices as those of Ali Shariati and (the formerly Tudeh intellectual) Jalal Aaal-e-Ahmed – walked into the breach. Eventually, and led now by Ayatollah Khomeini, they made the Islamic Revolution of 1978. There are all sorts of complications involved here, and the specific hierarchical structure of the Shiite clerical institution is itself a factor – but, on the whole, one can say that as of 1953, the time of the CIA-led coup, no one could have possibly foreseen or predicted that Iran would have an Islamic Revolution a quarter century later.

- As of 1965, Indonesia, the largest Muslim country in the world, had the distinction of also having the largest communist party outside China and the USSR, and the country was led by Sukarno, a leader of the anti-colonial movement and one of the key architects of the Non-Aligned Movement. Sukarno was as fond of lacing his speeches with references to Islam as Nehru in India was keen on invoking the Hindu or Buddhist achievements of classical India, but Indonesian politics were almost wholly secular, in a country where Muslim culture itself was highly ecumenical, with Hindu and even Buddhist elements embedded in it even more deeply than has been the case with Indian Islam. Then came the anti-communist, anti-nationalist coup of 1965, with the single biggest bloodbath of communists in post-Second World War history and half a million or more dead, leading to the Suharto dictatorship. The kind of Indonesia we now have – with a distinctly devout but politically mild Islam at the apex and a variety of millenarian, absolutist currents running through the lower echelons of society – is a direct consequence of what the military destroyed in the first place, and what it then allowed to flourish subsequently.

- As of 1948-52 in Egypt, there were essentially four centres of power, existing or emergent: the Palace itself, the mildly liberal-nationalist centre that may be symbolized in the broad sense by the word 'Wafd', the communists, and the Ikhwan al-Muslimun (the Muslim Brotherhood). The coup of Neguib and Nasser, out of which the authoritarian secular-nationalist Nasserist regime arose, destroyed all these centres of power and tamed whatever remained of them. The high point of the new regime was the nationalization of the Suez Canal in 1956 and Egypt's successful defiance of the British-French-Israeli aggression. Between that high point and the terminal decline of the regime after the defeat of 1967, Sayyid Qutb, the purported hero of today's politically absolutist currents in Sunni Islam, was hanged, with little immediate effect in Egyptian society. Then came the Israeli invasion of 1967, the destruction of the Egyptian armed forces, the occupation of the Sinai, the humiliation of Nasser, the fundamental shift in the balance of power within the Arab world from Nasser's Egypt to the Wahhabi'ite monarchy of Saudi Arabia, and the rise, out of that crucible, of the famous Jama'aat-i-Islamiya (the 'Islamic Societies', such as Takfir wa al-Hijra) who were responsible for the assassination of Sadat and who now dominate the more radical end of the religio-political field in Egypt, alongside the rejuvenated Ikhwan, the 'moderate' party of the pious, which now dominates the field of electoral politics – notwithstanding the extreme cruelties and electoral frauds of the Mubarak regime, America's favourite ally in the non-monarchical part of the Arab world.

These are stark examples, starkly condensed; many more could be added. Each could be enriched with nuance, detail, sense of complexity and contradition; each has been the object of book-length studies, some of them very good. At this point, though, let us allow ourselves the risky indulgence of playing with the counterfactual: the useless, melancholy history of what did not happen but could have. Suppose, for an instant, that the CIA had not made the coup in Iran and the communists and the liberal-nationalists had been allowed their role in Iranian politics, in which case the monarchy would have been overthrown by either a communist-liberal alliance, or by one of those secular forces, but not by the clerical ones; what sort of Iran would you then have? Suppose, further, that there had been no successful coup in Indonesia, no bloodbath of the secular political forces, communists as well as anti-imperialist nationalists, no Suharto regime; might there not have been a more liberal or leftwing but certainly a secular and enlightened Indonesia, entirely at peace with its religious ecumenism – and perhaps no branches of al-Qaeda there, no massacres in Bali, and so on?

Suppose, also, an Egypt in, say, 1954, that was allowed to find its own way into the world through its own internal dynamics. We know from what actually happened that the Nasserist regime claimed to be socialist but was at best a caricature of it, and that its nationalism was deeply scarred by its authoritarianism. But, suppose, then, in a counterfactual accounting, a Nasserist Egypt that was not constantly traumatized by the very real possibility of invasion or at least radical subversion from abroad, a Nasserist Egypt not forced to spend much of its national income on military buildup, not constantly on a war footing, not facing the war of 1967, not having been defeated so decisively in it. The Islamism that arose in the wake of that defeat levelled one unanswerable charge against Nasser: that he entirely failed to lead the Arabs to victory against Israel, to protect Egyptian honour and Egyptian territory, to prevent Israel from occupying the rest of Palestine. The charge was unanswerable because it was true. And, having filed an unanswerable charge of guilt, the Islamicists held out a millenarian promise of redemption: we shall deliver unto you – you the Egyptians, the Arabs, the Muslims everywhere – what Nasser could not; and we shall succeed because God is on our side, while He, the Lord, was not on Nasser's side because he was secular, in short heathen. In conditions of extreme social disorientation produced by the defeat of 1967 that millenarian promise held, and numerous among the young were swept by that kind of eschatology. When Sadat's assassins were put on trial a decade later, an impressive number of them said that they had been Nasserists in their youth and had come into the Islamicist political world after 1967.

In the meantime, by 1970, Nasser himself had travelled to Khartoum and made his peace with the Saudi king, and was in no position to offer any sort of protection to the Palestinians from the massacres of September 1971 in Jordan, in a contest of strength between a West-oriented monarchy and a secular PLO. Islamism among the Palestinians went from strength to strength after those massacres, after the massacres of Sabra and Shatila in the course of the Israeli invasion of Lebanon in 1982, and especially after the US-sponsored Oslo Accords of 1993. In the process, the PLO was first emasculated and then became a mere caricature of itself, endemic corruptions eroding it from within. That vacuum was then filled by Hamas.

But in order to imagine, in our counterfactual history, an Egypt in which so many of the secularists of yesteryear did not flee into the camp of the Islamicists thanks to the defeat of 1967, we shall also have to imagine a different kind of Israel; the kind that, say, Martin Buber had at times advocated. Buber seems to have believed that the sheer magnitude of the Holocaust in Europe required that the surviving Jews find for themselves a homeland in which they could guarantee for themselves a life free from those kinds of pogroms. But unlike Ben Gurion he also seemed to have believed that the Jews would never find enduring peace and safety in Palestine if they did not recognize that they had come to occupy other people's land, that those other people had legitimate rights of their own which predated the rights of the later Jewish immigrants, and that justice therefore demanded that Jews live in peace with their neighbours in a state where those neighbours had absolutely the same rights as themselves. Many Jews of that time were deeply sceptical of a certain sort of modular European nationalism which sought ethnically pure nation-states, and even of that majoritarian nationalism which sought special privileges for an ethno-religious majority within a territorial state; Zionism was precisely that kind of modular European nationalism. Many anti-Zionist Jews of that time certainly envisioned a community of Jews in Israel/Palestine but as a people who would consider themselves not as Westerners having to live corporeally outside Europe, but as a people who needed to learn a new ethic of belonging, as a new/old Middle Eastern people living among old inhabitants of the land.

In short, Jewish-Arab co-existence required great moderation in the purifying Zionist nationalism itself, for these newcomers in an ancient land. Not an attachment and self-definition in terms of a primordialist ethno-religious identity, an impermeable Jewishness, but a modern existence which is freely chosen and which arises out of a past European suffering and a present West Asian belonging. What follows from that is the vision of a multi-ethnic, secular democratic state comprised of Jews, Christians and Muslims alike, in a polity that grants no privilege to race or religion – an eternally open house, as it were. What Israel is, and what it ought to be – what it *can* be: much of the problem lies there, and hence, also, much of the solution.

Suppose, then, that the consideration of Islam and Islamism starts not from primordial and ageless belongings but from the precariousness *of a present* so bereft of secular justice that one finds no meaningful way of belonging to it, or in it; the sheer multiplicity of malignant contexts within which all sorts of cancerous growths become possible. Another way of putting this is that when human beings took upon themselves the task of managing the affairs of the material world, they also made the claim that they were capable of dispensing justice, a justice more whole than what the various monopolists of the holy books offer. The secular world has to be just twice over: in terms of what it has defined for itself, *and* also to ward off the claim that God would have given better justice. That is to say, the secular world has to have enough justice in it for one not to have to constantly invoke God's justice against the injustices of the profane. A politics of radical equalities, so to speak.

NOTES

1   In *Le Nouvel Observateur*, 15-21 January 1998, Brzezinski said: 'The day that the Soviets officially crossed the border, I wrote to President Carter: We now have the opportunity of giving to the USSR its Vietnam war... What is most important to the history of the world? The Taliban or the collapse of the Soviet empire? Some stirred-up Moslems or the liberation of Central Europe and the end of the cold war?'

2   For an early and incisive reflection on this connection of Islamic identity and conditions of immigration to advanced capitalist societies – in this case Britain – see 'Prologue: Muslim "Culture" and the European Tribe', in Aziz al-Azmeh, *Islams and Modernities*, London: Verso, 1992.

3   The Vatican's translation of the original speech, 'Three Stages in the Program of De-Hellenization' is available at http://www.zenit.org.

4   Ibid. The Qur'an's injunction 'There is no compulsion in the faith' (Surah 2:256) was frequently invoked by eminent Islamic jurists in deciding what rights and protections a Muslim ruler ought to offer to his subjects of other faiths.

5   Quoted in 'Ratzinger on Turkey in EU, European Secularism', *Catholic World News*, 11 August 2004, available from http://www.cwnews.com.

6   'Three Stages in the Program of De-Hellenization'.

7   Quoted in Paul Kokoski, 'Avoid "Challenge the Church"', *Catholic New Times*, 1 December 2002.

8   Samuel P. Huntington, *The Clash of Civilizations and the Remaking of the World Order*, New York: Simon and Schuster, 1996, pp, 20-21.

9   Ibid., p. 28; see also pp. 36, 46.

10   See especially Ervand Abrahimian, *Iran between Two Revolutions*, Princeton: Princeton University Press, 1982.

ISLAMISM AND EMPIRE:
THE INCONGRUOUS NATURE OF
ISLAMIST ANTI-IMPERIALISM

ASEF BAYAT

An animated debate is under way within the Left, the Right, and among Islamists themselves about the status of current Islamist movements vis-à-vis neoliberal imperialism. Rightist circles are clear that Islamism is a regressive, anti-modern and violent movement that poses the greatest threat to the 'free world'. Islamism represents, in their view, a 'totalitarian ideology', a 'cousin of fascism and communism', which stands opposed to modernity and to the enlightenment values enshrined in the capitalist free world.[1] In a sense, the idea of a 'clash of civilizations' captures the 'objective contradictions' of Islam and Islamism with Western modernity and its universalizing mission.

Leftist groups, however, seem to be divided. While some groups see Islamist movements as 'analogues to fascism', so that the best socialists can hope for is to break individuals away from the Islamist ranks and lure them into progressive camps,[2] others consider Islamism as an anti-imperialist force with which the Left can find some common ground. For the British Socialist Workers' Party, for instance, in the current conditions of mounting Islamophobia in the West, an 'internationalist duty to stand with Muslims against racism and imperialism' requires secular socialists to forge alliances with such admittedly conservative organizations as the Muslim Association of Britain,[3] whose misogynous stand on gender issues in Muslim communities is often overlooked on the grounds of cultural 'relativism'.[4]

Others suggest that 'Islam has the advantage of being simultaneously an ethno-nationalist identity as well as a resistance movement to subordination to the dictates of capitalist world economy'.[5] Thus, by mobilizing civil society against structural adjustment, by offering alternative welfare systems to the shrinking role of the states in fulfilling its responsibilities, Islamists currently present the most important challenge to global neoliberalism. Indeed for some observers, the seemingly proletarian profile of Islamists and their populist rhetoric render them *the* movement of the dispossessed. In this sense, their anti-imperialist stand, combined with religious language, makes the Islamist movement analogous to the Latin American liberation theology of the 1960s and 1970s, which took the liberation of the poor as its central moral objective.[6] Mike Davis's influential survey, *Planet of Slums*, for instance, portrays militant Islamism (along with Pentecostalism) as a 'song of the dispossessed' who survive in the misery of slums, as in Palestine's Gaza Strip, or Baghdad, defying the empire's Orwellian technologies of repression by resorting to the 'gods of chaos', daily explosions and suicide bombings.[7] Does this imply that Islamism represents the indigenous Middle Eastern version of global dissent against neoliberal imperialism?

The notion of 'anti-imperialism' has traditionally held a normative significance, referring to a just struggle waged by often secular progressive forces to liberate subjugated peoples from the diktat of global capitalism and imperial (economic, political and cultural) domination, and to establish self-rule, social justice, and support for the working classes and 'the subaltern' – women, minorities, and marginalized groups. Such anti-imperialism has been embraced, for instance, by the current anti-globalization movement to challenge the dictates of the 'new empire'. This notion of empire is distinct from the liberal concept, where 'leaders of one society rule directly or indirectly over at least one other society, using instruments different from (though not necessarily more authoritarian than) those used to rule at home'.[8] In the liberal conception, empire is not all that bad; the British empire spread the institutions of parliamentary democracy across the globe, and the US empire, as the Harvard historian Niall Ferguson stresses, not only seeks to ensure US national security and acquire raw materials, but also provides crucial 'public goods' such as peace, global order and 'Americanization' for the rest of the world through the export of commodities and ideas.[9] In contrast, the left-critical concept of the 'new empire' is one which consists, in the words of David Harvey, of a mix of 'neo-liberal restructurings world-wide and the neoconservative attempt to establish and maintain a coherent moral order in both the global and various national situations';[10] it results from the need of capital to dispose of its surplus, which involves geographical expansion. Put simply, capital needs the state to clear the way for a secure and less-troubled context for overseas investment.

What is the relationship of the current Islamist movements to neoliberal imperialism? Do they pose a genuine challenge, or are they no more than reactions which offer unfortunate justifications for neoliberal hegemony? I suggest that the fundamental question is not whether Islamists pose resistance to empire, nor whether they are anti-imperialist or fascist. The relevant question rather is what does Islamist anti-imperialism entail vis-à-vis the mass of Muslim humanity.

WHAT IS ISLAMISM?

Some of the problems involved in exploring the anti-imperialist position of Islamism lie in its multiple facets and meanings. Some observers focus on the political economy of certain Islamist trends, concluding that it stands against neoliberal orthodoxy; some highlight Islamist movements' welfare operations, focusing on Islamism's proletarian character; while still others concentrate on Islamism's ideologies, moral codes and religio-political visions, finding them conservative, regressive, or even fascist.

Not only does Islamism possess different facets; it also refers to different types of organizations, different visions of an Islamic order, and different ways in which to achieve such an order. While gradualist and reformist Islamists, such as the Muslim Brotherhood and its offshoots in Algeria, Syria, Sudan, Kuwait, Palestine and Jordan pursue non-violent methods of mobilizing civil society – through work in professional associations, NGOs, local mosques and charities – the militant trends, such as the Jama'a al-Islamiya in Egypt or the Algerian FIS, resort to violence and terrorism against state agencies, Western targets and civilians, hoping to cause a Leninist-type insurrection. And such militant Islamists also differ from current jihadi trends, such as the groups associated with al-Qaeda. Whereas militant Islamism represents political movements operating within the given nation-states and targeting primarily the secular national state, the jihadis are transnational in their ideas and operations, and represent fundamentally apocalyptic 'ethical movements' involved in 'civilizational' struggles, with the aim of combating a highly abstract 'West', and all societies of 'non-believers'. They invariably resort to extreme violence both against the self (suicide bombing) and their targets.[11]

Many Islamic-oriented groups are not even Islamist, strictly speaking. A growing trend that I call 'post-Islamist' wants to transcend Islamism as an exclusivist and totalizing ideology, espousing instead inclusion, pluralism and ambiguity. In Iran, it took the form of the 'reform movement' which partly evolved into the 'reform government' of 1997-2004. In addition, a growing number of Islamic groups, such as the current Lebanese Hezbollah, the al-Wasat Party in Egypt, the Turkish Virtue Party and the Justice and Development Party, and the Indian Jama'at Islami, are in the throes of transformation, increasingly exhibiting some aspects of 'post-Islamism'. Post-Islamist movements aspire for a secular state, but wish to promote religious ethics in their societies, while their economic positions range from promoting the free-market to some kind of social democracy.[12]

Global events since the late 1990s (the Balkan ethnic wars, the Russian domination of Chechnya, the Israeli re-occupation of the West Bank and Gaza, not to mention post-9/11 anti-Islamic sentiments in the West) have created among Muslims an acute sense of insecurity and a feeling of siege. This in turn has heightened their sense of religious identity and communal bonds, generating a new trend of 'active piety', a sort of missionary tendency quite distinct from the highly-organized and powerful 'a-political Islam' of the Tablighi movement (a missionary movement of spiritual awakening active among Muslims) in being quite individualized, diffused, and inclined toward Salafism. Its adherents aim not to establish an Islamic state, but to reclaim and enhance the self, while striving to implant the same mission in others.[13]

In this essay I take Islamism to refer to the ideologies and movements which, notwithstanding their variations, aim in general at establishing an 'Islamic order'– a religious state, Islamic laws, and moral codes. Concerns such as establishing social justice, are only supposed to follow from this strategic objective. Historically speaking, Islamism has been the political language not just of the marginalized but particularly of high-achieving middle classes who saw their dream of social equity and justice betrayed by the failure of both capitalist modernity and socialist utopia. They aspired to an alternative social and political order rooted in 'indigenous', Islamic history, values and thought. Segments of the poor may support Islamism when they feel it can increase their life chances. Even though different currents of Islamists have adopted different ways to achieve their ultimate goals, they have all used a religious, Islamic language and conceptual framework, favoured conservative social mores and an exclusive social order, and have had a patriarchal disposition and broadly intolerant attitudes towards different ideas and life-styles. Theirs, then, has been an ideology and a movement resting on a blend of religiosity and obligation, with little commitment to the language of rights.

AN ANTI-IMPERIALIST MOVEMENT?

What then is the status of such a movement vis-à-vis the new empire? A cursory survey of the discourses and practices of Islamists reasonably foregrounds critical and anti-imperialist tendencies. From their street marches and protests to their welfare programmes in the back streets of the Muslim metropolis; from their defiance of Israel and the US role in the Middle East to their populist anti-globalization rhetoric – everything seems to point to the implacable opposition of these movements to global domination. What political force has in recent years inflicted more economic, geopolitical, and physical injury to Western powers than militant Islamism?

The victory of the Islamic revolution in Iran and the subsequent seizure of the US Embassy and diplomats in 1979 heralded the advent of a new oppositional force. The revolution threw the major ally of the West, the Shah, out of power, and instigated similar movements that threatened to erode US interests and influence in the Muslim Middle East. The writings of the Sorbonne-educated Ali Shariati, a key anti-imperialist Muslim intellectual, had a significant impact on a generation of revolutionaries who presided over the state power in Iran after the Shah. Shariati brought the modern concepts of 'class', 'class struggle', 'revolution', and 'classless society' from Marx into Shiite Islamic discourse, giving a scientific legitimacy to what he termed 'red' or 'revolutionary Shiism'.[14] One of the 'God-worshiping socialists' of the late 1960s, and deeply influenced by Frantz Fanon's and Marx's social theories, Shariati nevertheless remained critical of the materialist conception of man in Marxism and other Western philosophies.[15] Yet for him it was the revolutionary struggle against imperialism, and not simply religious identity, that should guide political alliances. It was a position of this sort that informed the 'Islamic Marxism' of Iran's Mujahideen Khalq organization, a major player in the immediate post-revolutionary situation of 1979.[16] Also, influenced by developments in Iran, the Lebanese Hezbollah has moved since the late 1980s to center-stage in world radical politics, thanks to its relentless struggle to oust Israeli occupation forces from Lebanon. Sheikh Hassan Nasrallah, the head of Hezbollah, has been an avid reader of Frantz Fanon, Che Guevara, and other anti-colonial figures.

Revolutionary Third-Worldism has not been limited to Shiite militants. The Egyptian Sayid Qutb, a leader of the Society of Muslim Brothers, the oldest and largest Islamist movement in the Arab world, brought the concept of *jahili* state and society from the Indian thinker Abulala' Mawdudi, who was himself influenced by Lenin's perspective on organization and the state. Mawdudi's notion of Islamic 'theo-democracy' was not very dissimilar to a kind of communist state in which the capitalist economy was to succumb to the principle of 'justice'. In his long essay, the *Struggle between Islam and Capitalism*, the militant Sayyid Qutb urged fellow Muslims not to wait for the 'miracle of Stalin', communism, but stand up and fight for their own liberation, social justice and dignity.[17] The strategy of Al-Banna, the founder of the group, was remarkably similar to Gramsci's notions of war of manoeuvre and hegemony, even though there is no evidence that he, unlike the contemporary Turkish Islamist Abdelrahman Dilipak, had actually read Gramsci.

More recently, since the 1980s, many Sunni Marxists in Egypt (such as Tariq el-Bishri, Mohammad Emarah, Mustafa Mahmoud, Adel Hussein, Abdulwahab el-Massiri and others) have been turning to Islamism, bringing many Marxian visions and vocabularies into political Islam and offering Islamism as an indigenous Third-Worldist ideology to fight imperialism, Zionism and, more importantly, secularism.[18]

Islamists see their economy and polity, and especially their culture, as having become dominated by 'Western powers', and US-led globalization in particular, which subordinates Islam's core values. Mohammad Mahdi Akif, the current leader of Egypt's Muslim Brotherhood, regards the US design in the Middle East, its call for 'democratization', with great suspicion, because the US has invariably supported the region's secular dictators and spread its corrupting cultural products throughout the Middle East.[19] Even the Muslim Brotherhood's younger and more moderate leadership (such as Esam el-Eryan) continues to lash out at the US for its building of a 'global empire' under the guise of globalization,[20] and because it subverts the Muslim Brothers' objective of establishing an Islamic international entity (*kiyan Islami*) in the Muslim lands.[21] Indeed, the very process of 'globalization' is no less than a 'trap' to subjugate the down-trodden (*mustazafin*) of the world, in particular the Islamic *umma* (community) through modern technology.[22] For Islamists, imperialism is embodied not simply in military conquest and economic control; it manifests itself first and foremost in cultural domination, established through the spread of secular ideas, immorality, foreign languages, logos, names, food and fashion.[23]

Thus Ayatollah Mesbah Yazdi, a major theoretician of Iran's hardliners, formulates the dictates of the *kuffar* (or non-believers, or the 'West') over Muslims in four domains. *Military conquest* as in the crusades may be uncommon, but it goes with *political control*, or ruling through cronies and proxy regimes; and *economic dominance* which creeps in by changing consumer cultures, exploiting material resources and economic dependency. But the most ravaging aspect is *cultural command*, a sort of soft imperialism established through science, technology, films, entertainment, alien ideas and values which insidiously subvert Islam's hegemony. What instigates cultural domination is partly the Western fear of annihilation, a kind of Darwinian struggle in which cultures need to dominate if they are not to vanish.[24] The idea of 'global village', according to Egyptian Adel Hussein, is nothing other than world rule by a single village head, the US; in other words, the Americanization of the planet. Precisely because Islam believes in human diversity, it inevitably challenges the homogenizing tendency of US-led globalization.[25]

Clearly then the objective contradiction between Islamism and imperialism is real. The politics and value-system preached and practised by Islamists would allow little of the kind of 'freedom' that the current neoliberal hegemons so deeply cherish. The puritanical and largely exclusivist image of social order projected by Islamists conflicts with the free flow of cultural goods and ideas that globalization unleashes. Islamists lash out at what they see as the homogenizing onslaught of globalization against cultural diversity; and yet they strive to enforce homogeneous thought and life-styles in the societies they rule. They defend, as do most democrats, the right of Muslim women in Europe to wear what they wish; and yet many of them deny such rights to both Muslim and non-Muslim women in their societies. Islamists offer a doctrinal justification for this by arguing that Islam does not accept Muslims being subjected to the dominion of 'non-believers'.[26] However, the notion of 'non-believers' is often interpreted so broadly that it would potentially include any non-Muslim Westerner, even those who may express solidarity with 'Muslim cause'. In short, key to the anti-imperialist disposition of Islamism is the clash over hegemony. Islamists' desire to cultivate an exclusive morality and culture to facilitate their authority over the Muslim *umma* is subverted by the spread of Western cultural and discursive practices. These observations give some idea of the incongruous nature of Islamist anti-imperialism.

AUTHORITARIAN ANTI-IMPERIALISTS

It is certainly reductionist to attribute the rise of Islamism to Cold War politics – to US support for Islamists in order to undermine communism.[27] Islamist resurgence has crucial internal roots. Yet the fact remains that Islamists and the 'free world' have at certain junctures made tacit alliances against anti-imperialist secular movements in the Middle East. The US went along quite easily with Saudi Arabia's attempt to promote Wahhabism as an ideological bulwark against the sweeping secular nationalism and republicanism that the Nasserist revolution unleashed in 1960s. In the same decade and in the early 1970s, Islamists were deployed against the revolutionary movements (as in Oman) as well as against secular leftists, communists, and women's movements. It has now become an open secret how the US and UK allied with the Islamist Mujahideen in Afghanistan to combat the USSR, and especially how the US-backed government of Pakistan sheltered the Taliban in their formative years. In other words, imperialism has in certain periods benefited from groups of Islamist militants. These conjunctural convergences should not, however, conceal the deep enmity between the two forces, as outlined earlier. The key question is: what is there in this for the mass of Muslim subaltern and other social forces who also fight the new empire? Certainly Islamists' struggles undercut certain material and strategic interests of the West. But do they necessarily undermine its global ideological hegemony? Islamists' struggles may contribute to liberating Muslim nations from foreign domination. But do they herald liberty, democracy and well-being at home?

Islamists in Iran sided with a popular revolution (in 1979) that overthrew the autocratic regime of the Shah, backed by Western powers, seriously undermining foreign influence in the country. But once in power the ruling elites established a religious authoritarian state, an exclusive social order, and a strict moral discipline that have subjugated a large segment of the population. They systematically suppressed rival 'anti-imperialist forces'– the socialists, secular women's groups, independent labour organizations and student activism – violating many civil liberties and establishing draconian social control. Indeed, the labelling of any cultural practice disapproved by the Islamist authorities as a Western 'cultural invasion' (in the formulation of Ayatollah Mesbah Yazdi) has meant severe repression and the systematic disciplining of both youth and women, in particular.[28]

It is true that factional struggles within the Islamist regime between 'in-house' rivals have at times opened some breathing-space for dissent from below. Yet Islamist factions have invariably forged an alliance at the top when opposition from below has mounted; they have opposed inclusive democracy, pluralist ideas, and independent voices. It was only with the ascendancy to power of reformists led by President Muhammad Khatami (1997-2004) that a new hope unfolded for democratic governance. However with the reformists' defeat, by 2004, through electoral fraud, massive disqualification of their candidates, and popular dissatisfaction with their economic failures, Ahmadinejad's government brought a new round of repression. Since 2005 scores of independent NGOs have been closed down; key activists incarcerated; intellectuals and journalists detained; dissenting faculty and students removed, women activists put behind bars, and mass protests of teachers and bus drivers put down. Ahmadinejad's populist electoral campaign focused on fighting corruption, generating jobs, and a generous distribution of oil money. Yet under his presidency the number of Iranians below the poverty line has increased by 13 per cent.[29] His cabinet – closely linked to the military, intelligence, and security apparatuses – has been building a support base in the network of clients among segments of the provincial poor, but also among military veterans, and those benefiting from connections to the state – administrators of the Revolutionary Guards, informal credit associations, and the like.[30] However justified it is to oppose Israel's continuing subjugation of the Palestinian people, Ahmadinejad's anti-Israel rhetoric is another matter when it extends to a denial of the holocaust, making him a bedfellow with the most grotesque white-supremacists such as David Duke, a former leader of KKK.[31] The hardliners' demagogic rhetoric on Iran's right to develop nuclear technology may inspire anti-American sentiments in the Middle East. But it can also play into the hands of intransigent war-mongers in Washington and Tel Aviv, with potentially catastrophic consequences.[32]

The contradictory and self-serving nature of Islamist anti-imperialism is not limited to Iran. Egypt's Jama'a al-Islamiya not only moralized its constituency and imposed discipline on its followers' behaviour, but also terrorized unveiled women and non-Muslims, and murdered scores of Christian Copts and foreign tourists, while it fought fiercely against the US-backed regime of President Mubarak. Al-Qaeda's elitism, misogyny, and widespread violence against its critics, secularists, and Shiite Muslims are too well-known to require elaboration here. Even the 'anti-imperialism' of the Arab Mujahideen who in the early 1990s rushed to 'help' the Bosnian Muslims against the Serbian aggression meant, in the end, little to the victims. These Islamist internationals had their own Islamization agenda – one that the Bosnian Muslims resented. Instead of focusing on humanitarian objectives they concentrated on military operations and missionary work – spreading Salafi ideas through print, TV channels and websites. They challenged the local religious authorities and attempted to turn Bosnia into a base against the West, and the Bosnian conflict into a war between Islam and Christianity.[33] No wonder these kinds of activities created among Europeans a fear of radical 'white Muslims' in the heart of Europe, thus jeopardizing the legitimacy of the otherwise just Bosnian cause. Of course, such self-serving anti-imperialism is not restricted to religious, or for that matter Islamist, experience; one has only to note the sad destiny of the champion of secular socialist anti-imperialism, the Zimbabwean Robert Mugabe, who ended up leading a nation that has to endure 20-hour daily electric cuts, triple digit inflation, and a massive demolition of poor people's homes.[34]

So the fundamental question is not whether Islamism challenges imperialist interests, which it does. The question rather is to what extent this struggle entails an emancipation of the subaltern in Muslim societies. And this point lies at the heart of the difference between Middle Eastern Islamism and Latin American liberation theology, notwithstanding their shared religious languages and anti-imperialist positions.

A THEOLOGY OF LIBERATION?

While Islamist movements (notwithstanding their variations) have in general aimed at the establishment of an Islamic order (a religious state with Sharia law and moral codes), from which social justice and improving the life of the poor are to trickle down, for liberation theology the point of departure has been the 'liberation of the poor'; the Gospel is re-read and reinterpreted to achieve this fundamental goal. The principal question for liberation theology was 'how can we be Christians in the world of misery?' 'We can be Christians, authentic Christians, only by living our faith in a liberating way', they replied.[35]

Originally liberation theology was a reaction to, and a reflection of, the hideous imperial legacy of the Church in Latin America. For in contrast to the Islamic *ulema* (scholars) who were mostly involved in anti-colonial struggles in the Middle East, the Latin American Catholic Church was an instrument of Iberian colonialism, which was to bring riches to Spain and Portugal and to Christianize the colonies. Not only did the Church support colonial rule, it continued to back the wealthy conservative classes in society after independence was achieved. Even some rethinking during the 1930s, reflected in the 'New Christendom' and the subsequent emergence of Christian Democratic Parties, failed to overturn the Church's old conservative disposition. Yet dramatic social and political events (poverty and oppression, military coups, American support of the holders of power and property, the failure of the Christian Democratic Parties, the sudden victory of the Cuban Revolution and the wave of popular guerrilla movements) had pushed the Church to the brink of social irrelevance. There was a need to intervene to save Catholicism from the conservatism of the Church's elites.[36]

Thus unlike Islamism, liberation theology was not so much an expression of cultural identity in the sense of self-preservation vis-à-vis a dominating Western 'other'; it was imbedded in the indigenous discourse of development, underdevelopment, and dependency that Latin America was fiercely debating at the time. Indeed, the idiom of a 'theology of liberation' emerged in the context of clerics exploring a 'theology of development'. It was Gustavo Gutierrez who, during the Conference of the World Council of Churches held in Switzerland in 1969, replaced that term with the 'theology of liberation', popularizing the concept through his book, *Liberation Theology*. Central to this notion was, of course, the emancipation of the subaltern.[37]

In contrast, Islamism had a different birth and birthplace. Broadly speaking, Islamism arose as a language of self-assertion to mobilize those (largely middle class high-achievers supported often pragmatically by segments of the lower classes) who felt marginalized by the dominant economic, political, or cultural processes, those for whom the failure of both capitalist modernity and socialist utopia made the language of morality (religion) a substitute for politics. In a sense, it was the Muslim middle-class way of saying 'No' to those whom they considered their 'excluders' – their national elites, secular governments, and these governments' Western allies. So they rejected Western cultural domination, its political rationale, moral sensibilities and cultural symbols, even if in practice many of them shared those traits, as in their neckties, food, and technologies. As an alternative to existing models they attempted to offer an alternative utopian society and state for Muslim humanity. It was also a project that aimed to regain the self-respect of Muslims relative to Western cultural imperialism and to Zionism as a perceived component of this. And all these aspirations arose in the context of the Cold War, when the US's fear of communism and secular nationalism drew it close to Islamist movements.[38]

While Islamists aim to Islamize their society, polity and economy, liberation theologians never intended to Christianize their society or states, but rather to change society from the vantage point of the deprived. Liberation theology, then, had much in common with humanist, democratic, and popular movements in Latin America, including labour unions, peasant leagues, student groups and guerrilla movements, with whom it organized campaigns, strikes, demonstrations, land occupations and development work. Here, as a partner of a broad popular movement, liberation theology aimed not to proselytize, nor to make the coalition partners Christian, but to help advance the cause of the liberation movement in general. More important, liberation theology shared a great deal with humanist Marxism. Indeed, both Latin American Marxism and liberation theology had been influenced by the language of the radical *dependencia* of the 1960s and 1970s that originated primarily in the South American continent. Prominent priests such as the Boff brothers (of Brazil), Gutierrez (of Peru), Bonino (of Venezuela) and Torres (of Columbia) were intellectual theologians equipped with the discourse of dependency and Marxist humanism.

A reinterpretation of Christian theology was to facilitate the goal of emancipation. They began first with the practice of liberation, and then their theology was formed as a reflection of that praxis. 'There is no truth outside or beyond the concrete historical events in which men are involved as agents', argued Bonino.[39] The protagonists refrained from projecting a blueprint for the future. What they could present was a general direction and basic structures, or 'historical projects' – something half-way to 'utopia'. This 'human project' sought to transcend capitalism and to imagine a form of democratic socialism. It would be carried out by ordinary people, the grassroots. Such an imagined society was to be informed by the spirit of participation and cooperation. People were to move beyond struggles for equality and justice to a society in which they would achieve true social solidarity, organized around the concept of love.

In contrast, few Islamic activists self-consciously incorporated Marxist notions into their ideologies. As noted earlier, the Iranian Ali Sahriati and his followers, the Islamic Mujahideen Khalq Organization, had been influenced by Marx's economic analyses and his critique of capitalism. They adopted such concepts as 'class struggle', 'exploitation', and 'classless society', and mixed them with Third-Worldist language drawn from Fanon, Aimé Césaire, and other anti-colonial leaders.[40] By the 1980s and 1990s, however, even this small Marxist influence had gone among Islamist intellectuals, as they moved toward nativist ideas and their 'authentic' canons expressed in the Qur'an, Sunna, and the classic Islamic fatawi and treatises. 'Return to the self', or discursive self-reliance, was a key ideological feature of the new Islamism. Thus, while most liberation theologians in Latin America embraced Marxist notions of liberation, many Marxists in the Muslim Middle East (e.g. Adel Hussein, Mustafa Mahmoud, El-Messiri, Behzad Nabavi and Mohammad Emara) abandoned their previous ideology and turned to Islam as an indigenous model for social transformation.[41]

As a consequence, building an exclusive moral and ideological community was substituted for the social emancipation of the subaltern. *Da'wa*, an invitation to Islam, became a key objective for Islamists. Even though Islamists varied in their economic visions – ranging from distributive populism through the mixed-economy to the Friedmanite free market – they generally converged on the idea of a closed social order, a polity based upon Sharia, and adherence to cultural nativism. Although gradualist Islamists such as the Muslim Brotherhood in Egypt and Jordan, the Rifah Party in Turkey, and the pre-election FIS in Algeria, formed political parties and were active in professional associations, communities, educational institutions and parliament, they remained overwhelmingly politicist in approach and middle-class in profile. Radical Islamists – the Mujahideen of Iran, those in Algeria after the 1992 cancellation of elections, Egyptian militants, and Persian Gulf Islamist groups – opted for a vanguardist project of seizing state power through armed struggle. A few attempts by such Muslim intellectuals as the Egyptian Hasan Hanafi or the Indian Asghar Ali Engineer to build the intellectual basis for an Islamic liberation theology lost out to the populist fundamentalism of the growing Islamist trend. Elitism remained a key feature of Islamist politics.

CONCLUSION:
ANTI-IMPERIALISM OR EMANCIPATION?

What then of the anti-imperialism of Islamist movements? At one level Islamism has shown a formidable opposition to the new empire, contributing to undercutting certain strategic interests of the Western powers, and especially the US. Islamists have spearheaded protracted public protests against US policies in the Middle East, especially its support for Israel. They have also opposed the region's secular authoritarian regimes, and diminished or disrupted the normalization of US control in the region, particularly in Iran, Iraq and Afghanistan.

But has Islamism been able to offer, either in practice or in theory, a viable alternative to imperialist domination? Despite its practical failures, socialism managed, albeit only for some time, to articulate a powerful theoretical model of social justice and liberation of the oppressed that offered a solid alternative to capitalist hegemony. For a while, it undermined the ideological foundation of bourgeois values and the capitalist economic model. Things however have been different with Islamism. The largely culturalist thrust of Islamists' anti-imperialism has meant that they have little to offer in the domain of political economy. Even their 'distributive populism' remains largely a feature of their movement phase; the economic policies (even though they vary across different countries and time periods) of the Islamist *states* such as Iran, Saudi Arabia, the Sudan or Afghanistan, differ little from those of other non-ideological developing economies with comparable national incomes.

On the other hand, a preoccupation with particularistic cultural and religious struggles has allowed little room to work with global movements which pursue broader concerns such as the environment, livelihoods, and welfare systems. This culturalism, instead of forging alliances, has caused division and hostility at both national and international levels. Although a populist posture, affordable welfare provisions, moral language, and fierce opposition to corrupt Middle East regimes has earned Islamist movements support, they have failed to set up a viable alternative because of their patriarchal, exclusivist, authoritarian vision of social order and lack of a solid economic vision. If anything, Islamism, especially its radical version, has played into the hands of imperialist circles; its policies have in practice justified and dignified the position of its neoliberal enemies who preach individual liberty and open social order. The undemocratic precepts and practices of most Islamist groups have provoked widespread anti-Islamic reactions, security measures, illiberal policies, and global surveillance, which taken together have victimized ordinary Muslims in the West and in the Muslim world alike.

The 1980 Iran hostage-taking was bold, and a blow to the US sense of self-importance; but it led to surveillance at home and hostility abroad. On the same day that the Muslim militants climbed over the embassy walls, a large group of unemployed marched in the streets of Tehran to demand jobs and social protection. But the desperate appeals of those marchers were stifled by the nationalist outcry of the militants who were preoccupied with 'Islam against the Great Satan'.[42] The hostage-taking also pushed the US to support a devastating Iran-Iraq war which cost millions of lives and massive economic destruction. Only recently have some critics openly wondered who benefited from this hostage-taking – the *umma*, or imperialism? And now once again after more than 25 years history seems to be repeating itself, this time with a more tragic prospect. President Ahmadinejad's rhetoric over the holocaust and his populist language has already played into the hands of the most dangerous war-mongers in Washington and Tel Aviv, who are fantasizing about massive air strikes against the Islamic Republic.[43]

The good news is that Islamist movements can and do modify their positions under the test of time, by adhering to a certain democratic ethos, pluralist principles, and broader inclusive objectives. Some clear signs of change can be observed, for instance, in the organizations of the Muslim Brotherhood in Egypt and Jordan in recent years, in Hezbollah of Lebanon, and especially among the 1980s generation of Iranian Islamists who by the late 1990s had turned 'post-Islamist' in theory and practice. The anti-imperialism of the latter would have different, more meaningful, implications for the Muslim subaltern than that of the Islamist global jihad, for instance.

Far from demagogy and voluntarism, a meaningful anti-imperialism is about building a hegemony that rests on the universal ideals of justice, inclusion, and human dignity. This requires clarity, candour and, more than anything else, a sense of self-confidence. It is about winning the hearts and minds of global humanity to resist the diktat of the new empire in a patient, painstaking, and scrupulous strategy. This means opening up, connecting, negotiating, developing a global platform with and for those in the globe (from various races, religions and gender) who struggle for liberation – not simply liberation from foreign, imperialist, domination, but also liberation from political, patriarchal, economic and religious domination at home. This means transcending nativism, exclusivism, authoritarianism and xenophobia.

Any struggle, however heroic, that replaces imperialist supremacy with domestic forms of oppression will not serve the interests of the Muslim majority. For decades in the Middle East, the majority of people and libera-tory ideas have already been caught in the crossfire between nationalism and colonialism, Baathism and imperialism, and now Islamism and neoliberal empire, from which they are attempting to exit. Thus, the central question for progressive forces is not just how to challenge the empire, but how to realize liberation; for the ultimate end is not simply anti-imperialism, but emancipation.

NOTES

1   Expressed by the ultra-rightist commentator Gamie Glazov in 'Symposium: The Terror War: How We Can Win', 15 November 2004, available from http://www.frontpagemagazine.com.

2   See for instance Edward Ellis, 'The Left and "Reactionary Anti-imperialism" - The Theory of Accommodation', *Workers' Liberty*, 30 March 2002, available from http://www.workersliberty.org.

3   Dave Crouch, 'The Bolsheviks and Islam', *International Socialism*, 110, Spring 2006, p. 38.

4   See an interesting critique, for instance, in Chetan Bhatt, 'The Fetish of the Margins: Religious Absolutism, Anti-Racism and Postcolonial Silence', *New Formations*, 59, Autumn 2006.

5   See Paul Lubeck, 'The Islamic Revival: Antinomies of Islamic Movements un-der Globalization', CGIRS Working Paper Series, Number 99-1, University of California, Santa Cruz, available from http://www2.ucsc.edu/cgirs.

6   See for instance J. Haynes, *Religion in Third World Politics*, Buckingham: Open University Press, 1993; Phil Marfleet, 'Globalization and Religious Activism', in Ray Kiely and Phil Marfleet, eds., *Globalization and the Third World*, Lon-don: Routledge, 1998, pp. 185-215; John Esposito, 'Religion and Global Af-fairs: Political Challenges', *SAIS Review: A Journal of International Affairs*, 18(2), Summer/Fall 1998.

7   Mike Davis, *Planet of Slums*, London: Verso, 2006.

8   See Kenneth Pomernaz, 'Empire and "Civilizing Mission": Past and Present', *Daedalus*, Spring 2005, pp. 34-35.

9   Niall Ferguson, 'The Unconscious Colossus: Limits of (and Alternative to) American Empire', *Daedalus*, Spring 2005, p. 20. See also Ferguson, *Empire: How Britain Made the Modern World*, London: Allen Lane, 2003, p. 358.

10   Interview with David Harvey, by Alberto Toscano, *Development and Change Forum*, 2007, forthcoming.

11   Asef Bayat, 'Is There a Future for Islamic Revolutions? Religion, Revolt, and Middle Eastern Modernity', in John Foran, David Lane, and Andreja Zivkovic, eds., *Revolution in the Making of the Modern World: Social Identities, Globalization and Modernity*, London, Routledge (forthcoming). For a fine analysis of al-Qa-eda as an ethical movement, see Faisal Devji, *Landscapes of the Jihad: Militancy, Morality, and Modernity*, New York: Cornell University Press, 2005.

12 See Asef Bayat, *Making Islam Democratic: Social Movements and the Post-Islamist Turn*, Stanford: Stanford University Press, 2007, especially chapter 1.

13 This section draws on Asef Bayat, 'Is There a Future for Islamic Movements?'.

14 See Ali Shariati, *Shi'eh-ye Alavi and Shi'e-ye Safavi*, Tehran, 1979; see also his *Jahat-guiri-ye Tabaqati-ye Islam*, Tehran, 1980.

15 Ali Shariati, *Insan, Islam, va Marxism*, Tehran, 1977.

16 See Ervan Abrahamian, 'The Guerrilla Movement in Iran, 1963–77', 86 *MERIP Reports*, 86, March–April 1980; also see his *Radical Islam: The Iranian Mojahedin*, London: I.B. Tauris, 1989.

17 Sayyid Qutb, *Ma'rikat al-Islam wa al-Ra'sulmaliya*, Cairo: Dar al-Shorouk, 2006.

18 Indeed as early as 1954, Bernard Lewis wrote an essay in which he implied how the ethics of Islam was compatible with the spirit of communism. See Lewis, 'Communism and Islam', *International Affairs*, 30(1), January 1954.

19 See Akif, 'al-Wilayat al-Muttahida', February 2006, http://www.ikhwanonline.com; see also Akif in March and April 2006.

20 Esam el-Eryan, 'Al-Ikhwan al-Muslimun wa Amrika', December 2005, in http://www.ikhwanonline.com.

21 Ibid.

22 Adel Hussein, 'Al-'Awlama wa Sera'atna Ma 'a al-Gharb', in Muhammad Ibrahim Mabruk, et al., eds., *Al-Islam wa al-'Awlama*, Cairo: Dar al-Qawmiya al-'Arabiya, 1999.

23 Ahmad Abdelrahman, 'Al-'Awlama: Wojhat Nazar Islamiya', in Mabruk, *Al-Islam wa al-'Awlama*, pp. 91–100.

24 Ibid.

25 Hussein, 'Al-'Awlama wa Sera'atna Ma 'a al-Gharb'.

26 See Mesbah Yazdi, *Tahajom-e Farhagui*, Tehran, 1997. This volume is translated into Arabic as *Al-Ghazw al-Thiqafi*.

27 See for instance Mahmood Mamdani, *Good Muslims, Bad Muslims*, New York: Pantheon, 2004.

28 See Asef Bayat, 'Islamism and the Politics of Fun', *Public Culture*, vol. 19, no. 3, October 2007.

29 Reported in *Kargozaran*, 17 Ordibehesht 1386, p. 1.

30 For a good analysis see Kaveh Ehsani, 'Iran's Populist Threat to Democracy', *Middle East Report*, 241, Winter 2006, pp. 4–9.

31 Reported in Richard Landes, 'Strange Bedfellows: The Islamists and the far… What?', 18 May 2006, available from http://www.theaugeanstables.com.

32 For the message of such war mongers see Norman Podhoretz, 'The Case for Bombing Iran', *Commentary*, June 2007.

33 See Onder Cetin, 'The Bosnian Ulema and the Negotiation of Islamic Revivalism in Multi-Ethnic Bosnia', unpublished paper, ISIM Seminar, Leiden, 23 January 2007.

34 Nelosn Banya, 'Zimbabwe Heads for Dark Days as Power Cuts Loom', *Reuters News Agency*, 9 May 2007.

35 L. Boff and C. Boff, *Salvation and Liberation*, New York: Orbis Books, 1988, p. 13. The discussions in this section regarding liberation theology in Latin America draws primarily on this book as well as: Christian Smith, *The Emergence of Liberation Theology*, Chicago: University of Chicago Press, 1991; Michael Lowy, *The War of Gods: Religion and Politics in Latin America*, London: Verso Press, 1996.

36 In this sense, liberation theologians were similar not to Islamists but to post-Islamist intellectuals and socially conscious Iranian clerics whose mission was to save Islam as a tolerant religion from the authoritarian practices of fundamentalist Islamism. An undemocratic polity lay at the heart of Islamism, 'republican theology' became the central thrust in post-Islamist religious discourse; see Asef Bayat, *Making Islam Democratic*.

37 G. Gutierrez, *A Theology of Liberation*, New York: Orbis Books, 1988. Martin Lee and Pia Gallegos, 'Gustavo Gutierrez with the Poor', *Christianity and Crisis*, 47(5), 1987.

38 For elaboration see Bayat, *Making Islam Democratic*.

39 Jose Miguez Bonino, *Doing Theology in a Revolutionary Situation*, Philadelphia: Fortress, 1976, p. 88.

40 See Asef Bayat, 'Karl Marx and Ali Shariati', *Alif: Journal of Comparative Poetics*, 9, April 1990.

41 Yet the modernist Islamist intellectuals do receive input from outside Islam. Sheikh Fadlullah of Lebanon reads Fanon; Turkish Abdurrahman Dilipak offers a dialogue with Antonio Gramsci.

42 See Asef Bayat, 'Workless Revolutionaries: The Unemployed Movement in Revolutionary Iran', *International Review of Social History*, 42(2), August 1997.

43 See Seymour Hersh, 'The Iran Plans', *New Yorker*, 17 April 2006.

RELIGION AND POLITICS TODAY FROM A MARXIAN PERSPECTIVE

GILBERT ACHCAR

We had an excellent history teacher during the year before the last of my high school study in Beirut. I still remember listening with bated breath to him telling us the story of the Russian revolution. That was in 1967: revolution was in the air and I had been freshly 'converted' to Marxism. Like any good history teacher, ours used to discuss with us various matters of the past, present and future, after classes as well as during them.

One of these discussions remains engraved on my memory: a chat during a break about the issue of religion. I can't remember what brought us to this topic, but what I do remember is my deep frustration when the teacher contradicted the Marxist positivist that I was, fully convinced that the progress of science and education would wipe out religion in the 21st century. Needless to say, I imagined that century as the outcome of the worldwide triumph of socialist revolution, which I expected to happen during the next few decades. Our teacher held the view that the continuous material enrichment of society would actually enhance the search for spirituality. If my memory serves me right, he quoted approvingly the famous statement attributed to André Malraux, and much discussed since, that the 21st century would be 'religious'.[1]

Was my teacher right after all? Is the present vigour of religious creeds, movements and sects testimony to the religiosity of the 21st century? Well, what is beyond doubt is that my own youthful expectation proved wrong; but I do not concede victory to the opposite view for all that. The truth is that we all proved wrong, as the common assumption of our different expectations was that society in the 21st century would be one of abundance. Whether it would be atheistic or religious was a question deriving from that basic assumption. The question under debate could be phrased in the following terms: Does the satisfaction of material needs enhance a (supposed) need of religious spirituality?

We won't know the answer to this last question any time soon, as the prospect of a world 'free from want' is as remote as the prospect of one 'free from fear' – the last two of the famous 'Four Freedoms' defined by Franklin Roosevelt in 1941 as the pillars of the world he aspired to. The first of Roosevelt's Freedoms – freedom of speech – has surely expanded a lot, though it is still far from complete triumph. The second – freedom to 'worship God in one's own way' – is no longer chiefly threatened by Stalinist-imposed dogmatic 'atheism', as people supposed back in Roosevelt's time, but rather by fanatic-imposed single ways of worshipping God, or any deity for that matter – i.e. by various brands of religious fundamentalism. Nowadays, the freedom that appears to be most wanting and most threatened in major parts of the world is actually the freedom *not* to worship any deity and to live in one's own way. That is surely not progress, but the sign of an ideological regression of historic proportions.

The resilience of religion at the dawn of the fifth century after the 'scientific revolution' is an enigma to anyone holding a positivist view of the world, but not for an authentic Marxian understanding, as I came to realize since my first steps in Marxist theory. This essay aims not only to provide a clue to the resilience of religion in general, but also to account for the various religious ideologies to which history gives rise at different epochs, and their specificities. For not only did religion survive into our times as part of the 'dominant ideology', it is also still producing combative ideologies contesting the prevailing social and/or political conditions. Two of these have received a lot of attention in recent years: Christian theology of liberation and Islamic fundamentalism. A comparative assessment of these two phenomena from the standpoint of Marxist theory, enriched by further inputs from the sociology of religions, is a particularly challenging and politically enlightening endeavour, as I hope to establish.

MARX'S VIEW OF RELIGION

The boundaries of Marx's thinking on the issue of religion were announced in the programme he set himself when he started his transition from 'Young Hegelian' philosophy to class-struggle radical materialism, or what we call Marxism. The much-quoted passage on religion in the 'Introduction' to his *On the Critique of Hegel's Philosophy of Right* is the expression of a decisive moment in the formation of his thought. After having drafted the *Critique* in the summer of 1843 (it remained unpublished during his lifetime), Marx wrote the 'Introduction' at the end of the same year and the beginning of the next, and published it in 1844 in the *Deutsch-Französische Jahrbücher*. The fact that he deemed it good enough for publication is telling, as throughout his life Marx displayed a reluctance to publish any theoretical writing with which he was not fully satisfied. Along with his famous 'Theses on Feuerbach' written the year after, the 'Introduction' maps out brilliantly his course toward what Antonio Labriola was to call the 'philosophy of praxis'.[2] In the 1844 'Introduction', Marx wrote:

> The foundation of irreligious criticism is: The *human being makes religion*; religion does not make the human being. Religion is, indeed, the self-consciousness and self-esteem of the human who has either not yet won through to himself, or has already lost himself again. But the *human* is no abstract being squatting outside the world. The human is *the world of the human* — state, society. This state and this society produce religion, which is an *inverted consciousness of the world*, because they are an *inverted world*. Religion is the general theory of this world, its encyclopaedic compendium, its logic in popular form, its spiritual *point d'honneur*, its enthusiasm, its moral sanction, its solemn complement, and its universal basis of consolation and justification. It is the *fantastic realization* of the human essence since the *human essence* has not acquired any true reality. The struggle against religion is, therefore, indirectly the struggle against *that world* whose spiritual *aroma* is religion.[3]

Here Marx, after stating one of the key ideas of Ludwig Feuerbach's critique of religion ('The human being makes religion; religion does not make the human being'), draws the full implication of this statement, reproaching Feuerbach for his inability to do precisely that. The next statement, that 'the human is no abstract being squatting outside the world', is a direct rebuff to Feuerbach. Religion is an '*inverted consciousness of the world*' only because the human world itself, i.e. society and the state, is 'inverted': it stands on its head, to borrow another metaphor used by Marx in relation to Hegel's dialectics.

Following Feuerbach, and with Christianity mainly in mind, the young Marx fully acknowledged the psychological (spiritual) role played by religion, alongside its essence as a vulgar 'false consciousness': 'Religion is the *general theory of this world*... its logic *in popular form*... its enthusiasm... its *universal basis of consolation and justification*'. However, if one can find in religion a form of humanism — '*the fantastic realization of the human essence*' — it is only because 'the human essence has not acquired any true reality'. Thus, '*the struggle against religion is, therefore, indirectly the struggle against that world whose spiritual aroma is religion*'.

Marx then goes on to develop this insight:

> *Religious* suffering is, at one and the same time, the *expression* of real suffering and the *protest* against real suffering. Religion is the sigh of the oppressed creature, the soul of a heartless world, as well as the spirit of spiritless conditions. It is the *opium* of the people.
>
> To supersede religion as the *illusory* happiness of the people is to require their *real* happiness. To require that they give up their illusions about their condition is *to require that they give up a condition that necessitates illusions*. The criticism of religion is, therefore, in *embryo*, the *criticism of that vale of tears* of which religion is the *halo*.

Religion is an expression of '*suffering*': the sublimated '*expression*' of '*real suffering*' as well as '*the protest*' against it. This is a very perceptive statement indeed; however, Marx did unfortunately not pursue the 'protest' part of it. In the following two sentences, he only emphasized the 'expression' dimension. They are Marx's most quoted sentences on religion: '*Religion is the sigh of the oppressed creature, the soul of a heartless world, as well as the spirit of spiritless conditions. It is the opium of the people*'. Had Marx stuck to his initial insight and sought to capture the *incitement dimension* of religion – as well as its *resignation dimension* designated metaphorically by the soothing power of 'opium' – he could have written the last sentence differently, using another metaphor to designate a stimulant: *It is, at one and the same time, the opium and the cocaine of the people.*[4]

If one wants people to supersede religion in its function as their '*illusory happiness*', it should be in order to achieve '*real happiness*'. If one wants people to get rid of '*their illusions about their condition*', it means realizing a fundamental change of their real condition, into one that does not necessitate illusions anymore. That is why the criticism of religion leads potentially – it should lead, provided the '*embryo*' is allowed to develop – to the criticism of '*real suffering*', that '*vale of tears of which religion is the halo*'. The criticism of religion should, then, lead to the criticism of the human world, i.e. state and society, law and politics. Philosophy, after unmasking the '*holy form*' of human alienation, should strive to unmask its '*unholy*' worldly form.

> It is first of all the *task of philosophy*… to unmask self-estrangement in its *unholy forms* once the *holy form* of human self-estrangement has been unmasked. Thus, the criticism of Heaven turns into the criticism of Earth, the *criticism of religion* into the *criticism of law*, and the *criticism of theology* into the *criticism of politics*.

This line of thought is pursued in the 1845 'Theses on Feuerbach', with its conclusion on revolutionary praxis – 'revolutionary, practical-critical, activity'.

> Feuerbach starts off from the fact of religious self-estrangement, of the duplication of the world into a religious, imaginary world, and a secular one. His work consists in resolving the religious world into its secular basis. He overlooks the fact that after completing this work, the chief thing still remains to be done. For the fact that the secular basis lifts off from itself and establishes itself in the clouds as an independent realm can only be explained by the inner strife and intrinsic contradictoriness of this secular basis. The latter must itself be understood in its contradiction and then, by the removal of the contradiction, revolutionised...
>
> Philosophers have hitherto only interpreted the world in various ways; the point is to change it.[5]

Ironically, in roughly the last four decades, two religious movements have striven to 'change the world' in a subversive manner, in order to establish their own version of the Kingdom of God, an anteroom of 'Heaven', on Earth: Christian liberation theology and Islamic fundamentalism. A revealing clue to their respective natures is to be found in the correlation between the rise of each of them and the fate of the secular left in their respective areas. Whereas the fate of liberation theology is roughly parallel to that of the secular left in Latin America, where it actually acts, and is perceived, as a component of the left in general, Islamic fundamentalism developed in most Muslim-majority countries as a competitor of, and an alternative to, the left – in trying to channel protest against 'real misery', and the state and society that are held responsible for it. These opposite correlations – positive in the first case, negative in the second – are indicative of a profound difference between the two historic movements.

RELIGION AND RADICALISM TODAY: LIBERATION THEOLOGY

Liberation theology is the main modern embodiment of what Michael Löwy calls – aptly drawing on a concept that Max Weber coined, and named after one of Goethe's famous novels – the 'elective affinity' between Christianity and socialism.[6] Putting it more accurately, the 'elective affinity' draws together the legacy of original Christianity – a legacy that faded away, allowing Christianity to turn into the institutionalized ideology of existing social domination – and communistic utopianism. 'Communistic' is used here as something distinct from the communist doctrines formulated with the advent of industrial capitalism. Weber himself depicted quite well this dimension of original Christianity:

> During the charismatic period of a religion, the perfect disciple must also reject landed property, and the mass of believers is expected to be indifferent toward it. An expression of this indifference is that attenuated form of the charismatic communism of love which apparently existed in the early Christian community of Jerusalem, where the members of the community owned property 'as if they did not own it'. Such unlimited, unrationalized sharing with needy brothers, which forced the missionaries, especially Paulus, to collect alms abroad for the anti-economic central community, is probably what lies behind that much-discussed tradition, not any allegedly 'socialist' organization or communist 'collective ownership'. Once the eschatological expectations fade, charismatic communism in all its forms declines and retreats into monastic circles, where it becomes the special concern of the exemplary followers of God.[7]

It is this 'elective affinity' between Christianity in its charismatic phase and a communistic social programme that explains the ability of a Thomas Münzer in the early 16th century to formulate in Christian terms a programme that Friedrich Engels described, in 1850, as an 'anticipation of communism by fantasy'.[8] Engels's description was, however, problematic to the extent that he attributed what he deemed unsuited to the prevailing historical conditions to 'human fantasy'. Although he himself acknowledged the affinity between Münzer's 'communism' and original Christianity, he reached an inconsistent conclusion, at once crudely deterministic and oddly idealistic:

> *The chiliastic raptures of original Christianity offered in this respect a very serviceable starting point.* On the other hand, this reaching out beyond not only the present but also the future, could not help being violently fantastic. At the first practical application, it naturally fell back into narrow limits set by prevailing conditions. …The anticipation of communism by fantasy was in reality the anticipation of modern bourgeois conditions.[9]

Engels could have found the clue to what he described as 'anticipation by fantasy' and 'a genius's anticipation' in the affinity between what he called 'the chiliastic raptures of original Christianity' and the historical condition of a German peasantry faced with profound upheaval and a severe deterioration of its living conditions; indeed, for a 'historical materialist', to see it as a fantastic anticipation of a future state was a surprising assessment of the social program of a peasants' uprising. In reality, the various programmatic statements of the German peasants were not a product of 'fantasy' but of two basic ingredients, combined in different ways.

On the one hand, there was the utopian 'communistic' inspiration found in original Christianity. On the other hand, there was what could be described as 'romantic' longing for the ancient Germanic communal property system, on the part of peasants confronted with pauperization and proletarianization as a result of the gradual dissolution of medieval society – in the same way that, three and a half centuries later, the Narodniks expressed the longing of Russian peasants for the obshchina. In both cases, these were very specific instances of what Marx and Engels's *Communist Manifesto* characterized as the 'reactionary' attempt by 'fractions of the middle class' to 'roll back the wheel of history'.[10] However, as Marx would acknowledge many years later about the Russian case, in such instances where commitment to past social forms means preserving collective property, holding back the wheel of history could give, through a spring effect, a powerful impetus for a major leap forward – theoretically at least.[11]

The communistic dimension of original Christianity is actually what gives sense to Engels's own assessment of Münzer's program:

> His programme, less a compilation of the demands of the then existing plebeians than a genius's anticipation of the conditions for the emancipation of the proletarian element that had just begun to develop among the plebeians, demanded the immediate establishment of the kingdom of God, of the prophesied millennium on earth. *This was to be accomplished by the return of the church to its origins and the abolition of all institutions that were in conflict with what Münzer conceived as original Christianity*, which, in fact, was the idea of a very modern church. By the kingdom of God, Münzer understood nothing else than a state of society without class differences, without private property, and without superimposed state powers opposed to the members of society. All existing authorities, as far as they did not submit and join the revolution, he taught, must be

overthrown, all work and all property must be shared in common, and complete equality must be introduced.[12]

Here again the crude 'historical materialism' by which the young Engels tried to abide, thereby attaching the 'communist' programme exclusively to the proletariat under capitalism, is all too manifest. What Engels was trying to skip in order to comply with the dogma, although he acknowledged it indirectly, was the fact that (1) there is a recurrent communistic tendency that has appeared in various proletarian protests throughout history;[13] and (2) that this tendency can be readily expressed in Christian terms, due to the affinity between its aspirations and original Christianity. Instead, Engels tried maladroitly to explain Thomas Münzer as an instance of 'anticipation of communism by fantasy' and the Christian dimension as a mere garb imposed by the historical circumstances.

> If the class struggles of that time appear to bear religious earmarks, if the interests, requirements and demands of the various classes hid themselves behind a religious screen, it little changes the actual situation, and is to be explained by conditions of the time.
>
> The Middle Ages had developed out of raw primitiveness. It had done away with old civilisation, old philosophy, politics and jurisprudence, in order to begin anew in every respect. The only thing which it had retained from the old shattered world was Christianity and a number of half-ruined cities deprived of their civilisation. As a consequence, the clergy retained a monopoly of intellectual education, a phenomenon to be found in every primitive stage of development, and education itself had acquired a predominantly theological nature.
>
> In the hands of the clergy, politics and jurisprudence, as well as other sciences, remained branches of theology, and were treated according to the principles prevailing in the latter. The dogmas of the church were at the same time political axioms, and Bible quotations had the validity of law in every court. Even after the formation of a special class of jurists, jurisprudence long remained under the tutelage of theology. This supremacy of theology in the realm of intellectual activities was at the same time a logical consequence of the situation of the church as the most general force coordinating and sanctioning existing feudal domination.
>
> It is obvious that under such conditions, all general and overt attacks on feudalism, in the first place attacks on the church, all

revolutionary, social and political doctrines, necessarily became theological heresies. In order to be attacked, existing social conditions had to be stripped of their aureole of sanctity.[14]

These assertions beg two questions. First, how is it that, beside numerous instances of revolts inspired by religious heresies, several plebeian revolts in the Middle Ages did not produce any specific religious heresy, or were even void of any religious character, let alone a theological one? That was the case more or less, for instance, of the 1378 Florentine Revolt of the Ciompi, the 1380 French Revolt of the Maillotins, the 1381 English Peasants' Revolt, the 1382 French Revolt of the Harelle, and the 15th century Catalonian Rebellion of the Remences. As a matter of fact, sections of the 16th century German peasants' revolt itself, in the Black Forest and Southern Swabia, were initially based on social demands free of any religious coating. Second, how is it that the most socially radical expression of the plebeian revolt of the European Middle Ages – the one led by Thomas Münzer – was at the same time one of those most directly linked to a Christian 'heresy'?

The answers to these two questions lead to a relativization of Engels's thesis: the dominance of religious ideology during the Middle Ages was indeed such that one could not expect any *atheistic* ideology to prevail among a significant section of the plebeian masses. In an era when the religious *Weltanschauung* overwhelmed every aspect of thought, the tendency for social dissent to express itself within the boundaries of religious creed was likewise overwhelming. However, this does not mean that 'every social and political movement [was doomed] to take on a *theological* form', as Engels put it. They could very well merely invoke the creed with no pretence of producing a theological doctrine, while concentrating on social issues and demands in a quasi-secular manner – unless a specific interpretation of the creed was particularly conducive to the expression of their aspiration.

The fact that the most radical ideology of any of the plebeian protest movements against the medieval society, Münzer's communistic ideology – which actually appeared at a time when the Protestant Reformation was signalling the end of the Middle Ages and the beginning of the Early Modern Times – took the form of a Christian heresy, advocating 'the return of the church to its origins', points not, or not only, to an epochal constraint of religion on thought (Münzer, after all, was a contemporary of Machiavelli!), but to the convenience of *one aspect* of historical Christianity for such a communistic program.

Ernest Belfort Bax, in his remarkable history of the peasants' revolts, summarized the demands put forward by Michael Gaismair, one of the most radical figures of the 16th century German peasants' revolt, who led the uprising in Tyrol and Salzburg (demands that included the prohibition of the profession of merchant!), and then rightly added: 'All this is to a large extent an outcome of the general tendency of medieval communistic thought, with its Biblical colouring, and would-be resuscitation of primitive Christian conditions, or what were believed to have been such'.[15] As Bax aptly put it with regard to the German peasants' uprising as a whole: 'It was, it is true, primarily a social and economic agitation, but it had a strong religious colouring. *The invocation of Christian doctrine and Biblical sentiments was no mere external flourish, but formed part of the essence of the movement*'.[16]

It is this same 'elective affinity' between original Christianity and communistic utopianism that explains why the worldwide wave of leftwing political radicalization that started in the 1960s (not exactly religious times!) could partly take on a Christian dimension – especially in Christian-majority areas in 'peripheral' countries where the bulk of the people are poor and downtrodden. This was the case in Latin America above all, an area where radicalization got a great impulse from the onset of the 1960s thanks to the Cuban revolution and its socialist-humanistic message. The major difference between this modern wave of radicalization and the German peasants' movement was that in the Latin American case the Christian brand of communistic utopianism was combined, not so much with longing for some past communal forms (though one could find such a dimension among Native American movements, for sure), but with modern socialist aspirations such as those held by the Cuban revolutionaries and various Marxist movements.

RELIGION AND RADICALISM TODAY: ISLAMIC FUNDAMENTALISM

Let us now check the findings of the above discussion against the wave of Islamic fundamentalism that took off in the 1970s. The first aspect that imposes itself is the relative prevalence of religion in most Muslim-majority countries compared to the rest of the world. The *medieval* features that Engels described in *The Peasant War in Germany* – the fact that 'the clergy retained a monopoly of intellectual education', that 'politics and jurisprudence… remained branches of theology, and were treated according to the principles prevailing in the latter', and that jurisprudence 'remained under the tutelage of theology' – applies literally to the conditions prevailing in many Muslim-majority countries today.

There are many and complex reasons for that. In a nutshell: the strength of survivals of pre-capitalist social formations in major sections of the area concerned; the fact that Islam was very much, from its inception, a political and juridical system; the fact that Western colonial-capitalist powers did not want to upset the area's historical survivals and religious ideology, for they made use of them and were also keen on avoiding anything that would make it easier to stir up popular revolts against their domination; the fact that, nevertheless, the obvious contrast between the religion of the foreign colonial power and the locally prevailing religion made the latter a handy instrument for anti-colonial rebellion; the fact that the nationalist bourgeois and petit bourgeois rebellions against Western domination (and against the indigenous ruling classes upon which this domination relied) did not confront the religion of Islam, for the reason just given as well as out of sheer opportunism. (The one major exception to this was the borderline case of Kemalism, which developed in a formerly imperial state and actually aimed at westernizing Turkey.)

For all these reasons, the situation in most Muslim-majority countries never went thoroughly beyond the frame of what Engels described for the European Middle Ages. Recent times have even witnessed a dramatic reinforcement of the ideological, social and political prevalence of Islam, spurred by the spectacular resurgence and expansion of Islamic fundamentalism, after some real, albeit limited, progress towards secularization in previous decades. Various Marxist explanations of this resurgence have been offered.[17] What must be noted here is that Islamic fundamentalism, generally speaking, grew on the decomposing corpse of the progressive movement in its zones of expansion, contributing to the incineration of the latter's remnants. It has been a central feature of what was unmistakably a tremendously regressive historic turn: beginning in the early 1970s, with the demise of radical middle-class nationalism (symbolized by the death of Gamal Abdel-Nasser in 1970 after his defeat at the hands of Israel in 1967), reactionary forces using Islam as an ideological banner prevailed in most Muslim-majority countries, fanning Islamic fundamentalism as the most virulent antidote to the remnants of the left.

Filling the void created by the downfall of the left, Islamic fundamentalism soon also imposed itself as the main vector of the most intense opposition to Western domination – a dimension that it incorporated from the start, but which had gone into decline during the 'secular' nationalist era. Intense opposition to Western domination prevailed again within Shiite Islam after the 1979 Islamic Revolution in Iran, and regained prominence within Sunni Islam in the early 1990s after armed detachments of militant Sunni Islamic fundamentalists switched from fighting against the Soviet Union to fighting against the United States, following the defeat and disintegration of the former, and the latter's subsequent military return to the Middle East.

Thus two main brands of Islamic fundamentalism came to coexist in the vast area of Muslim-majority countries: one that is collaborationist with Western interests – the stronghold of which is the Saudi kingdom, the most fundamentalist/obscurantist of all Islamic states; and another that is hostile to Western interests – the stronghold of which among Shiites is the Islamic Republic of Iran, while its present spearhead among Sunnis is al-Qaeda. Both have in common not only their strict literal adherence to Islamic scriptures and their fundamentalist program, but also their hostility to the left, notwithstanding circumstantial convergences in some instances.[18]

All brands of Islamic fundamentalism share a common dedication to what is basically a 'medieval-reactionary utopia', i.e. an imaginary and mythical project of society that is not turned toward the future but toward the medieval past. All of them seek to re-establish on earth the mythicized society and state of early Islamic history. In that, they share, formally, a premise in common with Christian liberationist theology's reference to original Christianity. However, the programme of Islamic fundamentalists is not a set of idealistic principles of 'communism of love', stemming from an oppressed community of the poor living on the fringes of their society, whose founder was put to death atrociously by the powers that be – as is the case for original Christianity. Nor is it based on some ancient form of communal property, as was the case in part for the 16th century German peasants' uprising. Islamic fundamentalists share a common dedication to the implementation of a once 'really existing', albeit mythologized, social and political medieval model of class rule, founded little less than fourteen centuries ago and whose founder, a merchant turned prophet, warlord and founder of state and empire, died at the peak of his political power.

As is the case with any attempt to restore a centuries-old class society and polity, the project of Islamic fundamentalism amounts necessarily to a 'reactionary utopia'. By no stretch of imagination could '*the return of Islam to its origins and the abolition of all institutions that are in conflict with what Islamic fundamentalists conceive as original Islam*' (to adapt Engels's description of Münzer's program) lead to a '*a state of society without class differences, without private property, and without superimposed state powers opposed to the members of society*'. It could only mean a huge historical regression.

A question naturally arises at this stage, in light of the previous discussion, which could be phrased in this way: Is there an 'elective affinity' between Orthodox Islam – defined here as characterized by strict allegiance to the Sharia – and 'medieval-reactionary utopianism' that would contribute to explaining the way in which Islamic fundamentalism has swept through Muslim communities in our epoch? There are several reasons for arguing that it is indeed the case. Orthodox Islam, presently the most powerful current within Islamic religion, is conducive to religious literalism by its unequalled cult of the scriptures, especially the Qur'an, deemed God's final word.[19] What in most other religions had become the preserve of 'fundamentalism' as a minority current – basically a doctrine advocating the implementation of a literal interpretation of religious scriptures – remained the mainstream norm in Orthodox Islam, which plays a pervasive role within institutional Islam. Due to the specific historical content of the scriptures that it tries to stick to, Orthodox Islam is conducive in particular to a set of fundamentalist doctrines that regard the faithful implementation of the religion as involving a government based on Islam, since the Prophet of Islam fought bitterly to establish such a state. For the same reason, Orthodox Islam is particularly conducive to armed fight against non-Islamic dominations, as Islam's history, from the start, is one of war against other creeds for its expansion.[20]

FOR A MARXIAN COMPARATIVE SOCIOLOGY OF RELIGIONS

To acknowledge this 'elective affinity' between Orthodox Islam and me-dieval-reactionary utopianism, after having emphasized the 'elective affinity' between original Christianity and communistic utopianism, does not stem from any value judgement. It is based on elements of a comparative histori-cal sociology of both religions, in the tradition of Marx and Engels, and the late Maxime Rodinson, the most prominent contributor to a Marxian ana-lysis of Islam.[21] A comprehensive Marxian comparative historical sociology of religions, on the scale of Max Weber's famous one at the very least, is still badly needed. Although there have been modest attempts to engage in such a project,[22] for which there are many interesting insights to be found in the writings of Marx and especially Engels, as well as in Max Weber's own deep and rich materialistic analyses, it is a demanding project that remains unac-complished and must necessarily be a collective undertaking in order to be properly achieved. The different 'affinities' peculiar to each religious corpus are rooted in the peculiarities of the historical development of each religion, especially each religion's historical genesis, notwithstanding their ulterior convergence as institutionalized ideologies of class domination. Weber put it correctly:

> It is true that the great ecclesiastic religions differ greatly, especially during their early stages, in their structure of domination and their basic ethics, as it is expressed in rules of conduct. Thus, Islam de-veloped out of a charismatic community of warriors led by the mi-

litant prophet and his successors; it accepted the commandment of
the forcible subjection of the infidels, glorified heroism, and promised sensual pleasures in the here and the hereafter to the fighter
for the true faith. Conversely, Buddhism grew out of a community of sages and ascetics who sought individual salvation not only
from the sinful social order and individual sin but from life itself.
Judaism developed out of an hierocratic and bourgeois community that was led by prophets, priests and, eventually, theologically
trained intellectuals; it completely disregarded the hereafter, and
strove for the reestablishment of its secular nation state, and also
for bourgeois well-being through conformity with a casuist law.
Finally, Christianity grew out of the community of participants in
the mystical Christ cult of the Lord's Supper; initially, this community was filled with eschatological hopes for a divine universal
kingdom, rejected all force and was indifferent to the social order,
whose end appeared imminent; it was guided charismatically by
prophets and hierocratically by officials. But these very different
beginnings, which were bound to result in different attitudes toward the economic order, and the equally different historical fate
of these religions did not prevent the hierocracies from exerting
rather similar influences on social and economic life. These influences corresponded to the universally similar preconditions of
hierocracy, which assert themselves once the charismatic heroic
age of a religion has passed and the adaptation to everyday life has
been made.[23]

Furthermore, to acknowledge the different 'elective affinities' found in
Christianity and Islam does not mean that there are no countervailing tendencies in each of them. Thus Christianity has included from inception
countervailing tendencies, to which the subsequent development of the
church as an oppressive medieval institution added a huge corpus and a
very powerful tradition, nurturing various brands of reactionary Christian
doctrine and Christian fundamentalism.[24] Conversely, the Islamic scriptures
include a few egalitarian leftovers of the period during which the first Muslims were an oppressed community, which have been used for attempts at
devising 'socialist' versions of Islam.

Besides, the fact that there are different 'elective affinities' in Christianity
and Islam does not mean that the actual historical development of each religion flowed 'naturally' along the slope of its specific 'elective affinity'. It
flowed naturally along the slope of the actual configuration of the class so-

ciety with which each religion became interwoven – hugely different from the reality of its social origin in the case of Christianity, less so in the case of Islam. Thus, during several centuries, historical 'actually existing' Christianity was less progressive in many regards than historical 'actually existing' Islam. And it is in the realm of the same Christian religion, within the same Catholic Church, that nowadays an ongoing bitter fight is taking place between, on the one hand, an institutionally dominant and utterly reactionary version represented by the present pope Joseph Ratzinger and, on the other hand, the upholders of liberation theology, who are finding a new impulsion in the ongoing new left radicalization in Latin America.

The acknowledgement of the 'elective affinity' that exists between Orthodox Islam and medieval-reactionary utopianism bears no relation to what Edward Said described as 'Orientalism'[25] – it can only be so in the mind of enthusiasts of what Sadik Jalal al-'Azm aptly described as 'Orientalism in Reverse'.[26] Acknowledging an 'elective affinity' between a modern political ideology and features located within the historical corpus of a religion does not amount to an 'essentialist', timeless view of the political uses of this religion. The contrary is actually true. The clearest illustration of that is the aforementioned 'elective affinity' between Christianity and socialism: acknowledging it cannot possibly amount, by any stretch of the imagination, to believing that historical Christianity was essentially socialist! The very absurdity of such a proposition shows how far from 'essentialism' is the discussion of 'elective affinities' in this essay. Likewise, to acknowledge the 'elective affinity' between the Islamic corpus and modern-day medieval-reactionary utopianism, in the shape of Islamic fundamentalism, does not in the least amount to believing that historical Islam was essentially fundamentalist – it was definitely not! – or that Muslims are doomed to fall prey to fundamentalism, whatever the historical conditions.

The acknowledgement of the different 'elective affinities' of (original) Christianity and (orthodox) Islam is one of the clues to understanding the different historical uses of each religion as a banner of protest. This is what Engels tried to explain briefly in one of his very last writings, where he summarized his earlier views on early Christianity:

> The history of early Christianity has notable points of resemblance with the modern working-class movement. Like the latter, Christianity was originally a movement of oppressed people: it first appeared as the religion of slaves and emancipated slaves, of poor people deprived of all rights, of peoples subjugated or dispersed by

Rome. Both Christianity and the workers' socialism preach forthcoming salvation from bondage and misery; Christianity places this salvation in a life beyond, after death, in heaven; socialism places it in this world, in a transformation of society. Both are persecuted and baited, their adherents are despised and made the objects of exclusive laws, the former as enemies of the human race, the latter as enemies of the state, enemies of religion, the family, social order. ...

The parallel between the two historic phenomena forces itself upon our attention as early as the Middle Ages in the first risings of the oppressed peasants and particularly of the town plebeians. These risings, like all mass movements of the Middle Ages, were bound to wear the mask of religion and appeared as the restoration of early Christianity from spreading degeneration.[27]

At this point, Engels added the following interesting long footnote about Islam, containing insights that bear a striking resemblance to the famous theories of the 14th century Muslim Arab historian Ibn Khaldun, while ending with a reiteration of the reductionist 'flag and mask' thesis about the use of Christianity in social protests:

A peculiar antithesis to this was the religious risings in the Mohammedan world, particularly in Africa. Islam is a religion adapted to Orientals, especially Arabs, i.e., on one hand to townsmen engaged in trade and industry, on the other to nomadic Bedouins. Therein lies, however, the embryo of a periodically recurring collision. The townspeople grow rich, luxurious and lax in the observation of the 'law'. The Bedouins, poor and hence of strict morals, contemplate with envy and covetousness these riches and pleasures. Then they unite under a prophet, a Mahdi, to chastise the apostates and restore the observation of the ritual and the true faith and to appropriate in recompense the treasures of the renegades. In a hundred years they are naturally in the same position as the renegades were: a new purge of the faith is required, a new Mahdi arises and the game starts again from the beginning. That is what happened from the conquest campaigns of the African Almoravids and Almohads in Spain to the last Mahdi of Khartoum who so successfully thwarted the English. It happened in the same way or similarly with the risings in Persia and other Mohammedan countries. All these movements are clothed in religion but they have their source in economic causes; and yet, even when they are victorious, they allow the old economic conditions to persist untouched. So the old situation remains unchanged and the collision recurs periodically. In the popular risings of the Christian West, on the contrary, the religious disguise is only a flag and a mask for attacks on an economic order which is becoming antiquated. This is finally overthrown, a new one arises and the world progresses.[28]

The awareness of the different 'elective affinities' of each religion allows us to understand likewise why Christian liberation theology could become such an important component of the left in Latin America, while all attempts at producing an Islamic version of the same remained marginal. It also helps us to understand why Islamic fundamentalism could gain such a huge importance nowadays among Muslim communities, and why it came to supersede the left so successfully in embodying the rejection of Western domination, even though on reactionary social terms. In particular, the acknowledgement of the 'elective affinity' between Orthodox Islam and medieval-reactionary utopianism points to one reason for the facility encountered by Islamic fundamentalism in its expansion in modern times, one reason for what Abdelwahab Meddeb called 'the malady of Islam'.[29]

Other, historical, reasons for the expansion of fundamentalism in Muslim-majority countries have been described at some length elsewhere.[30] They fall basically under four headings: the defeat of middle-class nationalism and the shortcomings of the radical left; the fact that Islamic fundamentalism had been promoted for years as an alternative to the left by the Saudi kingdom and its US sponsor; the ever increasing exacerbation of the economic, social and political crisis in the 'broader Middle East'; the worldwide anomie resulting from both the neoliberal offensive and the collapse of Soviet 'communism'. To that should be added more circumstantial factors, such as the boosting power of the Iranian 'Islamic Revolution' and the Soviet defeat in the Afghan war at the hand of Islamic fundamentalists, as well as the huge impetus given to Islamic fundamentalism by the US aggressions in the 'broader Middle East' and the Israeli repression of the 'second Intifada'.

The superficial Orientalist impression, now widespread, according to which Islamic fundamentalism is the 'natural' ahistorical inclination of the Muslim peoples is sheer nonsense, of course. It overlooks elementary historical facts. As I have recently written,

Many people in the West don't understand that there is nothing 'natural' or ahistorical in the fact that Islamic fundamentalism is nowadays the most visible political current among Muslim peoples. They ignore or forget that the picture was completely different in other historical periods of our contemporary history – that, for instance, a few decades ago the largest nongoverning communist party in the world, a party officially referring therefore to an atheistic doctrine, was in the country with the largest Muslim population: Indonesia – of course, until the party was crushed in a bloodbath at the hands of the US-backed Indonesian military starting in 1965. They ignore or forget, to give another example of the same kind, that in the late 1950s and early 1960s, the most massive political organization in Iraq, especially among the Shiites in Southern Iraq, was not led by some cleric but was here, too, the Communist Party.[31]

To the possible objection that the above only proves that Muslim peoples have to get rid of religion in order to express progressive political views, one needs only to point to the post-Second World War decades, contemporary with the long boom of global capitalism, during which mass protest in Muslim-majority countries was dominated by radicalizing brands of middle-class nationalism that sought an accommodation with religion, fostering its modernization. Nasser was undoubtedly a sincere believer and practising Muslim, even though he became the fundamentalists' bitterest enemy. The influence he achieved at the peak of his prestige in the Arab countries and beyond remains unequalled.[32]

POLITICAL CONCLUSIONS

If the reductionist 'flag and mask' thesis does obviously not hold much water in the case of Christianity, its application to Islamic fundamentalism can also be politically very misleading. Thus, to pretend that movements like Lebanese Hezbollah or Palestinian Hamas are just peculiar expressions of mass social and political protest, using Islam only as a 'flag and mask' or merely as a 'language', is to understate considerably the very important reactionary limitations imposed on the radicalizing potential of their membership, and even their mass following, by their firm adherence to Islamic fundamentalist doctrines.

True, in the same way that it is necessary to locate every use of Islam, as for any other religion, in the concrete social and political conditions where it takes place – hence, making a clear distinction between Islam as the ideological tool of oppressive class-and-gender domination and Islam as the identity marker of an oppressed minority, as in the case of oppressed Muslim immigrant communities in Western countries[33] – it is necessary also to draw the necessary distinction between widely varying and contrasting brands of Islamic fundamentalism. Thus, there is a huge difference, for instance, between, on the one hand, an organization like the most reactionary al-Qaeda, which is waging in Iraq a bloody war of sectarian extermination along with its fight against US occupation, and holds a truly totalitarian conception of society and polity; and, on the other hand, a movement such as Lebanese Hezbollah, which condemns 'political sectarianism' in the name of its fight against Israeli occupation and aggression and, even while considering the 'Islamic Republic' of Iran as its supreme earthly model, acknowledges the religious plurality of Lebanon and consequently upholds the principles of parliamentary democracy.[34]

Still, whatever the case, the ideological fight against Islamic fundamentalism – its social, moral and political views, not the basic spiritual tenets of Islam as a religion – should remain for progressives one of their priorities among Muslim communities.[35] In contrast, there is very little matter for objection in the social, moral and political views of Christian liberation theology, whereas the ideological fight against its strictly spiritual component should certainly not be considered a priority – even for hard-line atheists of the radical left.[36]

NOTES

1   See Brian Thompson, 'The 21st Century Will Be Religious or Will Not Be: Malraux's Controversial Dictum', *Revue André Malraux Review*, 30(1/2), 2001.

2   For a discussion of the evolution of Marx's thought at this stage seen from the angle of 'proletarian self-emancipation' as the cornerstone of mature 'Marxism', see Michael Löwy, *The Theory of Revolution in the Young Marx*, Leiden: Brill, 2003. From the same author, an excellent introduction to the topic of 'Marxism and religion' is to be found in the first chapter of his remarkable book on Latin American liberation theology, *The War of Gods: Religion and Politics in Latin America*, London: Verso, 1996, pp. 4–18. I am indebted to Michael, a dear and long-time friend, for helpful comments on an earlier draft of this article – for which he bears no responsibility.

3   This and the following excerpts from the 'Introduction' are based on the commonly available English translation modernized and corrected in light of the German original: Karl Marx, 'Zur Kritik der Hegelschen Rechtsphilosophie', in *Marx Engels Werke*, Volume 1, Berlin: Dietz Verlag, 1956, pp. 378–79.

4   In a previous article on this topic, I have used 'heroin' as a metaphor for the *incitement dimension* of religion. 'Marxists and Religion – Yesterday and Today',

ZNet, 21 March 2005. A friend of mine, who is a medical doctor told me that the relevant metaphor is rather 'cocaine'. Since 'cocaine' is defined as 'a *stimulant* of the central nervous system… giving rise to what has been described as a euphoric sense of happiness and *increased energy*' (http://www.wikipedia.org), its metaphoric use seems indeed warranted here – with the obvious limitations of such metaphors in both cases.

5   Theses 4 and 11, in Marx, 'Theses on Feuerbach', translation by Cyril Smith and Don Cuckson, 2002, on *Marxists Internet Archive*, available at http://www.marxists.org.

6   In his above quoted *The War of Gods*, a major work of Marxist social theory dedicated to liberation theology. The truth is that conflicting 'affinities' were to be found very early in the Christian corpus.

7   Max Weber, *Economy and Society*, ed. by Guenther Roth and Claus Wittich, Volume 2, Berkeley: University of California Press, 1978, p. 1187.

8   In Friedrich Engels, *The Peasant War in Germany*, ch. 2, available on *Marxists Internet Archive*.

9   Ibid. (my emphasis) corrected in light of the German original in *Marx Engels Werke*, Volume 7, Berlin: Dietz Verlag, 1960, p. 346. Engels's tendency to present the Christian dimension in Münzer as a 'screen' is the reason Michael Löwy prefers the assessment of the leader of the peasant rebellion given by Ernst Bloch in his *Thomas Münzer als Theologe der Revolution* (1921). This last book was never translated into English; the latest German edition was printed in Leipzig: Reclam, 1989.

10   Marx and Engels, *Manifesto of the Communist Party* (1848), ch. 1, available on *Marxists Internet Archive*.

11   'Theoretically speaking, then, the Russian "rural commune" can preserve itself by developing its basis, the common ownership of land, and by eliminating the principle of private property which it also implies; it can become a *direct point of departure* for the economic system towards which modern society tends…'. Marx, 'First Draft of Letter to Vera Zasulich' (1881), available on *Marxists Internet Archive*.

12   Engels, *The Peasant War in Germany*.

13   The term 'proletariat' by itself indicates certain continuity: it is derived from the Latin *proletarius* designating in Roman Antiquity members of the lowest of the plebeian classes, those who paid no taxes and whose only 'wealth' was their children. Hence the origin of the word: *proles*, meaning 'offspring'.

14   Engels, *The Peasant War in Germany*. Engels reiterated the same idea thirty-six years later in his *Ludwig Feuerbach and the End of Classical German Philosophy* (1886), available on *Marxists Internet Archive*.

15   Ernest Belfort Bax, *The Peasants War in Germany 1525-1526*, London: Swan Sonnenschein & Co., 1899, p. 86, also available on *Marxists Internet Archive*. Quotes are here based on the original print edition, as there are some errors in the transcript on the internet.

16   Ibid., p. 33 (my emphasis).

17   For my own contribution to this endeavour, see in particular Gilbert Achcar, 'Eleven Theses on the Current Resurgence of Islamic Fundamentalism'

(1981), in Achcar, *Eastern Cauldron: Islam, Afghanistan, Palestine and Iraq in a Marxist Mirror*, New York: Monthly Review Press and London: Pluto Press, 2004, pp. 48-59, and Achcar, *The Clash of Barbarisms: The Making of the New World Disorder*, Boulder: Paradigm Publishers and London: Saqi, 2006, ch. 2.

18   Thus the Khomeinists tolerated the left in Iran until they got rid of the monarchy and achieved control over the state: the tragic fate of the Iranian left thereafter is well known.

19   Thus, a literal adherence to the letter of the Qur'an leads easily to uses like those of present-day Islamic fundamentalism, as Abdelwahab Meddeb aptly explained: 'The Qur'anic letter, if submitted to a literal reading, can resonate in the space delimited by the fundamentalist project: It can respond to one who wants to make it talk within the narrowness of those confines; for it to escape, it needs to be invested with the desire of the interpreter'. *The Malady of Islam*, Cambridge: Basic Books, 2003, p. 6. One of the key tasks that Meddeb set himself in his book is defined from the onset: 'We have to recognize exactly where the letter – the Qur'an and tradition – is predisposed to a fundamentalist reading' (p. 3).

20   There are, of course, many other features that derive more or less necessarily from the literal interpretation and dogmatic adherence to Islamic scriptures – too many to be discussed within the limits of this article.

21   For a good sample of reflections based on Marxian comparative historical sociology, see the interview that Rodinson granted me some twenty years ago, 'Maxime Rodinson on Islamic Fundamentalism: An Unpublished Interview with Gilbert Achcar', *Middle East Report*, 233, Winter 2004.

22   See Paul N. Siegel, *The Meek and the Militant: Religion and Power Across the World*, London: Zed Press, 1986.

23   Weber, *Economy and Society*, p. 1185.

24   For an attempt at showing how oppressive elements contradicting the 'proletarian' character of the original Christian message were introduced already by apostles Luke and Paul, see Anton Mayer, *Der zensierte Jesus: Soziologie des Neuen Testament*, Olten: Walter Verlag, 1983.

25   As is well known, Edward Said himself – in his *Orientalism: Western Conceptions of the Orient* (1978; reprinted with a new Afterward, London: Penguin Books, 1995) – bestowed the 'Orientalist' label on Marx (he ignored totally Engels, although the latter's writings on the Orient are at least as significant as Marx's, if not more). For a critique of Said's statements on this issue, see Aijaz Ahmad, *In Theory: Classes, Nations, Literatures*, London: Verso, 1992.

26   Sadik Jalal al-'Azm, 'Orientalism and Orientalism in Reverse', *Khamsin*, 8, 1981.

27   Engels, 'On the History of Early Christianity' (1894), available on *Marxists Internet Archive*.

28   Ibid. On the comparison with Ibn Khaldun, see Nicholas S. Hopkins, 'Engels and Ibn Khaldun', *Alif: Journal of Comparative Poetics*, 10, 1990.

29   Meddeb, *The Malady of Islam*.

30   See note 17 above.

31   Noam Chomsky and Gilbert Achcar, *Perilous Power: The Middle East and US Foreign Policy*, ed. by Stephen Shalom, Boulder: Paradigm Publishers, 2007, p. 213.

32   Despite the analogies drawn between Nasser's clout in the 1960s and that of Lebanese Hezbollah's chief Hassan Nasrallah during the 33-Day War of the summer of 2006, the truth is that Nasser's was hugely more important in that he was not only perceived by the tens of millions as a 'hero' but also – certainly so – as their leader.

33   I have underscored this difference in most of my writings on Islam. On the immigrant communities' Islam, see Achcar, 'Marxists and Religion'.

34   For my views on al-Qaeda, see Achcar, *The Clash of Barbarisms*; on Hezbollah, see Achcar with Michel Warschawski, *The 33-Day War: Israel's War on Hezbollah in Lebanon and its Aftermath*, London: Saqi and Boulder: Paradigm Publishers, 2007.

35   My 1981 'Eleven Theses on the Current Resurgence of Islamic Fundamentalism' ended with the assertion that: 'even in cases where Islamic fundamentalism takes purely reactionary forms, revolutionary socialists must use tactical caution in their fight against it. In particular they must avoid falling into the fundamentalists' trap of fighting about religious issues. ...At the same time [they] must nevertheless declare themselves unequivocally for a *secular* society, which is a basic element of the democratic program. They can play down their atheism, but never their secularism, unless they wish to replace Marx outright with Mohammed!'

36   Even on an issue like that of abortion rights, the ideological struggle can be fought without putting into question the spiritual convictions.

UNDERSTANDING IRAQ

SABAH ALNASSERI

The war in Iraq can be understood neither as a sectarian nor as a civil war. The notion of the Iraq conflict as a sectarian conflict, which is propagated by the occupier, suggests that the spiral of violence is due not to the occupation, but is a manifestation of the internal logic of Iraqi society. Thus the responsibility is shifted to the victims of the war. At the same time, the notion of sectarian conflict implicitly refers to internal struggles for power within the governing and ruling classes and their opponents.

There can be no civil war under the occupation. The idea that there is a civil war is put about by the occupiers and the governing cliques in Iraq to further legitimize the occupation and the presence of an ever-increasing number of troops and forces, on which the position of power of the governing cliques and the ruling classes relies. Rather than a civil war, the violence in Iraq today reflects the *correlation* of political power and economic interest between the Bush administration and the Iraqi ruling and governing classes.

Historical prejudices are long-lasting. The Bush administration and the present ruling class in Iraq have learned from Saddam Hussein that just as in Babylonian times the people between the Euphrates and the Tigris can be ruled only by brute force: violence, terror, and humiliation. Abu Ghraib is thus neither a mistake nor an exception, but a consciously chosen method. Another central element in their strategic war scenario is the acquisition of land for the purpose of creating extra-legal, extra-territorialized zones, under direct control of the imperial powers, re-designed as prisons, internment camps, and military bases. This scenario presupposes, however, that the collaboration of domestic forces will be forthcoming. In the context of the imperial war in Iraq, 'democracy' comes to mean a technique of control. The presence of occupying forces and troops, of private security companies and mercenaries, of international institutions and protagonists, plus the variety of political forces in Iraq, have contributed to fracturing the country's political map – a socio-economic as well as a territorial fragmentation. The division of the country into different zones of occupation, the dissolution of the state's economic, ideological and security apparatus, the wholesale dismissal of civil servants, as well as the destruction of the communication, health, electricity and water supply infrastructure caused by the embargo and the war, have led to a re-traditionalization of relations of power and rule.

The mass media representation of the conflict as a religious and cultural issue sensationally misrepresents the empirical reality and the actual struggles and resistances. In this way, ideas like Samuel Huntington's famous 'clash of civilizations' are deployed to legitimate imperial control and rule over geo-strategically and economically important spaces in the South. The discursive construction of these spaces as dangerous, terrorist, and uncivilized areas is a necessary condition for ensuring and perpetuating such control and rule.

To understand Iraq and situate the extreme violence and terror in their proper context, one must understand two specific moments: the *Guantàna-mo-isation* of Iraq, and the reactivation of *colonial* forms of rule and social forces under new circumstances. Although, to the misfortune of the occupier, there are two independent variables in this scenario – the ability of the ruling class to rule and govern, and the resistance of the subaltern – which could not be tested *a priori* and which could jeopardize the entire imperial project. Most of the governing parties in Iraq have no experience in governing, no experience of institutional politics and a narrow and instrumental understanding of the state, and remain divided and splintered. In terms of their relations to civil society, these political forces dispose of various power networks (tribal, confessional, local, familial), militias and paramilitary units.[1] All of their leading figures were either privileged beneficiaries of Saddam's regime (Allawi), or profited through an arrangement with the regime (Talabani and Barzani), or represent powerful families (clans) in Iraqi society (al-Sadr, al-Hakim, al-Chalabi). Each of these groups stresses its exclusive representation of a part of the Iraqi population and/or lays a claim to an institutional part of the state apparatus. The state becomes a mere conglomeration of particular interests. Gangsters, bandits, and militia groups have been organized through the occupation and the governing parties, and political alliances have been formed with some tribal forces in the hope that they will help secure the political and social dominance of these parties. What ensues are intra-parliamentary fights for political power, jockeying for key political positions – and political murders.

Still, despite being backed by the most powerful country on earth, with its troops, spin-doctors and exorbitantly paid consultants, neither Allawi, nor al-Jaafari and even less al-Maliki have demonstrated an ability to govern effectively. The more the government showed its inability and helplessness, the more backlash it provoked, the more violent the situation became, the faster were the changes of political camps and the shifts within political alliances. In the government equation there is a cumulative involution, to the point of collapse. The counter-tendency is the increasing reliance on armed force, and this, in particular, marks the present phase: more than 600,000 estimated dead,[2] twice as many injured and mutilated, three times as many refugees and migrants. This is the result of four years of *liberation imperialism* and a democracy which was, literally, bombed into the people.

The main challenges facing the current governing bloc – the Patriotic Union of Kurdistan (PUK), the Democratic Party of Kurdistan (DPK) and the Alliance (al-Da'wa, SCIRI, al-Chalabi's INC, among others) – cannot be easily overcome due to the persistence of a fatal equilibrium of innumerable particular interests and the continuation of the occupation, yielding what might be called a *transition in permanence*. Various changes in tactics such as the Baker-Hamilton Commission, the troop 'surge', and regional and international conferences, aim at reshuffling the political forces in Iraq and putting in place a new order in the region.

The tactics of the neoconservatives in the Bush administration have not implied the maintenance of an effective Iraqi state but a weakened Iraq whose unity would be ensured by multiple regimes of control (military, economic, 'democratic'). The transformation of the economic base of the state, oil, by the introduction of private property relations and redistribution in favour of war-profiteers (Iraqi as well as British and American) would weaken and destabilize Iraq as a regional power. This would also be a sharp blow to OPEC. However, Iraq is increasingly beyond political and military control. In addition to the occupation troops, recourse to private security firms, local and regional militias and mercenaries is increasingly necessary in order to discipline the subaltern classes, above all in the urban centres. They are used against politically inconvenient opponents, as well as trade unionists, human rights activists, critical journalists, and to secure important natural resources, trade and logistical routes.

In sum, the violence in Iraq must not be ascribed to fanatics or political extremists; rather the occupation has created a situation which provides a breeding-ground for all kinds of atrocities. The uneven development of the country, the precarious situation of the majority, the dramatic nature of the situation and uncertainty about further economic development, has thrown people back to a reliance on familial and local networks which are tied to particular patrons and institutions, or on corruption, or on crime. Once inside the state's apparatuses and institutions, protagonists take off their ethnic or religious veil if they want to survive and cement their political power under the institutional constraints, selectivity and internal dynamics of the state. This is why presenting the situation in Iraq in cultural or ethnological categories is not terribly enlightening. The debacle of the current *junta* in Iraq is due to the fact that it inaugurated a political catharsis through encouraging an *imperial war of liberation*, or what was really an imperial Trojan horse. But the new ruling class was unable to create a viable new state. Due to weak leadership, extreme corruption, and the increasingly lawless violence of the militias, the present al-Maliki government is under enormous pressure. Thus, the security issue – or more precisely, the insecuritization of the population – is the trump card in the transitional phase up to the next election, or putsch.

So what is really going in Iraq? First, there is an occupation by imperial troops, private mercenaries, and public-private militias, all of which are acting without legal constraints. Second, there is a provincial political regime based on clientelist networks rather than citizenship and national consensus. Third, there is a government lacking in both authority and legitimacy, despite (or because of) the elections and the passing of a constitution. Since the dominant groups in the state represent the old social classes which are now celebrating a comeback, and taking control of state affairs, this represents a massive historical regression. Fourth, since March 2003 there has been a situation of war with enormous social, economic, human, environmental, and institutional destruction; a war not against the former ruling clique, but against the country as a whole.

By means of the war economy and the propaganda about the war being a civil sectarian one, the governing parties and ruling classes appeal to their respective supporters to stand behind their policies. These forces have penetrated all state apparatuses with their own personnel. The war has gone through several phases and there have been many shifts in the balance of power both within and outside the state apparatuses. This war without end is creating the conditions of existence of a new type of polity: *a neo-feudal dictatorship*.

THE BACKGROUND

The way the social structure of Iraq is currently presented as predominantly ethnic-confessional is misleading. It is claimed that not only under the republican regime from 1958 to 2003 but also under the monarchy and British colonialism, the Shiite and the Kurds were repressed whereas the predominantly Arab Sunni dominated the state institutions as well as the economy and society. Of course, winners re-write history in ways that confer legitimacy on their claims to power. And this is a case in point.

The first phase in the restructuring of socio-economic relations in Iraqi history was inaugurated by the Ottoman administration.[3] Tribal Sheikhs and the Sadah (Shiite family clans supposed to be descendants of the prophet Mohammad, like the Sadr clan) got for the first time in history the right to register collectively-owned land in their own names, turning *waaqfs* (religious ownership) into the private possessions of the Sheikhs and the Sadah. The loss of collective land rights resulted in an extremely inegalitarian, hierarchical, and asymmetrical power structure that gave rise to a new class of powerful landowners as well as a new class of extremely exploited peasants.

Within the borders of Iraq arbitrarily drawn by the colonial powers after the First World War, changes in the law of landownership under the British occupation and after dramatically increased the landlords' power. Non-capitalist modes and forms of production were transformed by haphazard industrialization, raw material production, commercialization, proletarianization, and the creation of agricultural monocultures and markets. The new ruling class, mostly consisting of landowners, accumulated more capital and political power, while also holding important positions in the state apparatuses (parliament, ministries, security and administration), although the main protagonists in the mandate period and beyond were British experts.

Formal independence was arranged in 1932 in exchange for military bases and oil concessions, but the economic interests and political dominance of the new ruling class still depended upon protection by the British empire. The internal fractional struggles within the ruling class and their representative parties revolved around the economic interests and political power of family clans and clientelist networks from all sectors of the new state and society (Shia, Sunni, Kurds, Arab, Jews, Turkman). They used their dominant positions within the state institutions to pass new laws that secured personal titles to their enormous landholdings, allowed urban merchants and finance cliques to invest in land, gave landlords extensive judicial power, and considerably limited the rights of the peasants: without settling their debts to the landlords, they were not allowed to leave the land. The law therefore enslaved the peasants and increasing taxes and debts drove them to ruin. The consequence was massive waves of migration from rural areas to the cities that began in the late 1920s and accelerated over the next three decades.

Ruling class consensus was based on giving tribal Sheikhs and Aghas (the local landlords in Kurdistan) tax exemptions, legal power over their peasant tenants, property registration, and irrigation systems through which they controlled water distribution and made themselves enormously rich. By the late 1940s, the economically dominant groups of the new ruling class were predominantly Shiite: clerics, traders, merchants, and tribal Sheikhs-landlords, who 'were prime targets for denunciation by the modern "progressive" intelligentsia, nationalists and leftist, amongst whom Shiite intellectuals were strongly represented'.[4] Although Shia had traditionally been under-represented in the state (partly due to their refusal to recognize the legitimacy of Ottoman rule), in the last decade of the monarchy before the 1958 revolution they secured over a third of ministerial appointments. Six of the seven largest landowners in Iraq in 1958 were Shiite. Two of them were Ahmed Ajil al-Yawer, paramount chief of the Shiite Shammar tribes, with 160,000 acres, and Abdul-Hadi al-Chalabi, a rich Shiite merchant from Baghdad with 64,000 acres of rain-fed land. Al-Yawer was the grandfather of Ghazi Ajil al-Yawer, appointed president of Iraq in June 2004, while Abdul-Hadi al-Chalabi's son, Ahmed al-Chalabi, played a key role in Washington before 2003, and is the most prominent neoliberal figure in Iraq today. But 'if in 1958 the richest of the rich were often Shi'is, so were also predominantly the poorest of the poor… the correspondence between the sectarian and class cleavages was never complete… there were always very poor Sunnis… they and the Shi'i poor were brethren in adversity'.[5]

The socio-structural remapping and stratification of post-independence Iraq became more complex when the landlords became urban absentee landlords and a new stratum of foremen (serkals) was created who subjugated the peasants to intensive forms of exploitation, a mix between a slave and a capitalist mode of production, which contributed to one of the most terrible forms of poverty in the Middle East. Until the 1950s, the rate of poverty in Iraq was the highest in the region and Iraq had one of the lowest per capita incomes in the world due to the intensive forms of exploitation. With a time lag of almost two decades, the subaltern classes began to organize themselves on secular party lines (nationalist and left), and the class struggle began to take shape. The migration of peasants to the cities, and hence the drying up of taxes paid by peasants, plus the declining numbers of pilgrims to the holy cities, led to a crisis in the clerical institutions of the Iraqi Shia. Workers and peasants from all parts of the country turned to secular parties, above all the Iraqi Communist Party (ICP), which was the dominant political force in the 1950s, even in the holy Shiite cities, and reflected all segments of the subaltern within Iraqi society (Arabs, Kurds, Turkmen, Sunni and Shia Muslims, Christians, Jews), men and women alike.

Non-clerical Shiite secular intellectuals played a major role in the secular movements. The two nationalist parties (the Independence Party and the Baath Party) were both led by Shiite intellectuals during the 1950s. Shiite intellectuals also dominated the ICP's rank and file and made up the majority of the leadership. On the other hand, Kurdish members of the ICP also played a prominent role in the party leadership. In Kurdistan the party supported peasant uprisings against intensified exploitation, and the peasantry was for the first time able to challenge the dominant position of the Agha class, and to enforce a class compromise. During the 1940s and the 1950s the CP was more popular than Kurdish nationalists whose leaders (such as Mulla Mustafa Barzani, the father of today's KDP leader, Mas'ud Barzani) were marginalized.

Already at the end of the 1940s the monarchy recognized the danger of the nationalist movement, which was supported primarily by Shiite peasants and workers, and it was for this reason that Salih Jabr was appointed as Iraq's first Shiite prime minister in 1948. He was forced from office shortly after his nomination due to his clear pro-British position, which was one of the causes of the Shiite rebellion of 1948. His successor, another Shiite leader of the 1920 insurrection against Britain, Muhammad al-Sadr, was chosen to head a government charged with putting down this rebellion, although this also failed to effectively discipline the Shiite peasants and wage labourers who were questioning the authority of the government. As a reaction to the threat posed by communism and nationalism to clerical power, Mohammad Sadeq al-Sadr, a junior cleric in Najaf, in 1957 founded the al-Da'wa party and developed Islamist theories of economics and philosophy as alternatives to historical materialism.

In 1958 the monarchy was overthrown in a nationalist military coup led by General Qasim, with Communist support. One of the major achievements of the revolution concerned the oil industry. Under the monarchy, the British had created the Iraq Petroleum Company (IPC), which was jointly owned by British, Dutch, French and US oil companies. Qasim revoked the IPC's concession, created the Iraq National Oil Company (INOC), and contributed to forming the Organization of Petroleum Exporting Countries (OPEC). With the revolution, and especially with the implementation of the land reform law in October of 1958, aimed at reshaping the rural relations of exploitation, the social structure was shifted, weakening the position of the governing parties and the ruling class, whereas the position of the subaltern classes and the petit bourgeoisie was strengthened. The resistance in Kurdistan to the revolution of 1958 was not ethno-national, but rather class related, driven by the fear of the extension of land reform to Kurdistan which would have undermined the position of dominant feudal landlords like Barzani. Through the land reforms the rural areas in Kurdistan and the rest of the country witnessed intensifying class struggles, and peasants (Arabs as much as Kurds) began to seize the land for themselves. Elsewhere in the country, Shiite religious institutions and the al-Da'wa party took a consistently anti-communist and anti-nationalist stance, and strongly opposed the land reform which meant a decline in tribal Sheikhs' income (and, hence, the religious taxes that flowed to the clerics), and the equalization of female rights in inheritance law; they were, moreover, against nationalization, public property and pan-Arabism.

The political instability that engulfed Iraq with the overthrow of Qasim in 1963 (immediately followed by a brief period of Baath party rule and vicious suppression of the Communists, and then by another five years of unstable military rule) was only ended with the coming to power of the Baathist party in 1968 and its imposition of one-party rule. The Baathist state owed its subsequent stability to a relatively large middle class it created, mainly in the public sector, who enjoyed a high degree of prosperity and social privileges in the 1970s.[6] It is important to note that under the Baath regime poverty and wealth never coincided exactly with ethnic or religious identification; moreover individuals from all groups, provided they were not politically against the nationalist regime, benefited from the creation of a significant welfare state.

With the coming to power of Saddam Hussein in 1979 the Baath party was reduced to a disciplinary agency subsumed under the security apparatus and serving as a tool of control of the subaltern. Opposition forces, including the Communists, which had been present on the political scene through the 1970s, fell into oblivion, or were mercilessly suppressed. The state functioned as the *entire party* of the ruling classes and allied social categories. In the course of the war with Iran in the 1980s, the Iraqi state, with the help of a war economy, became increasingly based on a network of tribal clans, cliques, bureaucratic elites and military functionaries. Ideologically the regime developed a war nationalist discourse that articulated mythical and historical narratives of pre-Islamic, Arabic, Islamic and racialist, as well as anti-imperialistic, elements. But the social structure was radically transformed. Through capital inflows, the import of millions of workers from the poor Arabic countries, land redistribution in favour of allied tribes and clans (permitting some of their members to become agro-capitalists), partial privatization of finance, trade and services, and the development of a military-industrial complex, the regime managed to mobilize wider segments of the Iraqi society.

Since the 1950s the main axes of conflict in Iraq had not been between Sunni, Kurds and Shiites. In the 1970s not only did many secular Kurds join the Baath-Communist front and participate in national institutions, but also anti-Barzani feudal clans and their militias in Kurdistan were beneficiaries of the regime. As for the Shiites, their religious institutions lost their dominant status in Shiite communities, and the number of religious scholars in the Shiite institutions declined from over ten thousand in the beginning of the 20th century to a few hundred in the 1970s. The majority of Shiites supported secular parties which offered them social welfare and hope for the future. The Supreme Congress for the Islamic Revolution in Iraq (SCIRI) was formed by al-Da'wa members in Iran and other Iraqi Shiite Islamists in 1982, partly in reaction to the loss of their flock. During the Iran-Iraq War SCIRI had formed a militia, the al-Badr Brigade, recruited from Iraqi refugees in Iran with the help of the Iranian secret service. The war left many Iraqi Shiites mistrustful of al-Da'wa and SCIRI who fought against Iraq on the side of Iran. Through subsequent land reforms, peasant migration, and confiscation of property of Shiite religious institutions, the Baathist state marginalized the institutions, their clerics, and affiliated family clans. The main weight of Iraqi Shiism shifted outside the country where these clans created wealthy institutions, such as the al-Khoei and the al-Sistani foundations. Their major financial supporters were landlords, merchants, and financiers. Most of them were deported to Iran at the end of the 1970s and early 1980s.

With the end of the war with Iran, the Saddam regime entered a major crisis which could only be resolved by creating a new crisis: the invasion of Kuwait was pre-ordained. The US embargo after the war was a decisive condition for the stabilization of the regime after 1991. Iraq was deprived of some 300 billion dollars during the 13 years of the embargo, but the oil for food program, negotiated with and managed by the regime beginning in 1995, made the population directly dependent on it. The regime reactivated archaic, authoritarian and semi-feudal elements in such a way that the groups, clans and cliques it was now based on were able to monopolize markets, and engage in smuggling and the underground economy. The embargo forced a de-industrialization, and led to a deregulated and lawless urban economy, based mainly on informal activities by day labourers, land workers and child and female labour. Depopulation through hyper-emigration was the consequence.

In 1992, and as a means of gaining more legitimacy after the *de facto* hollowing out of the Baath party, Saddam moved to mollify religious resentments and enhance the position of the Sunni and Shiite institutions and teaching centres. Mohammad Sadeq al-Sadr, an Arab cleric, was backed up institutionally, publicly and financially against the influence of the Iranian clergy. Each Shiite religious institution now came to be dominated by one family clan against other clans and their related clergy, mostly outside of Iraq. To make things worse for the opponents of al-Sadr, he issued a religious order (*fatwa*), requiring wealthy Shiite to pay their *khums* (a religious tax representing one fifth of income or profit) directly to the poor and not, as previously, to religious institutions. This enormously increased al-Sadr's popularity, which upset not only Saddam, but above all his opponents within the Shiite institutions and communities, so that the murder of al-Sadr and two of his sons in 1999 can be equally perceived as the work of either Saddam, or Shiite clans opposed to al-Sadr.

Those who have been brought to power in Iraq today by the American invasion are primarily drawn from those Shiites outside Iraq who were opposed to al-Sadr as well as Saddam. The political schism within the Shiite clans is currently articulated by the young cleric Muqtada al-Sadr who is supported by the peasantry and the unemployed poor inhabitants of al-Sadr city, on the one hand, and the predominantly Shiite regime with its comprador and middle-class supporters, on the other.

THE STATE OF THE OCCUPATION

The imperial project of rule is not aimed at the re-building of a nation but at the fractioning of formerly politically-constituted space. A mosaic of ethnicities, cultures and religious communities comes into being, whose existence is then given as a reason for the intervention for the purpose of creating political order. The new state fulfils this role with the help of the imperial army and international political and economic institutions, as well as various NGOs. The formation of political institutions and the forms of sovereignty are not determined by the people of Iraq but by the imperial protagonists and their institutions. This includes not only the imposition of a neoliberal constitution but also the institutions of the extended state: parties, labour unions, civic associations, etc.

This represents a dual strategy: dissolution of the existing apparatus of the state and a simultaneous, but uneven, construction of a new one. This entails the deconstruction of social categories (dismissal of the staff of the administration and the security and ideological apparatus) to be replaced by new staff functionally disciplined for this purpose. It also means the destruction of the forms of representation of the ruling classes of the previous republican regime, and the creation of new forms of representation that serve to reactivate the old ruling classes and their parties: the state becomes a *general* party of the ruling classes. This carries with it the creation of new types of capitalist relations through different forms of appropriation of collective capital, involving a decomposition of public property through plunder, robbery, corruption and redistribution of land, creating new sectors of private property as the basis for new bourgeois fractions. The state apparatuses, parties, and economic institutions are so interwoven here that no economic activity or politics is possible without a party affiliation. The parties in all parts of the country are not merely representative of existing classes, but are the forms through which the new class fractions are created. This is epitomized by personages like Barzani, Talabanim al-Hakim, and al-Chalabi who are simultaneously holders of high state office as well as leading class figures.

However, in order to reproduce this form of domination and rule in the long run, it must be internalized. The dissolving of the social formation and the fractioning of the political space clear the path for an 'interior colonization'. Certain institutions (parts of the security, ideological and economic apparatus) and forces of the old order are conserved or reactivated, since they are functional for the new state project. They adapt themselves to the new materiality of authoritarian security institutions inaugurated by means of war and the laws that followed it, ensuring the assignment of important political, military, legal and economic functions and decisions to international institutions. Domestic forces function as transmission belts (locally, regionally, nationally, internationally) between different levels of power. The so-called 'police training' of security personnel in Iraq by the occupiers and NATO means installing imperial norms of governance aimed at disciplining the subaltern: ruling according to the ideas, expectations and general interests of imperial powers.

Insecuritization plays a major role in the formation of new class and gender relations. Security policy means freedom of movement for capital and total control of wage and non-wage labour, i.e. police and military control – prisons, internment camps, check-points, road blocks, razor wire, curfews, and arbitrary collective arrests. For 'security reasons' high and long concrete walls have been built in some districts of Baghdad, following the example of other cities, such as Fallujah. The whole country is changed into a prison landscape. Through these techniques the people are supposed to be effectively controlled, monitored and restricted in their movement and communication. In this context only geo-strategically and/or economically attractive zones are of interest, which means the exclusion of significant areas and their populations who can be instrumentalized in ethnic, religious, cultural, and sexist terms: nationalism dissolves into hybrid identity discourses.

A key moment in the evolution of the new state was the holding of elections in January 2005, following the 'democratic' narrative of the occupiers. US political foundations such as the National Democratic Institute (NDI) and the International Republican Institute (IRI) were active in advising the six largest political parties: the Iraqi National Accord (INA) led by the transitional prime minister Iyad Allawi; the Pentagon's favourite, Ahmad al-Chalabi's Iraqi National Congress (INC); al-Da'wa and SCIRI; and two Kurdish parties, the Democratic Party of Kurdistan (DPK) and the Patriotic Union of Kurdistan (PUK). The Iraqi voters had to choose between 7,471 candidates on 111 lists for the National Assembly. There were 75 parties, nine electoral alliances and 27 individual candidates. Perhaps only a tenth of the candidate's names were published because for *real* security reasons the majority did not dare to present themselves to the voters! Not names or programs but symbols distinguished the mass of candidates from each other.

The ethnification and confessionalization of the electoral system made it more difficult to build a government and secure compromises on questions of strategic importance (such as ending the occupation as well as still unsolved questions of federalism, privatization, gender relations, etc.) more difficult to solve, and this made it nearly impossible to call for the dismantling of military bases and timetables for troop withdrawals. Rather the new government requested, *because of fear of a civil war*, that the occupation troops remain in the country *for a while*.

The referendum on the draft constitution in October 2005 gave the voters even less choice than they had in the elections. The fact that the process of drafting the constitution was not organized nation-wide, or publicly and transparently, reinforced the danger of further fractioning the country. A broader as well as democratically-secured participation which would have guaranteed more legitimacy for the new constitution was jeopardized through the multiple segregations of space: the public sphere as a no-go-area. An oligarchy of powerful groups was cemented which facilitated the institutionalization of pre-fabricated drafts. Many of the drafters had no experience in state, administrative and government institutions so that they were dependent primarily on American experts and advisors who identified with the occupation and their interests, misunderstood the situation on the ground, and thus offered advice that addressed the wrong priorities. The draft constitution represented a regressive step in the social realm: all social and gender rights – work, education, health, pension, gender equality, and others – which were guaranteed in the former constitution since 1972 were systematically dismantled. The old patriarchal spirit and the colonial fetishism of private property permeated the whole document. Thus, the referendum on the new constitution – which read more like an anti-terror tract than a juridical document – was a masterpiece of democratic fraud. Indeed, the draft submitted to the public was not the same draft that was accepted by the National Assembly, having been amended in the meantime by executive decree.

The draft constitution was also saturated in patriarchal-theological discourse, with all the implications this entails for women especially.[7] The support of allied clerics and religious institutions provided the state with a new ideology: the construction of an *Islamic democracy*.[8] But this is a contradiction in terms which has provided, and will continue to provide, explosive material for conflict. Thus provisions of the constitution enshrined the fractioning rather than the unity of society and the state, by giving quasi-veto rights to minorities, i.e. ethnic-religious and spatial fixes were institutionally cemented and this contributes, in turn, to further conflict escalation. Like US administrator Paul Bremer's constitution, the current constitution is also transitory, since after the elections of December 15, 2005 a committee was formed to propose constitutional amendments. A new referendum will have to be held on the new draft. The transition in permanence is immanent in this political situation.

THE RELATIONS OF FORCES

This transition in permanence inside the state reflects the relations of forces, political and otherwise, outside it. It means that there can be no stable configuration of forces and no uniform political project; there exist instead contradictory state projects, each with fluid social foundations and continually changing political representation. Consequently, there are multiple centres of power and contradictory institutions in which a diverse mass of forces exists, with a militaristic ethos and no practicable politics. The return of the old social classes and their political representatives signifies the subjugation of urban life to the countryside, which entails multiple displacements: from national to provincial and local; from secular groups to tribes and clans; from industry to commerce and trade; from civic institutions to semi-feudal institutions and patriarchal law and customs.

The current power bloc in Iraq encompasses the following categories. First of all, the descendants of powerful families from old social classes of the country, which prevailed before the fall of the monarchy in 1958 (e.g. al-Hakim, Barzani, Chaderchi, al-Chalabi, Khoei, Pachachi, Sadr, Shirazi, Rubaai, and al-Saadun among others.).[9] The protagonists are mainly family clans who owed their social, economic and/or political power to the pre-republican regime and who are now celebrating a comeback. The rehabilitation of Shiite religious institutions and the status of their clerics is a clear indication of this development. which in the current situation acquires a geo-strategic and a geo-political dimension. The religious cities of Najaf and Kerbela have been revived as locations of pilgrimage for millions of Shiites world-wide, leading to an enormous economic boost for the Shiite institutions (religious taxes) and their clientele in trade, commerce, industry and handicraft, while also boosting the political-cultural promises of the Iraqi clerics.

The revaluation of Iraqi-Shiite culture is geopolitically also an affront to nationalist, socialist and pan-Arabist forces, collectively labelled as 'Sunnis'. The way 'Shiite' and 'Sunni' are used now really signifies 'provincial' and 'nationalist'. The conflict with the fallen regime is represented *post factum* as an ethnic-confessional and not as a political conflict. Since according to this scenario the victims of Saddam's regime were exclusively ethnic and confessional groups, their representatives now claim an exclusive right to *their* state. But Shiite and Sunni are not political categories. An oil minister, who is nominally Shiite, introduces a neoliberal law not because of his Shiite identity, or in the interests of his community or region, but in the interest of a class fraction of private owners created by the state's restructuring of property relations; this is also true *mutatis mutandis* of other groups like the Kurds.

The religious institutions, clerics and clerical groups, above all those associated with dominant, competitive family clans such as al-Hakim and al-Sadr, have assumed a central position. In their form of organization, and their social and political agenda, they are to a large extent an external fabrication; having had no deep roots in internal communities, they have exploited the situation of permanent violence in order to build their social base, which has brought them into conflict with the internal representatives of these communities. The conflict between al-Hakim- and al-Sadr clans and their respective militias (al-Badr and al-Mahdi) is an obvious indicator. The clerics can be seen as the intellectuals of a conservative-liberal bloc, manufacturing electoral majorities for its parties and using religious-cultural practices to articulate their neoliberal projects, while discrediting left and secular movements by branding them as atheist and Westernized.[10] In other words, it is not capitalist relations of production and rule that are Western, but the left! In this way the term 'west' has been ideologically shifted from its former, imperial meaning.

A second category of the bloc in power is the old nationalist middle class, whose social, economic and political ascent was owed to the Saddam regime. Above all, the former Baathists like Allawi have good contacts and connections to the dissolved security personnel, to the rest of the Baath party in Syria and in Iraq, and to other secular forces such as the communists, pan-Arabists, and liberals.

A third category consists of embargo and war profiteers who form the core of a new middle class, particularly drawn from the Iraqi exile communities who profited from the collapse of the economy during the embargo years and accumulated enormous capital in various forms: through the devaluation of the currency, from foreign debts, the black market for dollars, and the wave of privatizations in the 1990s – all at the expense of those subordinate classes who suffered from the substantial inflation and structural unemployment of that decade, and the dramatic lowering of their standard of living.[11]

A fourth category consists of the regional tribal forces whose status had already risen under Saddam's regime.[12] Some of them were transformed into a fraction of the bourgeoisie (agro-capitalist) through socio-economic restructuring in the 1980s and 1990s – which was not ethnically or religiously exclusive. The tribalization of the political field was advanced by the creation of the so-called 'office of the tribal chiefs' and research into so-called tribal genealogies, financed by the government in the 1990s, to promote allied tribal forces and to isolate opponents of the regime.

Besides these domestic social forces, there is a fifth category in the power bloc, consisting of the neoliberal internationalists of the occupation: MNCs, experts, technicians, political and military consultants, and managers. These external forces are central to the formation of an interior balance of power and have a determining position at all legal, economic and political levels. With more than 2,000 employees, the US embassy in Baghdad is the biggest in the world; it is like a fortress within the so-called Green Zone. The Iraqi government and its institutions are totally penetrated by American experts and advisers.

The current violent and unstable situation in Iraq is represented by the governing parties in the power bloc as having been brought about primarily by outsiders (al-Qaeda). This line is favoured by the occupiers, who require in turn the political and economic subordination of the ruling classes and their representatives. The political space has become defined in terms of institutional mechanisms negotiated with and enforced by the occupiers, which guarantee the government parliamentary majorities on any issue, including the dissolution of parliament and the declaration of a state of emergency whenever desired. This means that there is no legislature but only a consultative body with absolutely no power to control the government; no real executive, but American experts, domestic clans and militias; no independent judiciary to which the security apparatuses are subordinate; no effective state security apparatuses but militias and private agencies administering violence against citizens. The citizens, being under permanent, collective suspicion (every Iraqi against the occupation and the government is a potential terrorist) cannot control the arbitrary acts of the government, the militias, or the occupiers – which is why the citizens, in turn, also rely on violence and armed struggle.

The ruling classes respond by, on the one hand, organizing crowds and mobs to subjugate and discipline the majority, and on the other hand, using violence and corruption to destroy any unity of the people. This political practice aims at polarizing the people and directing their frustration against each other: massacring people with impunity, blackmail, taking people hostage and using them as human shields. Terror comes from the interior of the state. Both the ruling classes and their respective representative parties (e.g. DPK, PUK, al-Da'wa, SCIRI), and their opponents (e.g. al-Sadr) have organized militias and paramilitary groups which they recruit from the reserve army of the millions of unemployed, excluded and marginalized young men, and, to a lesser extent, women. Since Iraq has a very high urban density, the rationale behind the massive bombardment of the cities and the terrorization of civilian life is to displace a high percentage of the population into government- and occupation-controlled zones, and simultaneously deprive the resistance of its social basis.

Terror is in this sense a technique of governance, a public–private partnership in creative destruction. On the one hand, there is a coercive repression aiming at fragmenting and hampering popular resistance, armed and otherwise, and on the other hand the fractioning of public space, by barricades and check-points, which favours the movement of the army, the clerics and the militias, while creating barriers that prevent most people from moving about and taking actions such as strikes and protests. Public space becomes an exclusive right of the powerful. The consequence of this violent situation is to undermine social, economic and political rights, to cut people off from public life, and to deliver them to media indoctrination, making them intellectually and politically lethargic. This creates a sense of political passivity and scepticism about politics in general and liberation in particular.

For these reasons, the core form of organization, and the foundation of the social and political power of the ruling classes and governing parties, is the militias.[13] The militias of the governing parties underwent years of indoctrination in exile, and thus were out of touch with realities on the ground. They resorted to violence not only because their organizations were militaristic from the beginning, but above all because they were fed with hostility not only against the old regime but against society as whole, seen as something to be cleansed by new spiritual and political vanguards. Strategically there is a division of labour between parliamentary groups and the militias, inasmuch as the illegal acts of the latter are clothed by the former with the legality of the state. Who exactly has the authority to make and implement decisions about the responsibilities of the security apparatus in the Defence and Interior ministries is constantly contested. It is primarily the paramilitary groups and militias of the ruling parties that contribute to this confusion, but also the occupation's generals, the NATO experts, the private security companies, and the secret service agents from several regional powers who have a strong influence on various elements in the security apparatus.

The militias usually act autonomously, following the orders of their parties and local commanders rather than those of officials in government ministries. As a result it is often unclear with what legal authority and within what limits the militias are acting when it comes to questions of arrests, searches, incarceration, punishment, abductions, collective murders and executions. This strengthens the relative legitimacy of religious institutions, tribal alliances, and criminal organizations. In this sense, the question of violence and terror is not a matter of security policy: dissolving the militias would mean dissolving the allied parties as apparatuses, and with them the new state. Hence, brutalizing the civilian population is actually a form of political order, not 'collateral damage'. Fanon's argument about violence as a cleansing force, as means of liberation and catharsis, has been reversed here: violence becomes a counter-cleansing force in the hands of the occupation and the ruling classes; it creates an atmosphere in which liberation seems impossible and futile.[14]

THE POLITICAL ECONOMY OF OCCUPIED IRAQ

The economic meaning of the restructuring of state-society relations under the insecuritization and under ideological ciphers like de-Baathification, liberalization, sectarian and civil war, is exemplified by the draft oil and gas law – adopted by the cabinet early in 2007 and submitted to parliament for approval later in the year, but was destined to be enforced by the executive whatever the outcome in parliament.[15] The most problematic part of the law concerns the creation of the 'Federal Council for Oil and Gas', an 'independent (sic!) consultant bureau', consisting of 'executive managers and experts' of Iraqi and foreign companies. It will oversee Production Sharing Agreements (PSAs) which guarantee foreign companies a high average profit under very long-term contracts. The draft law produced massive resistance across Iraq, especially from the unions; and indeed approval of the law would entail the political suicide of parliament as it would hand over to an unelected body the crucial resources of Iraq. Moreover, since the oil producing regions have more juridical power than the federal government, it could lead to Iraq falling apart in a process of 'cantonization', paving the way for neoliberal strategies of accumulation, a value transfer from the south to the north, a marginalization of the expropriated majority and the formation of oases of prosperity for corrupt local and regional classes (old and new).[16] This in turn would lead to further instability, new conflicts and violent relations – inevitably requiring the continuing presence of the occupying powers.

The opening up of the country to foreign investment and the commodification of public and social goods and services, as well as unhindered access to the natural resources of the country, require in the long run a neoliberal constitution, a requirement which the former Iraqi government council already met by signing the US-designed 'provisional constitution' on March 8, 2004. Before the former Coalition Provisional Authority (CPA) administrator L. Paul Bremer, or as Iraqis called him, the caliph of Baghdad, left Iraq in June 2004, he did not forget to decree 100 neoliberal orders. According to Order 81, 'Patent, Industrial Design, Undisclosed Information, Integrated Circuits and Plant Variety', collective practices of cultivation that are thousands of years old were made illegal. 'The new law is presented as being necessary to ensure the supply of good quality seeds in Iraq and to facilitate Iraq's accession to the World Trade Organization (WTO). What it will actually do is facilitate the penetration of Iraqi agriculture by the likes of Monsanto, Syngenta, Bayer, and Dow Chemical – the corporate giants that control seed trade across the globe'.[17] Seeds no longer belong to the communities, but are instead considered to be the private property of international corporations.

The 'independence' of the central bank written into the new constitution, the setting of low tariffs and low taxes, the privatization of public goods and industries, all reflect the way the external debt incurred under the old regime has been used as a lever by various international protagonists and institutions to impose privatization and deregulation, and secure the interests of international capital.[18] The deregulation of labour markets provides a flexible reserve army, leading to high unemployment for the sake of wage cuts, while the renunciation of subsidies for the local economy protects foreign companies from national competition. Hence, MNCs from the occupation states seize Iraqi property and at the same time set privatization standards and technological norms which favour their own position against other imperial competitors. The privatization of state industries, services, public facilities and infrastructure, as well as the dismissal of the workforce and state personnel on a massive scale, was achieved in the name of the so-called 'deBaathification', which was an extremely effective code for the victimization of whole swathes of Iraqi society. The attempt at a radical neoliberalization of Iraq with regard to foreign capital, taxation, custom duties, investment and employment policies, as well as unhindered profit transfers abroad, is on a scale without precedent in international law and conventions in the way it transforms pre-existing national laws.

This is most clearly seen in the draft oil and gas law. But that law is about the future. The only economy currently functioning in Iraq is the 'security' and 'reconstruction' economy, and the only businesses flourishing are those concerned with insecurity and instability, and with looting the public. Accumulation is possible only within structures where the imperial army joins forces with private security companies and mercenaries, on the one hand, and where, on the other, criminal gangs, cliques, groups, and tribal forces unite in a predatory economy: the more essential the war becomes for them, the more they want to prolong it. This extra-legal looting is being promoted at home and abroad, for the purpose of awarding contracts for Iraqi oil, through dummy firms and commissions by some members of the government, and their clients or parasitical supporters which functions like a mafia network. Meanwhile, monies for the so-called 'reconstruction' of Iraq are allocated to MNCs based in the occupiers' countries who subcontract to still more dummy firms through which the loot is used to try to create a social and economic base for the newly constituted state.

CONCLUSION

Shock and awe' designates less a code name for the US–UK war in and against Iraq, than the unrestricted practice of violence and institutionalized terror as a technique of governance. The victims among the civilian population are not merely collateral damage. In the context of this war, their lives themselves represent a military surplus value which is realized through collective punishment as a blackmail tactic: the conscious practice of war crimes.[19] 'This is not a war on terror, this is a war of terror', as one Iraqi woman has characterized the occupation.[20] The victims of this terror are primarily women, wage labourers, the unemployed, farmers, slum inhabitants and the homeless. Regardless of who is behind the terror, be it imperial troops, mercenaries, militias, criminal gangs, resistance groups, or contract killers, those who are targeted represent all segments of Iraqi society: car bombs, suicide bombers, Apache missiles, IEDs (improvised explosive devices), and napalm or cluster bombs are indifferent to their victims. The earlier the occupying powers withdraw or are forced to retreat, the more probable will be the pacification of Iraq. This does not mean that there will be an immediate peaceful situation but there would be no further political polarization within the society, which is the precondition for pacification.

Because of the hundreds of thousands of *inadvertent* civilian murders, together with the innumerable civilians tormented in Abu Ghraib, thousands of Iraqi victims together with thousands of unemployed ex-members of the old regime's army have joined the resistance. The decision of the US administrator Bremer to dissolve the Iraqi army in May 2003 left approximately half a million people unemployed, armed men with no means of existence. A fair part of this army has been attracted by the Mahdi army and the secular resistance. The material base of the cleric Muqtada al-Sadr rests upon a net of social and economic welfare activities which he inherited form his father Muhammad Sadiq al-Sadr. In July 2003 al-Sadr created his militia, the Mahdi army, which functions more as an instrument in his struggle for power against other Shiite political and religious forces, and less as an anti-occupation force.

The resistance proper generally has a secular character and takes various forms, from armed struggle to civil disobedience, strikes and sabotage. The majority of the protagonists are liberal members of the old middle class, nationalists, pan-Arabists, and socialists and communists of various stripes. The ICP itself is not part of the resistance. The many splits it underwent from the 1950s onward, due to problematic political and strategic decisions and failures of leadership, resulted in the several communist parties and independent groups that exist in Iraq today, most of which oppose the occupation. But the leadership of the ICP from the beginning took an active part in the occupation regime, repeating the strategic political mistakes of the 1950s, '60s and '70s. The ICP has become social-democratic in character, primarily due to the shift of its class base from the working class to a new middle class based among the returning exiled ex-communists.

Those who are 'God's fighters' (jihadist, Salafist, Wahabbite, bin-Ladenist) are actually a minority, whose actions are sensationalized by the media. The depiction of the resistance as religious is useful to the present government as it allows it to stress its religious claim to power; it also serves the ideological purpose of the American 'neocons', since they can propagate their war as a 'clash of civilizations'. However, to claim that the resistance is secular does not mean that all its groups are progressive, or that anti-occupation attitudes are *per se* emancipatory, or that they do not pursue mutually antagonistic projects. It is merely to say that the basic evil is the occupation, and only once the occupation is removed can the situation be resolved internally. The fractioning of the resistance to this point has several causes: continual shifts in the balance of forces within the opposition; internal conflicts around incompatible interests; socio-structural displacements caused by the war (and with this a decline in the social base of the opposition); steady emigration and refugee waves; and, not least, attempts at interference by regional and other international interests.[21] But the question is not how to centralize all the multiple elements in the opposition. The question is how to get them to converge on the critical demand for an unconditional and immediate end to the occupation.

What are the prospects for this? Since the governing parties represent nothing but their own interests and have no popular recognition, this opens up the political field not just to violence but also to alternative projects. There is no sign of a dominant force within the power bloc which can keep the situation under control. And in 2006, exactly at the time of the propagation of the sectarian war, there was a growing fragmentation within the tribal forces between those who are close to the regime and those who support a popular politics. This was a very important development, since due to their social status tribal leaders can mobilize the rural population – which is indispensable for the legitimacy of a popular political project.

Moreover, whereas trade unions and workers' councils in Iraq have been divided along regional and political (not religious) lines, and have often adopted strategies that contradicted one another (above all concerning the occupation and privatization) with conflicting forms of organization (democratic and grass roots vs. hierarchical and paternalistic), there have been some positive developments. In January 2006 Iraqi trade unions issued a joint statement against the programs of the World Bank and International Monetary Fund in Iraq.[22] And in December 2006 all the unions declared their opposition to the draft of the oil and gas law for the first time. All this indicates the emergence, however tentative, of new political thinking and readiness to cooperate across the political divides.

Even in regard to the situation of women, some common struggles yielded positive results. Due to the supremacy of the religious institutions in the state and society old patriarchal and tribal practices have been revived. Women are not allowed to move about freely without permission and the company of a male member of the family. So-called 'temporary marriage' in the Shiite tradition, a sexist and class chauvinist form of exploitation of women, has been institutionalized (allowing primarily wealthy men to exploit young women sexually for a short period of time). Social deprivation and economic plight are the consequences of this sexist practice for the poor women and their families. That in the face of all this, women succeeded in securing the reservation of one-quarter of the seats in parliament was a considerable achievement.[23]

At the end of the day, the people of Iraq will determine the course and outcome of its contradictory development themselves. But a life of dignity is only possible if they break out of their passivity and collectively bring the current barbarism to an end. How the contradictions develop concretely, whether they reach a crisis point, and how the subaltern act, will determine the course of conflict and the forms of political change. One should not close the horizon of the possibilities of the present situation by an objectivistic or culturalist analysis but try to determine the conditions for it in a critical perspective of power relations. A peaceful and just solution is possible, even if arriving at it will be anything but free of conflict. For this it is necessary to build progressive forms of organization and experiment with radically democratic political practices, so as to engage in alternative political projects within and beyond the Iraqi state. In face of the violent and destructive character of the current situation, the increasing number of civilian victims and the depressing news the media bring daily, this appears no doubt to be naïve. Let me conclude by saying that it is not so, but is implied by an analysis that places the ongoing struggles at its centre.

NOTES

1   See Faleh A. Jabar, 'Postconflict Iraq', United States Institute of Peace, Special Report 120, May 2004, available from http://www.usip.org.
2   654,965 civilian Iraqis may have died in Iraq since March 2003, according to a survey conducted by the Johns Hopkins Bloomberg School of Public Health and al-Mustansiriya University in Baghdad. The population-based, active method of collecting mortality data was derived from a nationwide household survey of 1,880 households throughout Iraq, conducted between May and July 2006, see G. Burnham et al., 'Mortality after the 2003 invasion of Iraq: A cross-sectional cluster sample survey', *The Lancet*, 368, 2006; Richard Horton, 'A Monstrous War Crime', *The Guardian*, 28 March 2007.
3   Many of the tribes in present-day Iraq became Shiite only in the 19th century as a reaction to the aggressive Wahhabite movements in the Arabian peninsula. One of the characteristics of the Iraqi tribes is their mixed confessional relations, due to both intermarriage and conversion.
4   Sami Zubaida, *Islam, the People, and the State*, London: I.B. Tauris, 2001, pp. 91ff.
5   Hanna Batatu, *The Old Social Classes and the Revolutionary Movement in Iraq*, Princeton: Princeton University Press, 1978, pp. 49-50.
6   The middle class experienced a drastic impoverishment by the wars and sanctions of the 1980s and 1990s, and many of its members emigrated.
7   In the new constitution, the Supreme Federal Court will be also made up judges and experts in Sharia law (Islamic Law), and under Article 101 of the constitution 'the offices of (religious) endowments are considered financially and administratively independent associations'.
8   On this problematic see Sabah Alnasseri, 'Die Konstruktion "islamische Demokratie" und der mögliche Übergang zu einer postislamitischen Situa-

tion', in Alnasseri, ed., *Politik jenseits der Kreuzzüge*, Münster: Westfälisches Dampfboot, 2004.

9   See Batatu, *The Old Social Classes*.

10   Graham E. Fuller, 'Islamist Politics in Iraq after Saddam Hussein', United States Institute of Peace, Special Report 108, August 2003, available from http://www.usip.org.

11   Sabah Alnasseri, 'Die unendliche Geschichte. Die USA, der Irak und der Krieg', 2002 and 'Ende des Befreiungsimperialismus? Präzedenzfall(e) Irak, Teil I-IV', 2003/4, both available from www.links-netz.de.

12   See Zabaida, *Islam, the People, and the State*.

13   Some militias and killer commands in the security apparatus and in civil society were created, financed, trained, and armed by the US-occupation itself (the *El Salvador option*), to counter the resistance and inconvenient opponents and as means to weaken the central government. The formal subordination of these militias under the security apparatus or the ruling parties, however, does not prevent them from operating on their own initiative which makes decisions on security policy almost impossible.

14   Frantz Fanon, 'Concerning Violence', in *The Wretched of the Earth*, New York: Grove Weidenfeld, 1991.

15   During the whole drafting process and before submitting the draft to the parliament, only hand-picked MPs had access to the draft so that acquiring a copy and publication of the draft was a risky, clandestine task. The Iraqi blogger Raed Jarar was the first to publish the Arabic version of the draft and translate it into English, http://raedinthemiddle.blogspot.com. On the criticism and global opposition to the law, see http://www.handsoffiraqioil.org and http://www.iraqoillaw.com; See also Antonia Juhasz and Raed Jarrar, 'Oil Grab in Iraq', *Foreign Policy in Focus*, 22 February 2007, available from http://www.fpif.org; Kamil Mahdi, 'Iraqis will never accept this Sellout to the Oil Corporations', *The Guardian*, 16 January 2007.

16   Sabah Alnasseri, 'Ende des Befreiungsimperialismus? Präzedenzfall(e) Irak I, II& III', 2003, available from http://www.links-netz.de.

17   'Iraq's New Patent Law: A Declaration of War against Farmers', *Foreign Policy in Focus*, November 2004, available from http://www.fpif.org. They add that the 'new patent law also explicitly promotes the commercialization of genetically modified (GM) seeds in Iraq'. See also Daniel Stone, 'The Assault on Iraqi Agriculture – US Agribusiness Targets the Fertile Crescent', August 2006, available from http://www.globalpolicy.org.

18   On this problematic, see http://www.jubileeiraq.org/blog; Jeff Leys, 'Economic Warfare: Iraq and the I.M.F.', 19 September 2006, available from http://www.commondreams.org; Basav Sen and Hope Chu, 'Operation Corporate Freedom: The IMF and the World Bank in Iraq', September 2005, *Global Policy Forum*, available from http://www.globalpolicy.org.

19   Sabah Alnasseri, 'Falludscha: Über Kriegsverbrechen, Völker und Menschenrechtsverletzungen', in *Komitee für Grundrechte und Demokratie*, Köln, Jahrbuch 20, 2004/2005, pp. 61-72.

20   This is how Dr. Dahlia Wasfi (born to a Jewish mother and an Iraqi father from Basrah) characterizes the occupation. She described in her visit to her family in Basrah the daily life of Iraqis under the US-occupation on April 27, 2006 in a speech to the Iraq Forum, in Washington, DC, available at http://www.youtube.com.

21   One of the best sources in English on the nature of the Iraqi resistance is Susan Watkins, 'Vichy on the Tigris', *New Left Review,* 28, July-August 2004.

22   The statement was signed by the General Federation of Iraqi Workers, Oil Unions Federation in Iraq/Basra, Federation of Workers Councils and Unions in Iraq, Kurdistan General Workers Syndicate Union/Erbil, and the Iraqi Kurdistan Workers Syndicate Union. In December 2005, just prior to the elections, the al-Jaafri government signed a so-called 'Stand-By Arrangement' with the IMF according to which, among others things, public subventions for oil were to be de facto lifted. Henceforth the oil price and with it all other related prices sky-rocketed. See Jeff Leys, 'Economic Warfare'; Matthew Rothschild, 'IMF Occupies Iraq, Riots Follow', 3 January 2006, available from http://progressive.org.

23   On the current situation of women, see the Iraq section of http://www.peacewomen.org; the CODEPINK report on Iraq available from http://www.act-together.org; and reports of the Organization of Women's Freedom in Iraq at http://www.equalityiniraq.com.

ISRAEL'S COLONIAL SIEGE AND THE PALESTINIANS

BASHIR ABU-MANNEH

If there's one short phrase that can describe Palestinian reality under Israeli occupation today, it is this: *enduring under permanent siege, without surrender.*[1]

My aim in the following is, first, to defend the accuracy of this statement. Since the Oslo Agreements of 1993, Israel's occupation of the West Bank and Gaza has developed into a colonial siege, gradually atomizing and strangling Palestinian economy and society. Compounded by international boycott, poverty levels are now between 70 per cent and 80 per cent, with extreme and unprecedented levels of unemployment and rising dependency on food aid.[2] Second, although Israeli policy is mainly to blame for this drastic worsening of Palestinian living conditions since 1993, the Palestinian national secular elite is far from blameless. They have, in fact, played a junior yet pivotal role in bringing this new regime into being. By legitimizing their people's continued dispossession and domination by Israel, they have ended up corrupting Palestinian national aspirations for justice and self-determination. With no alternative left project in sight, religious fundamentalism was destined to carry the mantle of an abandoned nationalism and drastically increase its own popular political constituency. Third, siege and capitulation also eventually generated mass resistance. As with the first Intifada of the late 1980s that led to Oslo, Palestinians again revolted in popular protest against colonization and national denial. And with the al-Aqsa Intifada in September 2000, resistance was re-legitimized.[3] This time round, though, conditions were much worse: social power and political leverage were in even shorter supply. Suicide bombing expressed growing Palestinian captivity and despair, and armed struggle replaced an earlier emphasis on mass political participation. I examine these new forms of resistance and scrutinize their prospects of achieving decolonization under continuing conditions of siege, Hamas-Fatah factionalism, and an absence of unified strategy.

ATOMIZED AND ENCIRCLED

Siege (or closure) is arguably Israel's most pernicious instrument of colonial control and punishment. It basically means a denial of the Palestinian right to freedom of movement through the use of hundreds of roadblocks and checkpoints, numbering 546 in total. Closure doesn't just restrict movement of goods and persons *externally* between the West Bank and Gaza, as well as from either area to Israel or the outside world. It blocks freedom of movement *internally* within the West Bank as well. Initially imposed as far back as the first Intifada in 1991, this regime was consolidated and incorporated into Oslo, only to be massively intensified since the second Intifada began. As a result, 40 per cent of the West Bank is today inaccessible to Palestinians.

In a recent report by the World Bank on movement restrictions in the West Bank, Israel was strongly criticized for the way 'closure has been implemented through a complicated agglomeration of policies and practices which has fragmented the territory into ever smaller and more disconnected cantons'.[4] While acknowledging (but without going into the deeper roots of the conflict) that Israeli security concerns are 'undeniable and must be addressed', the report clearly states that '...it is often difficult to reconcile the use of closure for security purposes from its use to expand and protect settlement activity and the relatively unhindered movement of settlers in and out of the West Bank... It is also difficult to account for the discriminatory enforcement of zoning and planning regulations which minimize the amount of land available for the normal growth and development of Palestinian areas...'. As a result, the Palestinian economy has been thoroughly devastated and is on the brink of collapse: 'The practical effect of this shattered economic space is that on any given day the ability to reach work, school, shopping, healthcare facilities and agricultural land is highly uncertain and subject to arbitrary restriction and delay'.

Much of this has been known for years. Indeed, four years earlier Salem Ajluni, chief UN economist, described Israel's economic strangulation of the Occupied Territories as a deliberate 'mass impoverishment – indeed immiseration – a process that is unprecedented in modern Palestinian history'.[5] With the recent economic and political boycott of the Palestinian government following on the heels of Hamas's election victory in January 2006, siege has been compounded by even harsher restrictions. As part of what the special rapporteur on human rights in the Occupied Territories, John Dugard, called 'economic coercion for regime change', Palestinians have been strangled even more: 'In effect, the Palestinian people have been subjected to economic sanctions – the first time an occupied people have been so treated.... [they] have been subjected to possibly the most rigorous form of international sanctions imposed in modern times'.[6]

So what started as 'an ad hoc military-bureaucratic measure crystallized into a fully conscious Israeli strategy with a clear political goal: separation between the two peoples with an *appearance* of political separation, but with only one government – Israel – having any effective power to shape the destinies of both'.[7] If Israel's strategy before the first Intifada was the exploitation and partial inclusion of the Palestinian working class into the Israeli economy as daily migrant labour, since 1991 Israel has reverted to its original Zionist goal of complete exclusion.[8] Unlike apartheid, then, Zionism combines political separation with economic exclusion. Azmi Bishara has described the logic of Zionist colonialism as 'separation, within separation': 'This colonialism displaces people, confiscates their land or bypasses them (the term, often applied to roads, is pertinent). It "develops" the land for settlement, but not for the inhabitants'.[9] The process of Zionist conquest and siege is, thus, more reminiscent of whites' treatment of Native Indians in North America than it is of Blacks under South African apartheid.[10] As Fayez A. Sayegh put it: 'The people of Palestine has lost not only *political control* over its country, but *physical occupation* of its country as well: it has been deprived not only of its inalienable right to *self-determination*, but also of its elemental right to *exist* on its own land!'[11]

A major effect of such dispensability, inequality, and separation has been a growing sense of social and political alienation. Occupied Palestinians have become not only alienated from their own leadership, as it has failed to deliver political independence and continues to benefit from VIP passes allowing it to travel freely. They have also become alienated from their own collective powers and capacities. What Amira Hass calls Israel's collective 'theft of space and time' is thus experienced as a maze of bureaucratic measures and arbitrary restrictions which people have to face and navigate as individuals on a daily basis, killing their sense of spontaneity, ability to plan, and everyday normalcy, and resulting in a 'privatization of the occupation' through a growing sense of personal insecurity, uncertainty, and impotence.[12] Stratified and segmented, Palestinians have thus carried the heavy weight of siege on their shoulders as individuals and families rather than as a national collective: 'Once I used to dream of a state', a Palestinian cameraman told Hass, 'Now I dream of getting to the other side of the Erez checkpoint'.[13] Such atomization and helplessness would ultimately generate a very particular form of resistance, one that is isolated and disengaged from mass organizational politics, as I argue below.

The fact that this was actually the *intended consequence* of Oslo is made abundantly clear in a report issued by the Israeli human rights organization B'Tselem in 2002. *Land Grab: Israel's Settlement Policy in the West Bank* clearly shows how colonization has always been a 'vigorous and systematic' state-sponsored and state-driven project.[14] Involving a 'massive intervention' by the Israeli army and by both Likud and Labour governments since 1967, Palestinian land was seized and cordoned off in order to establish and expand settlements in contravention of international laws and UN resolutions. This process only intensified with Oslo, leading to a 'dramatic growth of the settlements' and to a near doubling of the number of settlers in the West Bank from 1993 to 2001. In fact: 'The sharpest increase [of settlement housing units] during this period was recorded in 2000, under the government headed by Ehud Barak, when the construction of almost 4,800 new housing units was commenced'. *Land Grab* is unequivocal in stating that the Israeli settlements in the Occupied Palestinian Territories constitute a serious violation of Article 49 of the Fourth Geneva Convention: 'The Occupying Power shall not deport or transfer parts of its own civilian population into the territory it occupies'. Settlements and by-pass roads also violate Palestinian rights to self-determination and statehood, to equality, property, adequate living standards, and to freedom of movement. As a result of ongoing colonization, Palestinian territorial contiguity has been shattered, and Palestinian economic development and access to lands and natural resources has been blocked. B'Tselem thus charges the Israeli government, acting with the collusion of the Israeli High Court of Justice, with 'the *de facto* annexation of the settlements to the State of Israel, while avoiding the problems that would be caused by *de jure* annexation, particularly in the international arena'.

Land Grab was published five years ago. The situation today is much worse. Today there are 450,000 settlers in the West Bank and East Jerusalem, an increase of nearly 100,000 settlers since 2001. Many of the same mechanisms of land expropriation and settlement expansion continue, but there has been one major drastic development in this period: the Wall. Mostly completed, the Wall is 703 km long and incorporates most of the Israeli settlements: 85 per cent of it is built within the territory of the West Bank, annexing 16 per cent of its territory. As the International Court of Justice advisory opinion clearly states: 'Around 80 per cent of the settlers living in the Occupied Palestinian Territory, that is 320,000 individuals, would reside in that area, as well as 237,000 Palestinians. Moreover, as a result of the construction of the wall, around 160,000 other Palestinians would reside in almost completely encircled communities'.[15] Qalqiliya, a city of 40,000, is already surrounded by the Wall, and residents can only enter and leave through one military checkpoint open every day from 7 a.m. to 7 p.m. By the time the Wall is completed, there will be over 400,000 Palestinians completely or partially surrounded by it. No wonder the Court warned about the dangers of continued daily subsistence and survival of occupied Palestinians and, significantly, of the possibility of 'the departure of Palestinian populations from certain areas'.[16] In order to facilitate its colonial objectives and *de facto* annexation of more Palestinian lands, then, Israel has yet again created the conditions for a massive forced exodus of the indigenous population.

The factual record of siege and ongoing dispossession is thus pretty damning: Israel is in permanent violation of international norms and customs. Human rights reports continuously and unfailingly list the international illegality of: settlements, the Wall, an arbitrary permit system, house demolitions, assassinations, killings, Jewish-only by-pass roads, checkpoints and roadblocks, and a cruel and brutal occupation regime bolstered by unending military operations and periodic large-scale invasions.[17] This is not to mention more than 4,000 Palestinians killed since the beginning of the al-Aqsa Intifada, 650 in 2006 (a triple increase from 2005, compared to a reduction by half over the same year of the number of Israelis killed, from 54 to 27 – six of whom were soldiers), or the more than 10,000 Palestinians still in Israeli prisons today.[18] Indeed, since 1967 Israel has imprisoned more than 650,000 Palestinians, equivalent to nearly 20 per cent of the population.

How then, one wonders, does a national elite that purports to be leading its constituency to statehood and independence end up, since 1993, participating in a process that has produced such a drastic worsening of Palestinian living conditions, weakening if not terminally undermining Palestinian national survival? Why hasn't the PLO elite utilized all the aforementioned international laws and conventions, which clearly safeguard and guarantee its people's inalienable rights and national aspirations, in its struggle against Israel's occupation? A short answer has been provided by Edward Said: 'No other liberation group in history has sold itself to its enemies like this'.[19] Political capitulation, or 'partnership' with the occupier, has been the hallmark of Oslo, leaving the majority of Palestinians completely vulnerable to the ravages of Israeli colonialism.

ELITE CAPITULATION

My intention here is not to review the diplomatic and political record of the PLO/PA, but to focus on two main issues relevant to understanding the nature of the Palestinian resistance that eventually emerged in the West Bank and Gaza.[20] One is legal-ideological, and the other is more purely political. On the legal-ideological level, Oslo undermined the legitimacy of international law as a basis for resolving the Palestinian-Israeli conflict, effectively de-legitimizing Palestinian rights of national self-determination and of resistance against occupation. In one stroke of the pen, self-determination was denied and resistance was criminalized. On the political level, the PA also systematically policed Palestinian society to ensure the security of Israel and of its illegal settlers. PA rule, therefore, was characterized by a combination of political repression, authoritarianism, and co-optation of local economic and political elites. Anti-colonial self-organization and resistance were de-mobilized, and the resources for independent political initiative and participation were effectively undercut. In the face of elite profiteering and collusion, popular apathy and despair grew, until the explosion of the al-Aqsa Intifada gave resistance another important lease of life.

Under Oslo, the PLO became Israel's colonial enforcer. As Arafat put it on 9 September 1993: 'The PLO considers that the signing of the Declaration of Principles constitutes a historic event, inaugurating a new epoch of peaceful coexistence, free from violence and all other acts which endanger peace and stability. Accordingly, the PLO renounces the use of terrorism and other acts of violence and will assume responsibility over all PLO elements and personnel in order to assure their compliance, prevent violations and discipline violators'.[21] Arafat declared a political end to the Intifada and unequivocally renounced his people's right to resist Israel's occupation. As Burhan Dajani put it: 'The Palestinian letter of recognition of Israel in effect renounces violence, the right to the Palestinian struggle. That letter amounted to throwing away the most important card the Palestinians had to play: Palestinian legitimacy versus the illegitimacy of Israeli occupation. The result is a series of negotiations that will be a process of entreaty on one side and of giving or refusal on the other'.[22]

What the PLO effectively did by signing Oslo was undermine its own people's national rights while legitimizing the illegal practices of the occupier. This didn't just mean that the sovereignty of an occupier was 'affirmed' and 'consecrated' by representatives of the occupied. It also meant that the agreement gave the occupied no legal powers to prevent further illegal expansion or expropriation of land by the occupier. As Dajani clearly predicted then: 'An unfortunate result of the DOP [Declaration of Principles] is that it makes it far more difficult to challenge Israel's further legislations, and indeed even to challenge, as in the past, Israeli laws permitting the expropriation of land and property and the violation of rights and liberties on the basis of the Geneva Convention on occupying powers'. Israel's illegal colonial sovereignty was ratified.[23]

Ambiguous phrasing and vague formulations about maintaining the status quo aside, Oslo facilitated Israel's continued violations of the Geneva Convention and international humanitarian law. As a result, the PA did the following: it agreed to continued control of East Jerusalem; made 60 per cent of the West Bank negotiable with an illegal occupier; legitimized illegal Jewish settlements; agreed to construction of by-pass roads; legitimized prohibition on freedom of movement, etc.[24] Such abrogation of Palestinian civilian rights under occupation is prohibited under the Convention. This clearly undermines the PA's own authority to flout international law or to sell off Palestinian national rights, and constitutes an important resource for re-legitimizing Palestinian rights and anti-colonial struggle.

The critics of Oslo, then, were proven right. The PA turned out to be what they predicted it would be: a collaborationist regime running bisected and repressed cantons. Achcar formulated it accurately when he wrote at the time that '...the Arafat leadership's "Palestinian self-government" will be an extreme case of indirect colonial administration, closer to a "puppet" government than to the neo-colonial governments emerging from decolonization. Either it will be this or it will not be. The Zionist government has decided to proceed by stages, beginning with Gaza and Jericho, to test the efficiency of the Arafat apparatus in the repressive task that has been allocated to it. If this apparatus proves itself incapable of fulfilling the task, the Washington Accords will end up in the dustbin'.[25] The effect on the Palestinians of what Said called 'a betrayal of our history and our people' was a growing sense of disillusionment and cynicism. Oslo became a crisis of national proportions: it 'plunged the Palestinian people and its political institutions into the most serious and profound moral, cultural, identity, and political crisis'.[26]

Such a degeneration and diminishment of national life can be gauged by examining the way in which the PA reconstructed occupied Palestinian society around its own capitulation and opportunism. This brings me to my second focus: the politics of national de-legitimization. If the PLO's suspicion of democracy and mass mobilization was reconfirmed in its relationship to the first Intifada, its heir, the PA elite, would take the PLO's tight political grip to its logical conclusion, substituting itself for the Palestinian nation. Bureaucracy and authoritarianism became the norm, and security the main means of control.[27] The PA actively undermined and co-opted the democratic and resistance forces that produced the first Intifada. As Glenn Robinson concluded: 'Put bluntly, the PLO in Tunis successfully captured political power in the West Bank and Gaza not because it led the revolution but because it promised to end it. The PA had to construct its own political base, which would diminish the position of the new [university educated and progressive] elite inside the West Bank and Gaza while consolidating its own power'.[28] With the support of traditional sources of power like clans and notable families, old forms of patronage and control were reactivated and revived. Nigel Parsons, who studied PA rule in meticulous detail, describes Arafat's new centralized apparatus as follows:

> Rather than harnessing the mobilizational capacities developed during the first intifada and leading resistance to colonization, the PA engineered social control through patronage. The expansion of the PA bureaucracy diminished the political salience of the NGO community – the heart of Palestinian civil society and a stronghold of the left – through centralizing the provision of services, redirecting resources away from the non-state sector, and widespread recruitment from the professional and technocratic middle class.[29]

Many Palestinians thus became totally dependent on the PA for jobs and work opportunities (140,000 today), and this entangled significant segments of the population with a regime which existed mainly to deny them sovereignty and political independence. With the labour movement either repressed or 'politically quiescent',[30] and with a weak and fragmented working class, reeling from Israel's closure policy, there was little social leverage to either withstand or transform PA mechanisms of rule. As Nina Sovich notes, 'the PA has co-opted and quelled union leadership as well as the grass-roots movements that occasionally arise; and the union leaders themselves lack the discipline, expertise, and political will to mobilize the workers'.[31] Such working-class de-mobilization was compounded by the political left's loss of bearings after Oslo. In a clear admission of failure, the head of the Popular Front for the Liberation of Palestine (PFLP) clearly stated, as he looked back on seven years of Oslo, that the secular opposition 'has failed to transform its political discourse into practical, material action', blaming disunity and factionalism for its near total absence from the Palestinian political scene.[32] Little has changed since then.

An important signifier of strong political discontent came from the Committee of Twenty in November 1999. Parsons recounts this important episode in Palestinian dissent, and reads it as 'presaging' the al-Aqsa Intifada. Signed by leading political figures, nine of whom were Legislative members for Arafat's own Fatah group, the petition was entitled 'The Homeland Calls Us' and attacked 'corruption, deceit and despotism':

More lands are robbed while settlements expand. The conspiracy against refugees accelerates behind the scenes. Palestinian jails close their doors to our own sons and daughters. Jerusalem has not returned and Singapore has not arrived. The people are divided into two groups: that of the select who rule and steal, and that of the majority which complains and searches for someone to save it.[33]

The signatories looked forward to the day when the 'collective efforts of the deprived' would overcome injustice and end the humiliations of Oslo.[34] Arafat responded with severe repression, imprisoning nearly all of the signatories and sparking off public uproar, demonstrations, and solidarity calls from all the opposition factions (Islamic Jihad, Hamas, PFLP, and Democratic Front for the Liberation of Palestine). Less than a year later, occupied Palestinians would revolt again. Deceived by a false peace process, disappointed by their submissive leadership, and besieged by more colonial expansion, Palestinians came out in their thousands to demonstrate and protest. The al-Aqsa Intifada had begun.

RESISTING BRUTALITY AND SIEGE

The nature of the second Intifada was very different than the first, however. One of Oslo's practical consequences was that the Israeli army had redeployed outside major population concentrations, making it extremely difficult for enclaved Palestinians to get at or confront the occupation forces, unlike in the first Intifada. Being fragmented by checkpoints and confined to their locales 'rendered mass action virtually impossible'.[35] Reflecting the effects of the siege regime through the 1990s, there has thus been a systematic weakening of the capacity of Palestinian society to act and organize as a national collective. As Rema Hammami and Salim Tamari argue, Oslo destroyed all resources for civil rebellion:

Save for massive candlelight marches and funeral processions within the cities, the population at large has been left with virtually no active role in the uprising. This is clearly not by choice, but as a consequence of the fact that the kinds of political structures that made grass-roots organizing the main thrust of the first intifada, at least in the early years, no longer exist. Popular and neighborhood committees as well as mass organizations (and most of the political movements that sustained them) began to collapse at the end of the first intifada under the cumulative weight of Israeli anti-insurgency methods. Their recovery was preempted by the Gulf War and, even more profoundly, by Oslo and the state formation process it set in motion. The demobilization of the population and their deepening alienation from political action (until the current uprising) has been one of the most salient outcomes of PA rule.[36]

The second Intifada suffered seriously as a result. It was disorganized and lacked leadership: 'Not only was the al-Aqsa Intifada essentially leaderless in the sense of organization, expression of objectives, and tactics; the PA [with its 40,000 armed police], in essence, abandoned its own people to the vagaries of Israel's punishing blows'.[37]

And the blows were indeed immediate and merciless. Three weeks into the Intifada, General Amos Malka, head of Israel's Military Intelligence, wanted to know how many bullets the Israeli army had fired since the beginning of the Intifada. Ben Kaspit broke the story in *Ma'ariv* in 2002:

> When the answer arrived by noon, most of the officers who were present, according to an eye witness, turned white. In the first few days of the Intifada, the IDF fired about 700,000 bullets and other projectiles in Judea and Samaria [the West Bank] and about 300,000 in Gaza. All told, about a million bullets and other projectiles were used. Someone in the Central Command later quipped that the project should be named 'a bullet for every child'. This astronomical number evinces the facts on the ground.[38]

Israel's severe repression and brutality after the outbreak of the second Intifada had a clear political objective: complete Palestinian submission. Arafat had not been in a position to provide that in the Camp David negotiations of July 2000, refusing to go all the way along with what the US and Israel wanted without getting significant Israeli concessions in exchange. Barak, in response, initiated Israel's long campaign to both de-legitimize Arafat as an interlocutor and 'partner for peace' and to destroy the PA.[39] In a matter of months, Arafat was transformed from a courageous Nobel Laureate of Peace to a mastermind of revolt and terrorism.[40] Israel's immediate use of massive force to crush the Palestinian popular dissent that broke out in September 2000 also had the immediate effect of militarizing the Intifada and pushing Palestinians towards armed operations, rather than trying to revive the conditions for sustained civil participation and mobilization. Betrayed, besieged, and defenceless, Palestinian support for armed resistance and suicide bombings was bound to increase.

Three main groups competed for primacy. The Tanzim/al-Aqsa Martyrs Brigades emerged out of grassroots disenchantment within Fatah, and had been active as an anti-Oslo force since the mid-1990s; it was led in Ramallah by Marwan Barghouti, who was captured by the Israeli army during the spring 2002 invasion. The Islamic Jihad was a military-nationalist group made up of fundamentalists active in Gaza since the 1980s and had no interest in social work or in participating in legislative elections. Hamas, the most powerful resistance group, was, like Jihad, a product of the Israeli occupation, and has been active since the first Intifada. Combining a military wing with social welfare and charity work, Hamas sees itself as the heir to secular nationalism and to the PLO's political programme of liberating Palestine, and has implicitly recognized the two-state solution based on full independence, sovereignty, and complete withdrawal and dismantlement of all settlements.[41]

Between September 2000 and up to a ceasefire in mid-2003, it was estimated that 96 per cent of the attacks against Israeli targets took place in the West Bank and Gaza, with only 4 per cent inside Israel itself.[42] This was a clear indication that the al-Aqsa Intifada was fundamentally an anti-colonial rebellion. Yet Israel managed to obscure this essential fact by arguing that suicide terrorism against Jews is the real core of and motivation behind the revolt. As Baruch Kimmerling put it: 'If the symbol of the first Intifada was Palestinian children throwing stones, the symbol of the al-Aqsa Intifada – for both sides – is the suicide bombers'. Israel exploited this 'to gain domestic and international legitimacy for the unrestrained use of Israeli military power'.[43]

Suicide bombing, however, was susceptible to such appropriation and misconception. Because it targeted civilians inside the Green Line, it could easily be misrepresented by Israel as part of the age-old Palestinian desire to destroy Jewish life and Israeli statehood. As a form of resistance, therefore, suicide bombing had insurmountable internal weaknesses. In their excellent 'On Suicide Bombings', Rema Hammami and Musa Budeiri have shown that both as a means of revenge and retaliation for Israeli terror and violence and as a strategy for forcing Israeli withdrawal, suicide bombing has severe costs and drawbacks: it is counterproductive, inefficient, immoral, and may even risk de-legitimizing the Palestinian struggle for emancipation and justice. Its main effect, however, has been on the domestic Palestinian front:

> [It] risk[s] transforming Palestinian society into one in which the only people with a political role are those willing to die or kill while they die. The rest are confined to the role of spectators.

They applaud, but are not called upon to shoulder any task in the ongoing struggle for liberation and independence. The history of political struggle teaches us that such actions belittle the role of the masses and reconcile them to their own powerlessness – they merely exaggerate the feeling among exploited and oppressed peoples that the matter of resistance has to be left to a few martyrs.[44]

Rather than being a means for overcoming siege and ending colonialism, suicide bombing is a symptom of atomization and disengagement. Rather than re-mobilizing people, it exacerbates their demobilization, and risks undercutting their potential for collective participation.

A critical evaluation of suicide bombing was eventually achieved by the Palestinian resistance groups, and an end to targeting civilians within Israel was declared. Nasser Jumaa, Israel's most wanted al-Aqsa Brigades leader, made the following assessment in an interview in 2005: 'We didn't have a clear strategy for the Palestinian resistance. We should have specified the place for its work as the occupied territories, and made its target the settlers and the soldiers that exist to protect them. It would have been possible this way to win a voice within Israeli society. It would also have prevented outsiders from denying our rights to defend our land and expel those who stole and occupied our land'.[45] Having been abandoned by the Fatah PA, al-Aqsa Brigades remains unable either to democratize or to reform Fatah, overcome corruption, or unite the various factions, which remain very loosely organized and localized. Nasser Jumaa concludes: 'We are searching now for a strategy to get out of this miserable abyss'.

ABSENT STRATEGY

The absence of a clear strategy for national liberation is the most urgent problem facing Palestinians today. Israeli military superiority is still overwhelming, and Oslo has only improved Israel's diplomatic standing in the world, as it de-legitimized Palestinian needs and national rights. Under Oslo, Arab 'normalization' with Israel intensified, and most Islamic and third-world states removed political and economic barriers with Israel. This has radically worsened official international identification with the Palestinian cause, which was very high during the first Intifada. The structural constraints on the Palestinians have thus only gotten worse. The collapse of the Palestinian national project has also made the subjective conditions of national self-realization even harder. The Abbas leadership of the PLO and PA has abandoned refugee rights and representation, a clear measure of the degeneration of the Palestinian cause.[46]

Under such dire conditions, nagging questions remain: Will the Palestinians be able to formulate a successful liberation strategy that can overcome both colonial siege and PA capitulation? What are the political tasks of the present moment, and what role does military resistance play in a reconstructed national project, if any? And how, finally, can the Palestinian question *return* to the realm of popular political contestation?

In the January 2006 legislative elections, Hamas had an answer which spoke to the majority of the occupied Palestinian electorate. Hamas's Reform and Change list declared its clear and unambiguous defence of the inalienable rights of the Palestinian people, including the right of self-determination in the West Bank and Gaza and the right of return for all Palestinian refugees. Committed to bolstering resistance against the Israeli occupation, Hamas vowed to reform the PA, end corruption and opportunism, work for unity, defend political pluralism, and support Palestinian steadfastness and resilience.[47] Hamas also flagged its regressive social agenda of Islamizing Palestinian society, but only a minority of Palestinians have ever supported that (13 per cent). What attracted most occupied Palestinians to Hamas was neither its elaborate welfare programmes nor its religious fundamentalism (though both played a part). It was, rather, Hamas's promise to revive Palestinian nationalism and lead it to victory.

The Oslo framework was, as a result, put into crisis. Oslo was not intended to facilitate real democracy: elections were a good idea as long as they guaranteed the continuation of the colonial regime, and were dispensable if they didn't. Israel recognized this and was therefore against holding the 2006 elections. The US, however, was caught in a contradiction: its messianic rhetoric on the democratic transformation of the Middle East clashed with its actual hostility to Palestinian nationalism and to Hamas. The US risked elections and hoped for a Fatah victory (as the polls predicted). When Hamas won, the whole might of US imperialism descended on the Palestinians even harder: siege was compounded by economic sanctions and diplomatic boycott. Palestinians would have to be 'starved' for their choice, as the *New York Times* stated. And, true to form, since then every possible means of 'regime change' has been tried by Israel and its allies, including: Israeli military attacks and massacres;[48] assassinations of activists; arrest by Israel of nearly a third of the newly-elected parliament; calls and threats by the US-oriented Abbas to conduct new elections; active marginalization by Abbas of his own government ministers; a politically-motivated civil-service strike that sought to cripple the workings of government ministries even further; endless threats from Muhammad Dahlan, Abbas's main security chief, to 'decimate' Hamas;[49] and, finally, Dahlan's attempt to topple the government by force, leading to serious factional armed clashes, which left scores of Palestinian dead and a looming threat of civil war hanging.[50] Hamas was, as a result, pushed towards a military and security build-up in Gaza, yet again deferring possibilities of popular political mobilization and organization. The danger that Hamas will be endlessly dragged down into fighting over the breadcrumbs of a prison regime rather than helping people break out of it is very real.

In spite all of this, Hamas – and the Palestinians generally – withstood the global onslaught. Israel, the US, and local Palestinian capitulators all failed to reverse Hamas's victory.[51] The US, mired in Iraq, also failed to prevent a new Saudi-sponsored power-sharing unity government from forming, which was motivated by Saudi fears of Iranian sponsorship of Hamas. This attenuated the push towards civil war and national disintegration, though clashes continue to erupt occasionally. What the new government failed to achieve, however, was an end to the international boycott: the tax-money Israel owed the PA ($700 million) was unreturned and international economic and political sanctions remained in place. Israel and the US did everything possible to ensure that the new government either collapsed or was unable to function effectively or properly. Internal contradictions were severely exacerbated by Dahlan (dubbed by Hamas as the 'leader of the American, putschist faction'), who was indeed armed and supported by the US and Israel and actively sabotages unity and pushes for armed confrontation and civil war.[52]

On 14 June 2007, the Hamas-Fatah contradiction was resolved by force. Fearing a US-backed military coup, Hamas rooted out Dahlan's apparatus and took over the internal security of Gaza.[53] While announcing very clearly that this was not a military coup but a 'necessary step' to remove the 'stumbling block' facing Palestinian unity and national conciliation, Hamas' action was deemed an illegitimate aggression by all Palestinian factions, objecting to the use of force in Palestinian politics.[54] Abbas exploited Hamas' strategic blunder and declared a national emergency. He also dissolved the unity government and formed a new government of technocrats led by the American-favoured Salam Fayyad. Israel and the Western world applauded this unconstitutional act, promising Abbas support and an end to the boycott and sanctions. This left Hamas isolated and cut off, and risks compounding the geographical separation between the West Bank and Gaza with a political separation between a Hamas-run Gaza and a PA-run West Bank, an outcome that Israel has been working towards since 1991.[55] Such a Fatah-Hamas dual power situation can only entrench Palestinian political division and fragmentation.

Whether unity is restored or new elections declared, one thing is certain: Abbas won't deliver the independent statehood and decolonization that most Palestinians want; while Hamas seems unable to organize a popular mass mobilization against the occupation.[56] The real alternative is still dormant: a nation looks on in discontent. The majority of Palestinians, who blame both Hamas and Fatah for the current crisis, are yet to re-mobilize against Israel's occupation and overcome the militarization of their politics.[57] Collective self-organization is now Palestine's only hope.

One positive recent development is the consolidation of popular non-violent civilian struggles against the Wall. The village of Bilee'n has become a symbol for such local resistance campaigns, with Palestinian-led peaceful protests attracting Israeli and international solidarity activists joining in to protect Palestinian life and land. Though village lands have rarely been saved (Budrus is an important exception), many recognize the value of such collective political practices both in building up international and Israeli popular support for the Palestinian cause and in communicating the justness and urgency of the Palestinian question.[58]

Still missing, however, is a comprehensive liberation strategy. Neither elite nationalism nor religious fundamentalism has succeeded in this task. The elections of January 2006 have again re-opened the question of resistance as a political project. As Azmi Bishara put it, how can 'the occupiers [be forced] to pay a price for their occupation that they are unwilling or unable to withstand morally, materially, emotionally, politically, economically, and socially'?[59] Collective mobilization by all Palestinians around coherent national objectives is still necessary, as is clear elaboration of both short-term tasks and long-term strategic goals. These cannot be achieved without democratic re-activation of grassroots forces both inside and outside Palestine. The closest Palestinians have ever come to such national-popular mobilization was in the first Intifada - what Edward Said called 'one of the most extraordinary anti-colonial and unarmed mass insurrections in the whole history of the modern period'.[60] Only when its revolutionary remembrance comes to animate future Palestinian political organization can sufficient political leverage be created in order to make Israel pay the price of its 40 year-old occupation and begin to rectify the wrongs it has committed against the Palestinian people. A new progressive political agent is now imperative. No less than the survival of an oppressed nation is at stake.

NOTES

1   I borrow this phrase from Amira Hass: 'Just as was the case in the Oslo years, three million individuals are drawing on immense personal reserves to bear the hardships of siege without surrender'. 'Israel's Closure Policy: An Ineffective Strategy of Containment and Repression', *Journal of Palestine Studies*, 31(3) Spring 2002, p. 20.

2   For Gaza's position after Israel's disengagement, see Gisha's report, *Disengaged Occupiers: The Legal Status of Gaza*, Tel Aviv, January 2007. See also Patrick Cockburn, 'Gaza is Dying', *The Independent*, 8 September 2006: 'Gaza is dying. The Israeli siege of the Palestinian enclave is so tight that its people are on the edge of starvation. Here on the shores of the Mediterranean a great tragedy is taking place that is being ignored because the world's attention has been diverted by wars in Lebanon and Iraq'.

3   It was called the al-Aqsa Intifada as it was sparked off by Sharon's 'visit' to the Dome of the Rock, accompanied by several thousand police.

4   *Movement and Access Restrictions in the West Bank: Uncertainty and Inefficiency in the Palestinian Economy*, 9 May 2007, available from http://www.worldbank.org. For the quotations used here see Clauses 3 and 37. In response, Israeli Deputy Defense Minister Ephraim Sneh accused the Bank of being 'one-sided' and said that restrictions on travel are there to prevent terrorism. See Avi Issacharoff, 'Sneh: World Bank Report Slamming Israel One-Sided', *Haaretz*, 10 May 2007. The new Palestinian Minister of Information Moustafa Barghouti welcomed the report and added that it accurately describes Israel's new apartheid system in the West Bank. See Joshua Brilliant, 'World Bank Pessimistic on Palestinian Economy', *World Peace Herald* (Online), 9 May 2007, available from http://www.wpherald.com.

5   Salem Ajluni, 'The Palestinian Economy and the Second Intifada', *Journal of Palestine Studies*, 32(3), Spring 2003, p. 69. See also Sara Roy, *Failing Peace: Gaza and the Palestinian-Israeli Conflict*, London: Pluto, 2007, especially 'Ending the Palestinian Economy', pp. 250-93.

6   United Nations General Assembly, 'Report of the Special Rapporteur on the Situation of Human Rights in the Palestinian Territories Occupied since 1967, John Dugard', United Nations Human Rights Council, 29 January 2007, p. 21.

7   Hass, 'Israel's Closure Policy', p. 18.

8   For an excellent class analysis of the Palestinian question and of the differences between Zionist settler colonialism and South African apartheid, see Mona N. Younis, *Liberation and Democratization: The South African and Palestinian National Movements*, Minneapolis: University of Minnesota Press, 2000.

9   Azmi Bishara, 'A Short History of Apartheid', *Al-Ahram Weekly Online*, 8-14 January 2004, available from http://weekly.ahram.org.eg.

10   Norman G. Finkelstein develops such a historical comparison in his *The Rise and Fall of Palestine*, Minneapolis: University of Minnesota Press, 1996, pp. 104-121.

11   Fayez A. Sayegh, *Zionist Colonialism in Palestine*, Beirut: Palestine Liberation Organization Research Centre, 1965, p. v.

12   Lecture at Barnard College, New York, 11 April 2005. See also Hass, 'Israel's Closure Policy', especially p. 10.

13   Amira Hass, *Drinking the Sea at Gaza*, New York: Henry Holt, 1999, p. 235.

14   B'Tselem, *Land Grab: Israel's Settlement Policy in the West Bank*, Jerusalem, May 2002, p. 69. The subsequent quotations in this paragraph are at pp. 15-16, 37 and 69.

15   International Court of Justice, 'Legal Consequences of the Construction of a Wall in the Occupied Palestinian Territory', 9 July 2004, clause 122.

16   Ibid., p. 122.

17   The worst was Operation Defensive Shield in March-April 2002, when Israel re-occupied all major Palestinian cities and killed 220 people. See Muna Hamzeh and Todd May, eds., *Operation Defensive Shield: Witnesses to Israeli War Crimes*, London: Pluto Press, 2003.

18   See Amnesty International, *Amnesty International Report 2007*, London: Amnesty International Publications, 2007, pp. 147-50.

19   Edward Said, *The End of the Peace Process: Oslo and After*, New York: Vintage, 2000, p. 345. After Oslo, Said became the PLO's leading critic. See his *Peace And Its Discontents*, New York: Vintage, 1996.

20   The most recent scholarly accounts are: Nigel Parsons, *The Politics of the Palestinian Authority: From Oslo to al-Aqsa*, London: Routledge, 2005; Cheryl A. Rubenberg, *The Palestinians: In Search of a Just Peace*, Boulder, CO: Lynne Rienner, 2003; and Roy's *Failing Peace*. Edward Said's essays are indispensable for understanding Oslo, as are Tanya Reinhart's two books: *Israel/Palestine: How to End the War of 1948*, New York: Seven Stories, 2002 and *The Roadmap to Nowhere: Israel/Palestine since 2003*, London: Verso, 2006.

21   'Israel-PLO Recognition: Exchange of Letters Between PM Rabin and Chairman Arafat', U.S. Department of State, posted online July 2003, available from http://www.state.gov.

22   Burhan Dajani, 'The September 1993 Israeli-PLO Documents: A Textual Analysis', *Journal of Palestine Studies*, 23(3), Spring 1994, p. 22.

23   Ibid., pp. 18, 19.

24   These are some of the section headings in Allegra Pacheco's 'Flouting Convention: The Oslo Agreement', in Roane Carey, ed., *The New Intifada: Resisting Israel's Apartheid*, London: Verso, 2001, pp. 181-206. In her important legal intervention, she states that: 'One of the greatest flaws of the Oslo agreements was that they did not commit Israel to abide by the [Geneva] Convention and cease its human rights violations' (p. 186).

25   Gilbert Achcar, 'The Washington Accords: A Retreat Under Pressure', in Achcar, ed., *Eastern Cauldron: Islam, Afghanistan, Palestine and Iraq in a Marxist Mirror*, New York: Monthly Review Press, 2004, p. 201.

26   Quoted in Samih K. Farsoun with Christina E. Zacharia, *Palestine and the Palestinians*, Boulder, CO: Westview: 1997, p. 255. The quotation is taken from Edward Said, *The Politics of Dispossession: The Struggle for Palestinian Self-Determination*, New York: Pantheon, 1994, p. xxxii.

27 Graham Usher dubbed this 'securitisation', leading to a process of the 'de-politicisation of Palestinian society' and corrosion of Palestinian nationalism. *Dispatches from Palestine: The Rise and Fall of the Oslo Peace Process*, London: Pluto, 1999, p. 79.

28 Glenn E. Robinson, *Building a Palestinian State: The Incomplete Revolution*, Indianapolis: Indiana University Press, 1997, p. 177. This also entailed a diplomatic sidelining of the Madrid peace negotiators, who insisted on upholding international law and obliging Israel to withdraw from all occupied territory and dismantle all settlements. See Rashid Khalidi's important interview with the head of the Palestinian Madrid team Haydar 'Abd al-Shafi, 'Looking Back, Looking Forward', *Journal of Palestine Studies*, 32(1), Autumn 2002.

29 Parsons, *The Politics of the Palestinian Authority*, p. 222.

30 Ibid., p. 184.

31 Nina Sovich, 'Palestinian Trade Unions', *Journal of Palestine Studies*, 29(4), Summer 2000, p. 66.

32 'The Palestinian Secular Opposition at a Crossroads: Interviews with PFLP's Abu Ali Mustafa and DFLP's Nayif Hawatimah', *Journal of Palestine Studies*, 29(2), Winter 2000, p. 84.

33 See Parsons, *The Politics of the Palestinian Authority*, pp. 185-6. For the PA's curbing of freedom of expression and torture, see Amnesty International, 'Palestinian Authority: Silencing of Dissent', September 2000, available from http://www.amnesty.org.

34 See 'The Homeland Calls Us!', *News from Within*, January 2000.

35 Rubenberg, *The Palestinians*, p. 329. Parsons quotes an estimate of only 5 per cent of Palestinian active participation in the Intifada (p. 265).

36 Rema Hammami and Salim Tamari, 'The Second Intifada: End or New Beginning?', *Journal of Palestine Studies*, 30(2), Winter 2001, p. 17.

37 Rubenberg, *The Palestinians*, p. 330.

38 Ben Kaspit, 'Jewish New Year 2002: The Second Anniversary of the Intifada', Part I, *Ma'ariv*, 6 September 2002. Israel's brutality led Palestinians inside Israel to rise up in protest and solidarity with their occupied brethren. Israel responded by killing 13 demonstrators and injuring hundreds.

39 Operation Defensive Shield in Spring 2002 did exactly that, 'the crux' of which was 'Israel's decimation of Palestinian civilian institutions', as Rubenberg has shown (*The Palestinians*, p. 351). For Israel's 'generous offer' bluff at Camp David II, see Reinhart, *Israel/Palestine*.

40 Sharon's biographer, Uri Dan, suggests that if Arafat was not actually assassinated by Israel in November 2004, it was not because they were not prepared to do it. In September 2004 Dan asked Sharon, then Prime Minister for a second term, about his 'precise intentions toward Arafat'. Sharon replied: 'We eliminated the leaders of Hamas – Sheikh Ahmed Yassin, Abdel Aziz al-Rantissi – and other terrorist heads when the time was right. The same principle goes for Yasser Arafat. We will treat him like the others. I see no difference between him and Yassin: they both murder Jews. For Arafat, we will choose the time that suits us best. Everyone will receive his due. The question will be debated when the time is right, as it was for the leaders of Hamas'. Uri Dan, *Ariel*

Sharon: An Intimate Portrait, New York: Palgrave Macmillan, 2006, p. 234. Dan also says that Bush knew that Sharon was planning an assassination: 'On April 14, 2004, Sharon was finally able to extricate himself from the promise that he had involuntarily made to the American president in March 2001 – not to touch Yasser Arafat' (p. 246).

41   For an excellent brief review essay of books on Islamic Palestinian fundamentalism, see Musa Budeiri, 'The Nationalist Dimension of Islamic Movements in Palestinian Politics', *Journal of Palestine Studies*, 24(3), Spring 1995. Khaled Hroub's two books on Hamas are indispensable: *Hamas: Political Thought and Practice*, Washington: Institute of Palestine, 2000 and *Hamas: A Beginner's Guide*, London: Pluto, 2006.

42   Parsons, *The Politics of the Palestinian Authority*, p. 271. He adds: 'The rough parity in casualties (355 beyond the Green Line, 393 within it) is due to the much smaller number of attacks within the Green Line being far more likely to be suicide bombings, and hence far more deadly'.

43   Baruch Kimmerling, *Politicide: Ariel Sharon's War Against the Palestinians*, London: Verso, 2003, pp. 161, 137.

44   Rema Hammami and Musa Budeiri, 'On Suicide Bombings', *al-Quds Newspaper*, 14 December 2001 (in Arabic). An English translation, from which I quote, can be found on www.musabudeiri.net under 'newspaper articles'.

45   'From the Heart of the Struggle', *Al-Ahram Weekly Online*, 14–20 April 2005, available from http://weekly.ahram.org.eg

46   Randa Farah, 'Palestinian Refugees', *Interventions: International Journal of Postcolonial Studies*, 8(2), July 2006.

47   For a detailed analysis of Hamas's electoral platform, see Khaled Hroub, 'A "New Hamas" Through its Documents', *Journal of Palestine Studies*, 35(4), Summer 2006.

48   As John Dugard has reported, from June to November 2006, Israel killed over 400 Palestinians and injured 1500, conducting 364 military incursions into Gaza alone: 'In November 2006 alone there were 656 IDF raids into the West Bank' (United Nations General Assembly, 'Report of the Special Rapporteur', 29 January 2007). All this, Israel claimed, in order to save one captured Israeli solider, while refusing all comprehensive ceasefire and prisoner-exchange deals.

49   Khaled Amayreh, 'Dahlan Vows to Decimate Hamas', *Al-Ahram Weekly Online*, 8–14 June 2006, available from http://weekly.ahram.org.eg.

50   As predicted by Gilbert Achcar immediately after the elections: 'First Reflections on the Electoral Victory of Hamas', *Znet*, 27 January 2006, available at http://www.zmag.org.

51   Nor should one ignore the political initiative called 'the prisoners' conciliation document', ratified by Hamas and Fatah in June 2006. The agreement consecrates resistance, advocates mass participation, and defends Palestinian rights. For details, see my 'Occupied Palestine: Prisoners, Colonial Elites, and Fundamentalists', *Znet*, 11 June 2006.

52   Dahlan was the main reason why the new Minister of Internal Affairs Kawasmeh recently resigned. He protested that he had no powers to implement a newly

agreed on security plan that would put an end to Gaza's 'fawda il-silah' ('chaos of arms'). Looking back at the period since Hamas' election victory, Danny Rubenstein concluded in 'The Original Sin', *Haaretz*, 22 May 2007: 'Without a doubt, a series of reasons – political, economic, social and others – have brought these troubles down on the Palestinians. However, the direct cause of what is happening now in the Gaza Strip is that the traditional Palestinian leadership (i.e. the top echelon of Fatah) was not prepared to transfer authority to the elected Hamas leadership'. See also Scott Wilson, 'Fatah Troops Enter Gaza with Israeli Assent', *Washington Post*, 18 May 2007.

53   Jonathan Steele, 'Hamas Acted on a Very Real Fear of a US-sponsored Coup', *The Guardian*, 22 June 2007.

54   Press conference by exiled Hamas leader Khaled Mishal on 15 June 2007.

55   Akiva Eldar, 'Sharon's Dream', *Haaretz*, 20 June 2007.

56   Commentators have also warned that worsening conditions may lead to more extreme versions of Islamic fundamentalism taking hold in Gaza. See, for example, Gideon Rachman, 'Missed Opportunities, Gaza and the Spread of Jihadism', *Financial Times*, 18 June 2007.

57   As the Palestinian Center for Policy and Survey Research reported, 75 per cent of Palestinians want new elections and 59 per cent said 'both Hamas and Fatah are equally to blame for the bitter factional fighting that led to the Hamas takeover of Gaza' (Avi Issacharoff, *Haaretz*, 21 June 2007).

58   For a powerful account, see Reinhart, *The Roadmap to Nowhere*, pp. 174-217. 'In the months to come [in early 2004], virtually all the anti-occupation groups of Israel were to join the Palestinian struggle along the route of the wall' (p. 198). Ta'ayush and Anarchists Against the Wall are two such groups.

59   Azmi Bishara, 'The Quest for Strategy', *Journal of Palestine Studies*, 32(2), Winter 2003, p. 43.

60   Said, *The Politics of Dispossession*, p. 137.

THE ISLAMIC ETHIC AND THE SPIRIT OF TURKISH CAPITALISM TODAY

YILDIZ ATASOY

Turkey was among the first countries to adopt neoliberal reforms in the early 1980s. Even though privatization has been a rather slow process, due to the presence of strong regulatory authorities and state-owned industries, the market orientation of the economy was gradually consolidated over the following two decades. Yet neoliberal restructuring gave rise to a series of major crises from the late 1980s onwards, the most recent of which, in 2000-01, resulted in a 9.4 per cent fall in GDP. The vulnerable, poorer members of society, along with salaried professionals and small to medium-sized company owners, shouldered most of the burden. Many skilled and well-educated workers lost their jobs and among smaller companies the bankruptcy rate soared. For the first time in Turkey artisans, shopkeepers, and small business-owning tradesmen went on strike, closing shops and demonstrating against neoliberal policies.

In the wake of this severe economic crisis, the pro-Islamic Justice and Development Party (AKP) came to power, supported by both prosperous and disadvantaged segments of society. Due to its broad electoral base, the AKP has been able to draw, ironically enough, on mass dissatisfaction with neoliberalism while also supporting the neoliberal economic model. The party promises to alleviate poverty and reduce extreme inequality, yet also advocates the privatization of public corporations, liberalization of trade, entrepreneurship, and private investment.

Alongside the AKP, other Islamic groups such as the Gulen Community Movement, or *Fethullahcilar,* have participated in the institutionalization of neoliberalism, especially under the banner of enlarging civic engagement in the economy. This has involved appealing to a variety of social groups affected by deep class- and region-based inequalities and culture-based grievances against Kemalism. All of these groups are subject, albeit in different ways, to the ebb and flow of the global market economy that create the material conditions of inequality. But Kemalist ideology, which allegedly eviscerated Anatolia's cultural richness by imposing a homogeneous secular culture, encourages such groups to think of themselves as victims of social injustice, what Mike Davis, in a very different context, calls 'unequally endowed groups'.[1] In the absence of a strong Leftist movement the connections between material and cultural tensions can make Islam an appealing political project. It helps to resist both Kemalist developmentalism, with its class bias in favour of large Istanbul-based industrialists, and secularism, as embodied in the authoritarian homogenizing culture of civil-military state bureaucrats. Islam appeals to those over whom Kemalist bureaucrats have cast shadows, questioning their cultural suitability for 'western' modernity.

These groups include capitalists from smaller Anatolian cities, some large firms established in Istanbul, highly-educated Muslim professionals from modest Anatolian families, and the urban poor and marginalized. All wish to reposition themselves in the state, which should be restructured on neoliberal lines but in a way that caters to their imputed Muslim cultural difference and regional background.[2] In regard to the economically privileged, it is not difficult to see why they might support a policy orientation focused on greater integration into the world capitalist economy. The difficulty arises in relation to the economically weak. Especially crucial here has been the political re-signification of an Islamic orientation that ties their claims for 'access rights' to the broader ideological frame of neoliberalism. References to the need to respect Muslim traditions within the domestic context of the state are thus linked to, draw on, and blur into, the globalized 'rights and freedoms' discourse of liberal democracy.

THE AKP AND NEOLIBERALISM

In building a cross-class coalition the AKP has reframed an Islamic moral stance to fit a 'Third Way' party image that emulates Blair, Clinton and Schröder. It charts a course of integration between the neoliberal market economy and citizen-empowerment politics. In this way it addresses the two central themes of contemporary Turkish politics: neoliberal restructuring of the economy, and transformation of the state along liberal-democratic lines. Both of these are central to the AKP government's push for Turkey's membership in the EU, which also requires a broader shift in Turkish 'political culture'. It is in relation to these transformations that an Islamic political stand has gained considerable ground in the discursive battles being waged in Turkey today.

The AKP's ability to bring disadvantaged groups together with globally competitive large firms rests on its promise to realign state–society relations in Turkey. Its coalition-building is explicitly premised on 'a new social contract that facilitates an engagement between society and the state on the basis of universal justice and human rights principles'.[3] As highlighted in its *Development and Democratization Programme*, the AKP argues for redesigning fundamental rights and freedoms in Turkey to make them congruent with 'universal standards' and with the EU's Copenhagen political criteria for new members. Indeed the AKP program is generally very much in line with the 'globalization' and 'democratization' discourses of the EU.[4]

This commitment to European norms comes with a particular political-culture twist by linking a neoliberal policy orientation to an Islamic version of what the World Bank calls 'human capital growth'.[5] It goes beyond conceptualizing this as an aggregate of free actors in society making rational choices, and the removal of state-imposed political, cultural, and administrative constraints. Rather, the AKP program argues that 'combining world economic and European democratic normative standards with Turkish cultural values and moral precepts can produce an ethics that would apply in all aspects of the economy as a precondition for permanent and perpetual growth'.[6] Islamic moral principles seen as a strategy for asset building in human capital are combined with the transformation of the authoritarian Kemalist tradition to achieve greater social solidarity.

Thus, for Prime Minister Erdogan, the implementation of the Copenhagen political criteria will enable Turkey to secure economic growth by aligning its own Muslim values, defined as 'authentic', with the European liberal principles of democracy, human rights, and individual freedoms, which are elevated to a level of 'universality'.[7]

The AKP's *Transition to a Strong Economy* platform explicitly outlined a neoliberal program which redefines development as participation in the world market. It differed little from what was contained in the previous government's crisis-management agreement with the IMF, which accompanied its US$ 8 billion bailout in 2001, on top of an existing US$ 11 billion loan package.[8] Most notably it included provisions for the wide application of financial discipline to the 'informal' sector, the marginalized, and the impoverished elements of Turkish society. After promising to implement such policies the AKP government received an additional US$ 26 billion from the IMF.[9]

It is by no means due to pressure from the IMF that the AKP openly proclaimed that it 'supports a free-market economy with all of its rules and institutions, and adopts the principle that the state should not directly engage in economic activity'.[10] It has intensified the process of privatization of public companies (approximately 170 public companies have since 1984 been completely privatized, and state shares have been sold off in 240 mixed companies).[11] Although these included key infrastructure industries such as telecommunications, as well as petrochemicals and other energy-related in-dustries, the fiscal returns from privatization are minimal – the amount of income generated has been only US$ 9.5 billion.[12] The most important outcome appears to be the creation of a context for state downsizing and regulatory depoliticization, undertaken under the influence of the interna-tional lending agencies, rather than revenue generation. Yet there is more at work here for the AKP than adhering to policies adopted in accordance with IMF stand-by agreements and the World Bank's conditionality terms. The AKP has its own reasons for wanting to dismantle the state-owned enter-prises which since the 1930s have constituted the backbone of the Turkish economy.

THE REALIGNMENT OF TURKISH CAPITAL

It is important to appreciate how private capital has been realigned during the rise of neoliberalism and its embodiment in the Islamic politics of the AKP. This is best seen in terms of the divergence of interests that emerged within the Turkish Industrialists' and Businessmen's Association (TUSIAD), and between it and the Independent Industrialists' and Businessmen's Asso-ciation (MUSIAD). TUSIAD, representing secularly-oriented big business interests concentrated in the Istanbul region, with strong ties to the Kemalist state, has largely kept its distance from the AKP's Islamic-political project, although it supports the AKP government's neoliberal policies. MUSIAD, on the other hand, representing both large and smaller-sized Muslim busi-ness interests, generally from smaller cities in Anatolia with very weak ties to the Kemalist state apparatus, is a key element in the AKP's cross-class electoral coalition. It is no longer possible, however, to see political Islam as aligned only with 'small and medium scale' and newly-growing Anatolian capital, versus a secularly-oriented big bourgeoisie based in Istanbul. Since the mid-1980s the more successful pro-Islamic groups have already entered the ranks of big capital, and some of them are now located in Istanbul while maintaining strong family ties with Anatolian towns and villages.[13] How-ever, the political legacy of Kemalist developmentalism (which historically marginalized Anatolian small capitalists) still has a profound ideological effect on the reproduction of differences between large Istanbul-based and small Anatolian capitalists. This relates to the cultural signification of a 'Muslim other', and has lead to a debate within business between secularists and Is-lamists on the best direction for Turkish society. In this debate, pro-Islamic business groups combine their economic success stories with the theme of

Islamic social justice, while secularly oriented groups are concerned with the political future of the Kemalist state.

TUSIAD was founded in 1971 by the largest private industrial and commercial capital groups in the Istanbul region. Its headquarters is in Istanbul and it has only one Anatolian branch, which opened in Ankara in 2000.[14] In 2005 TUSIAD had a membership of 458 firms which accounted for 43.2 per cent of total value-added in the Turkish economy, and 38.2 per cent of Turkish exports.[15] These firms are primarily family-owned and managed conglomerates with origins in the state-led industrialization project of the 1930s. Indeed, high-level state bureaucrats were actively involved in the founding of industrial firms, transforming themselves into a private industrial bourgeoisie. Industrialization in Turkey has long been synonymous with nationalism, which directed social change onto a secular trajectory. Strong connections with state bureaucrats and dependence on state backing explain TUSIAD's secularist political orientation.

TUSIAD member firms still maintain strong links to the state and enjoy easy access to government support, aided by joint ventures with the military in areas ranging from iron and steel, cement, automotive, pulp and paper and food, as well as artillery ammunition, small arms, military vehicles and rocket systems.[16] The close ties between some of its members and civil-military bureaucrats often cause friction within TUSIAD because they tend to lead to a lack of concern with the military's frequent intervention in civilian politics. Leading older-generation TUSIAD members were pleased when the military engineered a 'soft coup' on February 28, 1997, forcing the resignation of the democratically elected coalition government of the pro-Islamic Welfare Party. Many leading pro-Islamic businessmen were arrested, and 100 pro-Islamic companies were blacklisted: they were excluded from bidding for military contracts on suspicion of undertaking 'Islamic fundamentalist' activities against the secular state.[17] For the owners of younger-generation TUSIAD firms, however, with limited linkages to the state, this was harmful to democracy. Although charges against pro-Islamic business groups were never proven, the military's action served to dampen the competitive growth of Islamic capitalists. And while TUSIAD strongly supports market-driven policies its internal cleavages have tended to prevent it from giving unified support to depoliticized regulation of the economy and more democratic standards for the state.[18]

During the 1970s TUSIAD's primary focus was on the institutionalization of export-oriented industrialization to replace the post-war import-substitution model. It repeatedly argued that excessive state regulation was the source of Turkey's economic problems. During the 1980s TUSIAD worked broadly for the consolidation of market-oriented structural reforms (although they did so with some hesitation, as they felt increasingly challenged by the fast growth of smaller export-oriented companies), without paying much attention to the legitimacy problems associated with privatization and growing inequality. Since the 1990s, under the influence of younger-generation business groups, and in any case reflecting TUSIAD's overall support for Turkey's membership in the EU (which it welcomes as an agent of international discipline), TUSIAD has also supported the democratization reform requirements spelled out in the Copenhagen political criteria (the rule of law, respect for human rights, and protection of minorities). Thus, TUSIAD appears to have broken with the inhibiting social, cultural, and legislative arrangements of the old Kemalist state with which the older TUSIAD firms had been so closely associated.[19]

But although it broadly supports the AKP's *Development and Democratization Programme*, TUSIAD's historical connections with the state have so far kept it out of the AKP's cross-class alliance. MUSIAD, on the other hand, with a clear Islamic political orientation, is central to that alliance. Ten members of MUSIAD were among the founders of the AKP, and 20 members were elected as AKP parliamentarians in the 2002 elections.[20] MUSIAD rejects the Kemalist cultural hierarchy which privileged big Istanbul-based business. It represents itself as the champion of 'Muslimness', seen as a political category of those who have been marginalized in that hierarchy, even though many of its leading companies refrain from referring to Islamic symbols in their business activities. MUSIAD was founded in 1990 by a group of young businessmen called the 'Anatolian tigers'; they were generally from modest Muslim-family backgrounds and included children of Anatolian rural immigrants in *gecekondu* (shantytown) neighbourhoods in the large cities.[21] MUSIAD's membership now exceeds 4,000 firms, the majority of which are export-oriented, small and medium-sized affairs employing fewer than 50 workers. In contrast to TUSIAD, 80 per cent of whose member firms were established before 1980, 70 per cent of MUSIAD companies were founded after 1980.[22] Also in contrast to TUSIAD, MUSIAD has many branches throughout Anatolia.

The traditional sectors of concentration for these companies are labour-intensive industries such as textiles, garments, leather and carpets, construction, building materials, food processing and transportation. Since the mid-1990s, they have also been involved in big-box grocery retailing, furniture, computing and electronics, banking and the media. Although Istanbul has the highest concentration, with 523 MUSIAD members, most of its firms remain dispersed among smaller Anatolian cities. MUSIAD represents only

10 per cent of Turkish GNP (compared to TUSIAD's more than 40 per cent), but its strength lies in its export competitiveness.[23] It aims to improve trade ties with Muslim and Central Asian countries, in addition to seeking Turkey's membership in the EU. It regularly organizes an International Business Forum (IBF) and a World Economic Forum for the Muslim World, as well as annual trade fairs within the Organization of Islamic Conference. MUSIAD is the headquarters for the IBF, whose key objective is to utilize Islamic ethical virtues in wealth creation and support global-business networking among Muslim countries.

MUSIAD represents itself as a civil-society organization which seeks to reduce state power in politics and the economy. This is the theme repeated in its publications since its *Constitutional Reform and Democratization of Government* report of April 2000.[24] Like the AKP's *Development and Democratization Programme,* and in line with the democratization discourse of the EU, MUSIAD's reports call for immediate implementation of the Copenhagen political criteria and a reduction in the military's political power.[25] Although critical of the government's fiscal-discipline policy which it sees as having disadvantaged smaller capitalists, MUSIAD supports the government's commitment to the implementation of IMF policies that integrate Islamic financial organizations into mainstream banking and reduce the state's involvement in the economy.[26]

Insofar as it represents a newly-growing bourgeoisie from Anatolia with weak connections to the state, it is hardly surprising that MUSIAD supports IMF policies and has embraced the World Bank's advocacy of 'human capital growth', especially the shifting of the focus from state institutions to a reliance on the autonomy of the individual and giving primacy to human economic rationality.[27] This is embraced as a necessary precondition for the development of an entrepreneurial spirit among the Anatolian lower and middle classes. However, it is melded with the notion that Islamic ethics also assert the primacy of the individual – which MUSIAD connects to an alleged Islamic requirement that humans must be free from political and administrative constraints – in order to realize their full potential and talent. As one of MUSIAD's documents puts it: 'Allah requires only those individuals with reason, intelligence, and freedom to fulfil their religious duties'.[28]

The context of these claims is that the state's large role in the economy during the early years of the Turkish Republic, and its urban, industrial and westernizing biases, gave rise to a politics of resentment on the part of regional bourgeoisies, articulated around cultural issues. MUSIAD members often believe that because of their Muslim beliefs and rural Anatolian family backgrounds they have been looked down upon and discriminated against by government bureaucrats. They feel they are perceived as backward, lacking the secular, urban, modern cultural prerequisites for participation in Kemalist state-making. Reacting against this they have sought to gain economic success by adopting a strong Islamic work ethic, for both themselves and their children. Whereas the old Istanbul bourgeoisie embraced the Kemalist 'idea of the state', the Anatolian bourgeoisie resents the Kemalist state as an oppressive bureaucracy. As a culturally distinct fraction of capital they question the inclusiveness of the existing public sphere.

MUSIAD situates its wealth-creation strategies in the deployment of educational and disciplinary techniques at the individual level, whereby – consistent with its embrace of 'human capital growth' – an Islamic work ethic is combined with the need for high technical educational attainment. Although their upward social mobility is largely due to their achievement of a first-rate higher education at state-funded public universities, MUSIAD's members have generally received their religious education in the private Koranic schools in the towns of their birth, or from family members; they embrace Islamic ethics for the purpose of creating disciplined, responsible individuals, and seek to build a culture of capital accumulation that 'associates high morality and ethical values with modern technology'.[29] MUSIAD often cites statements attributed to the Prophet Muhammed such as 'poverty is close to heresy' and 'God loves those who earn'.[30]

In contrast to the member firms in TUSIAD, state involvement in the economy brought little or no direct benefit for MUSIAD firms, so that they are strongly behind neoliberal economic reforms, and an Islamic asset-building strategy appears to have helped many of them to improve their international competitiveness. The best sources of investment capital for MUSIAD firms are the so-called 'hidden wealth' of pious Muslims, accumulated in the form of gold jewellery; the inflow of remittances from Turkish immigrant workers in Europe; and public share-holding. Workers' remittances come through share-holding investments and as cash brought into the country in suitcases – mostly through the informal channels of religious communities.[31] Kombassan Holding, YIMPAS, Buyuk Anadolu Holding, Sayha, and Ittifak are all holding companies that have grown with Turkish workers' savings abroad sent home either as investments in equity shares or as cash donations.

Kombassan Holding, which owns 60 factories and 100 firms, was established in 1988 by Bayran Hasim, a teacher from Konya. It has grown significantly with monies received from Turkish workers abroad and now employs more than 30,000 workers. Although Hasim does not reveal his connections or the amounts he receives he has stated that Turkish workers in Europe constitute the largest group of company shareholders.[32] It is also well known that the Association for a New World View in Europe, a Turkish pro-Islamic organization, collects cash donations from migrants in mosques and sends them to Islamic corporations through private couriers. The holding companies Kombassan, YIMPAS and the ULKER Group have been engaged in joint ventures in Germany, the Netherlands and Denmark since the mid-1990s. The Turkish military, and the Capital Market Board, accused these companies of collecting very large investment funds from unregistered sources via religious communities, and Kombassan's and YIMPAS' accounts were investigated after the 28 February 1997 'soft coup', but no evidence was found to substantiate the claim.[33]

There are now five Islamic interest-free banks operating in Turkey. Two are joint ventures established in the 1980s with Saudi and Kuwaiti capital, and three were established in the 1990s by Turkish Muslims. They are Anadolu Finance House, established by Istikbal Group in 1991; Ihlas Finance House, established by Ihlas Holding and the Turkish Religion Fund in 1995 (Ihlas Finance House went bankrupt in 2001); and Asya Finance House, established by the Fethullah Gulen community in 1996. Another Turkish Islamic bank, Family Finance, was established by the ULKER Group in 2001.[34] These Turkish Islamic banks (excluding Ihlas) had about 4 per cent of total deposits in the Turkish banking system (profit-loss sharing accounts, which offer returns on savings without officially paying interest, constitute around 85-90 per cent of their deposits).[35] Together with the unregistered financial dealings of religious communities, these banks play a significant role in mobilizing the 'hidden wealth' of Muslims in both Turkey and Europe for Islamic finance.

It is noteworthy that newly rich medium- and small-sized firms have proved to be highly successful within those sectors of the economy that employ informal labour. The ILO's *Decent Work and the Informal Economy* report of 2002 defines the 'informal economy' as including not only wage employment in unregistered workplaces but also as encompassing paid work not covered by labour and social security legislation.[36] It is estimated that informal employment constitutes about half of total employment and over a third of urban employment in Turkey, compared to 5 per cent in the EU 15 and 11-15 per cent in the EU 25.[37]

Many MUSIAD companies specialize in textile and clothing production for external markets, a sector which tends to be labour-intensive. Their labour management philosophy is expressed by the idea of 'mutual social responsibility' based on moral values and duties, so that unregistered wage-employment is made socially acceptable.[38] Accordingly, wage earners in this context are not seen as members of a social class but as family members who are expected to provide services for the common social good based on mutual trust and respect.[39] The TUSIAD leadership has called these informal types of capital mobilization and deployment of labour power illegal.[40] For MUSIAD, however, the incorporation of 'hidden wealth', workers' remittances, and informal labour into the process of private capital accumulation facilitates the integration of Islamic trust networks within a dynamic market economy, and has the added benefit of doing so without state involvement.

THE ISLAMIC TRUST NETWORK

The Gulen Community Movement mentioned above, the *Fethullahcilar*, is one of the main mass-based civil society movements which emerged in the 1970s. It is named after Fethullah Gulen, an imam trained in state-run schools for higher Islamic learning and a follower of the teachings of Said Nursi, the Anatolian Kurdish Islamic intellectual. Nursi (1876-1960) re-interpreted the Koran to demonstrate that it contains scientific knowledge regarding the laws of order and harmony found in nature, so that Islam is seen as congruent with the ideas of science and progress.[41] This is the basis of the *Fethullahcilar*'s belief that an Islamic brand of modernity can emerge from an imaginative blending of Islamic values and scientific knowledge.

The *Fethullahcilar* is also involved in *da'wa* (preaching) work in the tradition of the Tablighi Jamaat of the Indo-Pakistan subcontinent.[42] They often describe their activities as *hizmet* (dedicated vocational work); their primary concern is moral self-renewal. The success of the *Fethullahcilar* lies in its simple, direct, and personal appeal. It does not maintain a formal membership and makes no demands on its followers to practise Islam. Rather, individuals engage in religious learning and other devotional activities in small, community-based groups. Participants meet regularly to read and discuss commentaries on the Koran, the *Risale-I Nur*, and the books of Fethullah Gulen. These groups foster strong interpersonal relationships and allow emotional engagement to flourish within a context of self-scrutiny and religious discipline.

The *Fethullahcilar* maintains an apolitical stance in regard to Kemalism, which helps the movement to grow with little government intrusion. It should be noted that its practices bear some similarity to Kemalist notions of social solidarity (which in turn reflect the influence of Ziya Gokalp and his ideas on the role of religion in society).[43] Kemalism made the state responsible for the management of national culture, including controlling the production and dissemination of religious knowledge. The *Fethullahcilar* builds on this legacy and argues that Islam contributes to the moral strength of the national society as a religion of self-development.

According to Gulen, Islam promotes the rule of law and rejects the oppression of any segment of society. He argues that Islam does not offer a totalizing ideology for reshaping society, nor a blueprint for an unchangeable form of the state. Gulen argues that 'the Koran is a translation of the book of the universe, an interpretation of... the universe. Reducing it to political theories or forms of the state is a great disrespect' to the spirit of Islam.[44] For Gulen, Islam is complementary to democracy; it should be left to the people to choose the type and form of government according to their time and circumstances.

Insofar as the *Fethullahcilar* movement is fundamentally concerned with individual moral renewal, it has two primary objectives: to reconstruct individual thought in accordance with the ideas, moral values, and normative standards of Islam; and to connect individualized pious belief to the transformation of individual behaviour in the public sphere. In setting these objectives the *Fethullahcilar* is motivated by the belief that Islam is more than a religion. It is actually a 'civilization for individual growth', concerned with individuals becoming better, socially responsible citizens of the state.[45] It advocates greater piety, to be attained through a high quality education that connects the spiritual and material worlds, but does not expect overtly religious behaviour. What is crucial is personal training in asceticism, piety, kindness, and sincerity.[46]

The *Fethullahcilar* believes in disciplining the self in a way that strengthens civil-society engagement with the economy, rather than retreating from it. Such self-discipline is believed to mobilize certain values which can assist in controlling the body and emotions. To this end the *Fethullahcilar* has developed a web of some 20,000 micro-communities known as the *nur evleri*. These *nur evleri*, the first of which opened in Izmir in 1968, are groups of apartments that are normally rented out to university students.[47] They also function as a kind of schools, insofar as they reinforce pious beliefs and moral values for self-development, and promote solidarity among members of the *Fethullahcilar*.

The *Fethullahcilar* has also founded primary and secondary schools, university preparatory *dersanes* (study rooms), and universities. These are privately run and governed.[48] They follow a thoroughly secular curriculum and do not teach religion but focus on the study of science and technology, and the application of the resulting knowledge to economic development. Young people learn how to establish a meaningful life by *temsil* (example) rather than by *teblig* (words or instruction). The institutions are funded through the philanthropic support of business communities.

The *Fethullahcilar* is now also one of the fastest-growing capital groups in Turkey, with about 500 affiliated firms, many of them very profitable and fully integrated into the market economy. Significantly, ethical discipline inculcated through educational *hizmet* is always supposed to be integral to the wealth-creation activities of the *Fethullahcilar*. In fact, the *Fethullahci* world-view resembles Adam Smith's view that the pursuit of self-interest must be restrained by morality.[49] For the *Fethullahcilar*, an ethical individual should not refrain from commerce but pursue it in a harmonious manner.

For Gulen, those who move with religious love '...are content and place their knowledge and understanding at humanity's service', while always respecting individual freedom – the 'key to the mysteries of human identity'.[50] Gulen's Islamism attempts to shape a culture of individual righteousness and responsibility that enlarges the scope of civic engagement with the public sphere. Yet perhaps the most significant aspect of his approach is the articulation of Islamic political thinking as closely tied to the key norms of democracy, justice, and individual freedom as defined in Western liberal thought.

THE CLASS AMBIGUITIES OF AN ISLAMIC ORIENTATION

Why do so many people who suffer under neoliberalism support Gulen's Islamism and sustain the AKP's cross-class coalition? At one level this may be accounted for by the phenomenal economic growth rate experienced since the crisis at the beginning of the decade – reaching no less than 9.9 per cent in 2004.[51] The fact that it was still as high as 6.1 in 2006 led a *Financial Times* report to exult: 'Cumulative expansion over the past five years reached 40 per cent, making it the longest and most stable stretch of uninterrupted growth since at least 1970'.[52] Moreover, the AKP government's fiscal discipline has meant that inflation has fallen to a single digit for the first time in the past 30 years. On the other hand, high economic growth has been sustained by short-term capital inflows that alongside the massive foreign debt (growing from US$ 130 billion in 2002 to US$ 184 billion in 2006) render the economy vulnerable to a fresh crisis.[53]

And in spite of the high growth rate the government has not been able to deliver what it promised in its social justice program. Unemployment remains a major social problem, reaching 11.9 per cent in 2006, and 87.4 per cent of agricultural workers, and almost all of Turkey's self-employed workers, have no social protection. Women are the most severely affected; as of February 2007 only 23.4 per cent of women in the economically active age-group were employed, compared to 69.6 per cent of men.[54] In the last two decades Turkey has created only 6 million formal jobs, although the working-age population has grown by 23 million.[55] In short, phenomenal growth in the economy has been achieved by heavy reliance on foreign borrowing and with limited formal employment.

The informal economy, however, is flourishing, absorbing otherwise unemployable labour. In 2004, 53 per cent of the employed labour force was unregistered – approximately one in three workers in urban areas and three out of four in rural areas.[56] The World Bank estimates that over three-quarters of unregistered employees were working in unregistered workplaces in 2003, while underreporting of workers and the wage bill in registered workplaces is estimated to be about 24 and 28 per cent respectively.[57] Employment for those with education has been particularly scarce. In 2006, the unemployment rate for young people aged between 20 and 24 with at least a secondary school education was 23.4 per cent, and for those aged 25-29, 12.2 per cent.[58]

Relative poverty (defined in terms of an ability to obtain food and basic non-food necessities, and measured by household consumption expenditure of less than 60 per cent of the median) affects 27 per cent of the population, more than in any of the EU's 25 member countries.[59] The 2005 data also reveal very acute income inequality: the incomes of the richest 20 per cent of the population were on average 7.3 times higher than those of the poorest 20 per cent. Regional inequality is worse: Kocaeli, the richest city in the Marmara region, enjoyed a per capita income level of US$ 6,165 which was 11 times greater than Agri, the poorest city in Eastern Anatolia, with its US$ 568 per capita.

Turkey's economic growth has thus led to an increasing number of people living in cities under substandard conditions and who are employed in the informal economy. Yet it is also highly significant that Turkey has a virtually zero poverty rate in terms of the standard measure of US$ 1 per person per day. The proportion of the population living below the food-only component of the national poverty line is also only 1.35 per cent, thanks largely to a very high degree of inter-household transfers of food, clothing, and housing – i.e. a high degree of social solidarity in the face of poverty).[60] About one third of the general population lives in *gecekondus* (houses built illegally overnight), with a 35 per cent poverty rate.[61] They obtain assistance to build their homes and find jobs from kin, neighbours, *hemseri* (persons from the same region), *es-dost* (friends), *tanidik* (contacts), *torpil* (influential contacts), and *kivre kardesligi* (fictive kin).

These networks remain highly significant in Turkish society today in translating feelings of *durust* (trust) and *durustluk* (trustworthiness) into poverty alleviation, labour commitment and wealth creation.[62] Symbolizing the importance of moral fibre and ethical solidity in Turkish society, *durustluk* underpins the political aspects of mutual reciprocity. Not only *gecekondu* dwellers, recent migrants, and the poor are integrated into the highly personalized networks of cash and employment in this way, but also capitalists seeking *durust* workers. Smaller capitalists prefer to hire *hemseri* as they trust them more; workers find jobs by informally mobilizing *hemseri, tanidik-esdost, torpil* and kin. The Ankara leather-processing industry, for example, largely clusters *hemseri* from Gudul, a small town near Ankara. In the context of economic hardship, the trust networks invoke a cultural consensus: employers expect *hemseri* to work for lower wages without social-security provision; labour is willing to do so but only in return for 'charity', care, and support when needed.

CONCLUSION

What are we to make of the Islamic commitment to social cohesion in the context of a neoliberal economic orientation which continues to generate massive inequalities? The AKP government has allocated funds for employment creation and job-training programs, offered credits to small entrepreneurs, and supported micro-credit, but this barely touches the real problem. More relevant is the fact that the AKP government bases its social welfare policies largely on family and social solidarity networks. Its family-centred social policy focuses on motivating and mobilizing civil society initiatives that can provide social assistance.[63] Non-government charitable organizations, such as Deniz Feneri (Lighthouse), channel funds donated by Muslim businesses to the needy. Municipal governments have also become key players in providing social assistance, with budgets heavily reliant on donations from private individuals, thus acting as mediators between the local poor and Muslim charitable donors. This serves to support the privatization of social welfare under neoliberalism, and is reinforced by the *Fethullahcilar*'s Islamic ethic that relies on individual righteousness and charitable initiatives to solve social problems.

The symbolic relations of reciprocity in terms of mutual responsibility, respect, and trust may strengthen the role of Islamic charities, but it may also snap. The reciprocal relations between capitalists and workers are highly exploitative. Representing the emergent Anatolian middle class, many MUSIAD member firms are overtly hostile to trade unions. They pressed the government to enact the 2003 Labour Law which excluded companies with fewer than 30 workers from job-security coverage (the law previously only excluded those with fewer than ten workers). Although it shares a similar world-view, the pro-Islamic Hak-Is trade union condemns the government for intervening in strikes which are seen as slowing down exports, and for not taking poverty, unemployment, and informal employment issues seriously.[64] Neoliberal reorganization of the middle classes through Anatolian resentment politics against the Kemalist state may yet give way to a new sense of resentment on the part of workers and the poor against class inequalities.

An interesting dialectic thus emerges from the dual character of an Islamic perspective: its embeddedness in both the liberal–democratic capitalist ideas emanating from the European Union and the Islamic narrative of righteous individuals seeking the 'good society'. Islamic groups aim to enhance individual capacities in a capitalist economy and also support civil-society-based agents of charity. It may be useful in this light to rethink Weber's famous thesis on the protestant ethic and capitalism. The Islamic emphasis on brotherly love and ethical discipline feeds into very personalized cultural processes of economic rationality which Weber seems to have ignored.[65] The effectiveness of this Islamic ethic in materially addressing inequality depends on the individual will of believers who devote themselves to fulfilling *hizmet* (vocational work) and place it at the very centre of their economic activity.

This can hardly offset the actual dynamics of neoliberal capitalism in generating more inequality. Nevertheless, these inequalities will themselves not mobilize the weak and the poor to form a social-protest movement against neoliberalism. This is not necessarily because the symbolic relations of reciprocity and solidarity 'contain' potential opposition. Nor is it because marginalized members of society are unaware of the inequality that is masked by the culture of mutuality under which neoliberalism has developed in Islamic communities in Turkey.

Equally important, I believe, is the way opposition politics work: not entirely, and not always, based on economic grounds, but always context-bound. The 'moral' politics of resentment needs to be taken into account in order to understand why Islamic solidarity may not necessarily snap, despite the existence of such significant inequalities. Cultural tensions are also important; at times they are even 'created' by the military to justify its frequent interventions in civilian politics. The military's opposition to the election of a pro-Islamic candidate as president, merely because his wife wears the *hijab*, is a case in point – although the massive public demonstrations in support of the military's position remind us that Kemalism also has a strong popular base. What is clear is that even as neoliberalism generates massive exploitation and subordination, in Turkey's circumstances this has reinforced a politics of Islamic resentment against the Kemalist state, which has in turn led to the mobilization of mass support for Kemalist ideology. Resentment against the exploiters in the wake of neoliberalism still awaits such mobilization.

NOTES

1   Mike Davis, *Late Victorian Holocausts*, London: Verso, 2001, p. 20.
2   See Yildiz Atasoy, 'Cosmopolitan Islamists in Turkey: Rethinking the Local in a Global Era', *Studies in Political Economy*, 71/72, 2003/2004, p. 139.
3   AK Parti, *Development and Democratization Programme*, Ankara, 2002, p. 21.
4   Yildiz Atasoy, 'Turkey, Islamism and the European Union: Neo-liberal Market Economy, Democracy and the State', paper presented at a thematic panel at the 101st Annual Meeting of the American Sociological Association, Montreal, 2006.
5   AK Parti, *Development and Democratization*, pp. 20-27. See also World Bank, *Turkey: Knowledge Economy Assessment Study*, Washington: Private and Financial Sector Unit Europe and Central Asia Region, 2004.
6   AK Parti, *Development and Democratization*, p. 34.
7   Yalcin Akdogan, *Ak Parti ve Muhafazakar Demokrasi*, Istanbul: Alfa, 2004, p. 13.
8   Paul Blustein, 'Stopping the Bailout Buck Here: O'Neill Taking A Tough Stance on IMF Loans to Countries', The Washington Post Service, 5 June 2001, available from http://www.jubileeresearch.org.
9   Data calculated from: IMF, *Turkey: Fifth Review and Inflation Consultation Under the Stand-By Arrangement, IMF Country Report No. 07/161*, Washington: IMF, 2007; BBC News, 'IMF Hands Over Turkey Loan', 16 April 2002, available from http://news.bbc.co.uk; Property Frontiers, 'Turkey: Economic Overview', available at http://www.propertyfrontiers.com.
10   AK Parti, *Development and Democratization*, p. 33.
11   TUSIAD, 'European Union and Turkey: Main Data', available from http://www.tusiad.org.
12   TOBB, *Ekonomik Rapor 2004*, Ankara: Aydogdu Ofset, 2005, pp. 87-91.
13   See Tanil Bora, 'Istanbul of the Conqueror: The "Alternative Global City" Dreams of Political Islam', in Caglar Keyder, ed., *Istanbul between the Global and Local*, London: Rowman & Littlefield Publishers, 1999, especially p. 56.
14   It has two international branches, one in Brussels opened in 1995 and another in Washington, DC opened in 1998.
15   See TUSIAD's brochure, available from http://www.tusiad.org.
16   See the website of the OYAK holding company founded in 1961 as an Armed Forces Pension Fund, http://www.oyak.com.tr. See also Hulya Arac, 'International Market Research Reports: A Guide to Commercial Military Sales and Contracting', Industry Canada, 30 January 2004, p. 7, available from http://strategis.ic.gc.ca.

17   Ji-Hyang Jang, 'Taming Political Islamists by Islamic Capital: The Passions and the Interests in Turkish Islamic Society', Ph.D Thesis, The University of Texas at Austin, 2005, p. 203.

18   Ayse Bugra, 'Class, Culture, and State: An Analysis of Interest Representation by Two Turkish Business Associations', International Journal of Middle East Studies, 30(4), 1998.

19   TUSIAD, 'Press Release: Turkish Business Commits to Playing Key Role in EU Accession Talks Focusing on Democracy, Economy, Society and Technology', Brussels, 8 November 2005, available from http://www.tusiad.org. TUSIAD published no less than three reports on democratization in Turkey between 1997 and 2001.

20   Ji-Hyang Jang, 'Taming Political Islamists', pp. 227-28.

21   Wendy Kristianasen, 'No Delight for Turkey: New Faces of Islam', Le Monde Diplomatique, July 1997.

22   Ji-Hyang Jang, 'Taming Political Islamists', pp. 214, 217.

23   Rafi-uddin Shikoh, 'Turkish Business Association Drives Strong Muslim World Ties', Dinar Standard, 29 April 2006, available from http://www.dinarstandard.com.

24   MUSIAD, Anayasa Reformu ve Yonetimin Demokratiklestirilmesi, Istanbul, 2000.

25   Ibid., pp. 7-32.

26   See Martha Starr and Rasim Yilmaz, 'Bank Runs in Emerging-Market Economies: Evidence from Turkey's Special Finance Houses', American University Department of Economics Working Paper Series, No. 2006-08, May 2006, p. 5, available from http://www.american.edu/cas/econ.

27   World Bank, Turkey: Knowledge Economy Assessment Study.

28   Sennur Ozdemir, MUSIAD: Anadolu Sermayesinin Donusumu ve Turk Modernlesmesinin Derinlesmesi, Ankara: Vadi Yayinlari, 2006, p. 162.

29   Ibid., p. 73.

30   These ideas are propagated in MUSIAD periodicals such as Homo-Islamicus (1993-97) and Cerceve, a Research Reports series, a newsletter called MUSIAD in Press, and an Internet-based Information Bank.

31   Omer Demir, Mustafa Acar and Metin Toprak, 'Anatolian Tigers or Islamic Capital: Prospects and Challenges', Middle Eastern Studies, 40(6), November 2004, p. 184. It is estimated that the Central Bank also receives around US$ 4 billion in remittances annually.

32   Gulay Dincel, 'Konya'nin Kombassan'i ve Hasim Bayram'in Yukselisi', in Oya Baydar and Gulay Dince, eds., 75 Yilda Carklari Dondurenler, Istanbul: Tarih Vakfi, 1999, p. 162.

33   Ji-Hyang Jang, 'Taming Political Islamists', p. 212-13.

34   The Turkish-Saudi joint venture Faisal Finance House was purchased by Kombassan Holding in 1998 and later by the ULKER Group in 2001, with financial contributions from American Islamic Finance House – LARIBA. Faisal Finance thus acquired the name Family Finance.

35   Ji-Hyang Jang, 'Taming Political Islamists', pp. 146-47, 165. See also Ayse Yuce, 'Islamic Financial Houses in Turkey', Journal of the Academy of Business and Economics, January 2003, p. 4.

36   ILO, *International Labour Conference 90th Session 2002, Report VI: Decent Work and Informal Economy*, Geneva: ILO, 2002, pp. 5-9.

37   ILO, *Sosyal Diyalog Yoluyla Kayit Disi Istihdam Sorununa Cozum Bulunmasi, 2005-2007 EU-ILO Projesi Nihai Raporu*, January 2007, pp. 31, 10-11, available from http://www.ilo.org; and World Bank, *Turkey: Country Economic Memorandum: Promoting Sustained Growth and Convergence with the European Union, Report No. 33549-TR*, Washington: World Bank Poverty Reduction and Economic Management Unit Europe and Central Asia Region, 2006, p. 137.

38   Engin Yildirim, 'Labor Pains or Achilles' Heel: The Justice and Development Party and Labor in Turkey', in Hakan Yavuz, ed., *The Emergence of New Turkey*, Utah: The University of Utah Press, 2006, p. 236.

39   In the absence of hard data, I can offer the example of female industrial home-workers engaged in towel production in Denizli region, with an overall 50.2 per cent informal employment rate. Globally oriented firms account for almost 70 per cent of the city's numerous towel firms. These women, both single and married with children, earn about US$ 2 an hour. Turkish towel producers established their reputation weaving towels on handlooms from pure cotton or linen, designed with unique traditional embroidery motifs, and often work at home, participating in the production of US$ 1.5 billion worth of towel exports from Denizli. These women see their paid work as a matter of 'helping out' the subcontractors, who will often be their male relatives and neighbours.
      See Yildiz Atasoy, 'Explaining Local-Global Nexus: Muslim Politics in Turkey', in Yildiz Atasoy and William K. Carroll, eds., *Global Shaping and Its Alternatives*, Aurora: Garamond Press, 2003, pp. 74-75.

40   TUSIAD, *Optimal State: Towards a New State Model for the 21st Century*, Istanbul: TUSIAD Yayinlari, 1995.

41   Said Nursi's writings were collected into a six-volume commentary on the Koran, the *Risale-I Nur*, Kazan: Kul'turno-obrazovatel'ny fond "Nuru-Badi", 2001.

42   Mumtaz Ahmad, 'Islamic Fundamentalism in South Asia: The Jamaat-I Islami and the Tablighi Jamaat', in Martin E. Marty and R. Scott Appleby, eds., *Fundamentalisms Observed*, Chicago: The University of Chicago Press, 1991, pp. 510-23.

43   This influential Ottoman-Turkish sociologist (who translated Emile Durkheim's work into Turkish) contributed to the Kemalist notion that Islam can be functional in bringing about social cohesion in society, as long as it remains under state control. See Ihsan Yilmaz, 'State, Law, Civil Society and Islam in Contemporary Turkey', *Muslim World, Special Issue: Islam in Contemporary Turkey*, 95(3), 2005.

44   Fethullah Gulen, *The Statue of Our Souls: Revival in Islamic Thought and Activism*, Somerset: The Light, 2005, p. 456.

45   Turgay Sirin, *Kisisel Gelisim Medeniyeti: Islam Medeniyetinin Kisisel Gelisim Dinamikleri*, Istanbul: Armoni, 2005.

46   Gulen, *The Statue of Our Souls,* p. 452.

47   Latif Erdogan, *Fethullah Gulen Hocaefendi: Kucuk Dunyam*, Istanbul: Ad Yayin-
     cilik, 1998, p. 114.
48   There are no publicly available, openly disclosed data regarding the exact
     number of *Fethullahci* schools and student enrolments. Estimates are about 500
     worldwide, of which some 150 are outside Turkey. It is well known, however,
     that the *Fethullahcilar* operates 7 universities in Turkey. See: Bayram Balci, *Orta
     Asya'da Islam Misyonerleri: Fethullah Gulen Okullari*, Istanbul: Iletisim Yayinlari,
     2005, p. 191.
49   Adam Smith, *The Theory of Moral Sentiments*, New York: Oxford University
     Press, 1976.
50   See Fethullah Gulen, 'An Ideal Society', 17 September 2001, pp. 2- and 'What
     We Expect from the Righteous Generation', 31 May 2002, p. 4; See also
     Fethullah Gulen, 'Humanity, Science, and Globalization', 1 January 2003. All
     available from http://en.fgulen.com.
51   TOBB, *Ekonomik Rapor, 2004*, Ankara: Aydogdu Ofset, 2005, p. 9.
52   'Turkish Growth boosts Erdogan ahead of Poll', *Financial Times*, 3 April
     2007.
53   Data from the Türkiye Cumhuriyet Merkez Bankasi, available at http://www.
     tcmb.gov.tr/ucaylik/ua10/a16.pdf.
54   T.C. Basbakanlik Turkiye Istatistik Kurumu, Haber Bulteni, Sayi 76, 15 May
     2007. These figures contrast sharply with the 2005 EU-15 rates of 64.8 per
     cent overall employment and 57 per cent female employment (World Bank,
     Turkey: Country Economic Memorandum, p. 42).
55   World Bank, *Turkey: Labor Market Study, Report No. 33254-TR*, Washington:
     World Bank Poverty Reduction and Economic Management Unit Europe and
     Central Asia Region, 2006, p. ii.
56   Ibid., p. iii.
57   World Bank, *Turkey: Country Economic Memorandum*, pp. 37, 138.
58   World Bank, *Turkey: Labor Market Study*, p. iii.
59   Turkey published its first official poverty statistics in 2004, following the State
     Statistics Institute's survey on *Household Budget Research Results* published in
     2003. The poverty report of 2004 defined the *poverty line* in terms of the abil-
     ity to obtain food and basic non-food necessities, whereas the *hunger line* was
     defined in terms of not being able to obtain basic food needs. For the data in
     this paragraph, see Ayse Bugra and Caglar Keyder, 'Poverty and Social Policy
     in Contemporary Turkey', Bogazici University Social Policy Forum, January
     2005, p. 20; EUROSTAT, 'At-persistent-risk-of-poverty rate', http://epp.
     eurostat.ec.europa.eu; T.C. Basbakanlik Turkiye Istatistik Kurumu, Haber
     Bulteni, Sayi 207, 25 Aralik 2006; Serkan Demirtas, 'Esitsizlikte Cozum Zor',
     Radikal Newspaper, 1 September 2005, http://www.radikal.com.tr; World
     Bank, *Turkey: Joint Poverty Assessment Report, Report No. 29619-TU*, Wash-
     ington: Human Development Sector Unit Europe and Central Asia Region,
     2005, p. 29.
60   World Bank, *Turkey: Joint Poverty Assessment Report*, p. 14.
61   Ibid., p. 34.

62 Amongst the unemployed in Turkey, 31.5 per cent looks for jobs within in-
    formal networks of friends/kin/community. See: T.C. Basbakanlik Turkiye
    Istatistik Kurumu, Haber Bulteni, Sayi 76, 15 May 2007. For the historical
    importance of trust networks in factory organization in Turkey see: Alan Du-
    betsky, 'Kinship, Primordial Ties, and Factory Organization in Turkey: An
    Anthropological View', *International Journal of Middle East Studies*, 7(3), 1976.
63 Bugra and Keyder, 'Poverty and Social Policy', p. 32.
64 Engin Yildirim, 'Labour Pains', pp. 248- 52.
65 Max Weber, *The Protestant Ethic and the Spirit of Capitalism*, London: George
    Allen & Unwin, 1930/1984. On Weber's own concern with brotherly love,
    see Michael Symonds and Jason Pudsey, 'The Forms of Brotherly Love in Max
    Weber's Sociology of Religion', *Sociological Theory*, 24(2), 2006; and Max We-
    ber, 'Religious rejections of the World and their Directions', *From Max Weber:
    Essays in Sociology*, Edited by H.H. Gerth and C. Wright Mills, New York:
    Oxford University Press, 1946.

TRANSFORMATIVE POSSIBILITIES
IN LATIN AMERICA

WILLIAM I. ROBINSON

Latin America has been the cutting edge of struggles worldwide against neoliberalism. Several alternatives to the dominant model of global capitalism appear to be emerging in the region. A new model of revolutionary struggle and popular transformation from below for the 21st century may be emerging, based on the Venezuelan experience, but more broadly, on mass popular struggles in Ecuador, Bolivia, and elsewhere. Yet global capital has been able to blunt some of these struggles from above and a reformist bloc allied with global capital seems to be competing to shape a post-neoliberal era. Neoliberalism, we should recall, is but one model of global capitalism; resistance to this model is not necessarily resistance to global capitalism. Behind the so-called 'pink tide' that has swept the region are competing configurations of social and class forces, ideologies, programs and policies. The crossroad that Latin America has reached is not about 'reform versus revolution' as much as it is about what social and political forces will achieve hegemony over the anti-neoliberal struggle, and what kind of project will replace the orthodox programs that have ravaged the region over the past 25 years.

As long as neoliberalism reigned supreme and the neoliberal states remained impenetrable fortresses, the refusal to deal with state power appeared reasonable. The neoliberal national state is not a space for engaging in politics; it is an apparatus for the technocratic administration of transnational capital accumulation, infrastructure, and social control. But what is the historical context here? The dominant groups in Latin America reconstituted and consolidated their control over *political society* in the 1980s and 1990s, but the new round of popular class mobilization in the 1990s and early 21st century pointed to their inability to sustain hegemony in *civil society*. The renewal of political activism by subordinate groups at the grassroots level has been outside of state structures and largely independent of organized left parties. Grassroots social movements flourished in civil society at a time when the organized left operating in political society was unable to articulate a counter-hegemonic alternative. The failure of the left to lead a process of structural change from political society helped shift the locus of conflict more fully to civil society. Latin America seemed to move in the late 1980s and 1990s to a 'war of position' between contending social forces in light of subordinate groups' previous failures to win a 'war of manoeuvre' through revolutionary upheaval and the limits to 'power from above'. But as crises of legitimacy, perpetual instability, and the impending breakdown of state institutions spread rapidly throughout Latin America in the early 21st century, conditions seemed to be opening up for a new kind of war of manoeuvre under the novel circumstances of the global economy and society.

THE BACKDROP

The new transnational order has its origins in the world economic crisis of the 1970s, which gave capital the impetus and the means to initiate a major restructuring of the system through globalization over the next two decades.[1] Latin America has been deeply implicated in this restructuring crisis. The mass movements, revolutionary struggles, and nationalist and populist projects of the 1960s and 1970s (all of which had their own internal contradictions) were beaten back by local and international elites in the latter decades of the 20th century in the face of the global economic downturn, debt, state repression, US intervention, the collapse of a socialist alternative, and the rise of the neoliberal model. This paved the way for the region's integration into the new global capitalism.

This has entailed, first of all, the spread of Maquiladoras from the US-Mexico border south to much of Latin America, while small and medium industrial enterprises – known by their Spanish acronym PYMES – have reoriented from national to global markets by becoming local subcontractors for transnational corporations, while a few countries have integrated into global capitalism via substantial domestic industrial and financial sectors. Second, every country has been swept up in the explosive growth of the global tourist industry in Latin America, which now employs millions of people, accounts for a growing portion of national revenue and gross national product, penetrates numerous 'traditional' communities, and brings them into global capitalism. Third, amidst the commodity boom of this decade, a new type of transnational agribusiness has replaced the old agro-export and domestic agricultural models. Every national agricultural system is being inserted into the new global agro-industrial complex. In Brazil, Argentina, Bolivia and Paraguay, the biggest export crop now is soy, having replaced coffee, sugar, beef, and so on. Soy plantations set up by transnational agribusiness are displacing millions of small-holders and eating up the rainforests. In Mexico and Central America corn and beans are being replaced by winter fruits and vegetables for the global supermarket. In Ecuador and Colombia it is flowers, in Chile, fruits and wines. Finally, the transnationalization of labour markets has made Latin America a major exporter of workers to the global economy. This immigrant Latin American labour, in turn, sends back remittances – some $60 billion in 2006.[2] In many countries remittances are the number one source of foreign exchange.

In comparison to today, in the 1960s there were still major pockets of society that were pre-capitalist or that at least enjoyed some local autonomy vis-à-vis national and world capitalism. But 21st-century global capitalism has penetrated nearly every nook and cranny so that capitalist relations are practically universal in the region. This new cycle of capitalist development has been facilitated by the neoliberal adjustment programs required by transnationally mobile capital, which every Latin America country, with the exception of Cuba, implemented in the last two decades of the 20th century.

Neoliberalism, however, increasingly exhibits deep structural and social contradictions. In particular, the model is highly dependent on attracting mobile and often volatile transnational finance/investment capital, with a high component of financial speculation. Second, the new export boom, based on a set of non-traditional activities involved in regional participation in global production and distribution chains, is fragile as a consequence of global market competition, overproduction, and the impermanent nature of production sequences in the global economy – while also accelerating ecological disaster. Third, the development model based on neoliberal integration into the global economy does not require (or is at least unable to couple the new accumulation potential with) domestic market expansion or an inclusionary social base. Fourth, as a result, the social contradictions generated by neoliberalism have led to heightened conflict, popular class mobilization, and political instability.

The hegemony of neoliberalism began to crack in the late 1990s as a new resistance politics took hold. The fragile polyarchic ('democratic') systems installed through the so-called 'transitions to democracy' of the 1980s were increasingly unable to contain the social conflicts and political tensions generated by the polarizing and pauperizing effects of the neoliberal model.[3] ECLAC data show that per-capita income declined by an average of 0.9 per cent every year in the 1980s, known as the 'lost decade' in Latin America, and then declined by an average of 1.5 per cent each year in the 1990s, the alleged 'decade of recovery', while poverty levels and deprivation indicators spiralled upwards in most countries over the past 20 years. A major economic downturn hit the region between 1999 and 2002, unleashing counter-hege-monic social and political forces that discredited neoliberalism and brought about a new period of popular struggle and change. There is currently an ongoing realignment of social and political forces throughout Latin America whose outcome is uncertain and open-ended.

THE 'PINK TIDE'

The pressures to bring about a shift in the structure of distribution – both of income and of property – and the need for a more interventionist state to bring this about, is one side of the equation in the constellation of social and political forces that seemed to be coming together, even before the turn of the century, to contest the neoliberal order. Political, economic, and aca-demic elites began to look for an alternative formula to pull the region out of its stagnation and at the same time to prevent – or at least better manage – social and political unrest. These regional efforts paralleled calls by the tran-snational elite elsewhere for a limited reform of the global system. Prominent left of center leaders and parties, for instance, including Cuauhtémoc Cárde-nas of the Party of the Democratic Revolution in Mexico, Ricardo Lagos of the Socialist Party in Chile, Luis Inácio da Silva (Lula) of the Workers Party (PT) in Brazil, Carlos Álvarez of the FREPASO in Argentina, and Jorge Castañeda from Mexico, drew up the Buenos Aires Consensus in 1998 that called for a renewed social democracy in the region. While the document called for 'growth with equity' and a greater role for the state in assistance to the poor, it was explicit that the logic of the market must not be challenged, nor should an open integration into global capitalism.[4]

If the social democratic elites were explicitly engaged in only modifying neoliberalism, in the decade since the Buenos Aires initiative was launched popular electoral victories in a number of countries brought to power gov-ernments that opposed neoliberalism, at least in discourse, and at least initially. These include: Hugo Chávez in Venezuela (1998); Lula and the PT in Brazil (2002); Lucio Gutiérrez in Ecuador (2002 – Gutiérrez was subsequently run from office in a popular uprising in 2005); Lagos and the Socialist Party in Chile (2002), followed by Michelle Bachelet (2006) of the same party; Néstor Kirchner in Argentina (2003); Evo Morales in Bolivia (2005); Tabaré Vázquez and the Broad Front in Uruguay (2004); Rafael Correa in Ecuador (2006), Daniel Ortega and the Sandinistas in Nicaragua (2006); along with near-wins (amidst charges of electoral fraud) for the FMLN in El Salvador (2004); Andrés Manuel López Obrador in Mexico (2006); Ottón Solis in Costa Rica (2006); and Ollanta Humala in Peru (2006).

These popular electoral victories – the so-called 'pink tide' – would seem to symbolize the end of the reigning neoliberal order, but they also demonstrate the limits of parliamentary change in the era of global capitalism. The case of Brazil was most indicative of this – and the most tragic for the popular classes. Lula, denied the presidency in three previous electoral contests, won in 2002 only after his wing of the PT moved sharply towards the political center. He forged a social base among middle-class voters and won over centrist and even conservative political forces that did not endorse a left-wing program yet were unwilling to tolerate further neoliberal fallout. Lula promised not to default on the country's foreign debt and to maintain the previous government's adjustment policies, thereby indicating that the real power was that of transnational financial capital. Portending what was to come, almost as soon as he took office in 2003 he slashed the budgets for health and education in order to comply with the IMF requirement that the government maintain a fiscal surplus.

Other 'pink tide' governments have attempted to expropriate popular power from below and undercut its transformative potential, most notably in Ecuador and Argentina. In Ecuador, Gutiérrez, a former army colonel, won the 2002 election with the support of that country's powerful indigenous and social movements after he promised to reverse the neoliberal program of his predecessors and implement popular reforms. Upon taking office he appointed several indigenous cabinet ministers as well as representatives of the local elite and transnational capital. But within months, Gutiérrez capitulated to these conservative political forces in the tenuous governing coalition and reverted to an open neoliberal program. In Argentina, Kirchner strongly criticized the neoliberal policies of his predecessors, yet his own program has been limited to minor policy modifications to favour domestic producers and consumers: low interest rates, capital controls, price controls on public services, and the restoration of some social welfare programs, alongside a clientelist cooptation of a portion of the *piqueteros* and other popular movements.

In perhaps what is the most illusory of pink tide governments, Ortega and what remains of the FSLN in Nicaragua have dressed with a leftist discourse what in the pre-neoliberal era would have been characterized as a routine attempt to establish a populist multi-class political alliance under the hegemony of capital and state elites. In the years since the 1990 electoral defeat new Sandinista economic groups developed close business and personal ties with transnationally-oriented capitalist groups, while the political leadership negotiated a heavily criticized 'pact' to divide up government power with the Liberals, one of the two historically-dominant bourgeois oligarchic parties. While the FSLN retains a mass, if dwindling, base among the country's peasantry and urban poor, many leading Sandinistas grouped around Ortega have become successful businessmen heavily invested in the new transnational model of accumulation, including in tourism, agro-industry, finances, importing-exporting, and subcontracting for the maquiladoras. Their class interests impede them from challenging transnational capital or organizing a transformative project, yet their legitimacy depends on sustaining a revolutionary discourse and undertaking redistributive reforms.[5]

In its first major policy document since taking office in early 2007, the FSLN declared that its project rested on two planks, one political and the other economic. The first, 'citizen power councils', are to incorporate local communities into the 'struggle against drugs, narco-trafficking, gangs, diseases, ignorance, degradation of the environment, and the denial of human rights'.[6] Absent is any reference to these councils as politicized forums or vehicles for popular self-mobilization; they seem to be conceived as instruments for a controlled incorporation from above of grassroots communities into the state's social control and administrative programs. The second plank, 'economic associations for small and medium producers', calls for 'reorienting economic policies towards these sectors so as to link them up to the large-scale private sector',[7] that is, to incorporate these small-scale rural and urban producers via credits and technical assistance into the dominant transnational circuits of accumulation through subcontracting and other ancillary activities. The document calls for 'respect for all forms of property', attracting transnational corporate investment, and an agro-industrial model of development.

In fairness, the Sandinista program also contemplates a renationalization of health and educational systems, greater social spending, progressive tax policies, and a literacy campaign, among other popular welfare measures. Yet it is clear that the Sandinistas are part of the same elected left populist bloc in the region committed to mild redistributive programs but respectful of prevailing property relations and unwilling or simply unable to challenge the global capitalist order. This is not very different from what had informed the social democratic thinking that defined the Buenos Aires consensus. Many leftist parties, even when they sustain an anti-neoliberal discourse, such as the PT in Brazil, Vasquez in Uruguay, and the Sandinistas in Nicaragua, have abandoned earlier programs of fundamental structural change in the social order itself. What stands out about such 'pink tide' governments is that: (1) there has been no significant redistribution of income or wealth, and indeed, inequality may still actually be increasing; (2) there has been no shift in basic property and class relations despite changes in political blocs, in discourse in favour of the popular classes, and mildly reformist or social welfare measures. In Argentina, for instance, the percentage of national income going to labour (through wages) and to the unemployed and pensioners (through social welfare subsidies and pensions) dropped from 32.5 in 2001, before the crisis exploded, to 26.7 in 2005. In Brazil the wealthy grew in number by 11.3 per cent in 2005 as inequality deepened.[8] Moreover programs to subsidize the consumption of the poor and the unemployed, such as *Zero Fome* and *Bolsa Familia* programs in Brazil, or social welfare payments plans in Argentina, are financed by taxing not capital but formal sector workers and middle classes. It is increasingly dubious whether viable redistributive strategies are possible without more fundamental changes in property relations. Will this new social democratic tide amount to better local managers of global capitalism than their orthodox neoliberal predecessors? How long can low levels of redistribution hold back the tide of rebellion?

On the other hand, Venezuela is leading a radical anti-neoliberal regional bloc that would appear to include Bolivia under Evo Morales and Ecuador under Rafael Correa. Redistributive reforms have been much deeper in Venezuela than in other 'pink tide' countries and have been linked to the goal of transformations in state structure and property relations to the end of an authentic empowerment of the popular classes, as I will discuss below. Bolivia and Ecuador seem to be following a similar path of more radical reform, even if it is too early to reach conclusions about outcomes. In all three countries there have been constitutional assemblies convened by popular referenda to redraft constitutions in favour the popular classes, a reversal of the most egregious neoliberal policies, a renationalization of energy resources and the use of those resources for social investment. There are ongoing land redistributions in Venezuela and Bolivia and promises of such programs in Ecuador.

Casteñeda, the anti-communist, anti-Cuban, and pro-Washington former Mexican Foreign Minister and a leading social democratic critic of the socialist left in Latin America, argued recently that there are 'two lefts' in the region – a 'right left' that would include Lula in Brazil, Lagos and later Bachelet in Chile, and Vázquez in Uruguay, and a 'wrong left' led by Chávez in Venezuela, and including, of course, Fidel Castro in Cuba, as well as Morales, López Obrador, Humala, and others. The former, 'the reconstructed, formerly radical left emphasizes social policy – education, antipoverty programs, health care, housing – but within a more or less orthodox market framework'. The 'wrong left', according to Casteñeda, has 'proved much less responsive to modernizing influences.... For all these leaders, economic performance, democratic values, programmatic achievements, and good relations with the United States are not imperatives but bothersome constraints that miss the real point. They are more intent on maintaining popularity at any cost, picking as many fights as possible with Washington, and getting as much control as they can over sources of revenue, including oil, gas, and suspended foreign-debt payments'.[9] Never mind the ideologically-driven absurdities in Castañeda's argument – Venezuela, for instance, has the best economic performance in all of Latin America, is rated the most democratic, and boasts the most impressive programmatic achievements. The fact is that there *are* two lefts – a reformist one that dominates the 'pink tide' and seeks to reintroduce a mild redistributive component into the global capitalist program in the region, and a more radical one that seeks a more substantial transformation of social structures, class relations, and international power dynamics.

Most analyses fail to capture the dialectics of class relations and social struggles that have produced distinct dynamics among the 'pink tide' countries. Progressive governments seeking short-term popular objectives spark both opposition from dominant groups and mobilization for more fundamental change from subordinate groups. This in turn opens up new opportunities, confrontation, and further politicization of masses. If transnational capital is able to emasculate radical programs through structural pressures exerted by the global economy, the popular electoral victories and near-victories involved as well the mobilization of new collective subjects and mass social movements show that progressive forces are not easily cowed by the transnational elite. The fate of the pink tide will depend considerably on the configuration of class and social forces in each country and the extent to which regional and global configurations of these forces open up new space and push such governments in distinct directions. Latin America in the early 21st century stands at a crossroad; it has moved into an historic conjuncture in which the struggle among social and political forces could push the new resistance politics into mildly social democratic and populist outcomes or into more fundamental, potentially revolutionary ones.

THE BOLIVARIAN REVOLUTION AND RENEWAL OF THE SOCIALIST AGENDA

The 'Bolivarian revolution' took Latin America by storm with the arrival in power in 1999 of Venezuela's charismatic and enormously popular socialist president, Hugo Chávez. By putting forward an anti-capitalist alternative to the more reformist post-neoliberal proposals and by organizing a regional anti-neoliberal power bloc, Venezuela's influence could tip the balance by encouraging social and political forces in Latin America to move beyond a mild reform of the status quo. The Bolivarian revolution is the first radical, socialist-oriented revolution in Latin America – and indeed, the world – since the defeat of the Nicaraguan revolution of the 1980s. The declaration by the *Chavista* leadership for the first time in 2005 that the Bolivarian revolution would seek to build a '21st century socialism' has major implications for Latin America – and the world – because it put socialism back on the agenda at a time when the ignominious demise of 20th century socialism seemed to discredit the very idea of a socialist project, and when the late-twentieth-century global justice movement stalled as it proved unable to move beyond a negative anti-capitalism.

Apart from the challenge it issues to global neoliberalism and US interventionism, the Venezuelan revolution is significant on at least three counts. First the Venezuelan revolution had impeccable bourgeois democratic legitimacy. Chávez won the 1998 presidential elections by the largest majority in four decades (56.2 per cent) and then went on, between 1999 and 2006, to ratify his democratic legitimacy in another eight electoral contests, including three further presidential votes (in 2000, with 59 per cent of the vote, in 2004 with 59 per cent, and in 2006, with 63 per cent), a constitutional referendum, and several parliamentary, gubernatorial and local elections. Second, the old bourgeois state was not 'smashed' in the revolution. To the contrary, by winning the presidency through an electoral process in an established polyarchic system and a well-institutionalized capitalist state, yet with the mass support of the poor and the popular classes, Hugo Chávez initiated the Bolivarian project from the Miraflores presidential palace while leaving in place a state bureaucracy that would work over the next few years to resist and undermine that project. And third, the poor majority has been engaged in its own autonomous and often belligerent grassroots and community organizing, especially in the teeming slums of the capital city of Caracas, home to four million of the country's 26 million people, and in other major urban areas.

The mass popular base of the revolution is not subordinated to a state and party at the helm of the process, as they were in most revolutionary experiences of the 20th century. What is unfolding in Venezuela is distinct from the old Soviet-statist model, in which political command (domination) emanated vertically from the state/party downwards, the means of production were nationalized and bureaucratically administered, and there was no autonomous space for the working classes and social movements. The Bolivarian model also defies the anarchist-autonomist ideas influential in the global justice movement. *Chavismo* has opened up a remarkable space for mobilization from below. It is in fact the ongoing and expansive mobilization of this mass base that pushed the *Chavista* leadership forward and led the charge against the decadent capitalist state and social order. Class struggle is breaking out everywhere. Popular classes in civil society constitute a beehive of organizing and mobilizing. So too do counterrevolutionary right-wing forces, which have, nonetheless, steadily lost initiative.

Venezuela may well be in a pre-revolutionary stage still. In its first eight years the revolution was able to reform the political system and pass a new constitution that lays the juridical base for a new society, to break with US domination, recover oil revenues and begin a process of transforming property relations and building a new economic model linked to a regional/transnational program of integration and cooperation. A deepening of these developments would entail a more dramatic re-creation of the state and the transformation of the means and relations of production.

Chávez first announced at the January 2005 World Social Forum meeting in Brazil that the Bolivarian revolution would construct a '21st century socialism'. 'It is not possible that we will achieve our goals with capitalism, nor is it possible to find an intermediate path', stated Chávez. 'I invite all of Venezuela to march on the path of socialism of the new century. We must construct a new socialism in the 21st century'.[10] Then after Chávez won the December 2006 presidential elections with nearly 63 per cent of the popular vote he announced in a series of speeches in early 2007 that 'a new stage in the Bolivarian socialist revolution has begun. The period between 1998 and 2006 was a period of transition. Now begins the stage of building Bolivarian socialism'.[11]

Chávez called for what would amount to a revolution within the revolution – to an opening up of all branches of the state to 'popular power' from below and to mechanisms that would permit a 'social comptroller' role by the grassroots over state and public institutions. He called for a 'war to the death' against corruption and bureaucracy, practices that were 'counterrevolutionary currents within the revolution', and for 'a new geometry of power on the national map' and a 'revolutionary explosion of people's power, of communal power' from below.[12] Chávez envisioned a deepening of the role of Communal Councils and their conglomeration locally, regionally, and nationally into a sort of alternative power structure from below, a Paris Commune on a national scale:

> We must move toward the formation of a communal state and progressively dismantle the old bourgeois state that is still alive and kicking as we put into place the communal state, the socialist state, the Bolivarian state; a state with the ability to steer the revolution. Almost all states came into existence to hold back revolutions, so this is our challenge: to convert the old counterrevolutionary state into a revolutionary state.[13]

If the Venezuelan revolution's formal democratic legitimacy is impeccable this also presents it with a paradox. As popular sectors mobilize from below, and have become concientised, and politicized, they confront resistance from state institutions that act to constrain, dilute, institutionalize, and co-opt mass struggles, to reproduce the old order. The Venezuelan state is corrupt, bureaucratic, clientelist, and even inert; this was the state inherited from the *ancien régime*. The civil service bureaucracy and old elites have remained in control of much of the state. It is likely that the popular sectors which achieved a foothold in the state will have to confront them and reconstitute the state on a much more profound level as the process deepens. The more than 20,000 *Consejos Comunales*, or community councils, that have been formed may be indicative of revolutionary possibilities here. Yet even though conceived as organs of popular power, some of these councils are subordinate to state directives and others have become co-opted by corrupt leaders or local bureaucrats. Community leaders I met with spoke of the struggle to convert the councils into autonomous organs of community power that exercise power from below over state and party institutions, to avoid having these local organs appropriated (*secuestrado* or 'kidnapped') from above. They complain that the 'process is moving too slowly', that the 'transition' is taking too long. They are keenly aware of the danger of usurpation by bureaucratic and elite forces from above, a danger just as serious for them as the counterrevolutionary efforts of the old elite and their international allies. The slogan among local activists in the barrios was: 'no queremos ser gobierno pero queremos gobernar' ('we don't want to be the government but we want to govern from below').

Some on the left inside and outside Venezuela, while supportive, criticize Chávez as authoritarian and charge him with cultivating 'personal rule'. The prominent Venezuelan intellectual Margarita Lopez Maya, for instance, has accused Chávez of a 'desire to be the one who is essential to the process' and 'to perpetuate himself in power'.[14] She observes, for example, that in early 2007 Chávez requested of the legislature, and was granted, special powers ('enabling laws') to legislate in 11 policy areas over a year and a half, bypassing deliberations in the parliament and other formal representative institutions, and that he is also attempting to remove limits to his indefinite re-election. These criticisms cannot be dismissed. An authoritarianism of the left, cults of personality, and usurpation from above of popular power from below in the name of subordinate class interests, remain just as much a danger in the 21st century as they were in the 20th. Yet the discourse critical of Chávez is somewhat contradictory. Lopez Maya acknowledges that 'Chávez has successfully mobilized the poor and excluded to fight for first-class citizenship, and among the great majority of Venezuelans, who have never been able to participate in politics and society, many now feel like full citizens'. Yet she is troubled by the measures that have moved the country and the popular classes beyond the limits of polyarchic institutions which have historically excluded or co-opted the poor majority.[15]

Popular mobilizations, Lopez Maya observed in early 2007, 'have created very conflictive processes, and the country is now experiencing a very powerful polarization. Over the past few months it has tended to deepen as Chávez has proposed a new break with the past, essentially the destruction of the very state he himself brought into being with the Constitution of 1999'.[16] This, it seems to me, is the crux of the matter. Polarization is less a consequence of Chávez's authoritarianism than an objective and inevitable outcome of the attempt to effect a revolutionary rupture with the old order. The target of Chávez' 'authoritarianism' is not the popular majority but the corrupt and cronyist state of the *ancien régime* and its parasitic bureaucracy through which Chávez came to power – a state he was barely able to modify during his first few years. If there is a strong personal link between Chávez and the masses, it may be explained less by Chávez' desire to cultivate 'personal rule' than by the historic failure of the institutional left in Venezuela and the chasm that exists between it and the popular majority.

CHANGE SOCIETY WITHOUT STATE POWER?

The Venezuelan problematic of revolution and socialism within a capitalist state underscores broader quandaries for popular alternatives to global capitalism in the 21st century. As the struggle for hegemony in global civil society heats up the issue of state power and what to do about it, including national states and the transnational institutions and forums through which they are connected with one another, cannot be avoided. John Holloway's book, *Changing the World Without Taking Power*[17] has elevated to theoretical status the Zapatistas' decision not to bid for state power. The claim that social relations can be transformed from civil society alone appears as the inverse of the old vanguardist model in which social and political forces mobilize through political organizations in order to overthrow the existing state, take power, and use the state to transform society. That model, pursued by much of the Latin American left in the 1960s and 1970s, often through armed struggles, has been recognized by most as a failure and as a dead-end in the new century.

In recent years the indigenous movement in Latin America has spearheaded a new model of horizontal networking and organizational relations in a grassroots democratic process from the bottom up. But at some point popular movements must work out how the vertical and horizontal intersect. A 'long march' through civil society may be essential to transform social relations, construct counter-hegemony from the ground up and assure popular control from below. Yet no emancipation is possible without an alternative project, and no such project is possible without addressing the matter of the power of dominant groups, the organization of that power in the state (including coercive power), and the concomitant need to disempower dominant groups by seizing the state from them, dismantling it, and constructing alternative institutions. The limitations of strict horizontalism have become evident in Latin America in recent years, all the way from Mexico to Argentina.

The Zapatista model generated hope and inspiration for millions through-out Latin America and the world in the 1990s. The January 1, 1994 uprising in Chiapas was an urgent and refreshing response to the capitulation by many on the Left to the TINA ('there is no alternative') syndrome. The Zapatistas insisted on a new set of non-hierarchal practices within their revolutionary movement and within the communities under their influence, including ab-solute equality between men and women, collective leadership, and taking directives from, rather than giving them to, the grassroots base, leading by following and listening, and so on. Such non-hierarchal practices must be at the very core of any emancipatory project. Yet they also hold strong appeal for the anarchist currents that have spread among radical forces worldwide in the wake of the collapse of 'actually existing socialism' and the old statist-vanguardist Left, and that are unwilling to deal with the wider political sys-tem and the state. These currents have a strong influence in the global justice movement and the World Social Forum, as well as among radicalized youth and middle classes in Mexico who provide a base for the Zapatistas beyond Chiapas.

But Zapatismo has not been able to draw in a mass working-class base, and as a result it has experienced a declining political influence on Mexican society. It may still be a force of counter-hegemony or even of hegemony in some communities inside Chiapas, but the fact is that global capitalism has made major headway within Chiapas itself between 1994 and 2007, while the Zapatista movement has stagnated. This conundrum came to a head when the Zapatistas refused as a matter of principle to participate in the campaign that the PRD and Manuel López Obrador waged for the presidency in the 2006 elections. As a result the Zapatistas were ill-prepared to throw their weight behind the mass struggles against the fraud perpetrated by the Mexi-can state and its two ruling parties, the PRI and the PAN. If it is true, as the Zapatistas observe, that there is no blueprint for revolution, then it is also true that revolutionaries need to be able to shift strategies and tactics as history actually unfolds. For the Zapatistas, horizontalism became a rigid principle rather than a general emancipatory practice.

In Argentina, the late 2001 uprising marked the beginning of a popular rebellion of workers, the unemployed and the poor, along with newly dispossessed sectors of the middle class. In the wake of the rebellion popular sectors created hundreds – perhaps thousands – of neighbourhood assemblies, workers occupied and took over hundreds of factories, and the unemployed stepped up their mobilization through *piquetero* and other forms of grassroots struggle. Horizontalist thought makes much of the fact that the rebellion erupted without leadership or hierarchy, and that political parties and elites played no role in the movement.[18] Nonetheless, in the ensuing years the occupied factories have not been able to present even a remote alternative to the domination of transnational capital over the economy and the country's ever-deeper integration into global capitalism, especially through the agro-industrial-financial complex based on soy beans, while assemblies and *piqueteros* have become divided in the face of expanding clientelist networks and cooptation by the state and Kirchner's Peronist faction. It is quite true, as the Argentine autonomists point out, that political parties are bankrupt and corrupt and that local and global elites control the state ('*Que se vayan todos!*' – 'Out with them all!').Yet the *autonomist* movement, with its strict horizontalism, has come no closer to challenging this structure of elite power, nor has it been able to hold back the onslaught of global capitalism.

To dismiss political organizations and the state because they are, or can easily become, instruments of hierarchy, control and oppression, is to emasculate the ability of the popular classes and their social movements and mass organizations to transform the institutions of power and to mount a systemic challenge to the social order.Without some political hammer or political vehicle the popular classes cannot operate effectively vis-à-vis political society or synchronize the forces necessary for a radical transformatory process. As the cases of Venezuela, and perhaps Bolivia and Ecuador, demonstrate, the situation of disunity between civil and political society is not stable. Popular forces and classes must win state power and utilize it to transform production relations and the larger social, political, and cultural relations of domination, yet they must do so without subordinating their own autonomy and collective agency to that state. A confrontation with the global capitalist system beyond the nation-state, moreover, requires national state power.

It is notable that the indigenous movements in Ecuador and Bolivia have not followed the Zapatista example.They did not opt to stay in the highlands and the Amazonian region and forego a frontal struggle against the state. Indigenous and popular sectors in Ecuador, led by the powerful Confederation of Indigenous Nationalities of Ecuador (CONAIE), have sustained a virtual permanent mass mobilization against neoliberalism (and for indigenous rights) since the 1990s. They brought down neoliberal governments on four separate occasions between 1997 and 2005. Yet each time these governments were removed, as one indigenous leader put it to me in 2003, they were replaced with yet another neoliberal government whose policies were equally unaccountable to these sectors. This predicament was due, in part, to the lack of a political vehicle that could serve the popular sectors as a mechanism for exercising some form of institutional control over the state beyond oppositional agitation from within civil society. In 2003 the movement had therefore to place its bets on an alliance with Lucio Gutiérrez, an army colonel who promised an alternative to neoliberalism while participating in the popular overthrow of the neoliberal government of Jamil Mahuad. When Gutiérrez betrayed the popular movement and delivered the country to global capitalism, CONAIE's credibility with its base suffered. In the October 2006 elections the indigenous forces faced a dilemma. Should they support another candidate and risk getting burned? Should they put forward an indigenous candidate along the Bolivian model? In the end CONAIE put forward its own candidate in the 2005 vote but supported Correa in a second round of voting. Since Correa has come to power the mass movement has provided him with critical support while jealously preserving its own autonomous mobilization. Similarly, in Bolivia the indigenous and popular movement threw out several neoliberal regimes and in 2005 put Morales in power, while continuing to mobilize in an autonomous manner, both against the elite and the right, and to pressure the Morales government.

THE GLOBAL CONTEXT

In the age of globalization there are limitations to the reintroduction of a redistributive project at the nation-state level. It is not clear how effective national alternatives alone can be in transforming social structures, given the ability of transnational capital to utilize its structural power to impose its project even over states captured by forces adverse to that project. If the (capitalist) state as a class relation is becoming transnationalized then any challenge to (global) capitalist state power must involve a major transnational component. Struggles at the nation-state level are far from futile. They remain central to the prospects for social justice and progressive social change. The key thing is that any such struggles must be part of a more expansive transnational counter-hegemonic project, including transnational trade unionism, transnational social movements, transnational political organizations, and so on. And they must strive to establish sets of transnational institutions and practices that can place controls on the global market and rein in some of the power of global capital.

Efforts to reform the global order can only be successful when linked to the transformation of class and property relations in specific sets of countries. The formation of the South American Community of Nations (CSN) under Brazilian leadership in 2003 and the proposal that same year by Lula and his Argentine counterpart Kirchner to move forward with the 'Buenos Aires Consensus' have been touted by some among the Latin American Left as a step towards a progressive regional challenge to global capitalism. But it is not clear that the CSN or the Buenos Aires Consensus are anything more than – at best – a mildly reformist path for regional integration into global capitalism. A regional program that attempts to harness market forces for more regionally balanced accumulation and limited redistribution would be an improvement over the rigid neoliberal model vis-à-vis the interests of popular classes, but is hardly a counter-hegemonic alternative to capitalist globalization. Such an alternative would have to be founded on a more fundamental shift in class power at the national and regional levels in Latin America, and would have to involve a transformation of property and production relations beyond limited social redistribution in the phase of surplus circulation. Local class and property relations have global implications. Webs of interdependence and causal sequences in social change link the global to the local so that change at either level is dependent on change at the other level. An alternative to global capitalism must therefore be a *transnational* popular project involving strategies, programs, organizations and institutions that link the local to the national, and the national to the global.

In Venezuela's popular parlance, 'endogenous development' refers to an economic strategy of localized, inward-oriented, and integrative economic activity by self-organized communities that draws on local and national resources, alongside (and apparently subordinated to) trade-related activities, along the lines of what, years earlier, Samir Amin, termed 'autocentric accumulation'. Clearly an alternative economic model to neoliberalism – in Venezuela and elsewhere – would have to emphasize such a community-centered integrative and self-sustaining economic orientation. Yet the Chavista leadership has also proposed not a withdrawal from international trade and economic integration but an alternative transnational development project – the Bolivarian Alternative for the Americas, known by its Spanish acronym, ALBA. Indeed, the debate about socialism in Venezuela seems to center on the question of how to build a popular economy that can also trade in the international area. The ALBA envisages a regional economic development plan for Latin America and the Caribbean involving solidarity with the weakest national economies so that all can cooperate and benefit from regional exchange networks and development projects.

'Revolution in one country' is certainly even less viable in the 21st century than it proved to be in the 20th. All national economies have been reorganized and functionally integrated as component elements of a new global capitalist economy and all peoples have experienced heightened dependencies for their very social reproduction on the larger global system. In the case of Venezuela, the oil and financial system is thoroughly integrated into global capitalism. What this integration points to is the structural power that global capital can exercise and the possibility that this structural power will translate into local political influence. Global capital has local representation everywhere and it translates into local pressure within each state in favour of global capital. Those groups most closely tied to global capital, transnationally-oriented business groups, seek to gain increasing influence and quash a more radical transformative project. Indeed, to take the case of Venezuela, the greatest threat is not from the right-wing political opposition but that parts of the revolutionary bloc will develop a deeper stake in defending global capitalism over socialist transformation, that state managers will become bureaucratized as their own reproduction will depend on deepening relations with global capital.

In Brazil the PT took state power largely in the absence of a mass autonomous mobilization from below so that the popular classes could not exert mass pressure to control the PT government so that it would confront global capital and implement a popular program. The Brazilian model shows that, even when revolutionary groups take state power – absent the countervailing force from popular classes below to oblige those groups to respond to their interests from the heights of the state – the structural power of global capital can impose itself on direct state power and impose its project of global capitalism. In other words, global class struggle 'passes through' the national state in this way. This lack of mass mobilization to generate popular pressure from below meant that the dominant groups could absorb the challenge to their interests represented by a PT government. Leftists who came to power in Venezuela faced similar pressures from the global system to moderate structural change. Yet in Venezuela, unlike Brazil, mass mobilization from below placed pressure on revolutionaries in the state not to succumb to the structural pressures of global capital but rather to carry out a process of social transformation.

The transformative possibilities that have opened up in Latin America cannot be realized without an organized Left and a democratic socialist program. Yet such possibilities will only end up frustrated if they fall into the pattern of top-down change by vanguardist command and military fetishism, along the lines of the 1960s and 1970s when armed struggle was converted from a means into an end. Nowhere is this more evident than in the 'military hypertrophy' of the Colombian Armed Revolutionary Forces (FARC), which sees independent political mobilization as a threat to its own efforts to hegemonize resistance.[19] The transformative moment of the early 21st century in Latin America will depend on the Left's ability to learn the lessons of the previous era of revolution, especially the need to relinquish vanguardism of party and state and to encourage, respect, and subordinate itself to the autonomous mobilization from below of the popular classes and subordinate sectors. In sum, the current round of social and political struggle in Latin America highlights the changing relation between social movements of the left, the state, and global capitalism.

This is precisely why the issue of political organizations that can mediate vertical links between political and civil society is so important. What type of political vehicle can interface between the popular forces on the one hand, and state structures on the other? How can internally-democratic political instruments be developed to operate at the level of political society and dispute state power without diluting the autonomous mobilization of social movements? The potential for transformation will depend on the combination of independent pressure of mass social movements from below on the state, with the representatives and allies of those movements taking over the state. To reiterate, this is why a permanent mobilization from below that forces the state to deepen its transformative project 'at home' and its counter-hegemonic transnational project 'abroad' is so crucial.

NOTES

1   My theory of global capitalism that forms the theoretical backdrop to the matters addressed here can be found in William I. Robinson, *A Theory of Global Capitalism: Production, Class and State in a Transnational World*, Baltimore: John Hopkins University Press, 2004.

2   World Bank, *Global Development Finance*, 2006 Report, Washington: World Bank, 2006.

3   Polyarchy refers to a system in which a small group actually rules and mass participation and decision-making is confined to choosing leaders in elections that are carefully managed by competing elites. See William I. Robinson, *Promoting Polyarchy: Globalization, U.S. Intervention, and Hegemony*. Cambridge: Cambridge University Press, 1996.

4   For discussion, see Roberto P. Korzeniewicz and William C. Smith, 'Poverty, Inequality, and Growth in Latin America: Searching for the High Road to Globalization', *Latin American Research Review*, 35(3), 2000, pp. 7-54.

5   On these details, see William I. Robinson, *Transnational Conflicts: Central America,* *Social Change, and Globalization,* London: Verso, 2003.

6   Sandinista National Liberation Front, *Cuaderno Sandinista No. 1: El Nuevo* *Proyecto Sandinista (Document de Consulta y Debate),* Managua, May 2007.

7   Ibid., p. 5.

8   Raul Zibechi, Raul, 'America Latina: La Nueva Gobernabilidad', *ALAI news* *service,* 23 June 2006 dispatch, datelined Montevideo, available at http://www. paginadigital.com.ar.

9   Jorge G. Castañeda, 'Latin America's Left Turn', *Foreign Affairs,* May/June 2006, pp.28–43.

10   Gregory Wilpert, 'Chávez Affirms Venezuela is Heading Towards Socialism of 21st Century', *Venezuelanalysis,* 2 May 2005, available at http://www.venezue-lanalysis.com.

11   Hugo Chávez, *Entramos a Una Nueva Era: El Proyecto Nacional Simon Bolivar,* speech on the occasion of the swearing in of the executive cabinet, Caracas, 8 January 2007, published and distributed by the Venezuelan Ministry of Communications and Information, p. 67.

12   Ibid., pp. 67, 69.

13   Ibid., p. 72.

14   Fred Rosen, 'Breaking with the Past: A 40th-Anniversary Interview with Margarita Lopez Maya', *NACLA Report on the Americas,* 40(3), May-June 2007, pp. 4–8.

15   Ibid., pp. 6–7.

16   Ibid., p. 5.

17   John Holloway, *Change the World Without Taking Power: The Meaning of Revolution* *Today,* London: Pluto Press, 2005.

18   Marina Sitrin, ed., *Horizontalism: Voices of Popular Power in Argentina,* Oakland: AK Press, 2006.

19   The phrase 'military hypertrophy' was coined by Forrest Hylton, in *Evil Hour in* *Colombia,* London: Verso, 2006.

VENEZUELA TODAY:
A 'PARTICIPATIVE AND PROTAGONISTIC' DEMOCRACY?

MARGARITA LÓPEZ MAYA

Since the electoral victory of Chávez and his supporters – the so-called 'Polo Patriotico' – in December 1998, Venezuela has been undergoing a process of change in all aspects of its social life. Chávez offered Venezuelans a radical political proposal: to replace the elite that had been in power since 1958, to put an end to the prevailing corruption, and to introduce a new constitution which would transform Venezuelan democracy into one that would be 'participative and protagonistic'. Eight years later, in December 2006, after overcoming a coup and winning a referendum for his recall, Chávez was elected president again. Speaking at a massive political demonstration after his election he reaffirmed his electoral promise to lead Venezuela rapidly toward a 'socialism of the twenty-first century'.

The main events of these eight years are more or less well known; the particular focus of this essay is on the prospects for the promise contained in the idea of 'socialism of the twenty-first century', and in particular, its promise of a 'participative and protagonistic' democracy. This promise, which started to be developed during his first term, aroused the enthusiasm of the poorest sections of the population who had been deprived of their essential rights in previous decades, as well as high expectations on the part of an international left still searching for a way to move beyond the sense of defeat induced by the collapse of actually-existing socialism after 1989. Initially, the international left distrusted Chávez for his military background, for his populist rhetoric and for the political coalition that supported him, made up of personalities and parties with very diverse ideological positions. However, once Chávez halted the processes of neoliberal change, and was strongly attacked for this by the international financial agencies and the US government, he aroused the curiosity and then the interest of an international left that today invests the Venezuelan process with its hopes for a viable alternative model to capitalism.

At home, in his first eight years in office Chávez managed to sustain and even increase popular support for his political project of participative democracy. Once he had survived the coup d'état of April 11, 2002, and the oil sabotage/strike at the end of that year, that project began to take clearer shape. With growing financial resources, thanks to the combination of reform in the oil sector and the rising price of oil, the government started to promote novel social and economic policies, through special taskforces called 'missions', whereby the popular sectors gained real access to some of the rights denied them during the previous decades of crisis and neoliberal adjustment. These policies, conceived as instruments to promote the organization and participation of the people and their communities, sparked a popular effervescence that continues until now and that has permitted poor Venezuelans especially to overcome the effects of two decades of economic stagnation, political apathy and pessimism about the future.

Yet the political process during these eight years has been contradictory and stressful, with incipient effects that threaten to undermine its positive tendencies in the medium term. This process has unfolded in a context marked by high political polarization, in which powerful and conflicting interests, not only in Venezuelan society but also in the wider world, confront each other. For these reasons, information about Venezuela's evolution is usually of poor quality, difficult to access and interpret. This makes it all the more essential to have a critical analysis pointing out weaknesses as well as strengths so as to contribute some clarity to the debates taking place around current developments. This essay seeks to do this. To set the issues in the necessary context, a brief account is first offered of some of the factors which brought Chávez to power, and the most important events and socio-economic processes which occurred during his first term as president, and which condition the prospects for his second term.

CHÁVEZ AND HIS MOVEMENT TAKE POWER: THE NEW CONSTITUTION

There is already an extensive literature dedicated to explaining how a military outsider, promising a radical socio-political transformation, succeeded in shaking to its roots what was considered one of the most stable of Latin American democracies.[1] While there are differences of emphasis, there is general agreement that it was the result of a combination of mutually-reinforcing factors. Twenty years of economic stagnation without an apparent solution in sight, structural adjustment policies which aggravated an already grossly unequal income distribution; the undermining of the 'modern' social structure built on the basis of the previous development model; the growth of the informal economy and the lack, for the majority of the population, of any prospect of social advancement or even social inclusion; all these factors contributed to the conjuncture of 1998. These same factors had already contributed to a popular rebellion in February 1989, known as the *Caracazo*, which indicated a radical repudiation of the old socio-political order and marked the beginning of a search for alternatives.

After the *Caracazo*, discontent directly affected the political system. Street protests, which from then on become more numerous and visible, reflected not only an increasingly widespread rejection of the dominant political parties; they also led to a mounting institutional crisis and undermined the system of political representation. With two attempted coups in 1992, the military added a new dimension to an already explosive situation. The attempts to overthrow President Carlos Andrés Pérez, although defeated, weakened him and led, first, to his removal from office by the National Congress, and then, in the following presidential elections in December 1993, to the collapse of the two-party system, when Rafael Caldera won without the support of either of the two hitherto dominant parties. Then, between 1994 and 1998, the failure of the Caldera government to overcome economic stagnation, together with the increasingly serious social imbalances provoked by a new set of neoliberal measures, finally produced a radicalization of political attitudes amongst the population. In 1998, there was a final ingredient: the collapse of oil prices on the world market. In December, the electorate opted for the military figure who had headed the first of the 1992 coups and who, with his polarizing discourse and the promise to displace the existing, discredited elite, offered the opportunity to punish the old political establishment and – perhaps – initiate a process capable of overcoming the legacy of the previous twenty years.

Once in office, Chávez and his movement began with a constitutional process designed to replace the 1961 constitution, as promised in the election campaign. The new constitution, sanctioned in a referendum in December 1999, introduced a series of mechanisms aimed at replacing Venezuela's 'representative' democracy with a 'participative and protagonistic' version. Running counter to the prevailing neoliberal tendency, the constitution ratified the central role of the state, the universal nature of social rights, and oil as an inalienable property of the state. The country was renamed the 'Bolivarian Venezuelan Republic'. Amongst the new mechanisms for promoting participation, the constitution incorporated several different kinds of referendum (approbatory, consultative, recall and repeal), legislative initiatives (to approve or revise the constitution or laws), open municipal council sessions and citizens' assemblies. Together, all these measures put an end to the neoliberal policies of the previous decade.

The eight years from 1999 to late 2006 (when Chávez began his second term as president) have witnessed intense popular mobilizations, political confrontations, an attempted coup in April 11, 2002, and an oil stoppage-sabotage by the elite in charge of the state-owned oil industry which paralyzed the industry from December 2002 to February 2003. In this last confrontation, the government emerged victorious, recovering its control of the industry and dismissing about half of its employees, mainly high-level executive staff.[2] As a result, the government was able to implement its oil reform. This involved the recovery of the state's control over the formulation, implementation and supervision of the public oil company's policies. In the nineties, these powers had been assumed by the company's executives under the neoliberal policy of 'Apertura petrolera', which tended to disregard the public interest in favour of the company's corporate interests and eventually tended towards a re-privatization of PDVSA. Chavez' victory brought with it increased oil revenues with which to finance his social and political programme. In August 2004, the opposition was able to activate a recall referendum against the president; this was converted into another victory for Chávez, confirming him in office until the end of his term. And in December 2006, as already mentioned, he was re-elected.

During his first eight years, the application of the participative democracy principle to social and economic policies attacking the problem of social exclusion has been one of the major achievements of the Chávez government. It has created the necessary conditions and institutional mechanisms to stimulate the self-management of the popular sectors, dynamizing the organization of the country's poor communities, and thus introducing not only an element capable of improving public efficiency, but also a carrier of self-development, self-esteem, and a sense of belonging and solidarity, which have expanded and strengthened citizenship and democracy.

Before 1999, the popular movement was prostrate and disorganized, its members hard hit by almost two decades of neoliberal economic policy.[3] Furthermore, before the Chávez government came to power the popular movement did not have the organic base, traditions, or a strong enough articulation to be able to operate autonomously and take initiatives vis-à-vis the power of the state. Venezuelan representative democracy had favoured the cooptation of popular movements – as well as of the trade unions – by the two-party system that emerged in the sixties. From a small, poorly organized, dispersed and fragmented movement, an extensive range of new popular organizations were stimulated into being through various policies and so-cial programs during Chávez's first term – especially from 2003 onwards when the government took control of the PDVSA oil corporation and its resources.

At the beginning of the president's new term of office, the context is complex and prediction uncertain. Though the government has rightly acted to stimulate from above the organization and mobilization of its base, there is a very strong asymmetry between a state rich in oil resources and a popular movement full of needs and historically weak as far as autonomy is concerned. This makes fostering popular organizational and participatory dynamics into one of the government's major challenges; protecting the plurality of social and productive organizations, while at the same time respecting their devel-opment so that they can advance to higher levels of autonomous participa-tion in public management, and acquire increasing capacities to control it. This is essential if the popular movement is to be fortified enough to act as an interlocutor with the various agencies of public management, thus guar-anteeing it the capacity to control them. Otherwise, there is a high risk of returning to the clientelistic and paternalistic patterns that prevailed in the old Venezuelan political culture of representative democracy.

THE CONTEXT AFTER DECEMBER 2006

One of Chávez's main strengths at the start of his second term was the sheer scale of the support he received in the December 2006 election, afford-ing an important legitimacy to his subsequent initiatives. Chávez won with 7,309,080 valid votes (62.9 per cent) against 4,292,466 (36.9 per cent) for his rival, Manuel Rosales. The polarization between these two candidates was the most marked in Venezuela's electoral history; the two shared between them 99.8 per cent of the valid votes; the candidate who came in third received less than 5,000 votes. Turnout was high at 74.9 per cent and invalid votes ac-counted for a mere 1.4 per cent.[4] Moreover Chávez increased his share of the vote in each successive election. In the recall referendum he received 59.1 per cent of the vote; in the 2006 election, he got 62.9 per cent.

This convincing electoral victory can be accounted for to a large extent by the vigorous and sustained economic growth of the Venezuelan economy since 2004, when the government had overcome the most violent phase of political confrontation. That year, the economy recovered from the impact of the oil stoppage with a GNP growth of 17.9 per cent. From then on, during the following two years, GNP growth averaged more than 9 per cent (see Table 1).[5]

Table 1: Some Macroeconomic Indicators, 2003-2006

Year	Price per barrel of Venezuelan oil exports (US$)	Internatonal Reserves (millions of US$)	Inflation (% change in consumer prices)	Change of GNP	Exchange Rate (Bs. x $)
2003	25.8	21.366	27.1	– 7.7	1600
2004	33.4	24.208	19.2	17.9	1920
2005	45.5	30.368	14.4	9.3	2150
2006	55.9	31.917*	13.4**	9.6**	2150

* First six months **Year to October.

Source: Banco Central de Venezuela, 'Información estadística', 2006, available at www.bcv. org.ve/c2/indicadores.asp and Ministerio de Energía y Petróleo, 'Precios del petróleo', 2006, available at www.menpet.gob.ve/preciopetroleo.

As can be seen from Table 1, this impressive economic performance was due, above all, to the price of Venezuelan oil in the international market, averaging $US 55.9 per barrel during the election year. This, together with the ability of the government to apply its oil reform from 2003 onwards, was reflected in a boom in available revenues, enabling it to pursue multiple social policies. Missions (programs bypassing uncooperative or ineffective state agencies), such as *Barrio Adentro* (free 24 hours a day primary health care and disease prevention for low income groups), *Mercal* (state distribution of food at subsidized prices), *Robinson 1 and 2* (literacy and primary education for adults), *Ribas* and *Sucre* (secondary and university education for those who had missed or not finished these), *Vuelvan Caras* (training for employment), and the Bolivarian schools, where a full day schedule has been restored, with two free meals and two snacks a day, plus free uniforms and textbooks: all these undoubtedly had a positive political impact. The government has also invested in the social economy, as in the 'ruedas de negocios', in which the creation of cooperatives is encouraged in order to supply goods and services to the state sector. The government has also created a system of micro-financing with the Women's Bank, the Sovereign People's Bank, and so on, which make small loans to lower income borrowers.

These and other policies help to explain how, in recent years, poverty has fallen, and unemployment has been reduced. At the same time, the country has attained one of the highest Human Development Indices in Latin

America. Table 2 presents the official statistics, indicating clearly why Chávez and his movement obtained the support of the majority in December 2006, especially among those with lower incomes.

Table 2: Some Socio-Economic Indices, 2003-2006

Year	Unemployment Rate (%)	Poor Homes (%)	Extremely Poor Homes (%)	Human Development Index
2003	16.8	55.1	25.0	0.76
2004	13.9	47.0	18.5	0.80
2005	13.0	37.9	15.3	0.81
2006	9.9*	33.9**	10.6**	---

★ Third quarter ★★ First six months

Source: Instituto Nacional de Estadística, 'Estadísticas vitales', 2006, available at http://www. ine.gov.ve/registrosvitales/estadisticasvitales.asp.

It is important to emphasize that these advances are almost exclusively based on oil revenues. According to the Venezuelan Central Bank, in 2006, 89 per cent of our exports were oil. We are as dependent on oil as in the past, if not more so. If we examine the current relationship between the state and PDVSA (the state-owned oil corporation) in terms of the hard currency earned by the firm, in 2006 the state received 68 per cent while 32 per cent remained in the hands of PDVSA. The oil sector represents 14 per cent of the GNP.[6]

'TWENTY-FIRST CENTURY SOCIALISM'

The promise of 'twenty-first century socialism', one of the key themes in the December 2006 election campaign, was also, until then, an open and barely-defined formula, susceptible to diverse interpretations. Chávez used the ex-pression for the first time in the 5th World Social Forum in January 2005 held in Porto Alegre but did little to define it, apart from declaring that it meant an abandonment of the 'Third Way' as a development model. He insisted that it should not be confused with a socialist state like those developed in the Soviet Union or the Eastern European countries, or in Cuba; what he had in mind was a less state-centred and a more pluralist society.[7] In mid-2006, at an event in Vienna, he affirmed that the basis for this new socialism was 'solidar-ity, fraternity, love, justice, liberty and equality' – that is to say, the traditional ideals of socialism. He argued that it was not a question of a predetermined model of socialism, but rather 'of transforming the mode of production in the direction of a socialism that needs to be built on an everyday basis'.[8]

Apart from these indications, during the 2006 election campaign there was little to suggest a more precise definition of the term, except for two details which suggested certain contradictions with the idea of deepening democratic participation. On several occasions Chávez said that when he won he would modify the constitution to introduce an unlimited possibility of re-election for the incumbent president. At the same time, Francisco Ameliach, his campaign manger, threatened the opposition by saying that if they boycotted the election the right to proportional representation contemplated in the constitution would be eliminated.[9]

Apart from these two elements, until late 2006 Chávez's proposed new socialism was vague and open-ended. Indeed, until the December elections, twenty-first century socialism was a concept without a precise content, understood by each and everyone in terms of his or her unsatisfied demands and aspirations. As Ernesto Laclau argues, phrases like 'twenty-first century socialism' are particularly attractive in societies with an accumulation of unresolved problems; a multiplicity of demands become related in a 'chain of equivalences', finally represented by just one of them. This 'empty signifier' – in the Venezuelan case, 'twenty-first century socialism' – is central to populist discourse; it has a notable capacity to mobilize for change.[10]

Once the electoral triumph had been achieved, however, President Chávez began to give a more concrete content to the concept. In three key speeches during the weeks following the election he talked in more precise terms of the ideas and instruments he had in mind to produce a profound transformation of Venezuelan society. In a speech on the 15th December, during an electoral victory celebration with his followers, Chávez invited all the parties which supported his government to dissolve themselves in order to found a single, united party: 'what the revolution needs is a united party: a party, not a soup of acronyms which leads us to deceive the people'. He warned that if they did not do so, 'of course, they leave the government, leave the government, they leave my government'.[11] He proposed that the new party should be named the Venezuelan United Socialist Party (PSUV). Although he thought of the PSUV as an instrument for 'electoral battles', he insisted that it should transcend this function and also do battle in the sphere of ideas: 'We must study a lot... read a lot, discuss a lot, organize round tables, square tables, meetings of socialist squadrons, of detachments to read...'.[12] He predicted that it would be the largest and most democratic party in Venezuelan history.

Shortly afterwards, Chávez made two more important speeches, the first in the largest theatre in the country – the Teresa Carreño – on the 7th January; and the second on the 10th in the National Assembly, on the occasion of the formal inauguration of his second term. In these two speeches Chávez offered more precise ideas on his strategy for advancing towards a twenty-first century socialism.[13] He announced the nationalization of the strategic industries which had been privatized during the previous administrations, and described 'five constituent motors' that were to drive the next stage of the Bolivarian revolution.[14] Before the members of the National Assembly and representatives of the other public authorities he announced the slogan for his new term: 'Fatherland, Socialism or Death, I swear it'.[15]

The constituent motors would 'turn on the engine' that would carry the country to socialism. The first, an Enabling Law, already in the constitution, gives the Legislature power to delegate to the National Executive, for a predetermined period, the capacity to make decrees with the force of law (Article 203). Chávez called this 'the law of revolutionary laws, the mother of laws'. The second motor was a proposed 'integral and profound' reform of the constitution, with the object, amongst others, of modifying the articles which, in relation to economic and political questions, could be interpreted as obstacles on the road to socialism. Chávez considered that these two motors should run in tandem and appointed the President of the National Assembly, Cilia Flores, to preside over and coordinate the commission dedicated to the constitutional reform. The third motor of the revolution was called 'morality and enlightenment'; this refers to a campaign designed to promote moral, economic, political and social education in all spheres of society – schools, workshops, the countryside, endogenous nuclei[16] and other popular spaces. The fourth motor Chávez called 'the geometry of power': this was a proposed new geographic distribution of political, economic, social and military power across the nation, in order to generate the construction of cities and federal territories more in line with socialist aspirations and current realities. Finally, he proposed a fifth motor, according to him the most important: the 'revolutionary explosion of communal power', according to which popular power would be promoted within the state, modifying its nature and making it socialist. Chávez talked of setting no limits to the communal councils, because these are the primary expression of popular power.

Chávez held that all these motors are interconnected and that 'the creative explosion of communal power will depend for its development, for its force, for its roots, for its expansion, for its success, on the other motors, on the Reform of the Constitution, it is going to depend to a great extent on the Enabling Laws, on the National Campaign of Morality and Enlightenment, it is going to depend on the new geometry of power, and on other factors'.[17] On several occasions the President underlined the need to 'accelerate the temporal rhythm and open up new spaces on the road to the new era which begins today'.[18]

Within a few days, the executive introduced its project for an Enabling Law in the National Assembly, asking for authorization to legislate for a period of a year and a half in ten broad areas of public administration, including civil and judicial security, popular participation, finance and taxation, economic and social policy, values in the exercise of the public function, energy, defence and security, science and technology, and boundary changes. Two weeks later the National Assembly unanimously approved the request, adding another sphere of action to those already covered – hydrocarbons. And in mid-January the President as part of these decisions also appointed a Presidential Commission for the Constitutional Reform (CPRC) and a Presidential Commission for Popular Power (CPPP) to help him employ his powers in these areas under the Enabling Law.

THE SIGNIFICANCE OF THE NEW MEASURES

It should be pointed out that the re-nationalization of the strategic firms, like the telephone company CANTV, and the new nationalizations, like that of *Electricidad de Caracas*, announced by the President in these speeches and carried out soon after, could be implemented without modifying the constitution. The 1999 constitution is sufficiently generous in the powers conceded to the state to abridge private property in the defence of social interests: it recognizes different forms of property and accords priority to the social economy. In consequence, these first presidential announcements appear designed primarily to promote a change of some importance in political institutions. We next consider the most important of these in turn.

The Enabling Law

This first motor is based on a constitutional provision that authorizes the President and the executive to elaborate and approve laws by decree. In this sense, it is in accordance with the rule of law. However, the President's request, for authorization for a period of a year and a half, and to legislate in ten broadly-defined areas – which then became eleven as a result of the Assembly's initiative – reveals the confirmation and acceleration of a tendency already apparent during the President's first term: a strengthening of the executive branch of government at the expense of the Legislative, a tendency which acquired a fresh impulse from 2006 on, since when Congress has been 100 per cent in the hands of the Bolivarian forces as a result of the decision of the opposition parties to withdraw their candidates during the parliamentary elections of December 2005.

The 1961 constitution had envisaged the possibility of an Enabling Law, which was then defined as a special law approved by Congress to empower the President to dictate laws as 'extraordinary measures of an economic or fiscal character when the national interest requires it' (Article 190, Section 8). This delegation of the legislative function to the executive was extended in the 1999 constitution, in that there is now no clause limiting it to a specific area; the law must simply specify a predetermined period of time. Since 1999, this broadening of the legislative capacity of the executive has generated controversy among constitutionalists, and this particular request – the third initiative of this type since Chávez came to power – has been considered unconstitutional by some on account of the generic nature of the areas to which it is applied and the length of the period during which it is valid, arguing that it effectively undermines the legislative function which is a prerogative of the Legislature.[19]

In any event, with government supporters in absolute control of the National Assembly, it was puzzling to many people that the executive should have made a request for powers defined in such broad terms. The President alleged the urgency of the changes which, according to him, did not permit a loss of time in legislative debates. However, beyond the question of the appropriateness of introducing profound changes at a forced pace, the rapidity with which the National Assembly accepted the request, approved two weeks after it had been introduced, above all revealed the passive attitude of the highest legislative authority in face of the executive. It meant a self-exclusion of the legislature from the reform process, and this, in turn, meant eliminating, for the Chavist masses who had elected it, the most natural institutional context for deliberating on, and taking decisions about, the shape of 'twenty-first century socialism'. Furthermore, the question of participation and popular power itself was included in the scope of the Enabling Law, which means that it will be the President, his ministers and those he deems appropriate to consult who will elaborate the proposal for popular power. This is evidently in contradiction with the participative democracy which it is supposed to promote. We return to this point below.

The constitutional reform

To activate the second motor, an 'integral and profound' reform of the constitution, the President, as already mentioned, appointed a presidential commission, the CPRC, consisting of 19 members headed by the President of the National Assembly, Cilia Flores. It includes, as executive secretary, the

President of the Supreme Tribunal of Justice, the People's Defense Representative and the Attorney General, together with representatives of various public institutions. Article 2 of the decree stipulates that the Commission is committed to keep its deliberations confidential: its members are not permitted to divulge their ideas, the terms of the debate or the proposals, without the permission of the President of the republic.

It should be pointed out that the Bolivarian constitution provides that the State Council is the highest organ for the purpose of government consultation on policy matters of national interest and particular importance. It is composed of the Vice-President as coordinator, five members appointed by the president, a representative designated by the National Assembly, another by the Supreme Tribunal of Justice, and another by the various state governors. The fact that Chávez ignored this constitutional instrument, made up of a clear majority of government sympathizers but at the same time permitting autonomy to the other state powers in choosing their representatives, suggests that the message of the Enabling Law was being reinforced: all other state powers are to be subordinated to the executive.

Furthermore, on the question of constitutional reform, the President and/or his spokespersons have been anticipating some specific proposals which point in the same direction. One is the proposal for unlimited re-election of the President. This proposal was first launched in the election campaign and has been repeated in numerous presidential speeches and in declarations by leaders and functionaries. More recently, there has been talk of extending the proposal to all publicly-elected posts. The principle of alternating in power, which was incorporated into all Venezuela's previous democratic constitutions (those of 1947, 1961 and 1999), is evidently undermined by this proposal.

Another related proposal is to eliminate proportional representation. This proposal emerged, as we noted earlier, as a threat to the opposition during the 2006 presidential election campaign, when the government thought that the opposition meant to withdraw its candidature from the presidential race at the last moment, leaving Chávez as the only candidate. Eliminating proportional representation, first established in the 1947 constitution, would mean the disappearance of small minority parties from legislative bodies.[20] A third proposal by Chávez is for multiple Vice-Presidencies, appointed by him, who he could send to coordinate national plans in the different regions of the country. This would involve inevitable tensions, with a potential weakening, or even elimination, of the state governors who are elected on the basis of a universal, direct and secret vote.

Apart from this, the fact that the constitutional reform coincides with the application of the Enabling Law suggests an additional and disturbing possibility. The Enabling Law is itself an exceptional measure which is limited only by the terms of the constitution. As its application coincides with the proposed constitutional reform, the president has the means to implement his proposals without any effective constraints.

THE COMMUNAL COUNCILS

In the presidential speeches dedicated to sketching the guidelines for achieving a twenty-first century socialism, the configuration of a new structure of popular power, made up of communal councils as vehicles for participation, self-management and popular self-government, is considered of central importance. As we have already noted, the president appointed a Presidential Council for Popular Power (CPPP) in conformity with the Law on Communal Councils sanctioned by the National Assembly in 2006. In addition, as also noted above, the executive included in the Enabling Law everything related to the question of participation, announcing the need for a reform of the Law on Communal Councils with a view to vitalizing popular power, a reform which would be included in the text of the new constitution.

According to the law currently in force, in cities communal councils are established on the basis of a maximum of 400 families each, sharing a common geographical area. In rural areas and in the indigenous communities the number of families covered can be substantially less. All the organizations active in the same location are to be incorporated within the councils: the technical water round tables, the health committees, the urban or rural land committees, the sports clubs, the women's groups, cultural groups, etc. The law, taking into account the leadership role anticipated for the councils, envisages a process of preparation prior to their formalization. First, a citizen's assembly is to be convoked to elect a provisional preparatory commission, which is entrusted with the task of creating the right conditions for the eventual formalization of the communal council, preparing a census of the community, organizing an electoral commission and electing a permanent promotion commission. Once these conditions have been fulfilled, a constituent assembly is convoked and spokespeople ('vocals') are elected for the various commissions of the council stipulated in the law (2006, Article 15).

The communal councils adopt decisions in citizens' assemblies. There, on the basis of a secret vote, the 'vocals' of the commissions are elected. It is also to be a different kind of representation from that of the past – as, for example in the neighbourhood associations – because those elected can be recalled by the assembly at any time. The commission 'vocals' are authorized to form intermediate organizations, such as federations or associations, with other councils. Their term of office lasts two years. Some public officials have suggested that this structure constitutes a sixth constitutional power, alongside the executive, legislative, judicial, electoral and citizens.[21]

According to the current legal provisions, the communal councils have to be registered in the office in the presidency of the republic and the monitoring of the projects to be undertaken, and control over the available resources, is in the hands of the CPPP (at its different administrative levels – national, regional and local), all of whose members are appointed by the president. There are no links to the mayors or governors. At the same time, communal banks have to be formed as cooperatives in order to receive resources from the government. This has provoked a great deal of confusion and contradiction, because the communal councils do not share the characteristics of cooperatives, which are voluntary civil associations, based on the financial contributions or work of their associated members, whereas the communal councils are part of the state structure and are basically financed by the state.[22]

It is a truism that in order for participation to contribute to genuine empowerment, it must be part of a dynamic which functions from the base upwards, strengthening the autonomy of the grass-roots organizations and their members, and providing incentives for the creation of intermediate organizations in a process of aggregation. As conceived of in the Law on Communal Councils, however, the contrary is the case. Dependency on the presidency is encouraged and there are ample opportunities for developing clientelistic relationships. The hurried way in which the councils are being formed, together with the very limited participation in the drafting of the law sanctioned in 2006, both conspire against the participative democracy they are supposed to advance, because this needs to be based on a massive participation and the time necessary for learning processes to mature. After all, what is being proposed is a profound cultural change which inevitably involves a prolonged and intrinsically difficult itinerary.

In terms of social participation, Venezuela is currently a laboratory in which the most diverse organizational forms are being created and tried out, with a view to promoting a self-development in the popular sectors. For that reason, it is risky to offer an evaluation of the results at this moment in time, when the experiences are fragmentary and information with an overall perspective, independent of official declarations and statistics, is hard to come by.

In recent months, however, while it is true that the general organizational dynamic continues, the process of organization and participation has been reflected above all in the communal councils, as a result of the insistence of the president in his speeches and the stimulus of the resources made available by the government. According to official sources, to date about 20,000 communal councils have been created which, on a conservative estimate of councils averaging 200 members and families averaging four members, would mean that more than two thirds of the entire population of Venezuela has been integrated into this form of participative activity. When the CPPP was formed, the funds available were increased from 2 billion to 4 billion Bolívares.[23]

The communal councils have provoked great expectations, but also doubts and controversies. There are many questions that can clearly not be answered unambiguously. One of them, as has already been suggested, is whether the current conception and dynamics, stimulated from above by the government, can effectively generate a genuine process of empowering autonomous popular power. In the field we can observe a wide range of councils, some of whose priorities were imposed from above, or by small groups; others frankly organized in order to take advantage of the oil revenues for particular individual interests; while yet others contribute to self-management and serve, with varying degrees of success, the needs of the shanty towns. The lack of clear rules in the current legislation, while perhaps understandable given the nature of the processes that are being promoted, which make flexibility necessary, nevertheless undoubtedly contribute to conflicts and confusions, and lend themselves to every type of abuse. There is therefore a clear need for a reform of the law, and for a regulation which will institutionalize the process, and this should be the product of a genuine democratic debate.

Many people also ask how to resolve the problem of maintaining and increasing the levels of citizen participation and that of the communities. It is well-known that it is not always easy to sustain high levels of participation. Up to now, the combination of readily-available money and empowerment has been an important incentive.[24] However, the failure to adequately control the money disbursed is a cause for concern and could end up reproducing old (or creating new) clientelistic patterns, especially in a society so accustomed to them.

In order for participation to be genuine, it needs time to take root, as a process assumed by those involved, cultivating values of solidarity. Furthermore, it requires a processing of the tension between the time people can realistically dedicate to these communal activities and the expectations which these forms of participation stimulate. Although it is not yet clear how this problem can be resolved, there is no doubt that the resources on which the Venezuelan oil-state can count are a help.

The small size of the councils is another controversial point, because it leads to the lack of an adequate perspective when it comes to more wide-ranging problems, such as the renovation of *barrios* in the large cities, where 400 families, the maximum permitted by law, can hardly offer solutions to the basic problems of communities consisting of three or four thousand families. They might well prove an obstacle in the way of efficient and rapid solutions, given the need to mediate between different points of view and divergent interests. When one thinks of the possibilities of participation in decisions over regional, national or international policies, these forms of organization would inevitably remain isolated from them. Moreover the councils are hardly suitable for furthering a pluralist culture, tolerant of differences, because their small size and territorial identity tend to imply a degree of homogeneity.

CONCLUDING REFLECTIONS

While the social dynamics of the revolution are characterized by their vital and open nature, in the sphere of politics, then, there appears to be a sort of regressive evolution, towards a closing of the space for participation and democratic decision-making. Venezuela, in this sense, appears to moving in the direction of a politically less democratic society.

The process which has led to the formation of the PSUV suggests the emergence of a new political system and tendencies towards the creation of a party-state, as we have known it in the failed socialisms of the last century, and as it continues to exist in Cuba and China. Currently, the government – without the least respect for the formal restrictions imposed by the law – uses public resources (money, public means of communication, etc.) to-gether with the social organizations created by the missions, technical water roundtables, and urban land committees, etc., to promote and coordinate its party, the PSUV. The frontiers between state, government, PSUV and the communal councils tend to vanish, in a statist logic of twentieth century so-cialism. Complaints about this do not have much impact and lack the politi-cal capacity to force any change. These irregularities place the government in an advantageous position in relation to any other organization which hopes to compete for the votes of the Venezuelan electorate, seriously compromis-ing the democratic principle of equality of conditions for competing in the political arena.

The declarations of the president in these first months of the year have accentuated a tendency already discernable during his first term: the con-centration of decision-making, in all key matters affecting the future of the society, in the hands of the president and a small group of loyal followers who depend on him. We can also observe how the suggestion that the communal councils represent a sixth state power, and their lack of links to the local governments as a result of their dependent relationship with the presidency, as currently proposed, would weaken the municipal structure of government, reinforcing a process of re-centralization which is also to be observed since the president's first term. Equally clear, as we have seen, are the tendencies towards the subordination of the other state powers to an executive dominated by Chávez. This was evident when the representatives of these other constitutional powers were incorporated into the CPRC, into a sort of pyramidal structure in contradiction with the horizontal logic of separate and independent powers, which was one of the basic features of representative democracy in Venezuela hitherto. President Chávez has argued that these developments are necessary in order to open the road to a twenty-first century socialism, to a profoundly egalitarian and libertarian society; but if this implies a restriction of its political democracy, are the means compatible with the ends?

In the light of the failures of the socialist attempts of the twentieth century, in which the authoritarian nature of the state played a key role, the answer to this question may seem to be obvious. However, it is necessary to review certain arguments that constantly circulate in Venezuela as well as elsewhere.

As a justification for the actions he has taken, President Chávez refers regularly in his speeches to the danger to the revolution posed by imperialism, or more precisely by Bush's government. With this argument, he stigmatizes those who do not share his ideas by making them responsible for debilitating and/or betraying the process and the country.

As is well known, high-ranking US officials knew about it and welcomed the 2002 coup d'état, and have been financing the organizations and leaders of Venezuelan opposition. However, it seems extremely improbable, after the successive and conclusive failures inflicted on the opposition by the government's forces, that the United States can, in the short term, intervene successfully in Venezuelan politics in a way that would weaken Chávez. The opposition forces are too discredited and dispersed to represent a political alternative. A military invasion or intervention by the United States appears still less likely, bearing in mind the political weakening of the Bush government, both internally and internationally. An adventure against Venezuela, a country which, without being a major power, is not a banana republic either, does not seem to be viable in the short term. US troops and resources are already involved on several fronts in other latitudes. On the other hand, Venezuela enjoys today support and sympathy in Latin American regional institutions such as the Caricom, the OAS, Mercosur, etc., which also has the effect of neutralizing US initiatives aimed at weakening Venezuela's presence in those organizations.

It is therefore very difficult in Venezuela to accept that it is necessary to restrict criticism and join together behind Chávez's personalistic power on the grounds that we would otherwise be assisting the enemy's plans. It seems more reasonable to think that Chávez, with his military training and his admiration for Fidel Castro, prefers a centralized and personalized model, in the style of Cuba, for his socialist project. Some point out that this tendency towards 'Cubanization' is all the more absurd, at a time when some space for political tolerance is being opened in Cuba, rather than closed down.

Tendencies towards the concentration of power and political intolerance are inexplicable if conceived as a strategy for strengthening the revolution against powerful domestic economic groups. It is true that between 2001 and 2004 almost all the economically influential groups collaborated with the insurrectionary strategies of the opposition to overthrow Chávez, but due to the defeats they suffered, most of them have preferred to accommodate to the situation and, in times of prosperity, to look after their businesses. Only a few of the privately-owned media still practise politics actively. The behaviour of the Venezuelan tycoon Gustavo Cisneros, one of the richest businessmen in Latin America, the owner of a television channel in Venezuela, Channel 4, and a shareholder in many other businesses in the region, is illustrative. Cisneros backed the strategies of the opposition until the 2004 referendum, then admitted that he had lost a lot of money and came to an agreement with the president, distancing his television channel from political controversies.

It should not be forgotten that the Venezuelan state, as an oil state, has a long entrepreneurial tradition. As the owner of PDVSA, it is the most powerful business in the country. It is also the owner of most of the electricity companies, of the reservoirs and of mining companies such as Venalum and Bauxiven. The recent nationalizations are not really novelties: even more took place in the seventies, during the previous boom in world oil prices. Carried out by President Carlos Andrés Pérez, it was then called 'state capitalism'. Until now Chávez's compensation for nationalized companies has abided by the law and has been accepted as satisfactory by most of their owners. The same has occurred with the large estates that have been expropriated. Although the presidential speech that announces the expropriation measure is usually very aggressive, in practice the measure is always in accordance with the law and compensation is paid promptly. And to date, the banking sector and importers have enjoyed extraordinary profits.

One of the most prolonged confrontations against the Bolivarian project has come from the private mass media. In contrast to Cisneros, Marcel Granier, a Venezuelan businessman who owned Channel 2, and was founder of an ideologically neoliberal political group in the 1980s, was far less inclined to establish a dialogue with Chávez or to negotiate with the government after the referendum in 2004. In December 2006, in the context of the set of announcements about hastening of the process towards a socialism of the twenty-first century, President Chávez, speaking from an army barracks and dressed in military uniform, announced his unwillingness to renew Channel 2's national licence which was due to expire on May 27, 2007. And he acted on this.

This gave rise to a complex situation involving various actors in various arenas acting from varied motives. In an already polarized society, it has made polarization worse. And this same polarization extends to the international sphere, where governments, political parties and mass media line up on one side or the other according to their interests.

By law, the Venezuelan state has the power not to renew a concession of space on the broadcasting spectrum. And the argument presented by the government that with this move it seeks to democratize the spectrum is also valid and fair, especially given its advocacy of the right to plurality and diversity regarding the mechanisms necessary for deepening participative democracy. Nevertheless, the lack of formal institutional procedure in the way Chávez made the announcement – military uniform, barracks, aggressive language, etc; the fact that on that same date Channel 4 was granted the renewal of its concession, having previously been as 'pro-coup' as Channel 2; his tendencies towards a personalistic concentration of power and intolerance of political differences in his new term; all this has given rise, since then and up to the time this essay is being written, to renewed polarized confrontations. It is not clear whether or not these have weakened Chávez politically, but surveys and opinion polls do show concern that this and other measures could contribute to those tendencies aiming at curtailing the right to freedom of speech.

These and other conflicts that have developed since the President's announcement of the radicalization of the Bolivarian process make the situation open-ended and difficult to predict. Chávez continues to enjoy strong support and legitimacy, which suggests that he will continue with his strategy of accelerating as far as he can the process of change through a centralization and concentration of decision-making power in his own hands. But it is also true that the society's organizational and participative dynamism, as seen both in those sectors allied to the president and in those of the opposition, may force him to rectify his practice in some aspects. Some actors, such as the university students' movement, began to mobilize at the end of May in order to express their dissatisfaction and demands in a less polarized way than in the past. Some new developments have also occurred within Chavism – for example, some of the pro-government political parties have rejected the presidential demand that they should join the PSUV without discussion, and have not dissolved themselves; and the President has himself stated that the constitutional reform may take more than a year before its definitive approval; all these facts can be seen as reflecting resistance to various presidential proposals.

Insofar as reforms and policies are opened up to the broadest participation of Venezuelans, they will guarantee greater viability, legitimacy and move in the desired direction. The better the procedures, the surer the attainment of the purposes of a better and deeper participative democracy.

NOTES

1   See, for example, Miriam Kornblith, *Venezuela en los 90. La crisis de la democracia*, Caracas: Ediciones UCV-IESA, 1998; Ángel Eduardo Álvarez, ed., *El sistema político venezolano: crisis y transformaciones*, Caracas: Ediciones de la Universidad Central de Venezuela, 1996; Steve Ellner and Daniel Hellinger, eds., *La política venezolana en la época de Chávez*, Caracas: Nueva Sociedad, 2003; Margarita López Maya, *Del Viernes Negro al Referendo Revocatorio*, Caracas: Alfadil, 2005.

2   For details on the struggle over oil and the oil reform, see Luis E. Lander, ed., *Poder y petróleo en Venezuela*, Caracas: FACES UCV-PDVSA, 2003.

3   See the quotes from Roland Denis and the discussion in Jonah Gindin, 'Chavistas in the Halls of Power, Chavistas on the Street', *NACLA Report on the Americas*, 38(5), 2005, also available at http://www.venezuelanalysis.com.

4   Data on the election available from the Consejo Nacional Electoral at http://www.cne.gov.ve.

5   The Tables 1 and 2 are taken from Margarita López Maya and Luis E. Lander, 'Venezuela: las elecciones presidenciales de 2006, ¿hacia el socialismo del siglo XXI?'. Paper presented in the Seminar *América Latina 2006: Balance de un año de elecciones II* at CEPC-Universidad de Salamanca, Madrid, Spain, 12-13 December 2006.

6   'PDVSA', in *Últimas Noticias*, 21 January 2007.

7   Gregory Wilpert, 'The Meaning of 21st Century Socialism for Venezuela', 11 July 2006, available at www.venezuelanalysis.com.

8   Ibid.

9   *El Nacional*, 27 August 2006.

10   Ernesto Laclau, *La razón populista*, Buenos Aires: FCE, 2005.

11   'Hugo Chávez Frías: Discurso sobre el Partido Socialista Unido de Venezuela', speech at Teatro Teresa Carreño, Caracas, 15 December 2006, transcriptión of TV Prensa, December 2006, in Venezuela Analítica, available at www.analitica.com.

12   Ibid.

13   'Vamos rumbo a la República Socialista de Venezuela', in *Aporrea*, 8 January 2007, http://www.aporrea.org; 'Discurso del Presidente en la juramentación del 10 de enero de 2007', 10 January 2007, available from www.minci.gov.ve.

14   He also announced changes in the cabinet, with the exit of José Vicente Rangel, Jesse Chacón, Aristóbulo Istúriz and other key figures during his first term as president. No information was given about why these changes happened; they were the object of much comment as some of these ministers – Rangel, Istúriz – were key players to Chávez's first period. None of the remaining or new ministers have the political status – i.e., the capacity to talk as equals with Chávez – of Rangel or Istúriz, or indeed Alí Rodríguez, who had also left the government a few months before.

15   'Presidente Chávez juró cumplir su mandato dentro del contexto del socialismo', in *Agencia Bolivariana de Noticias*, 10 January 2007, available at www.abn.info.ve.

16   Endogenous nuclei are territorial units where the government stimulates productive activities which are meant to take advantage of local socioeconomic, geographic and environmental conditions. The people or communities that establish such units receive various kinds of assistance from the government because they are supposed to be nuclei for the development of a new kind of socialist individual operating in a new kind of new economy. Until now they depend on government resources.

17   'Juramentación del Presidente de la República Bolivariana de Venezuela, Hugo Chávez Frías (período 2007-2013)', 15 January 2005, available from http://www.mci.gob.ve.

18   Ibid.

19   See Comisión de la Facultad de Ciencias Jurídicas y Políticas, UCV, 'La Ley Habilitante, por ser una "Ley de plenos poderes", está totalmente viciada de inconstitucionalidad', Caracas, February 2007, available from http://www.juri.ucv.ve.

20   In fact, this principle had already been weakened as a result of the use of the so-called 'morochas' (identical twins) lists.

21   Jesús Rojas, Interview in Caracas, 28 November 2006.

22   Bastidas in *El Nacional*, 5 February 2007.

23   'Gobierno asignó Bs 4 billones para los consejos comunales', *El Nacional*, 19 January 2007.

24   Josh Lerner, 'Communal Councils in Venezuela: Can 200 Families Revolutionize Democracy?', 19 March 2007, available at http://ww.venezuelanalysis.com.

BLOWS AND COUNTERBLOWS IN VENEZUELA

MARTA HARNECKER

The failure of the military coup in April 2002 (more than 80 per cent of the generals in operational positions remained faithful to Chávez and the constitution) constituted the first great defeat of the opposition and a real gift to Chávez. The new situation allowed for various actors to be unmasked and for the people to acquire a much higher level of political understanding – within both military and civilian cadres it was now known who could be counted on and who could not. It created favourable conditions in which to move forward with cleaning out the military. It divided the opposition. It reminded an ever-increasing number of the middle classes, who were previously against the process, of the anarchy which would result from the marginalization of Chávez.

The frustrated attempt to bring the country to a halt on December 2, 2002, was the second great defeat of the opposition. They could not bring the country to a halt. Chávez did not bow to their pressure. But most importantly, the oil industry came to be truly under the control of the Venezuelan state. This was the second great gift from the opposition. Due to their subversive and saboteur attitude, around 18,000 upper and middle-level managers who opposed the government – and who actually exercised control of the company – created the conditions in which they could be legally dismissed.

The ratification of President Chávez's mandate in the recall referendum of August 15, 2004 – a process without precedent in world history – was the third great defeat that the Venezuelan opposition suffered in attempting to terminate the government of President Chávez. The triumph, by a huge margin, and under the attentive gaze of hundreds of international observers, who unanimously ratified the results, was the third gift from the opposition.[1] It constituted, as one of the observers, the well-known Uruguayan writer Eduardo Galeano, put it, 'an injection of optimism in this world where democracy has lost so much prestige' due to the fact that it has been unable to resolve the problem of poverty.

It was not the victory of a single man, but rather of a humanist and solidarity-based project for the country, as much in the international as in the national arena; of a project for the country which had emerged as an alternative to the voracious and predatory neoliberal model – a model of endogenous development and social economy. It was a triumph of the current Venezuelan constitution, the only constitution in the world that contemplates the idea of a recall referendum for the presidency. But, above all else, it was a victory of the people, of popular organization, of the people from the barrios, but also of the people from the middle class, who responded to the call of the president to organize themselves in their local voting areas, taking the initiative without waiting to be constituted by the organizations that were heading the electoral campaign.

THE NEW POST-REFERENDUM STAGE

With this triumph, a new stage in the Bolivarian revolutionary process began. The media warmongers were left without ammunition. The opposition revealed itself; it lost a lot of credibility. Internal struggles between different factions intensified. But while the opposition had been defeated in this battle, it was clear that the forces supporting Chávez had not yet won the war. We must not forget that in a country of 26 million inhabitants, close to 4 million people voted in favour of revoking his mandate. Nor must we forget the expectations that were created by this triumph amongst the 6 million people who voted NO. The challenges to be met in this new stage were extremely varied: political, economic, institutional and communicational.

First, the Bolivarian revolutionary process had to make a qualitative leap forward in regard to the protagonistic participation of the people. President Chávez's most important idea – 'poverty cannot be eliminated if power is not given to the people' – needed to materialize in organizational forms and concrete participation. And that is what occurred. The concept of the communal councils emerged. On a rough estimate, Venezuela had around 52 thousand communities, and in each of these communities an entity needed to be elected which would play the role of a communitarian government. This entity was called the communal council, and a majority of them have already received government resources to begin carrying out small projects that the community has prioritized.

It was also crucial, secondly, to make headway with the development of a new productive model, as an alternative to capitalism. And that is what is occurring. Venezuela is being transformed from a country which survived on oil revenues and the export of primary materials, into a country with a solid agricultural and industrial base, which produces goods and services that are needed for popular consumption: a model based on new social relations of production that liberate wage labour from exploitation by capital, by promoting social production enterprises inspired by principles of solidarity, cooperation, complementarity, reciprocity, and economic and financial sustainability. A model that aspires to territorial balance, and harmonious and proportionate development of the regions, in order to overcome the housing problem and the degeneration of the five large cities in which 75 per cent of the population is concentrated. A model based on a new generation of basic goods companies oriented towards deepening endogenous development. I am referring to the creation of Compañía Nacional de Industrias Básicas (Coniba, National Company of Basic Industries) and its eleven affiliates, and the Corporación Petroquímica de Venezuela (Pequiven, Venezuelan Petrochemical Corporation), which aim to strengthen innovative technological capacities in order to transform primary materials into value-added products which will allow for import substitution and the diversification of exports. A model that promotes state investment in strategic industries like telecommunications (CVG Telecom) and those that have to do with food security and food sovereignty, such as Corporación Venezolana Agraria (CVA, Venezuelan Agrarian Corporation), the parent company of new enterprises in the agricultural sector. Meanwhile, a process of co-management has made notable advances in the electricity industry in the state of Merida, and in the aluminum company, ALCASA, in the state of Bolívar. And the number of factories closed by their owners and taken over by the workers has increased.

At the same time, one of the priority tasks is the need to solve the problem of employment. With this objective in mind, the state has being pushing forward with the reactivation of the private industrial sector which is willing to collaborate with the project of endogenous development and social economy proposed by the government. The framework of an agreement with this sector has been established, through which the government provides low-interest loans, as long as companies take on board their social responsibility, committing themselves to dedicating at least 10 per cent of their earnings to meeting the most pressing demands of the nearby communities.

Following the referendum there was a notable improvement in the correlation of forces in the institutional sphere. The results of the elections for governors and mayors were very positive for the government. The opposition now only governs two out of twenty-four states. All the deputies in the National Assembly are Bolivarian. The opposition candidates, seeing that they were going to lose, opted to not participate in the elections, hoping to discredit this legislative entity in doing so.

WEAKNESSES IN THE PROCESS

This quantitative accumulation of forces should have translated into a qualitative accumulation. An emphasis should have been placed on efficiency, on better performance in relation to the responsibilities that each person must assume in order to put into practice all the projects and initiatives announced by the government; but this is far from having been achieved. The old state model continues in force and, despite attempts by Chávez to change things, is very strong. The same is true of the issue of corruption.

Prior to the December 3, 2006 presidential elections little or no advance had been made in the formation of a political instrument better adapted to meeting the great challenges that the Bolivarian revolutionary process has set for itself. Disputes continued – and perhaps became even more acute – over positions at the different levels of leadership of the process. The Miranda Electoral Command, formed to lead the presidential electoral process, was hegemonized by the Movimiento V República (MVR, Movement for a Fifth Republic), provoking discontent among the other political parties that support the revolutionary process, as well as among the population. If anything, rather than advancing in the construction of a united instrument of the workers, the process took steps backward. Today, there continues to be too much dispersion. Old methods continue to be employed.

The opposition media outlets, which make up the great majority, exponentially magnify the errors and weaknesses of the government, and distort its project, re-creating a climate of opposition and influencing a significant number of Venezuelans. Of course the United States government – for whom Chávez has become a real obsession – has continuously been behind these campaigns.

Lastly, added to this daily and hourly media bombardment, was an opposition that finally began to unite around the figure of Manuel Rosales as the opposition presidential candidate for the December 2006 elections. Rosales, who had up till then been the governor of Zulia – one of the largest and most strategic states in the country, due to the fact that it shares a border with Colombia – carried out a well-orchestrated electoral campaign, promising to conserve all the good things that the Chávez government had done for the people, and demagogically announcing that he would also directly deposit into the bank account of every poor Venezuelan household a significant sum of money out of the oil revenues, so that instead of taking money out of the country to help other people, he would be handing it over to the people of Venezuela.

Becoming aware of all these limitations and obstacles, only weeks from polling day, the president began to personally assume the direction of the campaign, appearing everywhere in a tireless tour throughout the whole country, where the people of the barrios applauded him wildly. In the final two weeks of the campaign he began to involve the youth as the central motor of his campaign, and to point to this social sector as the moral force which would allow the process to overcome the vices that infected previous generations.

Although no one doubted that Chávez would win, given the notable gains that the Venezuelan people have obtained thanks to the Bolivarian government, for all the reasons just cited it seemed unlikely that the Bolivarian leader could secure a better electoral result than that achieved in the referendum. This appraisal of the situation was confirmed by a majority of the opinion polls, which made him the winner by a margin of some 20 per cent, the same 20 per cent as he had had more than two years earlier. Yet a clean election, with the lowest abstention rate in the political history of the country (less than 25 per cent), carried out under the attentive gaze of hundreds of international observers, ratified the mandate of the Venezuelan president by an overwhelming majority of votes. Hugo Chávez got 7 million votes, 1 million more than in the 2004 referendum, with the opposition, represented by Rosales, maintaining its 4 million votes. It was such a convincing victory that the US government had no other option but to recognize the triumph, publicly accepting that a democratic regime exists in Venezuela, and expressing its interest in establishing a positive and constructive relationship with the new government.[2]

This was Chávez's fourth great triumph, although this time it cannot be said that it was the fourth great defeat of the opposition because, although they lost, they came out strengthened from the battle. We need to accept that its most recognizable leaders demonstrated maturity in acknowledging their defeat with nobility, and stating their disposition to wage future battles within the rules of the game laid out by the Bolivarian constitution. For his part, President Chávez responded positively to these declarations, stating his disposition for dialogue, but 'without conditions or blackmail', and always so long as the opposition did not expect him to abandon his principles. 'Socialism of the 21st century is, and will continue to be, the objective we are aiming for', he affirmed.

THE CREATION OF A NEW PARTY OF THE REVOLUTION

In one of his first speeches after the election Chávez put forward 'as a strategic fundamental line, the deepening, widening and expansion of the Bolivarian Revolution... on the Venezuelan road to socialism', and made three fundamental announcements which reflect his clear awareness of the weaknesses that plague the political process in his country: the struggle against corruption and bureaucracy as two new strategic objectives of his government for the next period, and a call to construct the united party of the revolution.[3]

The first two announcements were not surprising, given that the president had repeatedly stated his preoccupation with these issues over the previous months, but the third announcement regarding his decision to create a new political party – which he provisionally called the United Socialist Party of Venezuela – was surprising. Not because he had not referred to the issue before, or had not discussed it with the leaders of all the political parties that supported him, but rather because the news was not preceded by a profound debate on the issue and because everyone was led to believe that what they would be dealing with, at least initially, would be more akin to the construction of a multiparty 'front', not a new political instrument that would imply the rapid dissolution of the existing parties, some with a long trajectory, such as the Communist Party.

But Chávez was very explicit: he rejected the idea of what he called 'a sum of acronyms', at the same time as he put forward the necessity to construct a new party with new figures elected from the grassroots. What we are dealing with, he said, is a political entity that would unite at its core all those Venezuelans willing to fight to construct socialism [in Venezuela]: whether they be militants from the political groups of the left, or members of the social movements, or those compatriots who up until this moment were either not members or, disappointed by the deviations and errors committed, had stopped being members, of some of the existing organizations.[4]

As part of this new political project tens of thousands of activists (Chávez called them 'promoters') travelled the country preparing a massive enrolment of all those who aspired to become members of the United Socialist Party of Venezuela, the largest in the history of the country. Up to June 3, one week before registration closed, more than 5 million people had enrolled. Unfortunately, everything seems to suggest that in order to obtain such a high figure, acts of 'stacking' or pressure were used on more than a few occasions, blurring the results obtained and causing discomfort amongst many people. The president has called on everyone to denounce this kind of behaviour, stating that it is necessary to 'take care of the process.... and denounce in time any deviation' which could cause a lot of damage in the future.

On the other hand during his 'Aló Presidente' television broadcast on Sunday, June 10, Chávez made it very clear that enrolment is one thing, while the later selection process of those who will go on to shape the new political instrument is another. His hope is that the leadership of the new party will be made up of tested militants, even if it will only be made up of a handful of people. What has not been discussed until now is who will carry out this selection, or how. At the moment, a review of all the enrolments is being conducted by the National Electoral Council (CNE). Afterwards, the registered members will meet in groups of 200 – the so-called 'socialist battalions' – to allow real, democratic participation by everyone, and to facilitate the selection from below of the best men and women from these battalions as *voceros* (spokespeople) at the Founding Congress. When it was previously calculated that some 4 million people would be enrolled as members it was estimated that around 22,000 socialist battalions would have to be constituted and that each battalion would elect a *vocero* to the regional assembly, which in turn would send *voceros* to the Congress. The Congress would therefore be made up of around 2,200 congress delegates. Today, given that inscriptions have risen to over 5 million, new calculations will have to be made. What this formula does not resolve is what will happen if several recognized leaders happen to be in the same community.

The Founding Congress is expected to last three months, debating all the issues related to the new party: its program, organizational forms, the type of membership and other issues, beginning with a debate over what type of country are they trying to build. After each session, these national *voceros* will go back to their respective grassroots assemblies to keep them informed and to deepen the debate at this level. It will be from these grassroots assemblies that those aspiring to fill positions at the different levels of leadership in the party will have to be nominated. No one who does not have support in their local base can be nominated to a position within this new political dispensation. It is expected that through this mechanism there will be a flowering of thousands of new faces, until now unknown, originating from the new leaderships emerging out of community work, workplaces and study centres.

THE FIVE MOTORS

On January 10, 2007, after being sworn in for his second presidential term, Chávez made another significant announcement: he proposed that the advance towards socialism of the 21st century should depend on 'five constituent motors'. The first would be the Enabling Law, which allows the executive to legislate on areas where this is necessary in order to speed up the transition to socialism. The second relates to the reform of the Bolivarian Constitution of Venezuela, which would allow, amongst other things, the modification of articles that in the economic and political sphere are not in accordance with the project of the socialist society whose construction is being attempted. There is nothing strange about the fact that the Bolivarian Constitution of 1999 has become too small for the revolutionary process, just as a child's clothes become too small as they grow up.

The third 'motor' envisages a campaign of moral, economic, political and social education called 'Morality and Enlightenment', which has to be as much present in territorial-based organizations (communal councils and other organizations) as in the workplace. The fourth, which the president called 'Geometry of Power', aims at revising the political-territorial arrangements of the country, generating the construction of city systems and federal territories with the objective of redistributing political, economic, social and military power more equitably across the national arena. The fifth, and most important, refers to 'The Revolutionary Explosion of Communal Power' and aims to promote communal councils and everything that has to do with popular power. According to the Venezuelan head of state, these five motors will be what drive the 'Bolivarian socialist project'.

ADVANCES IN NATIONALIZATION

In the last few months more progress has been made in the nationalization of companies than in the previous nine years of government, a dramatic move forward in the recovery of the country's economic sovereignty. 'Electricidad de Caracas', the largest company in the power sector, valued at $900 million, was nationalized. The US multinational AES signed an agreement with the Venezuelan government, handing over 82.14 per cent of its shares.[5] On May 1, 2007, the Venezuelan government also recovered its energy sovereignty by proceeding to nationalize the oil in the Orinoco Oil Belt, where the most important reserves in the world are located. There was a reduction of the power of the oil consortiums that operate in this region of the Orinoco river, where close to 400,000 barrels of oil are extracted daily, a figure which could rise to 600,000 barrels. This measure will affect various foreign companies. Those most affected will be the US companies Chevron, Exxon Mobil, Texaco and ConocoPhilips; the French company Total; the Norwegian Statoil; and the UK-based British Petroleum. For the Venezuelan company PDVSA, until now a minority partner in this consortium, the situation has been reversed: its share will now be 60 per cent.[6]

On June 8, 2007, Compañía Anónima Nacional Teléfonos de Venezuela (CANTV, the National Anonymous Telephone Company of Venezuela), the biggest private telephone company in the country, which had been publicly owned up until 1991, was renationalized. At the time of renationalization CANTV controlled 83 per cent of the internet market, 70 per cent of the national telephone communications market and 42 per cent of international calls. It owned close to 3 million telephone lines and 100,000 public telephones.[7] With this measure the Venezuelan state has advanced in the control of the strategic telecommunications sector. The renationalized company is attempting to extend telephone access to all areas of the country. In two years there will be a tripling of areas with fibre optic coverage. Its services will reach the most remote rural areas. As well as expanding the service, the aim is to make it accessible to the lowest income sectors, lowering the cost of calls.

VENEZUELAN YOUTH AND THE BATTLE OVER RCTV

During the night of May 27, the broadcasting concession granted to Radio Caracas Television, the most powerful opposition television station in the country, expired. I agree with the Venezuelan political analyst, Vladimir Acosta, that this was the second great revolutionary moment of the process after the recovery of control over oil in 2003.[8] To convert a private channel into a public service channel is not only a strong blow to the media hegemony of the Venezuelan opposition, it is also an act 'that goes to the heart of global power', because today this fundamentally depends on the mass media. Without a media monopoly to fabricate a consensus, the supremacy of this global power is enormously weakened.[9] This is why there has been such a virulent conservative reaction at the global level.

The measure was announced by Chávez months in advance. The opposition immediately prepared its response. It tried to make citizens believe that, with this act, freedom of expression would be mortally wounded, and that the government was advancing in an accelerated manner towards a dictatorial regime. After attempting various mobilizations of the adult sector, none of which achieved the scale hoped for, a new political subject appeared on the streets of Caracas: the students. Thousands of them, the majority coming from the private universities, came out onto the streets protesting against what they called the 'closure' of Radio Caracas Television. Although their intentions were peaceful, a group of them provoked disturbances, lighting bonfires in the streets, blocking traffic and forcing police forces to intervene to maintain order. Images of confrontations between students and police travelled the globe, as more proof of the authoritarian character of the government. What was not reported was the fact that most of those injured belonged to the police, who had assumed a dignified attitude, not allowing themselves to be provoked.

But what do these students represent? Are we dealing with a mere apolitical movement, as they themselves and the opposition media want people to believe? The strategy of the opposition has been, on one hand, to 'present the students as a unified mass', and on the other, to maintain their separation from the student movement, in order to underscore its independent and spontaneous character.[10] The first element of this strategy was rapidly pulled apart by an important sector of the students who supported the measure adopted by the government. They came out on the streets on a mass scale. In regards to the second element, new evidence is emerging daily which reveals the behind-the-scenes intervention of the opposition. There are not only re-corded telephone conversations and intercepted electronic messages which reveal their plans to use the students for political purposes, but there is also in addition irrefutable proof provided by one of the students' own leaders.

The small group of student leaders who protested the 'closure' of RCTV, convinced by media propaganda that the chavistas are against freedom of expression in Venezuela, decided to demand an audience with the Nation-al Assembly, believing that this initiative would be rejected. To their sur-prise, the opposite occurred: Cilia Flores, the president of the Parliament, broadened the proposal, deciding that the event would be used to open up a debate between students from the opposition and those supporting the government's measure. In an unprecedented gesture the National Assembly opened its doors to the students so that they could come and debate. It was decided that each current would be granted ten minutes to speak. The op-position students entered wearing red shirts, which was strange given that red is the color which has identified chavistas. Afterwards it was discovered why: 'far more than a safety strategy, they were an integral part of a profes-sionally-designed media strategy'.[11] The platform was given first to Douglas Barrios, a student at the Universidad Metropolitana, a university known for admitting only the elite of society. After a speech lacking in any substance, in which he called for a process of national reconciliation, he ended by say-ing that he 'dreams of a country where people are taken into consideration without having to wear a uniform', and having finished this phrase, he and the groups of opposition students removed their red shirts, allowing every-one to see the white shirts they had on underneath, covered with various slogans defending RCTV.

All this could have been interpreted to be an original, theatrical act of protest, if it had not been for the fact that the last sheet of his speech was left behind on the podium. On it, very precise instructions were given as to how they should conduct themselves in the National Assembly. The text was signed by ARS Publicity, a company owned by the Globovision group, which was implicated in the April 2002 coup. Taking off their red shirts, only speaking once, and then leaving immediately – all these were actions outlined in the instructions. This last action was halted, at least for the duration of the following speaker, due to the pressure exerted on them to stay by the chavista students and the deputies of the National Assembly. The self-proclaimed defenders of democracy were not capable of democratically debating; they made only one intervention and then retired from the scene. The self-proclaimed independents were actually pawns of Globovision. We should not assume, however, that all the students that marched against the decision not to renew the concession are as hypocritical as the student opposition leaders. It is quite likely most of them are open to healthy debate and to reconsidering their position on the Bolivarian project for society under President Chávez's leadership.

The events in Parliament not only put into relief the strategy of the opposition, but also, more importantly, revealed the remarkable student leadership that has been emerging in the country. One after the other, the ten student speakers supporting the measure adopted by the government began to dismantle, one by one, the arguments of the opposition, with freshness, intelligence, creativity and, above all, forcefulness. Who can argue, for example, with what the next speaker, Andreína Tarazón, from the Universidad Central de Venezuela, said, when she criticized the behaviour of the opposition students, comparing their conduct in not facing up to the debate, with that of Condoleezza Rice during the meeting of the OAS, where she spoke and then left?

Those watching television, who saw this live via a national broadcast on all frequencies, must have felt a strong impact thanks to the quality of the interventions. They were so good that it was not long before they began to be distributed via the internet. Thousands of people in all parts of the world were able to be impressed by the words of Andreína and her comrades. She became one of Venezuela's best ambassadors. But the blow dealt to the media by the left could not go unpunished. A few days later YouTube suspended the account of the user named 'Lbracci', through which this experience had been distributed in video format.[12]

On the other hand, new spaces for debate are opening up in all corners of the country. And the youth sectors are proving in practice that democracy exists in Venezuela. Once again, an attack by the opposition has had a very positive outcome for the Bolivarian process: a new social actor, full of force, of ideals, has entered the political sphere. There is no doubt that the students who support the government have everything to win: a project for a more humanistic and solidarity-based country, that puts its efforts into eliminating inequalities; that calls for the exercise of greater social control over all activities in order to struggle against the scourge of corruption; that restores the sovereignty of the homeland. It is a project that the Venezuelan youth cannot afford to be indifferent towards.

NOTES

This essay, forthcoming in Spanish in the 2007 *Abiven Yearbook,* was translated by Federico Fuentes for http://www.venezuelanalysis.com.

1   Among the most important groups present were: the European Union, the Carter Center, and the Organization of American States (OAS). Chávez obtained the support of around 6 million people; around 4 million voted in favour of revoking his mandate.

2   The United States expressed via Sean McCormack, spokesperson for the State Department, its desire to a have a 'positive' and 'constructive' relationship with the Bolivarian government. 'We congratulate the Venezuelan people for its conduct during this election', he declared, also expressing his desire to 'work with the government of President Chávez'. This seems to be a radical change given that not long ago, Washington classified Chávez as a 'destabilizing force for the region'.

3   Speech given at the Act of Recognition for the Miranda Command, 15 December 2006.

4   Hugo Chávez, 'Nota introductoria al libro El discurso de la unidad', 15 December 2006, Ediciones *Socialismo del Siglo XXI*, No. 1, Caracas, 2007.

5   Salim Lamrani, 'Se abre una nueva era en Venezuela', 26 February 2007, http://www.rebelión.org.

6   See Salim Lamrani, 'Soberanía petrolera, reformas sociales e independencia económica en Venezuela', 15 May 2007, http://www.rebelión.org.

7   Agencia Bolivariana de Noticias, 'Queremos que Cantv sea una empresa tan eficiente como PDVSA', 11 January 2007; Agencia Bolivariana de Noticias, 'gobierno nacional dio primer paso hacia nacionalización de la Cantv', 12 February 2007.

8   Vladimir Acosta, 'La no renovación de RCTV es un hecho revolucionario porque toca al corazón del poder mundial', Interview by Marcelo Colussi, *Argenpress*, June 2007.

9   The term 'fabricating consensus' was used by Walter Lippmann in *Public Opinion*, London: Allen and Unwin, 1932 and cited by Noam Chomsky in *Cómo nos venden la moto*, Barcelona: Icaria, 1996, p. 14, who also wrote a book entitled 'Manufacturing Consent'.

10   Georges Ciccariello-Maher, 'Who's Pulling the Strings behind Venezuela's "Student Rebellion"', *Counterpunch*, 9/10 June 2007, available from http://counterpunch.org.

11   Ibid.

12   Carlos Martínez, 'Antena 3 y YouTube censuran un debate sobre la no renovación de la concesión a RCTV', 12 June 2007, available from http://mrzine.monthlyreview.org.

THE CLASS STRUGGLES IN BRAZIL: THE PERSPECTIVE OF THE MST

JOÃO PEDRO STÉDILE
INTERVIEWED BY ATILIO BORON

Atilio Boron (AB): *The Socialist Register has long had a great appreciation of the Landless People's Movement in Brazil and of your role as a leader of the MST. We feel it is very important for readers of the Register in particular to learn more about the MST strategies and tactics to resist neoliberalism's encroachments, so we want to focus this interview on how the MST has reacted to the neoliberal policies carried out in Brazil by the Cardoso and Lula governments. But perhaps we should start by asking you for a panoramic overview of the evolution of class struggles in contemporary Brazil, in order to put this in an adequate historical perspective.*

João Pedro Stédile (JP): The MST and Via Campesina have developed a common understanding, a common reading, of the historical evolution of capitalism in Brazil.[1] We had four centuries of what might be called the 'agro-export model', which was inaugurated by colonial capitalism. Industrial capitalism was not really implanted until 1930, and as Florestan Fernandes said, it was a model of dependent industrialization, because it was so highly dependent on foreign capital.[2] It was not the result of local accumulation. It lasted until the early 1980s, and was quite successful insofar as in those fifty years the Brazilian economy grew at an annual average rate of 7.5 per cent. But by the early '80s it fell into a crisis – part of the general crisis of that model. Many people say that crisis still remains unresolved, because in the 27 years since then the Brazilian economy as a whole has become relatively paralyzed, growing only at 2-2.5 per cent per year. Others say that the Brazilian dominant classes have succeeded in implementing a new economic model – the neoliberal model. Even though we know that in practice this is a model that subordinates the Brazilian economy to international capital, especially financial capital, in our view we have made another transition in the last ten years. There is now a new economic model in Brazil in which

the most dynamic sector of the economy, aimed at the export business –
represented by the largest 200 firms, each of them embodying the alliance
between international capital, the banks and the large Brazilian economic
groups – has been growing at an average of 7 per cent per year. These 200
firms control 52 per cent of the economy and 78 per cent of all our exports.
This has been the economic journey of Brazil in the long historical period,
with the transition to neoliberalism leaving us today with an economy in
crisis for two decades but containing a dynamic pole that is growing very
fast, and reinforcing the dichotomy that exists between the interests of big
capital and the economy as a whole, an economy that should be solving the
general problems of the population.

There is, though, another reading of Brazilian history: the reading of class
struggles. The MST and Via Campesina, especially, work with the theory
of waves or cycles of the class struggle, as Lenin understood it in his own
time. A quick glance at the Brazilian history of class struggle in the past century shows that when the agro-export model entered into a crisis it brought
about an important wave of popular unrest. Many important social forces
were born; unions, political parties of the left, both socialist and communist,
emerged; and important actions took place, like Luís Carlos Prestes' 'Long
March' through the rural Brazilian interior, which mobilized broad segments
of the peasantry right across the country over a period of five or six years
during the 1920s. All this produced a big mass organization called Aliança
Nacional Libertadora, representing a broad working-class offensive – against
capital and for an alternative project. The rise of the popular movement led
to a clash with the dominant classes in 1935. By then the industrialization
model had already been consolidated and, led by Vargas, the bourgeoisie
unleashed a coup and smashed all the social and workers' movements. The
majority of their leaders were imprisoned, exiled or shot. Prestes, the great
leader of that first mobilizational wave, was held from 1936 to 1945 in soli-
tary confinement, under subhuman conditions.

This period of defeat – marking a descending wave of the class struggle –
ended in 1945, as the ascendancy of progressive and socialist forces in Europe
after World War Two also had an impact on Brazil; and this gave birth to a
new wave of mass mobilization in our country. The Communist Party was
revived, the Peasant Leagues were founded, the central labour organization
was rebuilt – indeed, all the class organizations were reconstructed. This
inaugurated a period of intense class struggle which lasted until 1964, when
a new confrontation or clash with the dominant classes took place and we
were once more defeated, this time by the military dictatorship, leading to
another phase of decline and disorganization of the mass movements. The

same scenario was played out again: leaders like Leonel Brizola, Luiz Carlos Prestes, Apolônio Carvalho and Carlos Marighella, among others, were exiled, jailed or killed. The downward movement lasted until 1978/79, when the industrial model began to show the first signs of crisis, creating the objective conditions for the working classes to begin to reorganize and fight: first against the dictatorship and then against the model. From 1979 on we witnessed a new impulse of social struggles, the rebirth of working-class organizations, the founding of the new Workers' Party, the PT, and the new trade union federation, the CUT. It is significant that the MST, while we were also the historical heirs of peasant movements that had emerged in the earlier phase and had been defeated in 1964 and later disappeared, was also born at this time as a part of the rise of the mass movements, a child of the accumulation of forces in a new period of upturn in the class struggle.

This new ascending cycle of the class struggle lasted until 1989. The peak of our accumulation of forces was the '*diretas já!*' campaign (a huge social movement demanding the direct election of the President) which between 1984 and 1989 was able to organize street meetings attended by two million people. There was great mobilization and political effervescence in the country. But all that ended with the victory of the *diretas já!* and the electoral competition of 1989. That election was about a lot more than a choice between two electoral projects: it was a confrontation between two different class projects. On the one side there was Lula, embodying a popular project to solve the crisis, and on the side of the dominant classes, we had Collor de Melo, as the unifying force around neoliberalism. Thus, when we were defeated in 1990 it was not only an electoral defeat. Collor's victory was much more than that, insofar as it signalled the end of the period of ascent. It was the defeat of a popular project, and the two successive electoral victories of Fernando Henrique Cardoso (FHC) ratified this defeat.

The new period of downturn has lasted until today – 17 years. The only popular sector that has managed to resist somewhat has been the peasant movement, because we focused on a struggle for the land, against the latifundia, and at first this was not seen as a problem for financial capital. Initially, our actions did not disturb them and they did not pay much attention to us. They said 'let those poor devils of the countryside fight the latifundio', and that was what allowed us to grow, even in a downturn in the class struggle. When everybody was demobilized, we were the only ones that were able to keep our struggles going. We projected a shadow much bigger than what we really were, and we became famous for that. In fact, the MST as an organized force of the workers in Brazil is very small: we cannot even organize all the landless of Brazil, who number four million. But since the others did not fight and we kept fighting, it was as if the small soccer team had started to play in the Premier League! We were the only ones really ready to confront the dominant classes, although some small sectors of the working classes also tried to do so, most notably in 1995, as soon as Fernando Henrique Cardoso won the elections, when the workers of the state-owned oil monopoly launched a national strike that lasted 20 days. FHC sent the troops to occupy all the oil refineries, militarized the conflict and smashed the workers. This strike was a symbol of the defeat of the working classes by neoliberalism.

AB: *It was the exact equivalent of what Thatcher did with the miners' strike in Britain.*

JP: Exactly the same. But there was an aggravation in the case of Brazil, which appeared to be emblematic of the cycle of defeat in our eyes: the oil workers remained more isolated and alone than the British miners. Nobody supported their struggle, except for the MST. Even Lula and the head of the CUT at that time, Vicentinho, made public statements saying that 'this is not a time for strikes' which appeared in all the newspapers at the time. We could thus see, already in those years, the ideological vacillations and the abandonment of the last sector of the working class which had the courage to oppose neoliberalism. And the defeat of the oil workers was a disaster for the working-class movement because the people saw the beginnings of labour flexibilization and outsourcing in the production process. Petrobrás, which before the strike employed 80,000 workers, laid off half of them after the strike; now it employs only 15,000. All the rest, about 80.000 in total, have been 'outsourced'. In other words, it was a major defeat of the class.

AB: *How then should we explain Lula's victory?*

JP: This is the classic question posed by everybody coming from abroad: how can you explain that Lula, a left-wing candidate, won the elections in 2002? How is it possible to win elections, with a candidate like Lula, in a period of downturn in the mass movement? Eric Hobsbawm asked this question when he visited us. As a historian of the working class who studied the history of waves of labour unrest in the twentieth century, he told us that the left only wins elections when the mass movement is on the rise, because then elections are transformed into one of the trenches of the class struggle. Nowhere in the world did the workers win elections in a phase of decline, as we can see with the elections in France this year. In Spain, Zapatero could not have won the elections as he did without hundreds of thousands of Spaniards taking to the streets against Aznar. They defeated the right in the streets. When the masses take over the streets the most progressive parties can win elections.

How then to explain Lula's victory in 2002? There are several factors which explain this anomaly – ideological, political and economic factors that created the conditions for Lula to win the elections, and afterwards, almost for the same reasons, to win again in the 2006 elections.

First, we need to put the 2002 election in the context of the Argentina revolt that mobilized hundred of thousands with pans in the streets (the '*cacerolazos*'), and ousted a president. The fear experienced by the Brazilian bourgeoisie at this time reflected their knowledge that their economic model was the same as that of the Argentinian bourgeoisie. They panicked with the Argentina crisis. It was for this reason that the bourgeoisie took the decision to go with Lula rather than Serra. They said to themselves: if Serra wins the elections and deepens neoliberal policies the outcome could be the same as Argentina, and this is too risky for us. It was too risky precisely because Brazilian society is not as stratified as Argentina, which is classically organized along capitalist lines in terms of a dominant class, middle classes and working classes. In a word: Argentina is an organized society. Brazil is not. Here we have 140 million poor and disorganized people, and the day they decide to rise and rebel nobody could control it, not even Jesus Christ! As our bourgeoisie is not foolish they know this quite well. But they were helped in this by the conversion to neoliberalism, alongside the rise of FHC, of many of those who had been our intellectuals in the ascending wave of the cycle. Former Marxist intellectuals – FHC himself, Francisco Weffort, José Arthur Giannotti, lots of them – changed sides, joined the government and became counsellors and advisers of the bourgeoisie, while still preserving a good command of Marxist concepts and theories of classes and class struggles.

The second factor in the explanation is that part of the Brazilian bourgeoisie realized that the principal goal of neoliberalism, the privatization of the strategic, large state-owned firms, had already been achieved. Having already taken over the critical firms in industry and finance, the most lucid sector of the bourgeoisie allied with Lula in practical and objective ways. It was an alliance that was political, supporting his candidacy, and economic as well. What is quite telling is that in 1998 Lula's presidential campaign spent only 8 million reais. It was a very modest, poorly-funded campaign, and depended on the mobilization of activists. We finished the campaign with a debt of 6 million, and the PT had to pay that debt with contributions from the congressmen and general activists. But in the 2002 campaign the PT spent 80 million reais, when the real was equal to one dollar. That was a lot of money. Where did this money come from? From the bourgeoisie who had decided to support Lula.

The third factor in the explanation, and the most important one, on which the above two rested, was that the PT, as the hegemonic force of the Brazilian left, abandoned the popular and socialist project, and moved towards the center. This ideological conversion removed the last fears that the PT might represent something threatening to the dominant classes.

AB: *What then are the MST's new challenges in light of this situation, especially taking into account the massive changes that have taken place in Brazilian agriculture?*

JP: This has to be seen in the context of the way in which MST had already inserted itself in the class struggle. More specifically, having emerged with the ascending cycle of the class struggle, we continued to fight even during the downturn, and our fame came precisely for that reason, which means that our reputation is larger than our effective force. Now, after the period of struggle against latifundio, the MST is confronting a much larger challenge. In fact, we are facing a veritable political cross-roads. Why?

Because from the time of our birth through the early 1990s, and up to the FHC government, our principal political thesis was that the MST must fight for a democratic and republican agrarian reform. That is, the movement tried to organize the poor in the countryside to ensure that they all gained access to the right to own the land, to work for themselves, produce their own food and sustain their families. That right is a republican one, not a socialist one. Strictly speaking, the agrarian reform we defended, and which was fought for everywhere in Latin America, was a republican project – although not a bourgeois one, because the bourgeoisie only defends private property for itself, it does not defend the democratization of the means of production. But it was republican in the sense that since the land is a gift of nature, not a classic means of production resulting from work, all the members of a society that owns a given territory should have the right to the land.

This being the case, what has changed in the last eight to ten years? It was a slow, barely visible process which made it difficult to have an appropriate understanding of the changes affecting the entire Brazilian society. What changed was that our enemy was no longer the old *latifundiários*, the big owners of large tracts of land who excluded us from access to the land. In the last ten years land and agriculture have come under the sway of neoliberalism: both were subsumed within the scope of the process of accumulation of large transnational enterprise and big financial capital. All around the world financial capital started to penetrate firms and economic units working in agriculture. This did not only happen in Brazil, but worldwide.

There was an excess of financial capital in the advanced capitalist econo-mies, accumulated thanks to the external debt and all the brutal transfer of resources from the South during the 1980s and 1990s (some calculations suggest that in the 1990s alone Latin America made a net transfer of one tril-lion dollars to the United States). So financial capital, which had previously limited its circulation to the core capitalist economies, now started to make inroads in the firms and corporations working in agriculture in the South, buying their stock on the exchanges of several countries. Take the case of Monsanto. Financial capital, especially American financial capital, began to purchase the stock of several firms involved in agricultural activities: one devoted to seeds, another to the production of herbicides, a third specialized in agricultural trade – and in a short span of time financial capital became the owner of 20 or 30 firms working in different branches of agriculture. And when it became the majority owner in them financial capital said: 'all of you are now Monsanto'. The Monsanto we know today is not the fruit of its own agricultural accumulation but the fruit of financial capital that was introduced into its veins and brought together these 30-odd original firms to make what today is Monsanto. I have the list of these firms. And who is today the 'owner' of Monsanto. It is not as in the past, family X or family Y. No, today the owner of Monsanto is financial capital.

The rise of financial capital quite swiftly brought about two major move-ments in the firms working in agriculture: first, business concentration took place very fast, with very few enterprises working in each sector; and sec-ondly, it unleashed the accelerated centralization of capital. Thus, Monsanto, which originally devoted itself only to trade in soy beans, today has a pres-ence in about 30 different branches of agriculture. Monsanto controls the production of herbicides and pesticides, and buys and sells soy beans, maize, wheat, sunflower, animal medicine, etc. A shining example is that one of the major firms devoted to this is Pfizer, which manufactures medicines both for humans and for livestock. Well, Monsanto is a major stock holder of Pfizer, Conversely, Pfizer also is owner of a large quantity of stocks of Monsanto. What made these two giants unite? Financial capital, which has bought both of them and promoted their unification in practice, if not in legal terms. Therefore, Monsanto is a huge conglomerate that works in several areas under the impulses provided by financial capital.

As a result of this process of capital concentration and centralization in Brazilian agriculture in the last five years a new mode of production in agriculture has been introduced which we now know by the name of 'agri-business'. When an association of firms involved in agriculture was founded it called itself 'Associação Brasileira de Agribusiness'; the Public Notary in charge of the registration of the association rejected the request, saying that 'agribusiness' was not a word in Portuguese. Well, they simply translated the word into 'agronegócios' and went on. This translation created a lot of confusion because in the dictionary 'agronegócios' means any commercial operation in agricultural goods. And, therefore, many in the media, in government, in multinationals or academia, hypocritically argued that 'any peasant in Brazil is involved in agribusiness!' But this is nonsense: in Brazil agribusiness is much more than simple trade in corn or wheat. It is a new mode of production in agriculture. Let me open a parenthesis: sociologists and historians of the colonial period created the concept of 'plantation' to explain a mode of production with slave labour. The concept of agribusiness, as applied to Brazil, refers to a mode of capitalistic agriculture that has as its major feature the big transnational firms that are the main actors.

The role of these primarily foreign-owned firms is to supply the necessary inputs that make production possible. They provide the tractors and heavy machinery needed for the exploitation of agriculture (all tractor manufacturers in Brazil are foreign-owned firms); the fertilizers; the herbicides; the seeds; and they guarantee the market. They say: 'don't worry. I will buy all your production'. But it is this handful of huge transnational firms which set the price of agricultural goods. It is not a market. These firms guarantee for the producers the realization of the commodities they produce, but the price is set by them. And they do not act alone. They have important partners in the person of the Brazilian landowner, the 'fazendeiro' capitalista. The multinational firms say to the Brazilian landowner: 'you provide the land; you super-exploit the peasants, rural workers, tractor drivers and the labour force in general; you do what you want with the environment, I have nothing to do with that; I will give you all the necessary inputs and in exchange you will give me your produce'. This alliance is what gave birth to agribusiness in Brazil: transnational firms provide the inputs and guarantee the realization of the produce, and the landowners provide the rest.

Incidentally, since the transnational firms provide the seeds the landowner is, from the technological point of view, locked into the system because of patent law in Brazil. The common seeds we use (called 'creole seeds') are a public good, but the transgenic seeds provided by the big firms are patented as private property (of course, this is itself an absurdity! Just by patenting a technique this makes them owners of a living being – which is what a seed really is). Anyone still can stick to the 'creole' seed. It is not necessary to buy the transgenic seed. But in that case he must pay royalties. In my state, Rio Grande do Sul, soy bean farmers don't use the transgenic seed but at the time of selling their produce Monsanto makes a test on the soy beans and if the seeds were not bought from it an 8 per cent royalty fee is charged. In Rio Grande do Sul every year we pay just 80 million dollars in seed royalties!

On the other hand, the Brazilian 'fazendeiro' is led to super-exploit his labour force. For example: the tractor driver working for him earns 600 reais monthly, about $300. The tractor driver looks around and says to himself: 'in a country with millions who are unemployed and badly paid, I am ok, I should be satisfied'. But this is a fetish that prevents him from seeing the super-exploitation involved. Dependency theory helps to explain this as follows: The product of the alliance between the transnational firms and the local landowners is the soy bean, and it is sold in the international market. It is internationally priced, there is an average price for soy and a world-wide average rate of profitability for the soy business. Our soy competes against soy from the US, where a tractor driver earns $1,000, or against soy produced in France where the same tractor driver earns $2,000, and against soy produced in Argentina where a tractor driver earns $500, while the Brazilian earns $300. This is the super-exploitation imposed on our labour force, because given international price formation in the soy business, the wage of a tractor driver should be something like the average of the wages in the US, France and all the rest.

No different is the super-exploitation of the environment. Just as in the North they use technologies that reduce the use of labour to increase profitability, here the predatory use of agricultural techniques also prevails, with intensive use of machinery that compacts the land and intensive use of pesticides that poison the land. They could employ peasants and agricultural workers instead, but landowners don't want to. They use poison that slowly penetrates the lower layers of the land and the water that flows from it. Moreover, this type of production imposes monoculture, soy for instance, suppressing biodiversity. The problem is that soy is a plant that does not accept cohabitation with any other type of plant. This produces all kind of detrimental effects on the environment. Diversity of plants helps to absorb the water produced by rainfall. Single-crop agriculture absorbs much less, creating the conditions for floods and allowing the land to be washed away by the rain. The suppression of biodiversity also affects the rain cycles as well as contributing to global warming.

What happened here was the imposition of a model of agribusiness in a manner not unlike what Lenin saw as the imposition of the 'Junker road' to capitalism in the nineteenth century. The backward 'latifundiários', who because of their old ways and shortage of capital had devoted themselves to cattle-raising, now received capital from transnational firms which furnished them with seeds, tractors, etc. Where did these firms get the money for this large operation? From the banks, from the financial capitalists who played a fundamental role in all this. Not even Monsanto had the capital to advance such large sums of money to our *latifundiários*. Therefore, what we had in Brazil was a type of 'Junker road' that transformed our old landowning class into capitalist entrepreneurs. In the past the MST had fought against the backward landowner and occupied his land in order to start a long process aimed at his disappropriation – *desapropriação*. (We use this term in the MST to signify that we do not seek expropriation ('*expropriação*') since this signifies that we regard the original 'appropriation' of the land to have been illegitimate.) But the MST is now fighting on a new terrain and against new enemies. We have realized that our struggle against the backward *latifundiários* is not enough because they were transformed as they were drawn into expanding the frontier of capitalist agriculture.

Take the case of Rio Grande do Sul, similar in some respects to the Argentine humid pampa, marked by cattle-raising latifundia. We occupied those lands. In 20 years of struggle we seized 100,000 hectares and settled 10,000 families. But in the last five years the new agribusinesses, in this case oriented toward the production of cellulose, bought 300,000 hectares. We occupied the latifundia in the night; the next day the fazendeiro perceived that our force was superior to his and went to the nearest city to sell his land to the transnationals. And when you went to reoccupy the land it was already fully planted with eucalyptus. And the peasants know only too well that once the land has been planted with eucalyptus its agricultural productivity will be almost zero, useless for cultivation. Even with a lot of work, and money, you would still need many years to make that land productive again, and even then only perhaps for some trees, fruit, etc. – not for grain.

Our struggle is also against a capitalist coalition that goes to the frontier to seize land and plant eucalyptus, soy and sugar cane for the production of ethanol, as here in São Paulo. With Bush's promotion of a US-Brazilian 'alliance' to promote biofuel production during his recent visit to Brazil, it was as if they had received a green light to move full speed ahead.[3] In São Paolo they have 4 million hectares of sugar cane. Now, they are planning to expand this to 6.6 million hectares, an increase of 50 per cent in three years – all in order to use sugar cane to produce ethanol.

AB: *Given these very significant changes, what happened under the first Lula term in office and how did you react to it?*

JP: Under FHC, with his classic neoliberalism, the MST continued its fight and our goal was a classic agrarian reform of the republican type. But we caught a glimpse then that things were starting to change quite fast. Since

Cardoso was very intelligent and perceived that the MST had the support of Brazilian society, and that we were strong, he sought advice from the World Bank and started to apply a policy of social compensation. He did not adopt a classic policy of agrarian reform himself, because he knew that model had been superseded by history. When we organized and took over farms he tried to solve the social problem in the following manner: he started to accept some of our occupations and paid cash, immediately, to the *fazendeiro*. It was a very good deal for the agricultural capitalist: he received the money from the government, and used it to buy new, and better, tracts of land elsewhere, or invested the money in some other business. This was what happened under FHC.

With Lula, we still had in mind the classic agrarian reform. Plínio de Arruda Sampaio, one of the greatest intellectuals in Brazil and one of the founders of the PT, was commissioned to develop an agrarian reform plan along classic lines. The goal of the National Plan of Agrarian Reform, which was presented to the government in 2003, was to settle 1,000,000 families within four years. This unleashed a big debate within the government. The government's whole economic team, then headed by Antonio Palocci as finance minister and to this day dominated by neoliberal ideas, opposed the plan, on the grounds it was too costly. It was denounced as a public expenditure that would jeopardize the 'superavit primário' (the primary fiscal surplus).[4] They claimed that the government had the money only for settling 80,000 families. Lula, as he had done all his life, as a union negotiator, applied his time-honoured formula: 'Let's cut it in half', and said he would compromise by settling 400,000 families. Of course, we accepted the deal, because in 20 years of struggle we had settled 400,000 peasant families, and if the government had kept its promise to settle another 400,000 families in the next four years that would have meant great progress for the MST.

What happened in these first four years of Lula's government? There was a permanent tension between the neoliberal wing of the government, whose bulwark was the Ministry of Finance, on the one hand, and the people at the Ministry of Agrarian Development (MDA), who still had in mind the classic program of agrarian reform, on the other. At this point we were allied to the MDA, while we kept saying 'we want 400,000'. But since Palocci restricted the budget of the MDA, and with an eye to the political crisis in which the government was mired, the MDA bureaucrats pursued a policy that allowed them to claim that they had settled 380,000 families; this was close to the goal, but 64 per cent of these families were sent to the Amazon, which avoided any 'disappropriation' of the old landowners. The government selected public land in the Amazon and redistributed it to our families.

The 380,000 families were settled, but not in a process of agrarian reform; and they are now completely out of the class struggle. It was a process of colonization instead, distributing public lands on the agricultural frontier far away from markets, cities, etc. Even worse, it still involved the peasants in having to fight, now against the lumber firms who went so far as to order a nun working with the peasants in one of our settlements to be killed. Our people are stranded in the Amazon, lost in a hostile environment. Not even a small market for their produce is available there. Another 20 per cent of the MST families were simply settled on land reallocated from previous settlement families who had proved incapable of working the land they had occupied. Therefore, strictly speaking, in Lula's first term of office only 80,000 families were settled, exactly what Palocci had determined from the very beginning.

What is our conflict with Lula today? We don't want to keep fighting over the exact numbers of settled in the Amazon, or over his unfulfilled promises. We are going to tell him: 'Lula, face the truth: if the peasants are to have a future in Brazil it will be necessary to confront agribusiness. That is the issue now. It is pointless to push peasants to the Amazon and fool yourself that you are solving the problem of poverty or redistributing the land properly'. Quite the contrary; all the empirical data we have has revealed that in the last eight years, four under FHC, and four under Lula, the concentration of land tenure has increased significantly in Brazil. As the 'fazendeiros' are buying land, and as the price of land increases, there is empirical evidence of growing concentration. What we are seeing is an agrarian counter-reform, where land becomes more and more concentrated instead of being re-distributed. There is an aggravating factor, evidenced in the last two years, because of ethanol: now there is a rapid process of transfer to foreign hands of very large tracts of land. The largest farm devoted to the production of biofuel in São Paulo, 36,000 hectares, the property of a traditional family, was bought by Cargill. The name of the estate remained unchanged and very few realized what happened. Many think that it still is a Brazilian farm, but it is not. This was brought home to the public on March 8, International Women's Day, when our MST women occupied the Cargill farm! Of course, we don't have the strength to 'disappropriate' it, but still we are able to denounce the situation, saying that the farm is property of Cargill, and that the Bush family is involved in several agribusiness firms which are buying land in Brazil.

When Bush came to Brazil he used Lula only as an alibi. Even though the members of the government said that there was no agreement with Bush, because no protocol or agreement was signed, the fact is that Bush spent 36 hours in meetings with entrepreneurial groups, while with Lula he only had a photo opportunity. The hotel in which Bush stayed employed not a single Brazilian worker. All of them were laid off until Bush left the hotel. It was completely staffed by Americans because they did not want any Brazilian to see who were the people and economic groups who came to strike deals with the Americans. The meeting with Lula, and the photo, was an alibi that allowed this whole operation to be covered up. It also shows that the capitalists don't need the Brazilian government to promote their businesses.

AB: *What about the national bourgeoisie?*

JP: Here in Brazil, Florestan Fernandes foresaw the decay of the national bourgeoisie before anybody else, and he helped us with his analysis.[5] We continue to have a powerful capitalist class, extremely powerful and rich. But it is no longer a class that conceives of a national project, that promotes a national project for Brazil. Their project is completely subordinated to imperialism, with an appalling degree of subservience to imperialist capital. Here the contributions of Ruy Mauro Marini and the theory of dependence are crucial.[6]

Let me offer an example to prove the point: Veracel is the largest cellulose factory in the world, located in the South of Bahia. Who owns Veracel? Well, it is shared equally between Aracruz (closely linked to one of Brazil's most powerful banking families via the Banco Safra), the Groupo Votorantim (owned by one of its most powerful industrial families), and the Swedish-Finnish conglomerate Stora Enso.[7] When the plant was inaugurated the Queen of Sweden, a Brazilian herself, came to the official ceremony. The cost of the plant was $890 million dollars, in machinery and buildings alone. Who financed that investment? $450 million were offered by European banks, and the remaining $440 million by the National Bank of Development of Brazil. The public savings of the Brazilian people are thus used by our national bourgeoisie to lend to international capital. A total of $852 million were spent on the acquisition of machinery in Europe, which served their own internal market, not ours. Even nails, screws, and nuts and bolts were imported, while all the production here is for export. The role played by the Brazilian bourgeoisie in this operation involved putting up half the money and all the land, importing the machinery, and exporting the product to Europe! The plant employs a total of 700 people, with high wages. You could say that the guy who cuts the eucalyptus is a Brazilian. Yes, he was trained in Sweden, and uses huge machines – each of which replaces 80 power saws (a power saw requires five workers). In other words, each machine dispenses with 400 workers.

This is a case study in dependency theory. Because the area where the plant is located is appallingly poor, the children of the 700 workers had no elementary school to go to. So the Queen of Sweden donated an elementary school for them! This is presented as European aid for the poor, but the workers of Veracel are a labour aristocracy earning one thousand dollars per month. In order to put the plant into operation Veracel bought 80,000 hectares of land, and expelled 1,200 peasant families, living in a very backward area of the country. Now they are all 'favelados', living in shanty towns, because they did not have legal titles to their land.

AB: *At this point in time, do you think that Lula is likely to confront this alliance between international and domestic capital, especially in agribusiness? And what is the MST strategy in this respect?*

JP: Lula will continue doing business with the TNCs. We expect nothing from the government. Our strategy is resistance, leading towards the accumulation of social forces on our side of the class struggle. At least for the time being, our strategy is defensive not offensive. Why? Because our theory of cycles in the class struggle shows that an offensive strategy is not possible during the downturn of the class struggle. We could only defeat agribusiness if and when the working class as a whole enters into a new upturn, in an offensive phase against capital. Then, and only then, we are going to launch an offensive against agribusiness, imperialism, neoliberalism. The MST alone in its struggle has no strength to fight agribusiness, no strength to defeat it or even to confront it. Our strategy, then, is to resist, and to denounce. If we cannot 'disappropriate' Cargill at least we are able to occupy one of their farms for one day, so as to let everybody know that farm is Cargill's.

What could Lula do? He could 'disappropriate' Cargill and place the peasant settlements near the markets, not in the remotest part of the Amazon. Or he could help us to build peasant cooperatives, in a way that would enable us to be owners of our own food, to achieve food sovereignty. If we don't develop our own dairy industry we will never shake off our dependence upon Nestlé, Danone and Parmalat. If we don't get the resources to compete with these firms – $5,000,000 is what we would need – how can we confront them? A progressive government could play a very significant role, even if nobody expected big changes from it. And that would help us in the process of the accumulation of social forces on our side.

Another thing Lula could do: The MST offers five courses in Agronomy in different regions of Brazil, with an 'agro-ecological' approach, specializing in the typical biomass of each region. The goal is the formation of agronomists with our ideology and with our techniques. How could the government help the MST? It could reproduce these courses in each one of the states of Brazil, helping us to accumulate the social forces and scientific knowledge for the next stage of the struggle. We know that the current model of agribusiness is doomed because it is environmentally unsustainable and will face a brutal crisis in the not-too-distant future. There is a region in Brazil, around Ribeirão Preto – considered the Brazilian California – in which this crisis has already arrived. Formerly a region of multiple crops: coffee, vegetables, fruits, etc., based on small farms, in the past 20 years they changed to sugar cane, eliminating all other crops. And because of the lack of biodiversity the rains are very heavy, which produces floods in two or three hours. Ribeirão Preto, a city of 50,000 when this began, grew to 300,000, and 100,000 live in favelas – this in a very rich region of Brazil! There are 3,813 people in jail as measured against only 2,400 people living in the fields. There are more people in jail than people living in the countryside, including children in this figure. There is no agrarian population any longer! This is an economic model only good for capital.

AB: *Let me play the devil's advocate. Being realistic, could Lula have promoted a different policy?*

JP: Yes. The people who say that there was no choice are those who don't want to confront capital. If you ally with the capitalists and with the neoliberals then you surely could not do otherwise. But this was Lula's option. If Lula had opted to ally with the working classes he could have helped the workers improve their organizations and reinforce their political weight in order to change the correlation of forces and fight against the capitalists, but the government did not make that choice. The assertion that there is no alternative is just a justification of the option chosen by the Lula government: to ally with capital and not with the workers.

AB: *What about the international policy of Lula? Is it as progressive as portrayed by many of his intellectuals?*

JP: Yes, it was progressive from a political point of view, recovering some degree of autonomy. Before, under FHC, Itamaratí (the headquarters of the Ministry of Foreign Affairs) was a local branch office of the State Department. It was pathetic! As Minister of Foreign Affairs Celso Lafer was much more concerned to defend the interests of international capital than to defend the interests of the Brazilian people. Cardoso's foreign policy was one of total servility to the Americans. It is a positive thing, then, that Itamaratí has recovered some degree of autonomy.

But now the international economic policy of Brazil is totally subservient to the TNCs. This is the contradiction in which Lula's government is trapped: an apparently self-confident foreign policy, under which Brazil no longer asks the US what it is allowed to say, but in economic matters it is totally congruent with the interests of the TNCs. The role of Brazil in the WTO is shameful; it only benefits the interests of the big export firms in Brazil. Lula's government lacks the courage to repeal the Kandir Law, enacted by FHC and named after his Minister of Planning, which exempted from taxes all the firms exporting raw materials and agricultural products. But, who exports soy in Brazil? Monsanto, Cargill, Bunge. We export 28 million tons of soy and they don't pay one penny in taxes. Is this a progressive foreign policy? Lula authorized the exporters to leave abroad 50 per cent of the value of their foreign sales. This is robbery! Brazilian soy exports are worth US$ 15 billion, and now these firms can leave half of their revenue overseas. This facilitates capital flight and concealed currency remittances. It also provides an incentive to speculation in the foreign currency market and in the domestic financial markets.

AB: *But many pundits said that we owe the failure of the Free Trade Agreement of Americas (ALCA) to Lula's determination. What do you think about that?*

JP: Yes, but this responded to the political position of the Foreign Minister Celso Amorim, who is opposed to any kind of continental agreement. But the same rules that Brazil supposedly rejected in the FTAA are accepted in the WTO! Even worse: the government did not reach an agreement with the European Union only because we in the MST launched a major campaign and held huge demonstrations against that agreement. They were ready to concede everything demanded by the Europeans. Our comrades in Europe told us at a recent meeting that the policy line in Europe these days is to gradually move away from the WTO because the international rules and norms restrict their room for manoeuvre. Therefore, the European governments are interested in bilateral agreements, with single countries or blocs of countries. What they want from Brazil is to open up its markets for services – banks, financial services, telephones, electricity, transportation and high-tech industries. They don't want restrictions or taxes to limit their activity in these fields. In exchange, what the EU offers is access to European agricultural markets, permitting us to export any quantity of soy, ethanol, or grain of all sorts.

The reading of the European peasant movements is that the European bourgeoisie, which controls industry and finance in Europe, is allying with the agrarian bourgeoisies abroad, including those in Brazil and Latin America generally. But the agrarian bourgeoisie in Brazil is subordinate, it has no autonomy. Who exports soy from Brazil to Europe? Bunge, Cargill, Monsanto: foreign firms, not ours. And as far as Europe itself is concerned, this alliance also results in the liquidation of the European peasantry. Even while it declined numerically after World War Two, it had won a critical ideological battle: food sovereignty, which requires that Europe should produce its own food supplies. But Europe today not only produces for itself but exports as well, and today governments in Europe are slowly abandoning the post-war consensus and are ready to let their own firms that operate overseas to take care of the whole business. They want cheap foodstuffs and in order to obtain that they are ready to let their own peasantry go down the drain.

What is Lula's position on this issue? Total agreement! Please, open your agricultural markets to our exports! He thinks that this is a good thing for Brazil, overlooking the fact that the only beneficiaries of this policy are the big transnational companies. Our government is an ally of the European governments against their peasants as well as our people. This reflects the fact that Brazil no longer has a national bourgeoisie. Look at this example: in Brazil people can't afford to buy meat. We consume 7 kilos of beef per head per year, against 70 kilos in Argentina. With our huge territory and very large population it is an absolute must for us to increase cattle raising in Brazil. We have cattle in all regions, except for the North East, almost 200 million head – but most of it is for export. These exports represent only $3 billion. But EMBRAER, a manufacturer of airplanes, with 1,700 workers has exports worth $2.5 billion. This is the model. EMBRAER was privatized, and now is controlled by American and Canadian capitalists, with only some 30 per cent of it belonging to Brazilian private capital. To sum up: we have an economic foreign policy subservient to international capital, and this is congruent with domestic economic policy.

AB: *What do you think about the US strategy of building 'small FTAAs' via bilateral trade agreements?*

JP: The American tactics are clear. They did not get the FTAA – not so much because of opposition to it from Lula's government but because it was an excessively ambitious project to try to get more than 30 countries to completely agree on a very complex trade agreement. That calls for total servility, which is impossible to find in this world. Even if Lula had accepted, the opposition of Venezuela would have been enough to derail the project. It was a megalomaniac desire on the part of the Americans, conceived at the apex of neoliberal domination in 1995, to try to win total agreement on neoliberalism across Latin America via the FTAA (apart from Cuba, which was excluded from the whole thing, of course). They are now trying to use bilateral negotiations to achieve the same goal and, as a second route to this, to press for a new juridical framework via the international financial institutions that would remove all fetters on the free movement of capital. Additionally, what we see is that agreements are being made between big American firms and strong local groups, alliances between capitalists that circumvent the state apparatuses. In a certain form the capacity of Latin American states to control the markets has been dramatically undermined, as you showed in your essay in the *Socialist Register 2006*.[8] As I said, when Bush visited Brazil he was only interested in Lula showing up for a photo.

AB: *Let us move on to some issues related to the popular organizations and the relationship of the MST with parties and unions in Brazil. What lessons should be drawn from the decay of the PT and the vanishing role played by the CUT?*

JP: Tentatively, let's start by saying that both PT and CUT were defeated, and are in a defensive position. Why? There are several hypotheses. Regarding the working class, the capitalist restructuring in favour of TNCs and financial capital led to the downgrading of labour. The sheer changes in the composition of the Brazilian working class are quite telling: in 1980, at its peak, the industrial working class amounted to 4,500,000. In 2007, when the total population had increased by 40 per cent, the number had fallen to 4,200,000. Increases in productivity have been very important in the defeat of the working class as an actor. If the class has been defeated, how could CUT and the labour unions, or the class organizations, move forward?

In the case of PT there was a move to occupy the centre of the political spectrum. The PT abandoned social struggles, the formation of cadres, and concentrated on the institutional arena: to elect deputies, councillors, the president, becoming an institutional party. And an institutional party, whether it intends to or not, becomes a party of order. The role of a congressman is to play by the rules of the prevailing order, not to make the revolution. We have peasants who are congressmen, but we know that their role is exactly that: to move within the limits of the prevailing institutional order. But the PT was defeated by the bourgeoisie when it changed to prioritize the institutional struggle alone. And we know that institutional struggle does not solve the problems of the common people because the state is totally controlled by capital. If the MST is not in crisis, it is because we did not devote our movements exclusively to electing congressmen. Had we done otherwise we surely would be in a terrible crisis today. But we did not.

Additionally, let us put things in perspective. We at MST helped to build PT and CUT. I am still affiliated to the PT, and I am not saying that the PT abandoned us, or betrayed us. The problem is to understand why these two political instruments were defeated. And this is not a matter of personalities but of the context of the class struggle. Every new wave of mass struggle produces its own organizational instruments. From 1945-1964 the instruments were the Partido Comunista do Brasil, (PCB), the CGT, and Ligas Camponesas (Peasant Leagues, headed by Francisco Julião). The mass upturn of 1978-1979 brought about the PT, the CUT, and MST, and the first two have now been defeated. What is our hope? That in the next wave of working-class ascent new organizational instruments will be created, more adequate to the necessities of the struggle. All this will happen not because one or another leader wants it to happen but because the necessities of the struggle promote the rise of organizational instruments fit to face the challenges of the epoch. Therefore, our concern is to be prepared when the new upturn in the class struggles takes off, well aware that new instruments will be created that can be better than the MST, and that new leaderships will be created.

And this is ok with me. I am not going to waste my time speaking poorly of Lula. Our task is to stimulate mass struggles in Brazil, social struggles, to change the correlation of forces vis-à-vis the bourgeoisie, and out of that confrontation new leaders will arise and new forms of struggle will appear, and new instruments will necessarily be created. These instruments will have to be political ones, but not political as they are today, locked in the institutional framework of the state. Parties that only elect congressmen are useless; we need parties able to be instruments of the class struggle, challenging the economic model, the state, etc, and leading to structural changes in Brazil.

AB: *What is the MST's strategy in terms of national and international alliances to carry on this struggle?*

JP: The struggle at the national level is the key one. Because of the long downturn in the popular struggle it is still very difficult for us to generate the necessary unity among the different social forces. In such a phase forces tend to disperse. We spent 15 years in total dispersion. Now we can see a few promising, even if still dim, lights at the end of the tunnel. Because of some ideological affinities there are four streams that are starting to join forces: First, there is Conlutas, a Trotskyite group linked to P-SOL, the party formed by dissidents from the PT. Second, there are a few militant labour leaders and unions, linked to socialist forces, but orphans in the CUT because of their militancy, critics of CUT but unwilling to break with it.

Third, there is CMS, the Coordination of Social Movements, which was meant to be a mass front but which has ended up becoming a peak organization, a rubber-stamp of big movements like CUT, Via Campesina, MST; we are part of this but not satisfied. Finally, in the last year, and still in a process of construction, the Popular Assembly initiative has brought together all social movements in Brazil under the strong influence of the Christian churches – these churches are very important in Brazil because of their capillarity, which allows them to have a broad popular base.

Insofar as these four currents are joining forces, this is the positive news. And as the MST participates in almost all these spaces we play an articulating role to promote their unification. Sem Teto, the Homeless Movement (literally, people without a roof) are also in the Assembly. Our goal is to unite all our forces against the government's economic policy, the social security reform, and against the' third amendment' to the labour law. The latter was introduced by the right-wing parties to promote a total flexibilization of labour rights which Lula vetoed under pressure from the CUT, but this could be over-ridden if the right gets 2/3rds of the vote in the Congress. If this were to happen the capitalists could hire employees on an individual basis and without any job definition, and without social rights.

We are then facing this responsibility, before any other international commitment, to use our prestige to help the process of convergence on the Brazilian social left. Without this unity we cannot escape the crisis. Our goal is to promote the growth of mass movements. Of course, there are differences, both ideological and tactical. For instance, Conluta's tactics are aimed at defeating the Lula government. They regard Lula as mainly responsible for the deepening of neoliberalism in Brazil, and their goal is to defeat Lula. The CMS supported the government in its first term, preventing its eventual overthrow by the right, marching and demonstrating against the right. Now they are in a position of 'critical support'. The Popular Assembly says 'forget the government, organize the people!' Therefore, if we concentrate on the Lula government we disagree, but in relation to the future there is a good deal of unity.

AB: *And your strategy on the international scene?*

JP: First, we have a historical alliance that we are trying to expand in the peasant world with Via Campesina, and we are making an effort to improve its articulation with environmentalists, consumer associations and the women's movement. The Mali World Forum on Food Sovereignty in February 2007 (where 128 countries were represented) was a fruit of that growing articulation, to bring other social groups into our struggles: fishermen and herdsmen, in addition to the other three I've just mentioned.

Second, we are devoting a lot of effort to organizing what could be called the World Assembly of Social Movements. This always took place within the World Social Forum, but we have come to feel that because of the WSF's own nature the assemblies there did not represent the real forces that resist neoliberalism. In the WSF the situation is rather chaotic. As you know, there is an unresolved quarrel within the WSF. There are people who want to transform the WSF into yet another 'International', able to lead struggles worldwide, and people who think that the WSF is just a space to meet people and exchange opinions and experiences. We are against these two polar positions, but believe that the popular forces should agree on a concrete agenda of struggles. In any case, we are a little bit disillusioned with the WSF. In the assemblies there, one finds a clear preponderance of European organizations, especially NGOs, because they have the resources to attend and extend invitations and offer tickets, and in Europe the social movements are dominated by anarchist visions that reject any form or organization or articulation. They don't accept any coordination, or any rules or organizational formats that could provide greater organic unity to the social movements. How can you possibly defeat neoliberalism without organization? They even refuse to set up a Secretariat that could serve as a reference point from one Forum to the next. We are very sober, because we know how difficult it will be to realize it, but we have a dream: the constitution of a World Assembly of Popular Movements.

The third path we are taking in the international arena is our partnership with the government of Venezuela in the process of advancing the ALBA (the Venezuelan-sponsored Bolivarian Alternative for the Americas) as an alternative to the ALCA (the U.S.-sponsored Free Trade Area of the Americas). For us ALBA is not only a name but the possibility of creating concrete mechanisms for the popular integration of the continent. These mechanisms could assume a variety of forms. We have been talking about the fundamental role that could be played by the Latin American School of Medicine (ELAM), based in Havana, with a branch in Venezuela, which will receive 600 students from all over Latin America, including 100 from Brazil. Cuba will also be increasing (to 500 per semester) the number of students – all from popular origins and with a sound formation – who are brought there to train as cadres and leaders. And if you start to have cadres with the same formation across the whole continent you will have, in the medium term, a very important substratum for your next political battles.

But we need more courses, beyond medicine: we need agronomists with a vision of agro-ecology and with alternative economic models in mind, to work with our peasants. They will be our technical cadres. This will be very important in the future, because you will have a similar ideological and technological matrix throughout Latin America. This will also be important in developing a common project for recovering 'creole seeds'. We have a lot of experience with this here in Brazil. We could provide advice and training to peasants of other countries and help them to escape from the control of the TNCs and their promotion of transgenic seeds. We need cooperatives to reproduce seeds adapted to our soils. If Venezuela's Bank for Economic and Social Development (BANDES) gave some support, we could recreate cooperatives around the region – a network of cooperatives developing new social cadres, always with an eye to the medium term, not the short term.

Fourth, we are also trying to seal an alliance with Asia. In Indonesia, Sri Lanka, South Korea, Thailand, the Philippines, in fact, all across the south of Asia there are strong mass movements that are anti-neoliberal and anti-imperialist. They are not in a downward phase of the class struggle as we still are here in Brazil. They have many techniques of mass mobilization and organization, of agitation and propaganda, including appealing to some religious sentiments, especially in Muslim countries where they are very active. We in the MST and Via Campesina Brazil think of those Asian movements as ideal partners for the exchange of ideas and experiences. On the other hand, Africa is a nightmare. African movements have a very low level of organization and are extremely poor, and many are still located at the tribal and local level. Few countries have a national movement. Mozambique is one, thanks to Frelimo, But Guinea, despite being a very small country, has three or four organizations, none of them national. Many countries in Africa have no peasant movements at all: and in those with oil – Sudan, Nigeria, Angola – the popular movements totally depend on the governments. There are 300 million Arab peasants in Africa, but they are totally dependent upon their governments. Unfortunately, Africa barely counts in the world correlation of forces and in the international social struggle. When they got rid of the European empires, their oil still went to them and to the Americans. But a new empire is arriving to exploit their natural resources: China. China is taking everything: coal, trees, mineral resources of all sorts, foodstuff, to sustain its economic growth. Maybe the next anti-imperialist revolt is going to be against China.

AB: *Do you have any hope that social movements could go upward in Europe, or the USA, helping your struggles in the South?*

JP: No, very little. We could point to the rising tide of the young immigrants in the periphery of Paris. But this is not a generalizable example, even in Europe. And in the USA, we could perhaps point to the migrant workers, since the Blacks are not in such a militant mood any longer. There are 8 million Mexican migrants that are sustaining the interior of Mexico with their remittances. But they have to face a very unfavourable correlation of forces, since the capitalist forces in the USA, Mexico and Canada have become fused, and this means that the migrants' struggle cannot be only national. It should be against the Mexican government as well as against the US and Canadian states and bourgeoisies. But the migrants are not engaged in a struggle to change the structures. Theirs is not a struggle for an emancipatory project. If somebody gives them a green card the fight is over.

AB: *Can the struggle against devoting the land to biofuel production as a capitalist response to peak oil and the ecological crisis unify the forces opposed to imperialism?*

JP: No. I don't think so, because the characteristics of each country are so different that what matters here in Brazil or Colombia is irrelevant in others, like Bolivia, Peru or Ecuador. They don't have much agricultural land available to allow them to take part in this project. The Americans said they would invest in a few selected countries. If we are to unify the anti-imperialist front we would need to discover other unifying issues. Perhaps the banks, or the telephone companies, offer some easier ways than ethanol to rally the forces together.

At the World Forum in Mali we asked ourselves: what could bring all the peasants together, worldwide? And we decided to set one day, October 16, as the international day of struggle against the transnational corporations. But we realized we could not do that against the TNCs in general. So then we asked: is there any possibility to personify TNCs in six specific firms that play a role in all countries of the world. In Brazil we have six: Nestlé, Coca Cola, Wal-Mart, Cargill, Monsanto and Bunge; other countries may have three or four. But these six are in all countries, and we will concentrate our fire on them. This will be a rallying point, and will provide us concrete targets against whom to fight.

NOTES

The two-hour long interview, conducted in Portuguese, took place in São Paulo on May 5, 2007.

1   Brazil's Landless Workers Movement, or in Portuguese, Movimento dos Trabalhadores Rurais Sem Terra (MST), founded in 1984, is the largest social movement in Latin America, with an estimated 1.5 million landless members

organized in 23 out of 27 states. Via Campesina is the international movement, founded in 1993, which coordinates peasant organizations of small and
medium sized producers, agricultural workers, rural women, and indigenous
communities from Asia, America, and Europe.

2   See Florestan Fernandes, *Mudanças sociais no Brasil: aspectos do desenvolvimento da
sociedade brasileira*, São Paulo: Difusão Européia do Livro, 1960 and *Sociedades
de classes e subdesenvolvimento*, Rio de Janeiro: Zahar, 1968.

3   The Brazil media played this up to the point of hyping the idea of the US and
Brazil forming a two-nation 'OPEC of ethanol', and Lula boasted to Bush that
'we have more than tripled the yields of sugarcane plantations, which are the
main source of ethanol'. See 'Brazil's Ethanol push could eat away at Amazon',
MSNBC online, 7 March 2007, available from http://www.msnbc.msn.com
and 'President Bush and President Lula of Brazil Discuss Biofuel Technology',
Press Release, 9 March 2007, available from http://www.whitehouse.gov.

4   The primary fiscal deficit is the nominal deficit of the central government,
minus the interest payments on the public sector debt. As an indicator of the
sustainability of the domestic debt, it is often used as a proxy for the risk of
default of the public sector. Conversely, a primary surplus (even if it is insufficient to eliminate the nominal deficit) indicates that the public sector is paying
at least part of the interest on its debt. In principle, this implies that the public
sector debt is sustainable.

5   See Florestan Fernandes, *Revolução burguesa no Brasil: ensaio de interpretação soci-
ológica,* Rio de Janeiro: Zahar, 1974.

6   See R.M. Marini, 'Brazilian Interdependence and Imperialist Integration',
Monthly Review, 17(7), 1965 and 'Brazilian Subimperialism', *Monthly Review*,
23(9), 1972.

7   Aracruz is the world's largest bleached eucalyptus pulp and paper manufacturer. The Banco Safra was founded by a venerable Jewish family of financiers to
the Ottoman empire who relocated from Beirut to Brazil in the 1950s. Ranked
sixth among the country's largest private sector financial institutions in terms
of total assets, the Bank is part of the Safra Group of financial institutions with
widespread international operations in the US, Europe, and the Middle East as
well as in Latin America and the Caribbean. The Grupo Votorantim, one of
the leading companies of Brazil and recently chosen as 'the world's best family
company' by the Swiss Institute IMD Business School, is primarily located in
the paper and cellulose sector.

8   Atilio Boron, 'The Truth About Capitalist Democracy', *Socialist Register
2006*.

ALL WE WANT IS THE EARTH: AGRARIAN REFORM IN BOLIVIA

WES ENZINNA

Coreino Martinez, whom I met only a few days before, has his pants un-buckled and is showing me the gruesome scar that runs from his belly button down past the waistband of his pants. 'This is where they shot me', he says. 'The bullet from a high-powered rifle entered me here, in my stom-ach'. Standing beside him, with burn scars tattooing her arms and hands, Angelica Cumasero adds, 'I was hiding in a hut, holding my baby – they set the hut on fire with me and my baby inside'.[1] Martinez and Cumasero are members of Bolivia's landless rural workers movement, Movimiento Sin Tierra (MST), a national organization of militant farmers who occupy, work, and live on unused lands; they are recounting an October 4, 2000 attack by paramilitary forces carried out on their squatters' community, *Los Sotos*, in the *Gran Chaco* in the province of Tarija.[1]

Stories like these – first told to me while visiting several MST settle-ments in Tarija during August 2006 – are not rare in Bolivia. The victims of government apathy and landowner violence, the efforts of landless peasants to gain access to land have often been met with ambivalence or force. Yet, today, these landless peasants find themselves in a different sort of spotlight.

On May 2, 2006 President Evo Morales announced a massive land re-form that aims to redistribute 20 million hectares (49 million acres) to the nation's 2.5 million landless peasants (Bolivia's total population is 9 million). Where currently it is estimated that 400 individuals own 70 per cent of the nation's productive land, claiming more than 100,000 hectares each, with the top 3,500 individuals together owning more than 20 million hectares,[2] the reform aims to distribute lands 'exclusively to peasants and indigenous communities without land or who possess insufficient lands'.[3] Agriculture accounts for about 15 per cent of the country's GDP, and major land re-forms have long been a demand of Bolivia's landless peasants. In particular, hope for what Morales might achieve runs high.[4] Born a poor peasant himself, Morales has worked as a llama herder and coca grower, rising to fame as a leader of the Six Federation of the Tropics, the coca growers' union. His presidential election came at the end of five years of unrelenting and highly effective popular resistance to neoliberalism and support for indigenous and national struggles in Bolivia, protests in which Morales sometimes participated. From the 2000 'Water War' in Cochabamba to the October 2005 'Gas War' in El Alto, these movements forced two neoliberal presidents out of the country and articulated a coherent anti-neoliberal program, often referred to as the 'October Agenda', leading Sinclair Thomson and Forrest Hylton to describe this period as the 'third major revolutionary moment in Bolivian history'.[5] Since taking office, Morales has echoed the demands of the peasant movements, insisting that 'In Bolivia the latifundio is illegal.... The unproductive latifundio has to be eradicated'.[6]

Morales' administration revolves around three central programmes: (1) 'nationalization' of the hydrocarbon industry, (2) convoking a 'Constituent Assembly' to re-write the nation's constitution, and (3) carrying out a large-scale land reform. That Morales has in fact gone forward with these three programs has proven he is far more committed to social change than any of his predecessors, and has served as evidence for his supporters that he is an 'authentic' revolutionary president and that his Movimiento al Socialismo (MAS) is an authentic revolutionary party. Yet there remains in Bolivia anything but a consensus that Morales is carrying forward the revolution begun in 2000, or that these programs are in fact fulfilling the demands articulated by the movements during the revolutionary period of 2000 to 2005.

While the land reform has not figured prominently in international media coverage, it is equally as important to the revolutionary project as gas nationalization or the Constituent Assembly. Morales has made explicit the connections between carrying out land reform and defeating the legacy of colonialism – 'eradicating the latifundio is about defeating colonialism once and for all in Bolivia's rural regions', Morales has said, alluding to the widely-acknowledged fact that the continued existence of the latifundio, or hacienda, is one of colonialism's clearest social-economic legacies in Bolivia.[7] In any case, MAS must carry forward an effective and sufficiently profound agrarian reform in order to satisfy a key segment of its constituency. As one analyst points out, 'although gaining control over Bolivia's hydrocarbons industry is the centerpiece of Morales' program... land reform is perhaps even more important for maintaining support from his indigenous base of peasants, many of whom are landless'.[8] Further, land reform holds the potential to incite a conservative backlash against the Morales administration. Land reform is the issue around which Bolivia's rabid right-wing in the east of the country has mobilized most effectively and virulently, organizing armed paramilitary militias to 'defend' their lands against MAS's reform and sporadically calling for civil war.

Understanding MAS's current land reform is thus central to understanding the larger political situation in Bolivia today. However, critical analysis of the reform is scarce. This is partly due to the fact that the reform is still under way and key developments still unfolding. Accordingly, any conclusions, including those made here, must be somewhat tentative. Nonetheless, by looking at the history of land reform efforts and focusing on one key movement that has fought for reform (the MST), landowner opposition, and the specifics of the reform itself, we can move towards a better understanding of this important effort.

PROFILE OF AN MST SETTLEMENT

The soil at *Los Sotos* is rich – darker and healthier than the sand that covers the ground everywhere else I've been in the *Chaco*. Thatched-roof huts dot the landscape, and rough-hewn fences cordon off cows, while chickens roam around as they please. Tall corn stalks grow everywhere. In the center of *Los Sotos* the land is cleared, and there is an impressive straw-roofed dome, the roof at the highest point reaching around thirty-five feet. In the center of the enormous hut is a large-bell – for emergencies and to convoke regular assemblies and meetings.

Los Sotos is disputed territory – occupied land. In May 2000, around 75 impoverished Bolivians, most of whom had worked for years as hired hands on massive *haciendas*, grew crops on small pieces of rented land, or worked in the cities as maids or manual labourers – or intermittently did all three – gathered to take over about 1,090 hectares (2,700 acres). The property had long been abandoned after being stripped for lumber, and when the settlers arrived the soil was barren, and the tree stumps left behind meant months of work before the land would bear any crops.

Once the farmers had occupied the area they christened it 'Los Sotos', and organized to clear the land, prepare the soil for cultivation, and later to plant crops. They began building huts for sleeping, constructed the large, high-roofed meeting place for assemblies, and later dug a well and put up pens for animals. Today, there are about 25 families living at *Los Sotos*, almost all of whom played key roles in the original takeover. They primarily grow corn, wheat, soy, and potatoes, half of which is for subsistence, and half sold on the market. Community members build their own private huts for homes, but all the land is worked, cared for, and defended in common, though women are charged with the brunt of child care, men with the most physically-demanding labour. Crops and profits – which total about $100 (US) a month for the entire community – are completely shared.

Los Sotos is one of more than 100 similar MST settlements in Bolivia, and virtually all of them have experienced violence in the form of paramilitary invasions orchestrated by local wealthy landowners. For example, on October 4, 2000, in the attack described above by Martinez and Cumasero, armed men attacked the settlers and shot and wounded several men, women, and children.[9] In the months following the initial May 2000 occupation, *Los Sotos* suffered other violent attacks. At the nearby *Pananti* settlement, on November 9, 2001, approximately 40 local landowners and hired men armed with guns and clubs raided the camp, determined to drive the squatters out. Six MST members were killed in the attack, and twenty others were badly wounded. Some of the attackers were arrested and the Minister of Government, Leopoldo Fernandez, acknowledged MST President Angel Duran's claim that the attackers had been given weapons by local police and military officials – yet the stiffest sentences given to the paramilitaries were three-year probationary sentences. On the other hand, when MST members later encountered a commander of the attack on a back road and beat him to death, those who participated in the beating were sentenced to eight years in prison.[10]

REVOLUTION, REFORM, AND THE PERSISTENCE OF THE LATIFUNDIO

Bolivia has a long and bloody history of land conflicts, stretching back to colonial times. If the period 2000 to 2005 was indeed 'the third major revolutionary moment in Bolivian history', the struggle over land has been important in each of them. The first of these moments was 1780-81 when Aymara and Quechua insurrections threatened to expel the Spanish. The second was the 1952 revolution, prior to which land in Bolivia remained distributed on an essentially feudal basis characterized by huge estates where peasants, overwhelmingly indigenous, often worked in exchange for nothing but the use of a small plot of the estate owner's land, often accompanied by a host of unpaid service requirements, called *ponguaje*. Such estates, called *latifundios,* were the most common type of land ownership scheme, and according to a 1950 census *latifundios* occupied 95 per cent of all cultivatable land in Bolivia, only 0.8 per cent of which was actually cultivated.[11] The national revolution of 1952 (and the land reforms that would come a year later) aimed to do away with such arrangements via the implementation of a massive land reform and the creation of the Agrarian Reform Council, whose purpose was to legally break up the *latifundios* and prioritize previously landless peasants by giving them land of their own to cultivate. To this end, the Council radically re-structured property law by creating the legal precedent – codified in the nation's constitution in Article 166, known as the Social Economic Function – that 'the land belongs to those who work it'; that is, the primary way to acquire and maintain ownership of land was to work it directly.

However, while the aims of the reform were quite radical, the new law was implemented unevenly across the country. In the western highlands the reform was somewhat successful, breaking the latifundios up into hundreds of small 'minifundio' plots. In eastern Bolivia the results of the revolution were quite different. While today the population of eastern Bolivia is about 4.5 million (half the country's total), at the time of the revolution this part of the country was largely unsettled forest and plains, on which some scattered and isolated communities of indigenous groups lived. While breaking up latifundios in the west, the administration of Victor Paz Estenssoro sought to simultaneously use the 1953 reforms to colonize eastern lands.[12] To this end, landless peasants of the west were encouraged to settle on small plots, and Bolivian and foreign elites were encouraged to settle on large estates. In search of land titles, landless peasants from the west migrated en masse to the east – until they were largely banned from doing so in 1988. As of 2000, these peasants owned only 4 per cent of all eastern lands.[13]

The settlement of large landholdings, on the other hand, continued at rapid pace. In particular, the dictatorships that took hold in Bolivia during the 1970s exploited the mechanisms of the reform created in 1953 (in particular the Agrarian Reform Council) to distribute land through favouritism and political cronyism.[14] In fact, MAS spokesman Alex Contreras has recently claimed that 90 per cent of the nation's land suitable for agriculture was corruptly given away between 1953 and 1992.[15] But perhaps more than numbers, a sense of the times can be gleaned from one exemplary episode. In 1977, dictator Hugo Banzer had charged his Undersecretary of Immigration, Dr. Guido Strauss, with attracting wealthy white immigrants from South Africa and Rhodesia to settle and create new lands in eastern Bolivia. The government offered 800,000 hectares (1.9 million acres) of land free of charge, as well as $150 million (US) in funds, part of which would be available for repressing the 120,000 indigenous peasants who already lived on the designated lands. Strauss, trying to entice the white Africans, assured them of favourable conditions: you 'will certainly find our Indians no more stupid or lazy than [your] blacks', he wrote.[16]

Thus, whereas in 1953 Bolivia undertook a land reform that explicitly aimed at the eradication of all latifundios in Bolivia, in the eastern lowlands the mechanisms of this reform, combined with the corruption of the military dictatorships, were used to create *new* latifundios. By the 1990s, 80 per cent of lands distributed were concentrated in the hands of just 10 per cent of landowners.[17] Summarizing the effect of this period, Miguel Urioste, director of the La Paz-based Fundacion Tierra, writes: 'The process of land distribution in the country was usurped by the military dictatorships... giving origin to the birth of latifundismo in the region'.[18]

After the restoration of democracy in 1982, the same pattern continued: 'Civilian governments did not substantially modify the discretional use of awarding eastern lands [which] continued being distributed and concentrated along the lines of new family networks of power and party adherence'.[19] In 1985, Estenssoro was again elected president and with Decree 21060 enacted sweeping neoliberal reforms that further polarized the countryside. Decree 21060 lifted all restrictions on imports, and as a result peasants across Bolivia suffered. Harry Sanabria writes, 'The terms of trade for key crops primarily produced by peasants declined significantly after the neoliberal project [of 1985], production costs rose, important crops barely competed with less expensive imports, and as a result, agricultural production fell by seventeen percent between 1985 and 1988'. By 1998 production had declined to 45 per cent of the pre-1985 level.[20] Sanabria concludes that 'neoliberal policies have relegated peasant production to an "economically marginal" role',[21] and a 1992 study by the UN's International Fund for Agricultural Development revealed that, seven years into Bolivia's 'economic miracle', 97 per cent of the rural population were below the poverty line – the highest level of rural poverty in the world.[22]

Neoliberal reforms further exacerbated peasant hardship by strengthening the eastern latifundios. With increased access to chemical fertilizers and monies from international finance institutions, including the World Bank, and with the economy geared towards exports, the latifundios were in a unique position to orient their already-industrialized farms towards monocrop production for export. A Center for the Study of Labour and Agricultural Development (CEDLA) report confirms that the only agricultural group to profit from the neoliberal revolution were the middle to large-scale farms.[23]

In response to widespread dissatisfaction, including intermittent protests, in 1996 President Gonzalo Sanchez de Lozada passed Law 1715, establishing the National Institute for Agrarian Reform (INRA). The stated goal of INRA was to carry out a major review of land titles in order to distribute to the landless state-owned lands, private landholdings that did not meet the Social Economic Function, and land obtained through corruption. Yet, the reality of INRA was disappointing. Specifically, what many found objectionable was that the new reform made an exception to the 1953 maxim, 'the land belongs to those who work it'. It now stated that the land also belongs to those who pay taxes on it – 1 per cent of the total property value, to be determined by the landowner. Many, like Manual Morales Davila, considered this antithetical to the spirit of '53, in that it legalized absentee ownership, speculation, and very large fallow holdings, characteristics favoured by wealthy landholders, not the peasants INRA claimed to benefit.[24] For many peasants the failure of INRA was the last straw in a long history of empty promises.

Consequently, a wave of peasant mobilizations erupted, beginning with the August 1996 'March for Territory, Land, Political Rights, and Development', led by the Trade Union Confederation of Indigenous Peasants and Labourers in Bolivia (CSUTCB), one of the country's longest-standing peasant unions. Peasants walked for 36 days from all corners of the country to arrive at the seat of government in La Paz, where they demanded, among other things, greater campesino participation in government, funds for indigenous and peasant land colonization programmes, and the modification of INRA.[25] Four years later, in September/October 2000, after hundreds more mobilizations, the nation's increasingly militant peasants orchestrated the shut-down of every major highway in the country, forcing the re-elected President Banzer to meet with the peasant leaders to discuss reforms. It was out of this period of militant peasant mobilization that the MST would emerge.

HISTORY OF THE MST

Since its birth in 2000, the MST has, almost alone among peasant groups, carried out land occupations to pressure local and national officials to carry out the *saneamiento* (revision of land titles) and redistribution of lands. Reflecting the lop-sided land distribution in the east of Bolivia, the MST has its strongholds in Tarija and Santa Cruz, with a significant presence also in La Paz, Beni, and Cochabamba. In contrast to the CSUTCB and other peasant unions, MST members overwhelmingly tend to have mixed origins and work histories that often include substantial amounts of time spent living and working in urban settings doing non-agricultural labour. The organization's members are 'born from the campesinos', as one of its leaders has put it, but they do not necessarily identify themselves exclusively as campesinos.[26]

Since the organization's birth, the MST's defining element has been the land takeover. In fact, the organization was born by the very act of a takeover. On February 20, 2000, a small group of landless farmers took over land in the *Gran Chaco*. Ten months later hundreds of landless families would peacefully occupy land in Pananti, an area in Tarija, and begin working it.[27] Much strategizing went into these initial occupations. The participants looked for a piece of land that had remained unused for a long time and thus didn't meet the Social Economic Function.

This direct-action tactic has both an immediate function and a more distant strategic goal. The immediate goal is to take land, live on it, and work it – that is, to immediately take steps to ameliorate poverty by acquiring land to live and grow crops on. In this sense, the land takeover is a powerful political act – through communal labour the occupied land becomes a site for personal and collective transformation, building solidarities, and prefiguring non-exploitative and convivial relations of production. This conforms with the express desire within the MST to organize and function horizontally and to eschew clientelism and co-optation. 'We think it is better this way', says Dionisio Mamani, regional secretary of a settlement named Collana, 'so that [MST members and leaders] don't have to accustom themselves to knocking at the doors of NGOs, political parties, or the government'.[28]

The takeovers also serve a long-term strategic function. While seeking to avoid clientelist relationships with the authorities, the occupation is simultaneously designed to pressure the government into action: to put pressure on regional and national government to assess the legality of landholdings in accordance with the 1953 land reform, thus clearing the way for redistribution. Further, the chances of actually being awarded land through the legal system have been proven to be greatly increased if that land is already occupied by the people making a claim for it.[29]

During the first months after the organization's founding, the 'MST [identified] between 18 and 20 key un-worked latifundios, the biggest being Pananti, where the movement succeeded in consolidating the presence of 200 peasant families settled on 3,000 hectares'.[30] As of early 2006, the group had continued to carry out occupations at a considerable pace. In 2000, the group had 3,000 members in Tarija, Santa Cruz, Cochabamba, and La Paz, later to expand to Beni and Pando; as of 2004, estimates put membership at 50,000, including the members of the 100 or so current settlements, as well as members still seeking settlements. The rapid growth of the organization is evidently related to the success of the occupation as a tactic. For example, in November 2003, after a barrage of occupations and mobilizations, the MST succeeded in pressuring the government to investigate and eventually turn over the titles to 14 settlements totalling more than 31,000 hectares (76,000 acres) of land. In their mobilizations 'the demand for *saneamiento* was articulated with extraordinary... precision on the part of the MST... The judicial apparatus, especially those in charge of land issues... were the object of intense pressure'. Despite its success, this tactic brings up a fundamental antinomy of the MST's strategy: while land occupation is a highly confrontational direct-action tactic, as employed by the MST it also relies heavily on claims to legality. This underscores one of the internal tensions of the MST, the intensity of which will increase with newfound access to the government via the MAS administration: their simultaneous desire for autonomy, and their desire for recognition from legal authorities. This is what prompted Álvaro García Linera to conclude: 'The position of the MST leaders towards the government is run-through with contradictions and ambiguities'.[31]

These tensions have sometimes led to conflict within the MST. In January 2004, the organization split, with President Angel Duran being dethroned by Moises Torres. The split was provoked by tension over how much the organization should pin its political aspirations to the rising MAS party, a point of contention that had become increasingly heated within the MST. However, mobilizations – by what were now dual MST organizations (though not antagonistic to each other) – persisted in the first years of the new century and the organization developed a coherent set of demands, echoing those of earlier peasant groups, focused on a modification or reversal of INRA, the redistribution of land, and the reversal of neoliberal policies.

These demands, and the fevered pitch at which land occupations were occurring – several hundred between 2000 and 2004, the most since the years immediately preceding the 1952 revolution – revealed a burgeoning radicalism on the part of the MST and the landless in general. In particular, the experience of MST members with rural-urban migration appears to have had a strong radicalizing effect. Although urban-rural migration was a long-standing survival strategy for agricultural workers, an increase in migration was sparked by the drop in crop prices for small peasants which resulted from the 1985 neoliberal reforms. Increased migration was combined with the simultaneous closing of work opportunities in urban areas for peasants. Urban experience and the re-embracing of agricultural work and campesino identity was a common experience among the MST workers I interviewed, and this accords with Bolivian journalist Victor Orduna's idea of 're-campesinazation', according to which urban-rural migration is a key radicalizing experience for uprooted agricultural workers. As a resident from the Chirimoyal settlement told me in August 2006,

> In 1998 I went to El Alto to work construction – my brother was there already. When I got there I could not find work, I could not even make enough money to survive. In the city, where I

had previously supplemented my family's earnings, now I couldn't even find enough work. So faced with the decision, go back to the countryside, defeated, or stay in the city and try to earn money, I decided: I will go back to the countryside, but not defeated, in fact, ready to struggle, more aware of the sources of our exploitation in the countryside. I will go back and, to ensure a better life, I will find land… This is the only way to survive, to survive with dignity.

When he returned from the city he participated in the occupation of the settlement *Chirimoyal* and joined the MST.

LANDHOLDER REACTION

While the MST has mobilized for land reform, the eastern agricultural elite has mobilized against the formation of landless settlements, and more recently against MAS's land reform. This elite derives much of its power and ideological coherence from their large landholdings. In fact, as previously mentioned, it is as beneficiaries of the corrupt resettlement policies of the 1970s, 1980s and 1990s that this new settler class was born.

While the new latifundios were getting rich through government-subsidized export farming, they were also depressing farm wages and leading a more general assault on agricultural work conditions. Workers on the latifundios are drawn mainly from the indigenous groups native to the east who were dispossessed of their land by latifundista logging and cattle-ranching, and from peasants who had migrated from west to east attracted by the (largely empty) promise of land titles. Conditions for these workers are dismal. Some have reported working from sunrise to sunset for $1.41 a day;[32] others report having their wages withheld entirely and being beaten on the job by bosses and overseers.[33] Yet even these experiences pale in comparison to other agro-industrial farms, like the latifundio in southeastern Bolivia where 600 families (3,000 individuals) of Guarani Indians were discovered to be enslaved for their labour by the landowner in 2005.[34]

The fact that poor landless peasants are the backbone of the export economy does not escape the attention of the latifundistas, who recognize the threat squatter exoduses pose to their labour supply. When their labourers defect from the latifundio labour force to squat other lands landowners typically unite to attack these settlements, irrespective of whether or not it is *their* land that is being occupied. This violence underscores a simple fact: in the agricultural economy of Bolivia, as in other third world countries, the interests of the latifundista and small peasant producer are diametrically opposed. This is why the chief demand of the peasantry in the 1952 revolution was the outlawing of the latifundio; why the MST and other groups today have demanded the eradication of the latifundio; and why latifundio owners will attack and kill landless squatters, even when it's not 'their' land that is being taken.

That the latifundio is the most significant source of anti-peasant violence can be clearly seen in the actions of the agricultural elite. Take, for example, the Agricultural Chamber of Eastern Bolivia (CAO), a group of agro-industrialists from Santa Cruz who in response to the May 2 announcement of Morales' land reform announced the formation of 'armed defence committees' to defend their land.[35] One mayor of a Santa Cruz rural area with protracted land tenure conflicts openly and enthusiastically supported the armed defence committees. He announced that they are prepared 'to spill blood with each eviction of [what they consider] illegal occupants of land'.[36] Or, take Nación Camba, a powerful group of Santa Cruz elites united around a white supremacist, separatist ideology, and their youth affiliate, Unión Juvenil Cruceñista. Brutal attacks by Juvenil Cruceñista and other groups have been numerous and well documented, and represent the vanguard of ethnic and regional hatred in eastern Bolivia. In one film the group Video Urgente shows a mob, including Juvenil Cruceñista members, beating MST leader Silvestre Saisari in the main public plaza in Santa Cruz, a beating the local press caught on tape but did not air; in another scene of the film, Juvenil Cruceñista members chase down and whip an elderly *campesino* man, and then kick and stomp him in the face while he is on the ground.

The group draws its name from the idea of the superiority of 'Cambas', the white settler residents of eastern Bolivia, relative to the indigenous Indians, an idea justified on the basis of their superior 'Spanish' culture and heritage. Nación Camba's literature typically refers to their indigenous fellow countrymen as 'collas', a paternalistic racial epithet. Juvenil Cruceñista members explained to North American journalist Ben Dangl that Cambas were friendlier and cleaner than Collas, and then added, perhaps with unintended candour: 'We are probably at the beginning of where you were in the US before the civil rights movements with whites and blacks'.[37]

The Cambas seek their own nation based on ethnic exclusion, claiming they are an oppressed group, a victim of Andean hegemony and 'Andinomania'. Echoing the west-to-east migrations of landless peasants, they write: for how much longer will Cambas 'continue to be converted into a "vaginal receptacle" by the pluricultural and multiethnic [Bolivian] society, where the country's various social diasporas are emptied? ...Because of such dramatic conditions we believe it is necessary to recreate the nation, *our* nation, our own state'.[38] The Camba political project, calling for regional control of resources ('autonomy') if not all-out secession, appeals to the large white population. While latifundistas represent a relatively small elite, a large percentage of Santa Cruz and eastern residents are white (perhaps as much as 50 per cent) and share the values and political aspirations of the agricultural elite. As Miss Bolivia 2004 infamously explained, 'we are [not] all just... poor people and very short people and Indian people. I'm from the other side of the country, the east side... and we are tall and we are white people and we speak English'.[39]

This Camba ideology provides powerful intellectual support for anti-Morales sentiment in the east, framing the parameters of debate and opposition to Morales's programs in racial terms, and fusing its economic and political critique with widely held racist views. In this perspective, Morales's administration is as much culturally repulsive as it is economically and politically objectionable. Thus the 'Andeanization' of the country is as much a problem to be combated as land reform or gas nationalization. That the rejection of, and separation from, the nation's 'collas' might be an adequate solution for the economic, political, and cultural concerns aroused in eastern residents by Morales's administration was reflected in the June 2006 referendum on autonomy, when a majority of citizens in all the eastern provinces voted 'Autonomia Si!': 65 per cent in the province of Tarija, 73 per cent in Beni, and 75 per cent in Santa Cruz.

And here, one cannot help but notice the similarities between the political project of a 'Nación Camba', and the experience of latifundismo. Writing presciently in 2004, prior to the widespread emergence of 'autonomy' as a conservative political project, García Linera predicted that the 'growing process of the formation of paramilitary bodies at the service of latifundio properties is such that until the government takes methods to carry out the *sanemiento* of lands established by law, until the latifundios are dismantled, they will continue to act as *mini-states with their own national sovereignty*'.[40]

MORALES' LAND REFORM

The eastern landholding elite has historically displayed a capacity and readiness for armed mobilization against those landless peasants that would threaten its interests. But it is the rise of the Morales administration that has provided the greatest rallying cry in the east, and in particular its land reform that has provoked this group's most militant actions.

The reform officially began on May 2, 2006, with a series of decrees, and was passed into law on November 28, 2006, amidst much tension. By 2011 the reform aims to distribute 20 million hectares (49 million acres), a fifth of the nation's total land area, to landless farmers. The law also establishes a process by which to prioritize women heads of household for titles, and to incorporate indigenous and peasant communities into its administration. It also aims to provide technical assistance to peasants. On August 2, 2006, in Ucurena, Bolivia, where the 1953 reform was inaugurated, 20,000 peasants, including leaders of the MST and CSUTCB, received 650 tractors and 700 land deeds. At the event, his voice harsh and ragged, with the MAS theme song blaring in the background, Morales reiterated his position: 'we're going to end colonialism and eradicate the latifundio. Today we're taking forward a profound agrarian revolution'.

The new law is largely in line with INRA, but with some important modifications. Firstly, it gets rid of the hated exception introduced in Law #1715 that allowed landowners to pay taxes on their lands to satisfy the Social Economic Function. Lands that do not do this (excluding lands left fallow for crop rotation, ecological reserves, and projected growth) will be subject to expropriation, as will lands determined to have been illegally acquired. The government body that will oversee the *saneamiento* and re-titling will be a newly-formed Agrarian Reform Council, comprised of indigenous organizations, government agencies and ministers, and CONFEAGRO, a Santa-Cruz-based group of large-scale landowners. Lands that do not meet the constitutional requirements will be expropriated without compensation; all others will be compensated in full, at market value. Further, the law states that no government official or family member can receive land, and only those without land can be given it. It also exempts small farmers, indigenous people, and campesinos, from paying property taxes, while introducing a 0.25 per cent surcharge to the tax base for all other agricultural landowners, and provides that 75 per cent of these tax revenues must be used for improvements in rural basic infrastructure and healthcare. The law also declares that only holdings larger than 50 hectares (120 acres) will be targeted for investigation, and aims to stimulate environmental-friendly production.[41]

In all of these respects Morales' land reform could be read as a mere extension and clarification of the 1996 law, designed to carry out the stated aim of this law more efficiently. As the Cochabamba-based Andean Information Network says in a December 2006 report, 'the text of the law merely updates and modifies the 1996 Agrarian Reform Law [INRA] passed during the first Gonzalo Sanchez de Lozada government'. Their report continues, 'What concerns the political opposition and large-scale landowners, though, is that it appears that this government will *actually implement the policy*, which had been ineffectual and subject to corruption and favoritism in the past'.[42]

Nonetheless, and contrary to its fiery rhetoric, to date MAS has been cautious about enforcing the law. Despite MAS spokesman Alex Contreras releasing a 'hit list' of the top offending landowners, some with as many as 48,000 largely unused hectares (120,000 acres), to date MAS has expropriated almost no latifundio land. Instead, with the exception of some reverted Brazilian-owned properties, almost all of the lands so far redistributed have been state-owned lands, including forest reserves. And in the few cases where lands have been expropriated, they were bought by the government at market value.

Yet despite the reform's moderation, the landholding elite did not allow it to become law without a fight. Morales sent his agrarian reform legislation to Congress in May 2006, but it was held up in the Senate, where MAS lacks a majority by three votes. Protesting the impasse, thousands of landless and indigenous marched from all over the country, arriving in November at the Congress building in La Paz. Upon their arrival, the conservative parties left the Senate, further stalling the vote. At the same time, Bolivian newspapers had discovered that Santa Cruz agricultural elites had sent two representatives to Spain to hire mercenaries to defend latifundio land and to overthrow Morales. At the final hour, the legal representatives of three of the abstaining opposition Senators switched sides and allowed the land reform to be passed into law on November 28, 2006.

Despite these conflicts, the reform effort has gone forward. As of August 2006 MAS had already given 3.5 million hectares (9 million acres) to indigenous and landless communities, and a further 2 million hectares (5.5 million acres) of the promised total of 20 million hectares had been taken over by the state in preparation for redistribution. Also very significant is the *Pueblos Unidos* settlement, the first MST-style settlement set up by the Morales administration. Composed largely of MST members evicted from previous settlements, *Pueblos Unidos* brings together 626 families on 16,000 hectares (40,000 acres) of land outside Santa Cruz. Despite the difficult access to the settlement and lack of basic services, *Pueblos Unidos* is a powerful sign of progress for Bolivia's landless peasants, intently monitoring the progress of Morales' reform.

LAND REFORM VS. 'ANDEAN CAPITALISM'

But despite the achievements of Morales' reform so far, there have been substantial criticisms of its shortcomings, ranging from observing that the residents of *Pueblos Unidos* are still labouring on marginal lands to pointing out that MAS has expropriated or redistributed virtually no latifundio land.[43]

Perhaps the most telling critique is offered by the Center for the Study of Labour and Agricultural Development, a La Paz–based independent research organization established in 1985 and dedicated to action and research on rural and urban labour issues. CEDLA argues that the continued existence of large-scale landholdings demonstrates that Morales' reform is deliberately continuing to rely on the neoliberal export model of agro-industrial development, in which the latifundios play a central role. In a report titled *The National Development Plan is neither Nationalist nor Anti-Neoliberal*, CEDLA points out that the main thrust of the government's 'National Development Plan 2006-2010 is, in its own words, that of "maintaining the competitiveness of the external sector"'.[44] This will mean a continuing emphasis on restricting domestic demand, which will in turn lead to the 'depression of the purchasing power of national salaries' and 'guarantee the overexploitation of the workforce'.[45] This, together with the stated goal of increasing foreign direct investment (including in agriculture) from 0.8 per cent of GDP in 2006 to 8.6 per cent of GDP in 2011, provides the grounds for CEDLA's conclusion that the National Development Plan 'preserves neoliberalism… [d]espite "the widening of State participation in certain sectors"'. Enrique Ormachea, the lead land researcher at CEDLA, sums all this up: 'the agricultural development model proposed by MAS in the National Development Plan is based on export agriculture and the privileging of the external over the internal market. In this model, the latifundio is the core productive unit of growth. And this is not going to change'.[46]

On May 28, 2007, Vice-President García Linera openly confirmed CEDLA's analysis when he said 'we have to work together with Cruceño landholders to re-strengthen the agro-export model of development…'.[47] According to García Linera, the prime architect of the administration's development strategy, MAS's strategy is based on 'capitalism with a big state presence', aiming for a 'pluralist modernization' combining 'the modern industrial economy… urban family micro-enterprises and…the communitarian campesino economy'. Linera calls this 'Andean capitalism'.[48] That the policy is to continue with the neoliberal development model is also confirmed by the nature of the new loan which the Morales government is currently negotiating with the World Bank to subsidize future phases of the land reform. As of June 2007 this loan had not been finalized, but the text of the loan, obtained by this writer, indicated that it would be used to support a 'land bank' micro-credit scheme, a programme that has already been implemented in Brazil and widely attacked by the Brazilian MST and other progressive sectors.[49]

The current land reform in Bolivia is based on a search for class harmony, offering state support for poor farmers, under the rubric of their incorporation into the larger scheme of maintaining a model of development that relies on large-scale agro-industrial exporters.[50] Perhaps the biggest danger here is that rather than either meaningfully incorporating peasant farmers or exploring alternative paths of agricultural development based on small-scale farming, peasants will be relegated to the status of economically quaint, folk novelties in the overall picture of 'Andean capitalism'. Yet, despite the dubious nature of their development plan, MAS has offered landless peasants some tangible benefits and has combined these with a radically pro-peasant and pro-indigenous rhetoric and symbolism. Because of the success of MAS's hegemonic project, and because of earlier contradictions within the landless movement itself, MAS's land reform, despite its significant shortcomings, has been overwhelmingly supported by the MST and others. Indeed, since May 2006 the MST leadership has respected a call from MAS that no more land occupations take place, so as not to jeopardize the legal process of government-led redistribution. But this also halts the very process by which MST members build solidarities and construct new political communities based on egalitarianism. It now shifts the MST's focus *entirely* to the legal terrain. Instead of putting pressure on the courts primarily via mass mobilizations – a tactic at which the MST has proven particularly capable – the key site of struggle has shifted to the legal realm, where landless peasants are seriously disadvantaged.

The typical justification of MAS's demobilization of the peasant movement has been the party's need to consolidate power in the face of intense pressure from all sides. And indeed, MAS has skilfully parried a host of real threats – their survival as a political party has no doubt depended on it. First, there are legitimate fears about agricultural development and production, particularly considering the crisis in productivity among peasant farmers. What effect would dismantling the medium to large-size latifundio land holdings and redistributing those lands to peasant farmers have on Bolivia's national economy? If it had a negative impact on the economy, would the Morales administration remain able to govern, or even remain in power? This fragility is further reinforced by the ever-present threat of massive right-wing violence, as well as by Bolivia's limited manoeuvrability due to its relative dependence on international financial institutions – a dependence it is in some ways reducing, but in other ways perpetuating.[51]

The effect for MAS's search for class harmony, as Thomson and Hylton have concluded, is that the 'Morales government has brought the current revolutionary cycle to a provisional close. It has partially fulfilled the major demands of the "October agenda", especially nationalization and the constitutional assembly, by quickening the administrative pace and centralizing power at the highest levels of the executive.... While the [present] reforms represent a response to the popular mandate, they are also a bid for state hegemony'. They continue, 'This, in turn, has demobilized and fragmented the movements that brought MAS to power'.[52]

The way MAS is navigating the tenuous political environment largely reflects its precarious position as a reformist party vis-à-vis the conservative and mobilized eastern elites at home and its relatively weak and dependent position vis-à-vis the international finance institutions in the global capitalist economy. Yet, it does not follow that the only option for Bolivia is 'Andean capitalism'. MAS's land reform seems to go too far in the direction of supporting the latifundio, when the latifundio monopolizes land and continues to be a key source of the racism, violence and inequality that MAS has vowed to combat. It is, of course, an obvious fact that there exist no clear alternatives to MAS's agricultural development plan. Yet, in an important sense, MAS itself is at least partly complicit in this lack of alternatives. While the administration has adopted the language of the Zapatistas, of 'mandar obedeciendo' (governing by obeying), its actions have largely been to the contrary.[53] For instance, in a much-criticized move, MAS sought to exclude virtually all grassroots groups from participating directly in the Constituent Assembly in the name of consolidating political power. One of the groups initially excluded was the MST, which has articulated some alternative proposals – albeit undeveloped – for agrarian reform. In their demand that the MST stop land occupations MAS has also adopted the dominant thinking about autonomous occupied settlements – that it is something to be stopped, not a source of creative regeneration to be supported. As Raquel Gutierrez has put it, 'today there is a tapering off of the social movements in Bolivia. The state is not acting as the interlocutor for the movements, but instead is subordinating them'.[54]

Contrary to Gutierrez's analysis, Pablo Stefanoni and Hervé Do Alto correctly point out that the vast majority of social movements in Bolivia support MAS and their reformist policies. They argue that the movements are no further to the left than MAS and that MAS and the movements essentially share the same political aspirations. 'The border between "moderates" and "radicals" is porous and does not refer precisely to a confrontation between socialism and capitalism', they write. Rather, Stefanoni and Do Alto say the key issue that divides moderates from radicals is the nationalization of hydrocarbons. According to this analysis, 'radicals' are those who support a 'radical version of state capitalism', 'moderates' the continuation of foreign direct investment under state control.[55]

Yet, something seems amiss with this attempt to unsettle the dichotomy between capitalism and socialism: in effect, it replaces it with the dichotomy between liberal or social-democratic capitalism and neoliberal capitalism. This would seem to suggest that the only desires of Bolivia's social movements, and the only realistic options for the country, are those of either social-democratic state capitalism (the 'radical' position) or neoliberal capitalism (the 'moderate' position). To be sure, it does appear to be the case that, whatever impressive changes MAS has introduced since it took power, socialism, at least as traditionally conceived, is not on the current government agenda. Indeed, García Linera confirmed this when he said at the end of 2005 that 'Bolivia will still be capitalist in 50 or 100 years'.[56] But to say socialism is not on the government's agenda is a very different thing from saying that there exists in Bolivia no real desire for socialism. This is a claim that sits uneasily with the demands of the country's social movements between 2000 and 2005, as well as with my own experiences at the MST settlements.

NOTES

Many thanks go to José Antonio Lucero, Enrique Ormachea, Caitlin Esch, and especially Jean Friedman-Rudovsky and the *compañeros* of the MST, in particular Justino, my brief *guía* in Yaquiba and Montero. Without their help, this essay would not have been possible.

1   Interview with author, August 2006.
2   Doug Herztler, 'Bolivia's Agrarian Reform Initiative', *Andean Information Network*, 28 June 2006; 'Propuesta para acabar con "latifundio ocioso" encuentra apoyo politico', *El Diario,* 22 May 2006.
3   Decreto Supremo 28733, Republica de Bolivia, 2 June 2006.
4   World Bank, *Bolivia Land for Agricultural Development Project*, Washington: World Bank, forthcoming, p. 136.
5   Forrest Hylton and Sinclair Thomson, 'The Chequered Rainbow', *New Left Review,* 35, September–October 2005.
6   Fernando Cabrera, 'Interview with Evo Morales', Radio Nederland, 1 December 2006.
7   Speech in Ucurena, 2 August 2006.
8   Michael Weinstein, 'Bolivia's Evo Morales Launches His Movement Toward Socialism into the Political Trenches', *Power and Interest News Report*, 15 June 2006.
9   Equipo Nizkor, 'Antecedentes de la matanza de los campesinos sin tierra de Bolivia', 9 November 2001, available from http://www.rebelion.org.

10   'Landowners Massacre Squatters', 18 November 2001, http://www.americas. org 'Massacre Verdict Protested', 24 November 2002, http://www.americas. org.

11   Silvia Cusicanqui Rivera, *Oprimidos pero no vencidos*, La Paz: Aruwiyiri, 2003, p. 110.

12   Based on the combined populations of Santa Cruz, Tarija, and Beni according to the Instituto Nacional de Estatistica, Republica de Bolivia.

13   Álvaro García Linera, Marxa Chávez León and Patricia Costas Monje, *Sociología de los movimientos sociales en Bolivia: estructuras de movilización, procesos enmarcadores y acción política*, La Paz: Diakonia, 2004, p. 546; Cabrera, 'Interview with Morales'.

14   Miguel Urioste, *La Revolucion Agraria de Evo Morales*, La Paz: Fundacion Tierra, August 2006.

15   Alex Contreras, *El Diario,* 24 November 2006.

16   June Nash, *We Eat the Mines and the Mines Eat Us,* New York: Columbia University Press, 1979, p. xxi.

17   Cabrera, 'Interview with Morale'.

18   Urioste, 'La Revolucion Agraria de Evo Morales'.

19   Linera, León and Monje, *Sociologia de los movimientos sociales*, p. 570.

20   Ibid., p. 545.

21   'The Antinomies of Bolivian Neoliberalism', *Comparative Studies in Society and History*, 41(3), July 1999, p. 539.

22   Duncan Green, *Silent Revolution*, New York: Monthly Review Press, 2003, p. 74.

23   Mamerto Luna Perez, *Apertura Comercial y Sector Agrícola Campesino – la otra cara de la pobreza del campesino andino*, La Paz: CEDLA, 2003.

24   Manuel Davila Morales, *INRA*, La Paz: U.P.S. Editorial, August 2005.

25   Linera, León and Monje, *Sociologia de los movimientos sociales*, p. 120.

26   Cited in Jean Friedsky, 'Land War in Bolivia', *Narco News,* 13 October 2005.

27   Linera, León and Monje, *Sociologia de los movimientos sociales*, p. 547.

28   Ibid., p. 558.

29   For a discussion of this, see Friedsky, 'Land War in Bolivia'.

30   The quotations and data in this paragraph are drawn from Linera, León and Monje, *Sociologia de los movimientos sociales*, pp. 548ff.

31   Ibid., p. 576.

32   'Landless Step up Occupations', 18 March 2006, available at http://www. americas.org.

33   Personal Interview, August 2006.

34   Luis Crespo, 'Bolivia: Guaranies "Desamparados"', 13 May 2005, available at http://www.BBCMundo.com.

35   'Agro del oriente crea Comités de Defensa y amenaza con violencia'. *Los Tiempos*, 31 May 2006.

36   Ibid.

37   Benjamin Dangl, *The Price of Fire,* Oakland: AK Press, 2007, p. 212.

38   S.R.A Gutierrez, 'Somos los Cambas una Nacion Sin Estado?', 2 October 2006, available from http://www.nacioncamba.net.

39   'Paupérrima imagen deja Miss Bolivia en el Miss Universo', 26 May 2004, available at http://www.bolivia.com.

40   Linera, León and Monje, *Sociologia de los movimientos sociales*, p. 571, my emphasis.

41   Andean Information Network, 'Bolivian Congress Passes Agrarian Reform During Tension',1 December 2006, available from http://ain-bolivia.org.

42   Ibid.

43   Regarding *Pueblos Unidos,* James Petras goes so far as to say that 'Government-promoted land settlements in remote lands with precarious soil, distant from markets, transport and credit facilities will doom recipients to failure, as has occurred in the past'. 'A Bizarre Beginning in Bolivia', *Counterpunch,* 4/5 February 2006.

44   Cited in Lorgio Orellana 'El Plan Nacional de Desarrollo no es nacionalista ni antineoliberal', *Alerta Laboral,* 46, September 2006, p. 7.

45   Ibid.

46   Personal communication to the author, June 2007.

47   'Las élites se redistribuyen el poder', *Econoticias,* 28 May 2007.

48   'We want a capitalism with a big state presence', Pablo Stefanoni interview with Álvaro García Linera, 18 May 2007, available from http://www.green-left.org.au.

49   World Bank, *Bolivia Land for Agricultural Development Project*.

50   Jeffery Webber, 'Bolivia: Evo Morales' First 100 Days', 21 December 2006, available from http://www.solidarity-us.org.

51   This is seen, on the one hand, in the MAS government's participation in the Boliviarian Alternative for the Americas and its pulling out of the World Bank's International Centre for the Settlement of Investment Disputes, and, on the other, in its participation in the pending World Bank land reform loan, discussed above.

52   Forrest Hylton and Sinclair Thomson, *Revolutionary Horizons,* London: Verso, p. 158.

53   Morales titled a speech given on January 22, 2006, 'Mandare Obedeciendo' (I will govern by obeying).

54   Interview with Raquel Gutierrez by Veronica Gago, 'La seduccion del chavismo', *Brecha,* 28 September 2006.

55   Pablo Stefanoni and Hervé Do Alto, *Evo Morales: de la coca al Palacio*, La Paz: Malatesta, 2006, p. 115.

56   Interview with Alvaro Garcia Linera by Pablo Stefanoni, 'MAS is of the Centre-Left', *IV Online Magazine,* 373, December 2005, available at http://www.internationalviewpoint.org.

ON THE FORMS OF RESISTANCE IN LATIN AMERICA: ITS 'NATIVE' MOMENT

ANA ESTHER CECEÑA

In the last fifteen years Latin America has been the scene of very different kinds of resistance and struggle. Each case is at the same time universal and singular; a condensation both of the major fault-lines of the system of domination and of particular local practices of power and expropriation – and of self-determination and autonomous political organization. Every people involved in struggle has its own means of expression and spaces where its project develops and is articulated. In some cases people burst onto the streets, take over public squares or schools, or block roads. In others they rely on silence, absence, invisibility. Masked faces and uncovered faces, metal weapons and wooden weapons, or just paper weapons – the power of printed images; marches and hunger strikes; the seizure of lands, or staying away from work. The reasons for the protests are as varied as their forms, and as motley and complex as the individuals who come together and dissolve again according to the circumstances and motives of each struggle. In face of such diversity, all have to remain open to change; so different are they that people must be content to agree on essentials; so numerous are they that they are able to surprise each other.

So, after its first disruptive and demobilizing impact, neoliberalism in Latin America has had to face mounting discontent: little by little, real social alternatives have begun to emerge, by combining reconstituted older organizations with a wide range of newly-active individuals, often not formally organized, without party discipline (and even allergic to it), and with new ways of understanding the world, constructing new imaginaries and mobilizing for struggle. Urban and rural collectives, people forced into precarious employment, displaced people, informal workers, nomadic collectives, men and women of every background interlinked in the creation of new codes of subjectivity and new forms of community. Among the unifying forces behind all this are water supplies, the tropical rain forests, destroyed and denuded forests, lack of access to land, pollution, the FTAA, the IMF, the World Bank, the USA and multinational companies, the Puebla–Panama Plan, militarization, the foreign debt, the denial of self-determination. In reply, autonomy, multiculturalism, land reform, direct democracy, a different relationship with nature, and popular sovereignty are the demands repeated from the tropics to the glaciers.

Revolts often begin in communities firmly rooted in a particular place. In general this is true of indigenous movements, like the Zapatistas, and many peasant movements. The same holds for insurrections in parts of cities, as in Cochabamba. But the problems that generate such revolts are world-wide problems, experienced also by people who are geographically dispersed, and it is this that has led to the setting-up of coordinating committees or networks that extend the boundaries of the communities in struggle and unite them with other similar communities, or other people worried about the same problem, often in very distant places. Thus the Coordinating Committee for the Defence of Water and Life in Cochabamba became a point of convergence for all struggles over water, and led to the building of a world-wide network. The same happened with apparently very particular challenges, such as those special to the Zapatistas, leading to the coming together of such widely different groups as, for example, the natives of Chiapas and European and Korean youth, who identified with the Zapatistas' aims despite having such different backgrounds; and older Latin American activists too, in spite of the fact that the Zapatistas do not represent the revolutionary subject – the urban wage-worker – who had for so long been considered the only real one.

And out of these experiences, continental, or at least regional, movements have emerged, not identified with a particular territory but with shared feelings, which sustain a great deal of cohesion based on their commitment to certain central ideas, such as the fight against the FTAA, or against free trade agreements in general; opposition to militarization and the repayment of foreign debt; the demand for the abolition of foreign military bases world-wide; the demand for people's self-determination with regard to their form of government and the use of the products of nature and industry. It is through these experiences that a new concept of emancipation has been discovered and articulated, often in a utopian way, yet also attempting to live the utopia in the process of struggle. The Zapatistas, the fighters for water in Cochabamba, the Ecuadorians' struggle to control their oil, the landless of Brazil, the Argentine *piqueteros* organizing the blocking of highways, the *mapuches* of the Southern cone fighting, as they have done for 500 years, against subordination – all those who demand demilitarization, and so many others, who, at different

scales of organization and with different degrees of visibility, and making different kinds of intervention in the construction of that other world glimpsed
on the horizon – all are part of a great liberatory cycle now occurring across
Latin America, combining millennial visions with immediate ones and making the region stand up with dignity again.

TRANSFORMING THE TERRAIN OF STRUGGLE

The working-class struggles which developed with Latin America's industrialization – often obscuring the problems of the countryside, the land, and indigenous, peasant life – have been seriously weakened by the global restructuring of work. Factory-based modes of organization have lost their purchase
as factory production has been reconfigured internationally, as plants have
been modernized and workforces downsized, and as more and more jobs
have become precarious or informal. The focus of organization has gradually been displaced from the factory to where the unemployed live – the
'margins', broadly understood. The key organization in people's lives can no
longer – or at least can not only – be one based on their place of work, at
a time when the workplace is losing its old salience, shifting the boundaries
between public and private, work and leisure, production and reproduction.

This shift of the terrain of struggle towards the sphere of everyday life has
reduced the centrality of the factory worker as the subject of struggle and
social transformation, and opened up the role of agent of resistance to all its
other constituent elements: women, peasants, 'Indians' (in its Latin American
sense of the descendants of aboriginal inhabitants), students, migrants, other
kinds of employees, undocumented workers, etc, each one with its particular
experience of oppression, specific views and claims, perceptions of reality,
modes of adaptation or rebellion, histories and memories.

Among all of these new modes of struggle the most significant has been
that of Latin America's Indians, its native Americans. In constant interaction
with a culture and a way of running the world based on relations of domination, appropriation through dispossession, and the predatory subordination
of the environment, they are engaged in one of their modest processes of
'everyday' resistance, not always clear or explicit, but this time leading towards the assumption of a leading continent-wide role: a role which also
involves a new perspective on the meaning of life and a new conception of
social relations. The recent Indian mobilizations of the continent have been
distinctive from one another in many important ways, yet they all have issued a similarly profound challenge to the existing order. Their perspective
focuses on the 'civilizational rupture' involved in capitalism's irruption into
America, and their reinterpretation of history is one in which this irrup-

tion is a mere *incident* in a millennial process. In their view Western history, a history of the emergence of Europe and a history of the rest of the world understood in terms of its linking-up with a civilization constructed in Europe and the USA, is not the history of America's native people. They, instead, after centuries of despotic rule, which have also been centuries of learning and resistance, are proposing their own version of history: a history of people who came from far away, who carry remote imaginaries, ancestral cultures and understandings of the world much older than that of appropriation and accumulation; a history of people who have lived together as *defeated* people for five hundred years without losing their collective memory, without ceasing to construct utopias, and without ceasing to resist; a history of a people whose deep historical roots enable them to look beyond the present to broad horizons that offer a glimpse, not of the end of history, but of its openness – precisely because they can perceive, and fight for, an end of the history of *capitalism*.

Although many of them have known the urban and industrialized world, have worked in construction or textiles, have migrated to the United States and encountered the problems associated with wage work and proletarian struggles, their deepest identity led these rebellions – the Zapatista one in Chiapas most explicitly – to see themselves as searching for the construction of a new historic epoch, the creation of a new world in place of the current one, which can no longer be patched up. And the route to this reconstruction or re-creation entails the reconstitution of the community – or, better, of communities – within a new, enriched culture, arrived at by recognizing *diversity* as the essential ontological element in social relations. This new culture assumes a society without exclusions, but with many differences; it implies a process of mutual recognition and the creation of new bonds which pay attention to the necessarily 'horizontal' nature of a society based on these principles.

Spatially dispersed, and often with scant connections between them, contemporary uprisings bearing the stamp of the last five hundred years show many similarities. In the Amazon forest the native people grouped in the Indian, Black and Popular Resistance Movement (MRINP) say they are struggling against 'the barbarity of the enslaved society that exploited the African people, sacrificing and separating families and communities, [and against] the atrocious cruelty, that wounded and wounds daily the popular sectors'.[1] In the Lacandona forest in Chiapas, an insurrection of *México profundo*, the Mexico of deep indigenous roots, the Zapatistas declare that a 'world order that destroys nations and cultures brings us together. Money, the great international criminal, has today a name that reflects the incapacity of power to create new things. A new world war is suffered today. It is a war against all peoples, all human beings, all culture, all history'.[2]

Even in Cochabamba, where the people in revolt do not see themselves as indigenous, they too stress the rights of indigenous people, and non-capitalist social relations: 'The workers of the city and the countryside, the communities and indigenous *ayllus,* have for decades or centuries practised non-neoliberal ways of managing the common good, forms of assembly power, ways of communal, union and town democracy. These institutions allow the direct and permanent participation of everybody, restrict the concentration of power and are resistant to corruption'.[3] But while the deep roots of resistance and ways of community organization are invoked, the protest is directed against the total dispossession to which people have been subjected, and which has now reached unbearable extremes: 'The neoliberal regime has eliminated the national economy. No natural resource belongs to us; the water, the land, the railways, the oil, the gas are in the hands of foreign businessmen whose sole desire is to make profit from somebody else's work... there is no work, no money, no investment, no growth.'[4]

Five hundred years of domination and looting have today reached the point of expropriating the conditions of life itself. The land is now converted into a mere platform for the exploitation of resources; nature is converted into codes that allow organisms to be reconstructed in laboratories, or the knowledge obtained from thousands of years of experimentation to be applied to circuit engineering; plants are reduced to their active principles; minerals to energy to drive machinery which robs the earth of its capacity to give shelter to life; water is turned into a commodity; in order to find work people are forced to migrate; human beings are turned into undocumented people, pariahs in their own country, legally *non-existent.*

People feel the threat to their culture, their history and their moral integrity much more than the threat to their jobs or their wages. Their ability to reproduce themselves independently declines, and they are excluded from all decisions about the future of their region, or anything else that matters to them. Neoliberalism has pushed the long process of dispossession to extremes, verging on the complete negation of what it is to be a human being. In face of this shift in the limits of the possible, all the victims of the system emerge to fight for their very existence, which today, more obviously than ever, means overcoming capitalism. At this point, two elements make the challenge a rebellion, rather than a mass suicide: the dignity of a people who prefer to die for reasons of their own choosing, and the hope of a people whose collective memory evokes the historic possibility of a different future.

HORIZONS AND UTOPIAS

Broad horizons, utopias and dreams are by their nature unattainable, precisely because they are always changing. But images of the future are what make it possible to construct the present. Utopias do become real; dreams are dreamed and eventually lived. They are not absurd, as neoliberal pragmatism would like them to be, but plans for building the future in the here and now. That is why they do not de-mobilize but on the contrary, offer a path to follow and a sense of life that allow people to deal with the squalor of their daily lives by creating an alternative culture – and a way of acting and understanding – that underpins different forms of resistance, organization and struggle. They combine the memories or imaginaries of the history of other times and other worlds with ideal representations of desires and longings.

With the homeland as a basic reference, and with an intersubjective relationship with land and nature, the utopias and dreams of Latin American people extend the history of capitalism both forwards and backwards. As John Berger has written:

> These two movements, towards the past and the future, are not as contrary as they might first appear because basically the peasant has a cyclical view of time. The two movements are different ways of going round a circle. He accepts the sequence of centuries without making that sequence absolute. Those who have a unilinear view of time cannot come to terms with the idea of cyclic time: it creates a moral vertigo since all their morality is based on cause and effect. Those who have a cyclic view of time are easily able to accept the convention of historic time, which is simply the trace of the turning wheel.[5]

The utopias constructed by half-breed, *mestizas*, baroque cultures (by virtue of which they are also non-linear) are not utopias of abundance but of finitude, and respect. What moves people in such cultures is clearly related to the impossibility of surviving in a world which tries to deny them both the essential conditions of subsistence, and any chance of being able to create such conditions for themselves. Their conviction, however, comes from something positive – a utopia that allows them to glimpse a society in which it is possible for human beings to work and realize their capacity to construct their own lives. To quote Berger again:

bourgeois and marxist ideals of equality presume a world of plenty; they demand equal rights for all before a cornucopia... to be constructed by science and the advancement of knowledge....The peasant ideal of equality recognizes a world of scarcity, and its promise is for mutual fraternal aid in struggling against this scarcity and a just sharing of what the work produces. Closely connected with the peasant's recognition, as a survivor, of scarcity is his recognition of man's relative ignorance. He may admire knowledge and the fruits of knowledge but he never supposes that the advance of knowledge reduces the extent of the unknown. This non-antagonistic relation between the unknown and the known explains why some of his knowledge is accommodated in what, from the outside, is defined as superstition or magic. Nothing in his experience encourages him to believe in final causes, precisely because his experience is so wide.[6]

I am well aware of the danger of ascribing to utopias a mobilizing potential which is not always realized in reality, at least not explicitly or obviously. Many contemporary revolts are due to some particular defeat, a particular situation which people rightly see as an outrage to both custom and law, to the moral economy (as in the case of water distribution in Cochabamba); or they are seen as resulting from a diverse set of problems that find their explanation in an abstract structure of relationships, such as neoliberalism, which is provoking similar reactions in other places, unconnected to their own.

But while it is not always consciously invoked, the utopia is as present in the re-conquest, or at least the reconsideration, of the moral economy, as it is in the fight against neoliberalism. Both involve memories and dreams, both implicitly contain the idea of a different world. Sometimes only a slight possibility of it is glimpsed, a diffuse horizon, but one which still, as Eduardo Galeano would say, guides us on the way. It is impossible to imagine a fighter without hope, much less an organized people with no concept of an intention to change its current circumstances. But decoding utopias is a task which not all movements explicitly undertake, and this is true of those which arise from particular defeats, such as the privatization of health services, or of water or other resources.

Throughout history there are numerous examples of revolts which have not paid much attention to making clear their image of the desired future, or which have done so only in a very summary or tangential manner. In some cases this has to do with values common to the group which are expressed in a way, or in a language, not easily grasped by people who are foreign to it; in others, it is something not even explicit in the group's own culture, but nonetheless inherent in the participants in the revolt. As Edward Thompson says, in order to understand these movements

> it is not enough to merely describe the popular symbolic protests (burning of effigies, putting on ilex sheets, hanging boots): it is also necessary to recover the meaning of these symbols with regard to a broader symbolic universe, and thus find their strength, both as an affront to the hegemony of the powerful and as an expression of the multitude's expectations.[7]

It is also necessary to work out the different perceptions of the problem, and their distinct tempos, that co-exist within any revolt, if one is to understand its meaning. It is clearly a matter of a complex meaning, which synthesizes an enormous number of determinations and is built up from numerous significations that converge at a critical point, where they acquire both expression and a broad significance. The meanings of a revolt are never trivial; they cannot be grasped by attending only to those demands that are openly articulated. It is essential to disclose a revolt's concealed codes, the messages from the depth of the history, the culture, the values and shared utopias of those involved. We cannot wait for the patience of a historical craftsman to do this – we need to begin to do this now, albeit without haste or vanity.

THE NEW SYMPTOMATOLOGY OF RESISTANCE

The neoliberal stage of capitalism involves profound transformations of pre-existing technological, organizational, political and conceptual paradigms. The scenery of class struggle has changed, socially, politically and geographically. Among the most important changes, on account of their recurrence in most of the contemporary movements of revolt, we may mention the following:

1. Revolts are led by heterogeneous subjects

New actors appear, making up what could be described as a 'blurred' class in search of new features, with perceptions of reality coming from diverse experiences of domination that are much more complex than those growing out of the labour relation alone, much more difficult to identify and recognize. It becomes difficult to think in terms of a single polarity, or a privileged dimension of conflict. As the Cochabamba rebels declared: 'The workers' trade-union movement is no longer the main context of discussion. It is the new world of work that has created new models and structures of organization and public interpellation in streets, the road blockages, in assemblies and meetings to entwine their solidarities…'.[8] The ethnic contradiction that coexists with relations of slavery or wage-earning, and which has served as a rationalization for the greatest cruelty and plunder, is by no means secondary to the capital-labour relation; nor is gender domination. Today a convergence seems to be occurring between all these dimensions, producing a complex, multidimensional kind of resistance, not disjointed or hierarchical as in earlier periods, but with strong indications of contact and mutual recognition between the parts, indicating a *reshaping of class* through the experience of struggle in accordance with the unforgettable Zapatista slogan – 'behind us we are you': 'the same forgotten men and women. The same excluded. The same untolerated. The same persecuted. We are the same you'.[9]

It is difficult to know if this is a class in the process of reconstitution, and in any case we need to reflect seriously on the character or the content of 'class' and 'classes', and the pertinence of maintaining that conceptualization. Many movements themselves speak of 'civil society', in order to differentiate themselves from the politicians and businessmen in the power structure, and to highlight their diversity and their collective detachment, their attitude of resistance, to all corridors of power, whether those of the parties, or even of working class organizations. Other movements refer to 'working people', pointing to the variety of the sectors which make up the working people, the signs of a collective identity and their distance from the circles of power. In all cases there seems to be a certainty that the insurgent subject today does not correspond to the narrow and clearly defined framework of what used to be thought of as a 'class', among other reasons because these new individuals come, to a large extent, from the countryside, or from the sectors which Armando Bartra called '*orilleros*' (semi-urban marginals), and which the dominant tendency within Marxism used to see as obstacles to progress, or even as counter-revolutionary.[10]

2. Radical questioning of the political system, and a search for new means and spaces of political expression

Revolts are themselves an indication of the inadequacy or irrelevance of the system of political representation, and are largely due to the inability of the system to construct a social contract that includes, however contradictorily, all sectors of the population. In most cases there is an outright rejection of the institutions and mechanisms of politics, and the very conception of politics and the political as a separate sphere of social life. For the insurgent Zapatistas, for example, the construction of a new world was seen as a deep cultural transformation in which politics becomes a means to generate a consensus, not a weapon of domination. For them, it is in the process of making contact, meeting and holding dialogues with others that real transformation of society occurs; a new way of doing politics, without mediations, without delegations, without secret agreements, without haste – constructing a solid base of collective agreement that does not exclude minorities, but could be worked out with everyone's assistance.

3. Rejection of vanguards and the construction of horizontal relationships

This too was a utopia, but involved a very relevant questioning of all political institutions in which parties or representatives seen as 'popular' or 'leftist' often participate. It meant trying to work out a new role for the organizations of the rebellious left, and a shift of focus towards 'civil society' or 'the people'. Dialogue with the state continues, but changes its character. Decisions are taken in the course of deliberation, implying that decision-making should be collective. Advocating direct democracy, unity in diversity, recognition of and respect for differences, implies deliberative practices in which 'all are equal because all are different' (in the words of the EZLN). The Zapatistas thereby advanced the argument that the only way of not reproducing relationships based on power is ensuring that no one is more important than anyone else, that relations between equals can only be horizontal.

4. The construction of a different society implies a complete revolution of culture and of the conception of the world

The protagonists of the insurgent movements are perceived much more as excluded than as exploited – excluded and dispensable, excluded and useless. The present system has nothing to offer to the vast majority of the world's population; market forces have made some of them redundant, while others are paid paltry wages. In either case, they are seen as victims of economic genocide, gradual but inevitable. The existing system offers no way to reverse the levels of poverty now reached on the planet, its progress and development plans are premised on poverty and robbery, a disaster only sustained by the seizure of political control and its counterpart, militarization. Exclusion and material appropriation depend on the exclusion and expropriation of people and their culture; on expropriating also their history and their utopias; on the fatalism of 'the end of history'. Society is seen as going through an extreme situation in which life itself is at risk.

The restoration of collective self-determination, then, involves a recuperation of history, memory and imagination. Culture, costumes, accumulated knowledge, hope and the capacity to imagine different worlds are the seeds of a project of emancipation with manifold faces, with scant concrete resources, but always with the same certainty: the world *must* be recreated, and to do this it is necessary to make use of age-old knowledge, human generosity, patience, respect and imagination. And in the process all colours, all experiences, all cultures must be present. The horizon is the creation of a world in which all the worlds, all the struggles and all the utopias have a place.

This process is taking shape every day in different places. Sometimes, as in Cochabamba, defending water, the struggle is for life; new relations are created, new ways of understanding and moulding the world of our hopes, with the help of all and sundry. Sometimes it is marches, actions and campaigns against neoliberalism in Latin American cities that are building, step by step, new relations and new frontiers. Sometimes, in the heart of a forest once forgotten, but today competed for, in the fight for autonomy a great leap forward occurs.

NOTES

1   Indian, Black and Popular Resistance Movement (MRINP), 'Brasil: 500 anos de resistência indígena, negra e popular', 1995.

2   Zapatist National Liberation Army (EZLN), *Documents and Reports*, Mexico: ERA, 1995, p. 440.

3   Coordinating Committee for the Defence of Water and Life (CDAV), *Declaración de la Coordinadora de Defensa del Agua y de la Vida*, 2000.

4   Ibid.

5   John Berger, *Pig Earth*, New York: Pantheon, 1979, p. 201.

6   Ibid., p. 202.

7   E. P. Thompson, *Tradición, revuelta y consciencia de clase. Estudios sobre la crisis de la sociedad preindustrial*, Barcelona: Crítica, 1989, p. 46.

8   CDAV, *Declaración*.

9   EZLN, 'Discurso inaugural de la Mayor Ana María', *Chiapas*, 3, 1996, pp. 102-3.

10   Armando Bartra, 'La llama y la piedra. De cómo cambiar el mundo según John Holloway', *Chiapas*, 15, 2003.

MEXICO'S OAXACA COMMUNE

RICHARD ROMAN
AND EDUR VELASCO ARREGUI

This essay explores the extraordinary experience of the Oaxaca Commune in Mexico, an experience of grass-roots rebellion and self-government that has put forth an alternative model of struggle to the electoralist model of the PRD (Partido de la Revolución Democrática – Party of the Democratic Revolution) and to that of the Zapatistas and their Other Campaign, with their opposition to 'taking power' and their indifference or opposition to participation in elections. The Oaxaca uprising of the Spring of 2006 was an urban insurrection in one city, with important resonances elsewhere in the state of Oaxaca. It developed novel and participatory forms of organization, struggle, and self-governance. The Oaxaca rebellion developed 'assembleist' forms of direct democracy in the Spring of 2006 in order to organize itself democratically, as the people of Paris did in 1870-1871, and Russian workers did in 1905 and 1917. The APPO (Asamblea Popular de los Pueblos de Oaxaca – Popular Assembly of the Peoples of Oaxaca) became the organ of struggle and self-government of the popular rebellion. The Oaxaca uprising was a working-class revolt with strong support from other sectors. It started as a strike by the militant section 22 of the teachers union (a union that at the national level is corrupt, authoritarian and linked to the federal government). When the state government moved to brutally repress the movement on June 14, 2006, the people of Oaxaca City rose up and drove the state government out of the city. After five months of self-government and resistance, the national government carried out a massive assault on the people of Oaxaca on November 25, 2006. A state of siege was imposed, hundreds were arrested, disappeared, tortured. The movement suffered a great defeat but has not lost the war. It has reappeared publicly and is continuing its battle. This essay examines some of the dynamics and processes of the Oaxaca uprising and commune, its strengths and weaknesses as well as the conjuncture within which it emerged.

The Oaxaca uprising developed into an insurrectionary movement that dreamed of a new society, but acted with realism in the context of a national situation that was not revolutionary. The popular insurrection asserted dignity, raised consciousness and challenged the rights of capital, but always continued to bargain, or seek to bargain, with an intact national state, though one with a crisis of legitimacy. The pragmatic approach to bargaining (akin to what Hobsbawm once famously called 'collective bargaining by riot') posed its own dilemmas, however. Revolution limited to only one area in a national state would only be tolerated by the national state as long as the government believed it had to bide its time or that it served its tactical or strategic objectives. The political and social breadth of the movement encouraged the government to make limited and vague promises to try to divide the more moderate forces from the more radical. But the government could not or would not respond positively to the key unifying demand, a demand that the movement said was non-negotiable – the removal of a hated governor.

A perennial problem of many local or regional popular movements in Mexico has been the relationship between the local or regional and the national. Movements have been coopted, marginalized or smashed if they remained both local or regional *and* insurgent. Local and regional movements must converge into national movements for the consolidation of gains and the transformation of even the local and regional. Otherwise victories and local/regional transformation will be precarious, dependent on fleeting conjunctures of the national situation and subject to defeat when the national situation changes.

MEXICO'S CRISIS OF RULE

Mexico is in a protracted crisis of rule. The regime is in transition from the old *Estado Nacional Popular* (an authoritarian, one-party regime, but with aspects of a welfare state for some and hope for inclusion for many) to a still ambiguous and contested destination. There is a tension between the partial democratization of the electoral system and the continuing state-linked authoritarian mechanisms of control over the popular classes. As well, the neoliberal assaults on the lives and rights of ordinary people have produced massive popular discontent. Mexico's crisis is rooted in the general effects of neoliberalism and neoliberal continental integration, the decay of the old mechanisms of domination, the disappointed hopes for a transition to democracy and better living standards, and the continued assault on the quality of jobs, incomes, social rights, and the national patrimony. The concentration of wealth has grown by leaps and bounds in recent years. Three-tenths of one per cent of the population control 50 per cent of the tangible wealth of the country, as of 2007.[1] The real wages of the best-paid workers, those with a collective contract, fell by 18 per cent between 1995 and 2007, while the real value of the minimum wage fell by 34 per cent. Only 13 per cent of the Mexican population has a regular salary; the rest are precarious workers. 70 per cent of Mexicans live in cities of over 100,000 that form a constantly growing chain of impoverished ghettos.[2] Starvation wages combined with the neoliberal assault on the countryside continue to push millions of Mexicans northward to the US. State repression and corruption remain unabated. One in every 700 Mexicans enjoys exorbitant wealth while 80 million Mexicans experience devastating poverty. The new ruling bloc has not been able to consolidate a new mode of legitimation and has relied more and more on blatant political fraud and state terror to maintain control. This crisis of rule has not produced a revolutionary situation as people have not lost all hope in a quasi-institutional resolution of the crisis and mass-based left projects have continued to be limited by either their reformist goals or the dilemmas of transformatory projects in the context of a still intact national state with a monopoly of coercive power.

The hopes that the replacement of the one-party regime of the PRI (Institutional Revolutionary Party), a regime that lasted for over 70 years, would equal a transition to democracy have been dashed by the actions of the Fox administration (2000-2006). Those who advocated strategic voting for the PAN (National Action Party), the traditional party of the Catholic right, to bring down the old political structure of domination failed to see – or did not want to see – that the victory of the right would continue the power of the coalition of the business right and the PRIista neoliberals, but now with the addition of the Catholic right. The neoliberal policies would continue and the de facto alliance of the dominant neoliberal sections of the PRI with the PAN would continue. Massive corruption, constant attacks on working people and peasants, support for the most gangsterist union leaders, were all continued by President Fox of the PAN.

Some of the key goals of this new power bloc (privatization of oil, labour law reform) had been frustrated because of popular pressure and the political stalemate in Congress. The big obstacle to this project of continuity of the right in power was the tremendous popularity of the PRD's mayor of Mexico City, López Obrador. He lived a simple life style, carried out some significant welfare reforms aimed at the poor and senior citizens, and expressed solidarity with the poor while pursuing urban renewal in partnership with capital. The new power bloc and its political operatives were determined to derail any possibility of López Obrador becoming the new president, an outcome which could jeopardize the more radical elements of their agenda as well as possibly subject them to investigation for corruption.

The July 2006 electoral fraud that denied López Obrador the presidency was just the latest attempt to guarantee continuity of their rule. Their first clumsy attempt was the *desafuero*, an attempt to disqualify López Obrador from eligibility to run for president through a petty and spurious legal manoeuvre. When the *desafuero* failed in the face of popular opposition and its transparent purpose, they resorted to a combination of the normal methods of a bourgeois democracy and those of the old PRI. The duopoly of private TV, Azteca and Televisa, vilified López Obrador as a far leftist, a Chavéz, who would destabilize Mexico. They, in collaboration with the national government, sought to create a climate of fear and a desire for stability.

The face of the new presidency of Felipe Calderón is that of the IMF underwritten by fierce repression. The new Secretary of the Interior (Secretario de Gobernación), Francisco Ramírez Acuña, has been widely condemned for human rights abuses as governor of the state of Jalisco. He took great pride in his tough handling of the anti-corporate globalization protests in Guadalajara on May 28, 2004, a 'handling', it should be noted, which was widely condemned by human rights groups for their brutality, arbitrary detentions and the use of torture. His appointment has been praised by business leaders who have said that disorder and protests in Mexico need to be handled with a 'firm hand'. Certainly, it was Ramírez Acuña who along with Calderón decided (a few days before the latter's official swearing-in on December 1, 2006) to use extreme force, arbitrary arrests and torture in their attempt to smash the Oaxacan popular movement. And the economic ministries went to extreme neoliberals. Agustín Carstens (a 'Chicago boy') resigned a top position at the IMF to become Secretary of the Treasury. Luis Téllez, former Secretary of Energy (1997-2000) and a directing manager of the Carlyle Group since December 2003, was appointed Secretary of Telecommunications. The members of the cabinet in charge of social issues come from the Catholic far right. This is a regime that has announced by words, cabinet appointments and actions its intention to deepen neoliberal reforms, which would include changing labour law and privatizing oil and electric power.

The reaction to the fraud of July 2, 2006 was immediate. Hundreds of thousands of people participated in unprecedented street mobilizations that lasted for weeks. Major parts of the downtown were occupied and temporary tent cities created that became sites of intense political discussion, cultural activities, and communal food preparation. Some of these activities were organized by local political organizations but many by popular grassroots organizations, new and old, neighbourhood and workplace. The López Obrador leadership formed an organization, the CND (Convención Nacional Democrática – National Democratic Convention), which held two massive rallies at the Zócalo (the main plaza of Mexico City), the first of over a million that declared López Obrador president (September 16, 2006) and the second of several hundred thousand in which he was sworn in as 'legitimate president' along with the cabinet he had chosen (November 20, 2006).

The López Obrador leadership was optimistic that popular mobilization could effectively pressure key elites to get the electoral tribunal to order a full recount of all votes, which they were confident would show that they had won the election, and that popular pressure would get the old political establishment to acquiesce in the victory of the PRD. But they also felt that they needed to reassure these key elites – as they had when governing Mexico City and throughout the campaign – that they would govern 'responsibly', that there would be boundaries to the popular mobilization. López Obrador therefore was very careful to limit the actions of the mass movement to those that would not bring the country to the brink of ungovernability. His approach to the popular uprising in Oaxaca was similarly cautious. In addition to not wanting to do anything to scare key elites, he also did not want to burn his bridges to the PRI, which governed Oaxaca, and whose acquiescence in a PRD presidential victory was viewed as necessary and possible. The PRI held a majority of state governorships – sixteen – and these governors could have created serious problems of governability for him as president. The political leadership of the movement was not seeking to transform the regime; they were fighting for governmental power.

The only formal organizational structure that developed was the plebiscitarian CND, a convention in name, a rally in practice, controlled from above by López Obrador. The anti-fraud movement had two souls – the elite bargaining, plebiscitarian soul and the popular, participatory soul. Both were real features of the mass anti-fraud movement. That the participatory, associational aspects of the movement dried up cannot be attributed solely to the limits of López Obrador's perspective and goals.

The left was not strong or cohesive enough to effectively promote the more radical social and political ideas of the anti-fraud movement that were submerged within that movement's overarching target of getting a vote-by-vote recount of the presidential election. Nor was it strong or cohesive enough to link this anti-fraud rebellion to the Oaxaca rebellion, which had already begun in June, 2006. The left was sharply divided and not all of it supported an assembleist, struggle-from-below, perspective, as exemplified by the APPO. Some of the old left and leaders of radical organizations and social movements had, over the years, been incorporated into the PRD apparatus and PRD governments of Mexico City and developed more cautious, institutionalist and electoralist perspectives. Others, such as the Zapatista leadership, refused to participate in a movement that they saw as tainted by electoralism and the leadership of ex-PRIistas. At a rare moment of mobilization and politicization of the popular classes, the moderate voice of López Obrador was strong and the voices of the left were weak and divided.

The Zapatistas rejected the López Obrador campaign from the start, and also rejected participation in the anti-fraud movement, though they condemned the fraud. They launched their own campaign, the 'Other Campaign', to coincide with the electoral campaign and to present a different approach and a different vision. They made their harshest attacks on the PRD and López Obrador. They expressed scepticism, if not contempt, for political parties and the electoral process, and tacitly supported abstentionism. They were largely invisible during the campaign and the post-election mobilizations against the fraud. Their campaign consisted of meetings and discussions with communities and movements in various parts of the country, usually away from the areas of major crisis and struggle.

The Zapatistas' political intervention foundered on the question of the relationship between López Obrador and a section of key PRD leaders, on the one hand, and the mass base of the popular movements that supported López Obrador, on the other. They anticipated, as López Obrador himself did, that he would be elected president and that he would seek to maintain a neoliberal capitalist regime, albeit with a more nationalist and human face, as he likely would have. This was, after all, his program and his track record as Mayor of Mexico City. They failed to see, as López Obrador himself failed to see, that the right in Mexico would not let him win the presidency. The Zapatistas prepared themselves to fight betrayal by the PRD while the right prepared an electoral coup, a sharp deepening of neoliberalism and continental integration, and increased use of the military to control social protest.

Although much of the Zapatista critique of López Obrador and the PRD was merited, they ignored the dynamic and contradictory character of the broader democratic movement of which the PRD was a key hub, but with limited control over the many constituent movements and milieux. While the PRD is an electoral machine that sought to build on electoral support from the popular movements, the broader democratic movement is a giant umbrella under which most of the left, progressive unions and social movements live with significant autonomy and fluid alliances. The PRD remains the most important national expression of the democratic and plebeian revolt against the authoritarian and neoliberal regime that had its peak moments in 1987-1988 and again in 2006-2007. It has been full of contradictions since its beginnings in 1987-1988. It has mostly been led by top-down, politically moderate dissidents from the old ruling party but based on a nationalist program that challenges the neoliberal integration of Mexico and its resources into the US empire. It has been the repository of hope for a republic of social justice among plebeian forces. The struggles between the more radical, moderate, and conservative elements of the PRD have been continual and have, to date, been contained by their lack of national power. This complex and contradictory character of the PRD cannot be reduced to the politics of some of its key leaders.

The PRD itself includes layers of former PRIistas but also currents and movements that have long fought the PRI as a party and PRIismo as a political culture of corruption, opportunism, and repression. Many elements of the reformist and revolutionary left were founding components of the PRD. And the anti-fraud movement that developed after the elections was even broader and more heterogeneous than the PRD base. The ideological heterogeneity and diffuseness of the mass base of the PRD and the anti-fraud movement includes strong anti-neoliberal, anti-imperialist and anti-capitalist elements. These different moods, hopes, meanings, and currents co-exist in an extremely fluid situation. The challenge for the Zapatistas, as for the left in general, was how to be part of this mass upsurge without being coopted by its moderate leadership. The tensions and contradictions within the PRD, between its top-down and electorally opportunist structure and its mass plebeian base, are as important in understanding its potential as are the politics of particular compromised leaders. Many of these same tensions – between accommodation, reform and revolution, between caudillistic verticality and horizontal democracy – also exist within the key organizations of the popular movements.

THE OAXACA COMMUNE

The Oaxaca uprising developed in this context of the deepest post-election crisis in Mexico since 1910 – the start of the Mexican Revolution – and slightly more than 12 years after the Zapatista revolt began in 1994, and 20 years after the democratic insurgency that started in 1987. The character of the national crisis gave the Oaxaca uprising impetus and space to grow while at the same time constraining its possibilities. Oaxaca is one of the three poorest states in Mexico and is, by far, the state with the highest percentage of indigenous people, approximately 67 per cent of the 3,700,000 Oaxacans living in Oaxaca. Another 250,000 Oaxacans live in the Mexico City area and the government estimates that at least 300,000 Oaxacans have migrated to the US in the last 15 years. As well, many Oaxacans live and work in the nearby states of Puebla and Veracruz and the agribusiness and maquila states of Sinaloa and Baja California. The Oaxacan population is composed of a variety of indigenous peoples and has one of the most, if not the most, trans-regionalized and trans-nationalized populations in Mexico. Oaxacans labour not only in Oaxaca but in the Mexico City area, in the agribusiness and maquila zones of the north, and throughout the west coast of the United States. Their communities live in a transnational space, harassed and oppressed by two national governments and their state government. In the US, their undocumented status is increasingly criminalized. In Oaxaca, their social protests and civil participation have been criminalized by the state and national governments. Many Oaxacan communities depend on remittances from the north. And not only remittances but nostalgia and family sentiments flow from the north to the south; stories and experiences and 'lessons' of individual and collective struggle are shared. Oaxacan networks – as other immigrant networks – are conduits of experiences and locations for interpreting and reinterpreting the character and nodal points of the local, national, and global.

Oaxaca is also a pivotal place in the drive to open up the resources of southern Mexico and Central America to exploitation by international capital. Plan Puebla Panama (PPP), proposed early in the Fox administration, proposes to solve the problems of regional poverty and underdevelopment by inserting Mexico's nine southern and southeastern states, as well as the seven countries of Central America, into globalization. But, in fact, these areas have long been inserted into international capitalism through enclave economies that have produced and reproduced poverty and 'backwardness'. The new plan, which has met major popular resistance, is a plan to deepen this integration as well as further open up the resources of the area to capital and to privatize those that are presently public (oil and electric power). The World Bank has had a plan for a number of years for Oaxaca and three of these Mexican states and Central America to foster biodiversity, a plan that many in the region feel is a plan for biopiracy. As well, the plan to develop a fast rail link across the Isthmus of Tehuantepec in southern Oaxaca is aimed at facilitating the movement of commodities from Asia to North America and has little to do with the needs of Oaxaca.

Oaxaca has long been a highly politicized state. It is one of the richest states in indigenous traditions, including that of participatory self-government at the community level. The two most important figures of the 19th century in creating modern Mexico were Oaxacans of indigenous origin, one Zapotec, one Mixtec. Benito Juárez, who served five terms from 1858 to 1872, was the most revered president in Mexico history, and led the war of national liberation against the French occupation; and one of his key military leaders in that war, Porfirio Díaz, led the capitalist modernization of Mexico as president and dictator from 1876 to 1910.[3] There is also a long history of popular resistance to tyranny in Oaxaca. Two of the most important leaders of the anarchist wing of the Mexican Revolution, the Flores Magón brothers, were Oaxacans. And the major democratic insurgency in the railway workers union in 1958 that led to a major national strike – and massive governmental repression – was initiated by a rank and file movement of railway workers in southern Oaxaca.

There is an overabundance of discontents in Oaxaca: long-term poverty, a result both of traditional exploitation and more recent neoliberal rapaciousness; fraudulent state elections; a history of human rights violations and repression by the state government; the long-term corruption of uninterrupted one-party rule. These discontents had intensified during the first three years of the governership of Ulises Ruiz (2004-2010), a period of even sharper repression than previously, as well as of deepening divisions and splits within the state and national PRI. Popular discontents combined with those of the impoverished teachers, with strong organic links to impoverished communities as well as to a three-decade long national teachers' insurgency against the authoritarian national union. The splits in the PRI, the intensified repression of Ulises Ruiz, and the ambience of vulnerability of the national regime in the midst of a presidential election campaign, in which it seemed the PRD had a chance of winning, created the context in which the rebellion had the time and space to flourish for a period. In the earlier periods of relatively stable one-party presidentialist rule, a popular challenge to a state government had little chance of success, as the national ruling party would use whatever force necessary to protect its governor. But now there were many complex cleavages not only between the three national parties but also within the PRI. And this seeming vulnerability of the national regime and the bitter intra-PRI battles would combine with the deepening historical discontents and the especially crude and brutal character of the government to produce a popular uprising beyond anyone's expectation

The Oaxaca rebellion started out as a strike by Section 22 of the national teachers union, in early May 2006. The teachers of Section 22 had long played the role of organic intellectuals to popular movements while, at the same time, collectively playing the role of a militant union and convenor of broader union and worker alliances. They are a key component of a national alliance of democratic teachers within the authoritarian national union. Their presence in all parts of the state, their links with parents and communities, their inclusion of demands for better schools, supplies and meals for the kids – all this gave them a powerful influence and credibility among the popular classes. The demands were a mix of demands for improvement in teachers' salaries and demands for financial help for poor schoolchildren. After negotiations completely broke down, the teachers and their allies organized a *plantón* (occupation) of the central plaza and surrounding streets. *Plantones* are a traditional form of protest that often accompany strikes. This *plantón* was larger (35,000 to 60,000 people) and more geographically extensive than usual, but was not otherwise different from what had occurred many times before. The intransigence of the governor in face of the union's demands, his history of repressiveness and contempt towards the patrimony of Oaxaca, led to a rapid politicization of the struggle. The removal of the governor from office came to be a central and non-negotiable demand.

Marches in support of the teachers were frequent and grew in size. On June 2, 80,000 marched in support of the movement; on June 7, 120,000 marched. But, on June 14, the governor sent in the state police to brutally attack the encampments in the pre-dawn hours while the teachers, their children, and their allies, were asleep. The teachers and their supporters fought back. Residents in the surrounding areas quickly joined the battle on the side of the teachers. And after four or so hours of fighting, the state police were driven out of the center of the city. The governor called for federal intervention but the federal government refused to do anything in these weeks leading up to the July 2 national elections. The movement reinforced its defences in the center of the city, setting up barricades with commandeered commercial and government vehicles, including police cars, as well as appropriating them for the transportation needs of the movement. On June 16, two days after the defeat of the police assault, the second mega-march was held in which most of the poor population of the central valley (Oaxaca City and surrounding areas) participated, a march that overwhelmed Oaxaca City. As well, the teachers union and the popular movements organized the APPO in an assembly held from June 17-21, which declared itself the supreme authority in Oaxaca. The government and the PRI sought to counter with their own march, a march that only drew 20,000. The APPO had the largest march in the history of Oaxaca on June 28, a march to which all seven regions of the state sent contingents in the tens of thousands to join with the poor of the central valley. This march had the overwhelming support of the people of the central valley and all seven regions. The state government had been forced to vacate the city and to go through the motions of governing from remote locations. The APPO ran the city.

The struggle over radio and television was crucial for the spread and deepening of the popular movement. The teachers had set up a radio station, *Radio Plantón*, with an extremely limited range, barely two kilometres. When the government attacked the *plantón* on June 14, it smashed the equipment of *Radio Plantón*. In response students at the Universidad Autónoma Benito Juárez de Oaxaca (UABJO) took over the university radio station in support of the rebellion, a station with a much more powerful transmitter. Thus began a struggle over the air waves that would last for the duration of the Oaxaca commune. Throughout the struggle, the radio and television stations controlled by the state government, as well as the private media, ignored, misrepresented and vilified the popular movement. On August 1 women organized a large march in support of APPO, a *marcha de las caserolas,* (banging pots and pans as they marched). Some of the women went to the state television and radio stations to request air time to present the views of the movement as well as to ask the stations to be more truthful. The brusque negative to both requests angered the marchers and they peacefully invaded and took over the stations, stations that could broadcast across the length and breadth of the entire state. From August 1 to August 21, the station became the voice of the people and the popular movement. Discussions were held about events elsewhere in Mexico and the rest of the world. Ordinary people voiced their views and aired their complaints. When the government destroyed the equipment for the transmission tower of its own stations, various APPO groups invaded 12 commercial radio stations, all but two of which were released back to the owners the next day. The two that the APPO continued to control were used as voices of the movement for several months. The popular movement of Oaxaca broke through this iron curtain of the media oligopoly by peacefully taking over the media, which was made possible by the absence of governmental power in Oaxaca City. The media then became a voice of the people. Media pluralism across class lines temporarily existed in Oaxaca.

Efforts were made over the next months by the teachers and APPO to negotiate a solution with the federal government in relation to the union's demands, the more political demands of the APPO, and the demand for the removal of the governor. The federal government made various attempts to coopt or split the movement, without great success. And though the national government did agree to some demands – generally without following through on fulfilling them – it would not agree to the fundamental demand for the removal of the governor. Thus there was a period of five months in which APPO controlled and ran the city, negotiations with the federal government took place sporadically, the state government was isolated from the state capital, but during which the state government and its para-military squads carried out a campaign of selective terror. There was an ambiguous mix of 'collective bargaining by insurrection', and a dual power situation in one city. The perspective of mobilization-negotiation-mobilization was constant, with the national government viewed as the necessary negotiating partner.

The APPO was composed of a great diversity of movements and organizations that ranged from NGOs, unions, neighbourhood associations, indigenous organizations, to newly formed associations such as the barricade committees. Some were not democratic at all and some had been viewed as having compromised relations with this or previous governments. Others were formally democratic but not all of these were very participatory. But as the masses of Oaxacans erupted in the streets, began to organize to fight back, to seize and run radio and TV stations, to man barricades, to debate and make decisions, to police and organize themselves, the APPO was transformed. The popular barrios joined in the movement and organized themselves; the indigenous communities – already organized – also joined. The original, more vertical, more formal core of union and left organizations was swamped by popular organizations, both new and traditional, giving the movement an energy and a character that overspilled formal organizational boundaries. As the APPO developed into a mass uprising and self-organizing movement, control over it was limited.[4] Luis Hernández Navarro well describes the heady mixture of movements and organizations that the APPO became: 'The APPO synthesizes the local political culture born of popular assemblies, teachers' unionism, indigenous communalism, municipal self-government, Church community activism, the radical left, regionalism, and the ethnic diversity of the entity. And it expresses, furthermore, the new associational forms created in Oaxaca through the pacific popular uprising: organizations of the poor neighbourhoods of the city of Oaxaca and its surrounding zone, libertarian youth networks and those of the barricades'.[5]

The APPO became the movement of the vast majority of the people of Oaxaca against the governor and his political machine. It was a multi-class coalition with proletarianized teachers at its core. It had the support and participation of other sectors of unionized and non-unionized workers, the informal sector, sectors of small business, intellectuals, university professors and students. It was a broad popular alliance within which labouring classes of various kinds played a crucial role. The strength of the APPO was in large part based on the social and political breadth of its support. The movement started with the struggle of teachers who were joined by parents and working people of all kinds. But sections of the middle strata and discontented elements of the PRI and the PAN in Oaxaca also joined the movement; some of them were also motivated by an agenda of democratization, an end of state repression, a desire for social justice, etc, but others were seeking to ride to political power on the back of the mass protest without a previous track record of commitment to the issues of the popular movement. APPO's very breadth thus presented and will continue to present important challenges for and tensions within the movement.

CONCLUSIONS

The para-revolutionary situation in Oaxaca has to be seen as a type of insurrectionary reformism, combining revolutionary forms of struggle with goals of increasingly radical reforms. This model of struggle has the potential to influence the discourse and imagery of existing and emerging movements seeking to transform Mexico. It provides an alternative to electoral struggle backed by mass pressure against fraud (PRD and López Obrador), and to the path the Zapatistas have chosen since their national march for indigenous rights in 2001. The generalization of the lessons of the forms of struggle and of self-organization ('dual power' within the city of Oaxaca and, to a lesser degree, within the state of Oaxaca) to significant parts of the bases of the anti-fraud movement, to the trade union dissidents, and to the base of the 'Other Campaign', would have a radicalizing impact. But it would be a mistake to see the Oaxaca struggle itself and at this time as the beginning of a revolutionary conjuncture in Mexico. This could develop as neoliberal reforms are deepened and repression continues to be intensified. But it is not that yet.

The López Obrador anti-fraud movement and the APPO remained apart and wary of each other, as did the Zapatistas 'Other Campaign' in relation to both. López Obrador sought to distance himself from semi-insurrectionary mass revolt from below and feared that the APPO would cut a deal with the national government that would grant some change in Oaxaca while, at the same time, helping to legitimate the national government. The APPO did not join the national anti-fraud movement and was willing to negotiate with the outgoing and incoming PANista governments. As well, there were elements in the APPO (PANistas, PRIistas) that did not even support the anti-fraud movement for political reasons, and other elements that were anti-electoralist or suspicious of Obrador's top-down approach. Thus though much of the rank and file of the anti-fraud movement supported the APPO struggle, and much of the APPO base supported the anti-fraud struggle, the two kept their distance from each other. There were symbolic expressions of solidarity but no real attempt at alliance. And the Zapatistas kept their distance from both. They distanced themselves from the anti-fraud movement because of the character of its political leadership. And while they praised the APPO, they also kept their distance from it.

The fact that the national context is not revolutionary presents the movement with a deep objective dilemma. The APPO was a revolt in one city and one state with resonances throughout Mexico but not with insurrectionary upsurges elsewhere. The national state is, for the moment, intact. Many Mexicans, even those with bitter and growing discontent, still believe there may be a way out of Mexico's deep crisis through some combination of mass protests and electoral activity. Though a large portion of the population feels the president is not legitimate, they do not, in the main, feel that the existing electoral system itself is illegitimate, but rather in need of fundamental reforms. And the relative democratization in congressional and state elections has helped sustain hope that change can come about within the political system, though with the necessity of mass extra-parliamentary pressure. This non-revolutionary context – the coercive power of the state remains intact and the people have not exhausted their hopes in a quasi-institutional process of change – had, of course, a major impact on how the strategy and goals of the APPO developed.

The combination of mass insurrectionary action in Oaxaca with bargaining with the national government represented an obvious realism toward the national situation. But this realism presented its own dilemmas in a national context in which a mass movement was challenging the legitimacy of the president. The 2006 elections to the national Senate and Congress were not in dispute but the legitimacy of the presidential election was being fervently disputed. The anti-fraud movement vowed to use mass action to prevent the fraudulently elected president from taking office. The APPO was pressuring the Senate to remove the governor of Oaxaca, which the Senate had the constitutional power to do, and bargaining with the outgoing and incoming presidents, both of whom were part and parcel of the process of precluding a presidential electoral victory by the center-left. The attempts to bridge the demands of APPO and the anti-fraud movement were fraught with difficulties and dilemmas. Both were complex, multi-tendencied mass movements with demands for important reforms but the APPO, in its attempt to force out the governor of Oaxaca, was pressuring the Senate and bargaining with the outgoing and incoming presidents. The movements, even had they shared a revolutionary ethos and strategy, would have faced the perennial dilemmas around radical demands in a non-revolutionary context: how to make real gains without either a complete showdown with intact state power and, at the same time, how to avoid the cooptation of leaders or sections of the movement. These dilemmas are inherently difficult; they require a clear perspective about power and the national state.

The APPO and the anti-fraud movements were both mass movements based on the labouring classes but they were radically different in their internal structures and dynamics. The APPO, in the main, was a deeply participatory and horizontal movement, although like most Mexican movements, it had *caudillsta* elements and potential. The anti-fraud movement was a top-down controlled movement with tremendous popular energies and participation that may have had the potential of spilling beyond the limits of a top-down structure and towards a more horizontal participatory process. These differences, mutual suspicions about goals, and the bargaining situation of the APPO, along with the absence of a political leadership or ethos that could confront the dilemmas and bridge the struggle, made working together difficult. Only the convergence of the various local, regional and national opposition movements into a national force could transform the situation from one of a deep organic crisis with regionally-segmented revolts to a pre-revolutionary situation. But the government is very well aware of the danger of discontent deepening and spreading. Its response is to carry out an active anticipatory counter-revolution through the increasing use of the military and state terror to control Mexico. The continuing fragmentation of the opposition forces facilitates this.

The Achilles' heel of many popular revolts in Mexico, from that of the original Zapatistas in the 1910s to that of the Zapatistas of the 1990s, has been the failure to realize that radical change at the local and regional levels can only be consolidated on the basis of fundamental change at the national level. A perspective involving national political power is indispensable. Local power – be it the Zapatista communities of present-day Chiapas or the APPO-Oaxaca commune of the spring and summer of 2006 – can only last as long as the national government has reason to let it continue. In isolation from a national movement of resistance, the national government, unless it is itself crumbling or dividing in fundamental ways, can smash it at its will, though it may pay a significant political cost.

Though there is much suspicion and scepticism toward all political parties, Oaxaca's popular movements and the Oaxacan left do not, in general, have an anti-electoralist position, nor do they have a position against assuming governmental power. Local, national and state elections are seen as tools in the struggle for change but not as the whole toolbox. The teachers and the APPO participated in the 2006 national elections by calling for a protest vote against the PRI and the PAN and devoted major energy to getting out the vote and being vigilant against electoral fraud. The protest vote meant, in fact, a vote for the PRD – and the PRD, in fact, won the vote for president in Oaxaca, nine of the eleven congressional seats and both of the senate seats. It was a dramatic sweep in a state where, before the rise of the APPO, the PRI had been expected to deliver the vote for its candidates yet again.

The Oaxacan revolt has combined extra-parliamentary struggle, electoral participation, insurrectionary activity with aspects of a self-governing commune. It has exhibited complex tensions between centralized coordination and 'spontaneous' self-organization and activity. It has shown the amazing creative potential of participatory self-organization and rebellion from below. It has also shown the limitations of rebellion in one city, one state, and the dilemmas of rebellion without a national movement. The enemies of the people of Oaxaca are powerful – the PRI state government and the local *caciques* (political bosses), the Mexican national state and bourgeoisie, the US state and global capital. But the tenacity, democratic and egalitarian spirit, and combativeness of Oaxacans is powerful. Oaxacans, with few exceptions, know that the state still matters.

The movement, in its diversity and tensions, is groping for a path that would combine electoral and extra-electoral struggle as well as bring together social, political, and economic demands around both indigenous and proletarian issues. It is a model of heroism and possibility that shows that it is mistaken to see the strategic choice as being between aspiring to manage the existing capitalist state apparatus, or ignoring it. This is a false dichotomy. The strategic task is to transform the nature of power through popular insurgency and organizational forms of control from below. This is the only way the people can rule and transform themselves as they transform society. The people of Paris in 1870-1871, the workers of Tsarist Russia in 1905 and 1917, and the people of Oaxaca in 2006, understood this in practice. Marx would express it in words in 'The Civil War in France'. The Oaxaca Commune has revived the image of democratic insurgency and popular control. When the next upsurge develops in Mexico – as it will, given the relentless neoliberal assault – the images, rhetoric, and experiences of the Oaxaca commune will resonate widely.

NOTES

1   *El Financiero*, Mexico, 31 May 2007.
2   Gómez Carlos and Vázquez Rivera, *Evolución Demográfica y Potencial de Desarrollo de las Ciudades de México*, México: Consejo de Población, 2006.
3   Porfirio Díaz was president all those years with the exception of 1880-1884 when he remained the power behind the throne. Contrary to current mythology, Evo Morales is not the first indigenous president in Latin America.

4   Gustavo Esteva, 'APPOlogía', *La J*, 18 December 2006.
5   Luis Hernández Navarro, 'La APPO', *La J*, 21 November 2006 (our transla-
      tion).

THE CONTRADICTIONS OF 'DEMOCRATIC' NEOLIBERALISM IN ARGENTINA: A NEW POLITICS FROM 'BELOW'?

EMILIA CASTORINA

By the end of 2001, the neoliberal model of capital accumulation imposed in Argentina since the late 1970s, reinforced by the economic and institutional reforms carried out during the 1990s, encountered a series of social, economic and political limits. The external debt rose from US$ 7.8 billion in 1976 to U$$ 128.0 billion in 2001; unemployment hit a record of 18 per cent in 2001 (and 22 per cent in 2002); by 2002 54 per cent of the population of Greater Buenos Aires were living below the poverty line.

For the first time in Argentine history a democratically-elected government was overthrown by a popular insurrection, which became known as the *Argentinazo*. In 2001-2 the country went through one of the deepest financial crises in the world through a massive (spontaneous) popular upheaval under the slogan *Que se vayan todos!* ('out with them all!'), giving way to a novel and generalized state of social mobilization which threatened the precarious neoliberal hegemony that had been built around convertibility and a triumphal belief in economic success. Heralded during the 1990s as the international poster-child for market-oriented economic reforms, thanks to its exceptional combination of far-reaching liberalizing policies and democracy, Argentina now came to be seen by the IMF as an 'unfeasible country'. This was certainly a setback for those who had extolled Argentina's unparalleled capacity to carry out radical stabilization programmes without an authoritarian regime (such as that of Chile or many South Asian countries), or an *autogolpe* [self-coup] (as in Peru), or harsh labour repression and states of siege (as in Bolivia). Overnight, Argentina went from being the 'best student' of the IMF's orthodoxy to a potential troublemaker.

Many different demands came together unexpectedly in the December 2001 insurrection: from the poorest sectors of society calling for food, jobs or unemployment subsidies, to the middle classes demanding the devolution of bank deposits confiscated by the financial *corralito* or punishment for corrupt politicians and judges. And there was a disturbing point of convergence for the guardians of order: a demand for the resignation of every person responsible for the ruling regime as a whole. The confluence of previous forms of popular resistance to neoliberalism such as those of the *Piqueteros*, *Puebladas*, independent unions (CTA), and those which emerged directly out of the events of December 2001, such as the movement to occupy abandoned factories, neighbourhood assemblies and several forms of cooperatives across the country, evolved during the insurrection into a new social force. This was mainly expressed in the widespread slogan: *piquetes y cacerolas, la lucha es una sola* (roadblocks and cooking pans, there is only one struggle). This convergence was far from expected, given the conservative attitude of most middle class sectors towards the convertibility regime during the 1990s, and it contributed to an accelerating process of political instability. The institutional crisis of 2002 can hardly be exaggerated: five consecutive presidencies in less than a year, politicians being violently assaulted or 'exposed',[1] the Parliament under attack, the number of road blockages (*cortes de ruta*) rising from 1,383 in 2001 to 2,336 in 2002, when default on the foreign debt was officially declared.[2] The leading political parties were in chaos. The year 2002 was characterized by a deep sense of rupture and despair.

Mainstream institutionalist perspectives, from those of the IMF and the World Bank to those of more liberal scholars of democratization, coincided in arguing that the crisis was more 'political' than 'economic', meaning that the problem was not the 'content' of the economic policies implemented during the 1990s but the inefficient way in which they were administered.[3] For these commentators the monetarist gospel continued as usual: corruption and politics were too costly, raising the burdens of fiscal deficit and subsequently indebtedness, a process that got even worse when political instability weakened the trust and credulousness of unfortunate foreign investors. Of course, an analysis that attributes the crisis in Argentina exclusively to its fiscal deficit is very convenient as it relieves the IMF of any responsibility for the making of the crisis (and for the overall macroeconomic setting of the 1990s). But, more importantly, it enhanced a widely-shared vision of Argentina as a 'persistently unconsolidated democracy',[4] or a 'weakly institutionalized democracy' – in other words, some sort of anomaly and deviation from the ideal type of 'representative democracy' for its recurrent instability and lack of enforcement of formal rules.

On the other hand, it didn't take long for progressive intellectuals and activists from very different perspectives to declare the official death of neoliberalism and, while burying it, to formulate a new set of prophecies based on new forms of politics from 'below'. A broad range of participants and observers, from the traditional revolutionary left[5] to supporters of the 'new social subjects',[6] shared the view that a fundamental change had emerged in the way politics is practised. Moreover they all seemed to be pointing towards new forms of political action directed at superseding the capitalist mode of production. Even at the international level, Argentina became a paradigmatic case of the rise of the 'multitude',[7] 'anti-power',[8] or a more vague concept of a new social subject[9] able to overthrow capitalist society. Advocates of this optimistic view generally focused on the fostering of social movements because party politics was said to be unfit for the task.

More sober observers, while dismissing the revolutionary thesis, nevertheless saw the new social movements as harbingers of a radical change in Argentine political culture. The conventional diagnosis was unanimous: the crisis of 2001 was the product of a 'crisis of politics', a 'crisis of the state', a 'crisis of representation', a 'crisis of the political parties', a 'crisis of legitimacy' and so on and so forth. A more demanding citizenry was said to be emerging, 'determined to redefine pre-existing ideals of democratic representation and to create a civic concern for governmental accountability'.[10] A growing industry of studies in the new politics from 'below' regularly invokes a 'holy quartet' consisting of the *Piqueteros*, the seized factories, *asambleas* and barter clubs as the most dynamic social movements in search of new forms of organization, new imaginaries and a new kind of democratic subjectivity.[11]

Beyond their particularities, there seems to be a general consensus among progressive scholars regarding the crisis of 'old politics' (i.e. the politics of politicians, institutional politics anchored in the state, corruption, clientelism, etc.) and the emergence of a 'new politics' (i.e. the politics of social movements). But this consensus is based on three problematic points. To begin with, as Carrera argues, there is an illusion that the apparent rise in the political awareness of the Argentine people will *per se* engender a radical change in the overall process of capital accumulation.[12] Second, there is the idea that 'horizontal' organization represents an effective way of challenging traditional, 'vertical' forms of organization, obviously taking it for granted that popular organizations have indeed replaced vertical forms with horizontal ones. Third, there is an idea that democracy has become a 'parody' or an 'empty shell', where formal rules are frequently ignored or overlooked, and an assumption that abstract subjects such as 'the people', the 'citizenry', 'civil society', the 'multitude', or 'the working class', will construct a new kind of democracy for an emancipatory project.

Paradoxically, the left (in its various forms) relies heavily on the same diagnosis of weak democratization as do mainstream institutionalists. One side is inspired by the hope of radical social transformation, the other by the perennial fear of the mob; but they all agreed that Argentine democracy is fragile, unstable and weak. Obviously the explanation is different in each case: the advocates of the radicalization of resistance argue that democracy was undermined by market policies, while the guardians of order attribute it to corrupt politicians (when not to 'backward' political culture).

The actual historical process that evolved from mid-2002 onward challenges (if not contradicts) both the progressive prophecies and the institutionalists' fears. The presidential election of 2003 marked a fundamental rechannelling of social struggles within the boundaries of capitalist (neoliberal) democracy. Some prophets of the left expected high absenteeism and spoiled ballots to predominate, as a manifestation of a supposedly popular advance beyond institutionalized, representative democracy, or at least some form of protest against the lack of legitimate political representation. Yet as some scholars have pointed out, spoiled ballots fell from their 20 per cent peak in the 2001 elections, to 1.6 per cent in the 2003 election; electoral absenteeism even went down in absolute terms compared to the previous parliamentary elections of 2001; and blank ballots went down to the smallest figures registered since the 1946 elections, and the number of annulled votes was negligible.[13] Despite the peculiarities of the election, the PJ – the Peronist Party (Partido Justicialista) that represents everything the left has defined as 'old politics' – got an overwhelming majority of votes, if the three Peronist candidates are taken together. Not to mention that Menem, whose ten-year rule of harsh structural adjustment made him the paradigmatic target of *Que se vayan todos*, led in the first round with no less than 24 per cent of the votes.[14] This pattern of social rage against a politician, followed by electoral victories by the traditional political parties, is not new in Argentina, as the case of the *Santiagazo* and other *puebladas* shows.[15]

Over the years that have passed since the crisis and insurrection of December 2001, a considerable reconstitution of the regime has taken place. Argentina has shown remarkable signs of economic recovery: Presidents Duhalde (2002-2003) and Kirchner (2003-2007) re-negotiated the debt payments with the IMF, based on an unprecedented discount on the foreign debt, and reversed the passive default of 2001; GDP rose 8 per cent in 2003, and 8.5 per cent in 2006. Investments and external credibility also grew. The new phase of economic expansion may seem to be taking a renewed 'populist' or even Keynesian shape, given Kirchner's discursive assertions of 'national sovereignty', the increasing levels of import substitution investment and also of inflation, along with fiscal and monetary policies (such as a floating exchange rate with a devalued peso as a competitive exchange rate for exports, and some minimum level of control on foreign exchange transactions) aimed at controlling inflation and managing the exchange rate through central bank intervention, all of which departs from the monetarist orthodoxy of the IMF. But the nature of this post-convertibility macroeconomic regime should not be misconstrued as 'anti' neoliberal, but rather as a pragmatic – and certainly, heterodox – strategy aimed at stabilizing the economy, and the domestic financial market in particular, within the prevailing neoliberal context of financial globalization. Not only had some of these policies already been implemented in other export-oriented market economies, but it should also be noted that some of the 'golden rules' of neoliberal social adjustment remain untouched: labour flexibilization (indeed, the real basis of the 'economic recovery' has been the further fall of wages that followed from devaluation and inflation), privatizations of public utilities, deregulation of pensions and mutual funds, and structural unemployment (although reduced from 22 per cent to 12 per cent, to some extent due to unemployment subsidies and the overall process of economic re-activation).[16] This regime also lacks redistributive policies, despite having increasing fiscal surpluses; so poverty and exclusion have certainly not been overcome and social inequalities have increased. At most, the new economic recovery should be seen as a 'successful' attempt at keeping neoliberal financialization within manageable and competitive macroeconomic conditions once the convertibility regime was no longer viable.

Moreover politicians did not face any serious efforts at impeachment and many faces from the 'old politics' were back in office. In fact, the political picture of the post-2003 era contrasts sharply with the romantic hopes of progressive intellectuals. First, a series of right-wing mobilizations (two consecutive demonstrations of 100,000) against 'insecurity' – led by a citizen whose son was kidnapped and killed after a ransom had been paid – redirected public and media attention to calls for more repression and 'security' as the poor and excluded became increasingly stigmatized as criminals and a threat to the 'included'. This definitely broke the alliance between the middle and the popular classes which had jointly rejected the existing system of democracy at the height of the crisis in 2001. Second, the *Peronization* of the larger fractions of the *Piqueteros*, with a base in La Matanza, gave increasing popular support to Kirchner's administration. Indeed, Duhalde and Kirchner dialogued and negotiated concrete governmental offices, social plans (2 million 'social emergency' packages in the form of unemployment subsidies, known as *Plan Jefas y Jefes de Hogar,* and later *Planes Trabajar*) and resources for local projects and micro enterprises – things that *Piqueteros* could hardly reject – in exchange for active political mobilization and support for the administration. Overall, the increasing media stigmatization of the excluded and criminalization of social protests, along with the government's capacity for attracting contentious individual leaders as well as entire groups of the unemployed, which played a key role in destabilizing the regime, signalled an unfortunate reverse for the calls of *Que se vayan todos:* old politics was back.

Social movements and their struggles also declined considerably between 2003 and 2006. Some argue that this decline is natural, since social protests always have cycles of ebb and flow. Yet that doesn't explain why Argentina experienced neither a revolution nor some alternative move towards wider social reforms, as envisaged by progressive forces. So, what happened to *Que se vayan todos*? What happened to all those new social actors who emerged defiant at the end of the Menemist era and grew powerfully against de la Rúa's government, but were increasingly de-mobilized after Kirchner took office? What does this decline of social movements actually say about Argentina's current conjuncture: is this just a temporary retreat within a wider 'pre-revolutionary' process, as some leftist activists believe, or a 'post-neoliberal' government that is really solving social problems as some advocates of Kirchner state; or is it rather a more complex process of political recomposition of neoliberalism? More importantly, if neoliberal democracy was so 'weak', how could it possibly survive what in many ways was its toughest challenge?

All these questions point to the need for a more complex and dynamic understanding of 'neoliberal democracy' in Argentina than is offered in conventional theorizations. Contrary to a general tendency to understand this regime as 'weak', or in the process of 'degradation', 'decadence' and/or terminal crisis, Argentine democratic neoliberalism as a form of domination has proved remarkably strong in politically recomposing the neoliberal crisis of 2001-2. In fact, the democratic regime has shown a remarkable capacity to react to challenges from 'below' and has proved highly successful in taming them without really giving in to their demands – or threatening the interests of the establishment – for two interrelated reasons:

(1) Unlike the optimistic prophecies of the left, 'old politics' was far from 'exhausted'. In fact, Peronist politics was revitalized by Kirchner's government to the extent that it was able to resort to the clientelistic and patronage-based structures of co-optation, de-mobilization, de-politicization and disciplining of subaltern classes built during the Menemist era to cope with the new politics from 'below'. As a result, the process of re-stabilization was

able to avoid any significant distribution of power and wealth to the 'losers' of the crisis.

(2) The political incapacity of the new social forces to build a unified, plausible alternative from 'below' that could effectively resist co-optation from 'above'. This is mainly due to the increasing political fragmentation of the new social movements, which is an indicator not of the 'reinvention of politics' but, on the contrary, of old and persistent dilemmas within left politics – i.e. the far from 'new' political divisions between reformist, revolutionaries and autonomists. The *Piqueteros* movement is an illustrative case in point.

This conjunctural hypothesis brings to the fore some broad theoretical questions, which have been largely ignored, or misconstrued: in particular the specific relation between democracy and neoliberalism. In a broad sense, prevailing explanations of the crisis of 2001-2 in Argentina mainly focus (some more mechanically than others) either on the problematic of capitalist (neoliberal) development and the subsequent forms of resistance, or on the inherent problems of democratic institutionalization as a formal regime. But very little effort has been made to bring these two themes together in a systematic theorization of democratic neoliberalism that might be able to account for the ups and downs of the new politics from 'below', and consequently, for the political strengths, rather than the institutional weakness, of contemporary Argentine democracy.

The failure to account for this has been especially evident in those determinist Marxist explanations of why a revolution didn't accompany the economic crisis of 2001-2 in Argentina. Since the crisis proved 'the objective conditions were there', all they could fall back on was simply that 'it was just a lost opportunity'[17] – as if such an 'opportunity' did not entail a very complex ensemble of power relations and ideological struggles. Those who have assigned a more decisive role to class struggle – usually referring to the works of Negri, Holloway, Clarke and Cleaver – to analyze the Argentine crisis of 2001, however, cannot explain satisfactorily the crisis of convertibility as being a result of class struggle.[18] As some critics have pointed out, this kind of approach generally relies on a somewhat ethereal version of class struggle that fails to be rooted in any kind of concrete analysis of capitalist forces of production. This way, class struggle and social relations are portrayed as though not subject to any material conditions, as if they were forged in 'ether' – i.e. only in people's consciousness. As Grigera argues, within this framework there is never a risk of being wrong: 'this sort of class struggle comes in and out as a real *deus ex machina* "explaining" cycles of capital accumulation, the end of regimes, political crises, and so on. Moreover, being unpredictable and omnipresent, class struggles account *post facto* for every event following both high and low tides of struggle'.[19] As a result, these critical approaches, no less than the 'deterministic' ones, tend to underestimate the extent to which democracy may contain the threat of class struggle within certain boundaries, and miss a fundamental aspect of neoliberal hegemony.

Also in this tradition of overestimating the will of new social subjects to challenge liberal democracy and turn it into a collective, horizontal enterprise of human development are many studies of social movements.[20] It is very common among students of social movements and, in general, advocates of the new politics from 'below', to stress (or maybe overstress) the extent to which neoliberalism has radically changed politics, especially in relation to the forms of resistance to it. The process of crisis and recomposition that took place in Argentina, however, warns against drawing a stark dichotomy between 'old' top-down forms of organization and 'new' bottom-up forms. As some scholars have recently argued, many of the most dynamic social movements in contemporary Argentina (*Piqueteros*, *Puebladas* and other forms of popular protests) combine important elements of both new and old.[21] Empirical evidence increasingly points to a deeper imbrication between the forms of protests and survival by the poor and excluded, which relies heavily on clientelist networks and patronage-based structures in which Peronist brokers (*punteros*) are key players.

Moreover, social movement studies tend to reify the process of building alternatives to neoliberal development by suggesting that the transformation of the development order will not come from 'grand structural transformations' but rather from the construction of identities and greater autonomy through modifications in everyday practices and beliefs. This last idea is particularly problematic given its resemblance with the World Bank's approach in *Equity and Development*, according to which the poor and marginalized will eventually overcome inequality by improving the terms in which they are 'recognized' by others, something that involves building a 'capacity to aspire' and a 'capacity to engage'.[22] In a fundamental sense, therefore, these approaches lack an adequate understanding of the way struggles for identity, autonomy and grassroots initiatives can be co-opted by and reshaped for the purposes of sustainable forms of capitalist neoliberal development, rather than for its transformation.

On the other hand, those who have indeed theorized democracy in a systematic way have largely taken capitalism (or neoliberalism) for granted, as more or less naturally given. This is hardly surprising considering that most of the research on democratization in the South derives from modernization theory's Eurocentric and linear view of development, whereby the future of democracy in peripheral countries is supposedly represented by the present modernity of 'representative democracy' in the core countries. In this perspective, the new democratic regimes are supposed to follow a series of necessary stages –'transitions', 'consolidation', etc. – to become fully developed (efficient, stable) democracies like those of the North. This approach to democratization as a normative teleological adaptation of the South to the North was coupled with the World Bank's discourse of 'democratic governability of social conflict' or 'democratic governance' in the construction of the neoliberal project in Latin America. It was a politically convenient project because it was confined within definite limits, based on the idea that a 'stable', 'efficient' and 'legitimate' democracy demanded the eradication of 'corporatism', 'populism', favouritism and all sorts of 'irrationalities' inherent in the developmental state, and of any form of popular intervention that may use democracy as a 'Jacobin' instrument of social progress.[23]

But the excessive emphasis on formal institutional design that dominated democratization studies became increasingly unable to account for a series of more complex political questions. In a context of market discipline, structural adjustment programmes, increasing inequality, social polarization, exclusion, unemployment and all sorts of social dislocations, how can the institutions of 'polyarchy' in the classic definition of Robert Dahl – secret ballots, universal adult suffrage, regular elections, open competition, associational recognition and access and accountability – 'process social conflict' without transforming the sources of inequality and exclusion or without resorting to military repression? In other words, what makes 'polyarchy' sustainable at all in a context of massive social exclusion, and more importantly, of increasing disenchantment with democratic institutions?

In the case of Argentina, the narrow emphasis on formal democracy cannot explain the political functioning of 'really existing democracy', which entails moving beyond formal institutional design to the complex terrain of political *strength*. Given the actual historical process of democratization in Argentina it seems much more interesting to analyze the specific mechanisms through which neoliberal democracy has been able to avoid major governability crises in the context of social restructuring during the 1990s. And in so doing, to ask whether it created new contradictions and to what extent the crisis of 2001-2 may be an expression of such contradictions. In order to understand why and how Argentine democracy proved strong enough to restore stability after the 2001-2 crisis, it is necessary to explore the overall project of democratization and its inherent contradictions by looking at less visible but more enduring forms of power relations.

In other words, to what extent must this particular project of democratization, far from eradicating 'populism', clientelism, patronage, partisanship, corruption, favouritism, etc., 're-pack' them to be sustainable at all? And, consequently, should the increasing reliance on these 'non-liberal' informal practices be seen not as an 'anomaly' or a 'deviation' from an ideal type of democracy, but rather as a condition for market discipline and therefore a constitutive aspect of the 'durability' of neoliberal capitalist development in a peripheral country like Argentina? This may challenge liberal, pluralistic rhetoric regarding what is to be defined as 'efficient democracy', since a closer look at the way this 'other institutionalization' (in O'Donnell's phrase) works may point to a politically effective form of neoliberal domination. It may also contradict the widespread assumption that neoliberalism and 'populist' politics (clientelism, patronage, etc.) are incompatible.

The concept of sustainability involved here refers to the political feasibility of a project of class and state formation. From this standpoint, we must understand democratization not as series of stages leading towards an 'ultimate (ethical) goal', but as a socially and politically contested process. The question shifts from one concerning the weakness or strength of formal institutions, as neutral spaces, to one concerning the relations of power between capital and labour under democratic conditions. To a large extent, what seems to be missing from the general vision of 'weak democracy' is some conception of the state as a social relation deeper than the electoral systems of today.

For instance, the assertion that neoliberalism 'undermines' democracy, because it creates political apathy and indifference among the citizens and an increasing gap between the citizens and their representatives (the so called 'crisis of representation'), can be misleading if liberal democracy is not measured in its own terms. It is important to bear in mind that representative democracy has never been conceived of as translating the 'popular will' into the 'public will'. On the contrary, the dominant approach in the theory of representation, as classically summed up by Schumpeter, has explicitly been about securing popular consent to the decision making by elites. For this reason, the neoliberal project of democratization can be best understood in the words of Diamond as a system where 'citizens care about politics but not so much'. The indifference and/or incapacity of ordinary citizens to influence governmental policy decisions vis-à-vis that of the concentrated fractions of capital, is not a sign of weakness or failure but rather of the political success and strength of the neoliberal project of democratization, as a project of political disempowerment of subordinated classes and an institutional mechanism to explicitly pre-empt either progressive reforms or revolutionary changes

As many critical scholars have consistently argued, the neoliberal project of democratization in the South involves a strategy of state reform and transformation of power relations – i.e. a project of capitalist restructuring based on a new form of class domination.[24] The neoliberal ideology of democracy that came to prevail over socialist or populist ideologies was deeply anti-political and anti-state, which had a decisive impact on the way political power was conceived, and on strategies for challenging it. At the core of most of the misconceptions regarding the Argentine political process there is a converging vision of the state as in crisis or in retreat, both in the project of democracy from 'above' and in the minds of those who seek to challenge it from 'below'. Neoliberals neglect the state as an agent of 'globalization'; the dynamics of our times are seen as driven by impersonal and inevitable forces such as technology or 'the market' – forces which are also seen as somehow inherently 'democratic'. At the same time, and probably as a result of an uncritical acceptance of the neoliberal interpretation of the current phase of capitalism, those who promote a politics from 'below', and most of the literature on 'new social movements', neglect the state as a site of resistance and transformation.[25] This may have led to their underestimation of the power of the state to control social mobilization and discipline new social actors in a crisis such as Argentina's at the beginning of this decade.

The reality is, however, that neoliberalism entails a transformation rather than a 'retreat' of the state, and therefore a transformation of fundamental power relations between classes. Several critical Marxist scholars whose work addresses debates on state and globalization argue that neoliberal reform is thus best thought of as a governing strategy, which does not entail a simple shift in power from 'states' to 'markets' as reified categories.[26] Rather, what has changed under neoliberalism is the *way* that the state intervenes in the economy, and the ideological justifications that are provided for these new forms of intervention.

Understanding the *project* of democratization in Argentina therefore involves re-addressing the relation between state, class and democracy in terms of the specificity of the offensive strategy of capital towards labour. Democratic neoliberalism is neither a 'political' regime based solely on rules and procedures detached from the material conditions of accumulation, nor a mere 'economic' system, but a specific historic articulation between the political and the economic – a particular form of capitalism (neoliberalism) that evolves under democratic, or at least electoral, conditions. The term *democratic neoliberalism* – as distinguished from 'neoliberal democracy' where the neoliberal aspect is only an adjective – serves to highlight the intrinsic contradiction between the political and the economic; that is, between the political form of universal freedom and the anti-democratic structure of inequality in a market-based capitalist society.[27] It is therefore a particular form of social domination that rests on a historical *hegemonic* 'solution', which is socially contested and not permanent. What follows is the transformation of an integral model of domination under neoliberalism (rather than the 'crisis of the state') and of the specific modes of creating consensus and social discipline contained within it – in other words, the transformation of hegemony. To use the words of Gramsci and Poulantzas, it is a transformation of the extent to which the state manages the tension between capitalism and democracy by functioning as the factor of political organization of dominant classes and as the factor of political disorganization of subaltern classes.

In the context of Argentina, this is closely related to the changing historical relation between the traditional labour-based party (Peronism) and democracy. Despite its working-class rhetoric, Peronism, both traditional and neoliberal, has to be seen as an effective vehicle for subordinating and disciplining working classes. What needs to be conceptualized are the specific mechanisms through which contemporary Peronism has managed to do this in ways that differ from traditional populism.

In a recent study Levistky explains the successful adaptation of the PJ to the neoliberal era, based on its extraordinary capacity to redefine its relationship with organized labour, dismantling traditional mechanisms of union participation and replacing its union-based linkages with clientelist linkages. In a context of working-class decline and increasing unemployment,

> the consolidation of clientelist links created new bases upon which the PJ could sustain its ties to the urban working and lower classes. Clientelist organizations are better suited than unions to appeal to the heterogeneous strata of urban unemployed, self-employed, and informal sector workers generated by de-industrialization. In urban zones characterized by high structural unemployment, unions tend to be marginal or nonexistent, and corporate channels of representation are therefore ineffective. A territorial organization, and especially one based on the distribution of particularistic benefits, can be more effective in such a context.[28]

What changed under neoliberalism, then, was the mechanism for absorbing and re-integrating lower classes. While old Peronist populism was based on a corporatist integration of social and labour rights and 'universal' measures of distribution, neoliberal Peronism is based on more focused strategies of poverty alleviation. As Roberts has consistently argued, through a range of empirical analyses proving the compatibility between neoliberalism and populism in Latin America, neoliberal policy adjustments may facilitate the provision of more selective, targeted material benefits to specific groups, which can be used as building blocks for local clientelist exchanges. Targeted programmes have a more modest fiscal impact than universal measures, but their political logic can be functionally equivalent, as both attempt to exchange material rewards for political support. Moreover,

> Besides their lower cost, targeted programs have the advantage of being direct and highly visible, allowing government leaders to claim political credit for material gains. By allowing leaders to personally inaugurate local projects or 'deliver' targeted benefits, selective programs are highly compatible with the personalistic leader-mass relationships of populism. As... selective incentives provide more powerful inducements to collective action than do public goods, selective benefits may create stronger clientelist bonds than universal benefits, especially politically obscure ones like permanent price subsidies and exchange controls.[29]

Not only does this tend to reduce the space for lower-class mobilizations against neoliberalism, but it also helps to create a popular political constituency for electoral success: the PJ orients its extensive informal networks of clientelism and patronage-based relations to maximizing its share of the vote. Although patronage was never absent from traditional populism, material exchanges aimed at vote-maximization strategies were rarely primary. This was mainly because after 1955 Peronism was proscribed from the electoral arena and so was not structured as a party machine but rather as a counter-culture, where traditional *punteros* maintained close ties of friendship, loyalty and ideology among their neighbours. In contrast, neoliberal Peronism is based on new de-politicized forms of social activism where the 'clientelistic *punteros* are more "entrepreneurial" so the patronage organization is being run like a business'.[30] For electoral purposes, Kirchner has used the PJ with even more flexibility by building larger electoral coalitions than traditional or Menemist Peronism would have allowed for, bringing *Piqueteros*, human rights organizations and members of the Radical Party (known as 'Radicals K') under the umbrella of the *Frente para la Victoria*. This party was created for the 2005 parliamentary elections that led Cristina Kirchner, his wife, to the Senate, and will probably take her to the presidency in 2007.

The remarkable new capacity of the PJ to control lower classes from 'above' (from the state) may also disprove any naive presumption that the increase of poverty and social inequality 'undermines' neoliberal democracy by inevitably producing a popular backlash in favour of progressive alternatives. On the contrary, the Argentinean case highlights the extent to which neoliberalism is both 'a cause and a consequence of the weakening and fragmentation of the popular collective actors who are essential to any progressive alternative'.[31]

This form of domination is not, however, cost-free, as it entails a series of disjunctures. First, the exclusionary nature of neoliberalism is at odds with the promises of democracy as encompassed in the famous inaugural speech of the first elected president Raúl Alfonsín (1983-1989), according to which 'democracy feeds, cures and educates'. Democratic neoliberalism promises social goods at the same time as it dismantles the institutional capacities to deliver them. In addition, the legitimacy of these regimes is built upon 'successful' economic results (monetary stability in the case of Menem or sustained rise of GDP in the case of Kirchner), which can be a source of political strength in a context of increasing commodification of citizenship, but also of great vulnerability when these results are not forthcoming (as demonstrated by the collapse of Alfonsín's government with the hyperinflation crisis and de la Rúa's with the end of convertibility).

Second, an increasing number of excluded people tend to be more reliant on clientelism and patronage than on 'free elections', 'accountability', and so on, creating a deep disjunction between formal institutions and everyday strategies of survival. Third, as the Peronists are more effective in using patronage than non-Peronist parties – indeed, this has been recently defined as the 'new iron law of Argentine politics'[32] – the stability of the political regime therefore becomes too dependent on the PJ's capacity and access to state resources for sustaining the informal networks that hold popular classes back. Consequently, when this capacity is reduced either by the fiscal restraints of a long economic recession, such as that which began in 1998, or by the rise of a non-Peronist party to the presidency (as that of the Alianza with de la Rúa between 1999 and 2001), the growing number of unemployed workers (or the 'losers' of the system in general) tend to look for alternative channels of action and organization. Indeed, from 1997-1998 onwards Argentina saw a unique explosion of popular forms of mobilization and resistance to neoliberal policies, completely detached from institutional politics, in response to the unfulfilled promises of democracy. This suggests that the limited version of democracy can 'tame popular sectors' only partially and temporarily when the 'hidden' or popular face of democracy takes the form of strikes, demonstrations, road blockages, occupations and many other forms of direct expression and demands for equal rights.[33]

So it can be argued that democratic neoliberalism in Argentina exists under a basic contradiction. On the one hand the disenchantment with conventional political practice combined with strategies of patronage and clientelism that is constitutive of Argentine democracy has been quite productive for the neoliberal political project aimed at locking-in the power gains of capitalist elites (transnational and local) and locking-out or de-politicizing the forces challenging these gains. On the other hand, and at the same time, it has opened up a new space for the mobilization of opposition by the excluded, new forms of struggle and organization.

This double movement of de-politicization and re-politicization of subaltern classes raises fundamental questions about the nature and scope of the challenges posed by this new form of politics based on a complex (and dialectical) relation between autonomy and dependency vis-à-vis the state. The process of recomposition may also point to some disturbing conclusions for progressive politics: the political reproduction and extension of clientelism *through* crises. In fact, the new 'losers' and unemployed that the Argentine crisis created became more vulnerable and dependent on state emergency programs, and discretionary ways of distributing them, thus extending the range of influence of Peronist clientelism over the excluded.

This is mainly because the process through which the movement of the unemployed – symbolized by the *Piqueteros* – emerged and evolved was contradictory. The heterogeneity and autonomy that were crucial for their successful mobilization in the first place also proved to be a source of political weakness. The movement first emerged in open confrontation with traditional forms of politics, rejecting the involvement of official unions (CGT), political parties and any other political leadership. The *Piqueteros* organizations led the way to a new politics from below that took shape through direct political action (road blocks) and direct and horizontal democratic procedures of decision-making (assemblies), which differed from the traditionally vertical and pyramidal structures of Peronist unions. The terrain of this new politics was no longer the factory but the community. The *Piqueteros* increasingly became the channel for a process of politicization of the communitarian experience in the neighbourhoods ('the barrio') promoting new forms of self-organization and self-management. Basically, these organizations turned the *Planes Trabajar* (unemployment subsidies) and other forms of aid into productive undertakings for satisfying social needs, such as cooperative farms and bakeries which provide food for soup-kitchens and public hospitals, and also some undertakings in public construction such as schools or housing.

On the other hand, the *Piqueteros'* preoccupation with organizational autonomy sat uncomfortably with the fact that they were completely dependent on state programs. Even though this aid was a product of continuing struggles, their productive and organizational autonomy ultimately came to depend on the state's capacity to provide these subsidies. The increasing institutionalization of the *Piqueteros* movement around the demand for *Planes Trabajar,* which enabled unemployed workers to mobilize new forms of politicization 'from below', at the same time made them intrinsically vulnerable to clientelistic integration and political fragmentation. In fact, the *Planes Trabajar* were an effective strategy of *divide and rule* as well as for re-integrating unemployed groups into a dependent relationship with the state, since more and more unemployed organizations concluded that a measure of cooperation with the government was the most effective way to secure some of their interests.[34]

Even though their fragmentation was not a problem until 2001 – as this was a period of *cooperation* among the different organizations, especially under de la Rúa's administration – the massive extension of the coverage of these state programs (from three hundred thousand to two million people) created *competition* and *conflict* among the different fractions.[35] This partly explains the movement's recurrent failures at creating a National Assembly of *Piqueteros* when the political and ideological differences between reformists (FTV and CCC with a unionist tradition), revolutionaries (at least ten factions ranging from Trotskyists to Guevarists to Communist, Nationalists, Socialists and so on) and autonomists (MTDs inspired by the Zapatistas experience) came to the fore, and the conflict among them for the leadership of the movement, disabled the unification of the *Piqueteros.*

The political fragmentation that characterizes the *Piqueteros* movement also highlights the complex relation between change and continuity within left politics, as well as the fundamental limits of the new forms of politics from below in challenging democratic neoliberalism. The *Piqueteros* movement illustrates the conflict between horizontal, anti-institutional forms of organization and vertical ones, as well as the particular struggle between Peronism and any leftist alternative for the leadership of subaltern classes. The case of the *Piqueteros* raises *the* key questions regarding the disciplinary effects unemployment may have within neoliberalism, the viability of autonomous strategies, the extent to which the new politics from 'below' is a politics of social transformation rather than mere survival (and in that case, how sustainable a mere survival strategy can be without transforming the power structures that create exclusion in the first place); and, ultimately, whether the ideological and political fragmentation of the working class is a source of empowerment or is, on the contrary, disempowering.

The case of the *Piqueteros* illustrates the political fragmentation of labour (workers and unemployed workers) as a force able to challenge the political unity of capital – i.e. the state. This is not just a theoretical, philosophical or ideological challenge for the 'left'. It points to a political and material problem, for the left seems unable to compete with Peronism and its privileged access to state resources, which sustain their base of power within the lower classes. Ultimately, this points not only to the political strategies at stake but also to the institutional flexibility of democratic neoliberalism in keeping its own contradictions within manageable limits.

NOTES

1   This is a form of protest called *escraches,* inaugurated by the children of the disappeared who 'exposed' their disappeared parent's repressors by painting and marking their homes, throwing eggs and other things.

2   Edward Epstein, 'The Piquetero Movement of Greater Buenos Aires: Working Class Protest During the Argentine Crisis', *Canadian Journal of Latin American and Caribbean Studies*, 28(55/56), 2003.

3   For instance, G. Perry and L. Serven, *The Anatomy of a Multiple Crisis. Why was Argentina special and what can we learn from it?*, Chief Economist Office, LAC, World Bank, 2002; also M. Mussa, *Argentina and the Fund: From Triumph to Tragedy*, Washington: Institute for International Economics, 2002.

4   Larry Diamond, *Developing Democracy. Towards Consolidation*, Baltimore: The John Hopkins University Press, 1999; Philippe Schmitter, 'Transitology: The Science or the Art of Democratization?', in Joseph S. Tulchin (with Bernice Romero), ed., *The Consolidation of Democracy in Latin America*, Boulder: Lynne Reinner, 1995.

5   Jorge Altamira, *El Argentinazo. El Presente como Historia*, Buenos Aires: Rumbos, 2002; Rubén Dri, *La Revolución de las Asambleas*, Buenos Aires: Ediciones Diaporías, 2006; the Journal *Cuadernos del Sur*.

6   R. Zibechi, *Genealogía de la revuelta. Argentina, Sociedad en Movimiento*, Buenos Aires: Letra Libre, 2003; Ana Dinerstein, 'The Battle of Buenos Aires. Crisis, Insurrection and the Reinvention of the Political in Argentina', *Historical Materialism*, 10(4), 2003; Alberto Bonnet, 'Que se vayan todos. Crisis Insurrección y caída de la convertibilidad', *Cuadernos del Sur,* 33, 2002; the Journal *Colectivo Situaciones*.

7   Toni Negri et al., *Diálogo sobre la globalización, la multitud y la experiencia argentina*, Buenos Aires: Paidos, 2003.

8   John Holloway, 'Argentina: Que se vayan todos', *Herramienta*, 20(VII), 2002.

9   James Petras and Henry Veltmeyer, 'Argentina: entre la desintegración y la revolución', in Petras and Veltmeyer, eds., *Las Privatizaciones y la Desnacionalización de América Latina*, Buenos Aires: Prometeo, 2004.

10   Enrique Peruzzoti, 'Demanding Accountable Government: Citizens, Politicians and the Perils of Representative Democracy in Argentina', in Steve Levitsky and Victoria Murillo, eds., *Argentine Democracy: The Politics of Institutional Weakness,* University Park: Penn State University Press, 2005, p. 230.

11   Juan Grigera, 'Argentina: On Crisis and a Measure for Class Struggle', *Historical Materialism*, 14(1), 2006.

12   Juan Iñigo Carrera, 'Argentina: The Reproduction of Capital through Political Crisis', *Historical Materialism*, 14(1), 2006.

13   Ernesto Calvo, 'Una fuerte participación enterró el voto bronca y dio paso al voto útil', *Clarín,* 28 April 2003, p. 12; Carrera, 'Argentina'; Alberto Bonnet, 'Que se vayan todos!: Discussing the Argentine Crisis and Insurrection', *Historical Materialism*, 14(1), 2006.

14   Kirchner finished second with 22 per cent, but seeing that a second run-off would give Kirchner an overwhelming victory Menem decided to drop out of the race.

15   For instance, in 1993 the PJ won 63 per cent of the votes in Santiago del Estero, after a paradigmatic *pueblada* took place involving burning the local legislature, the Justice Palace and the governor's house, in a protest over unpaid salaries and massive layoffs from the public administration; 61 per cent in Tierra del Fuego, after a worker was killed in a massive demonstration against the government; and 47 per cent in Jujuy, after several protests and popular upheavals.

16   An incipient attempt at re-nationalizing a few public services, such as *Aguas Argentinas* (water) and *Correos Argentinos* (General Post Office), has however not yet amounted to a systematic and structural reversal of the privatization process of the 1990s.

17   James Petras, 'Argentina: valoración tras dieciocho meses de lucha popular', in Petras and Veltmeyer, eds., *Las Privatizaciones*.

18   Dinerstein, 'The Battle of Buenos Aires'.

19   Grigera, 'Argentina', pp. 2-3.

20   For instance, Arturo Escobar, 'Imagining a Post-developmental Era', in Jonathan Crush, ed., *Power of Development*, New York: Routledge, 1995; G. Cieza, *Argentina: Ideas para el debate sobre los nuevos movimientos socials autónomos.* Paper presented at the Taller Autogestionado sobre Reconstrucción del Movimiento Popular at the Foro Social-Buenos Aires, 2002, available at http://www.lahaine.org.

21   Javier Auyero, *La Política de los Pobres. Las Prácticas Clientelistas del Peronismo*, Buenos Aires: Manantial, 2001.

22   World Bank, *Equity and Development*, Washington: World Bank, 2006.

23   As paradigmatically stated by Francis Fukuyama, neoliberal prophets claimed that this limited form of democracy constituted the 'end point of mankind's ideological evolution and the final form of human government'. *The End of History and the Last Man*, New York: Free Press, 1991, p. xi.

24 See for instance, B. Gills et al., *Low Intensity Democracy: Political Power in the New World Order*, London: Pluto Press, 1993; W. Robinson, 'Globalization: Nine Theses on our Epoch', *Race and Class*, 38(2), October–December 1996; J. Saul, 'Globalism, Socialism and Democracy in South African Transition', *Socialist Register 1994*.

25 As can be found in A. Negri and M. Hardt, *Empire*, Cambridge: Harvard University Press, 2000; J. Holloway, *Change the World without Taking Power*, London: Pluto Press, 2002; and other exponents of the so-called 'Open Marxism'; in Latin America, many 'post-structuralist' scholars such as A. Escobar, 'Imagining a Post-Development Era'; in Argentina: Raúl Zibechi, *Genealogía de la Revuleta*, La Plata: Letra Libre, 2003; and I. Lewcowicks, *Pensar sin Estado*, Buenos Aires: Paidos, 1994.

26 For instance, Leo Panitch, 'Globalisation and the State', *Socialist Register 1994*.

27 This notion of democratic neoliberalism is a partial adaptation of the notion of 'democratic capitalism' recently put forward by A. Borón, 'The Truth about Capitalist Democracy', *Socialist Register 2006*.

28 S. Levitsky, 'Crisis and Renovation: Institutional Weakness and the Transformation of Argentine Peronism, 1983-2003', in Levitsky and Murillo, eds., *Argentine Democracy*, p. 195.

29 K. Roberts, 'Neoliberalism and the Transformation of Populism in Latin America: The Peruvian Case', *World Politics*, 48(1), 1996, p. 91.

30 S. Levitsky, *Transforming Labour-Based Parties in Latin America. Argentine Peronism in Comparative Perspective*, Cambridge: Cambridge University Press, 2003, p. 207.

31 K. Roberts, 'Neoliberalism and the Transformation of Populism, p. 115.

32 Ernesto Calvo and Victoria Murillo, 'The New Iron Law of Argentine Politics? Partisanship, Clientelism and Governability in Contemporary Argentina', in Levitsky and Murillo, eds., *Argentine Democracy*.

33 J. Saul, 'Globalism, Socialism and Democracy'.

34 J. Wolff, '(De-)Mobilising the Marginalised: A Comparison of the Argentine *Piqueteros* and Ecuador's Indigenous Movement', *Journal of Latin American Studies*, 39, 2007, p. 23.

35 For a detailed analysis of this fragmentation, see M. Svampa and S. Pereyra, *Entre la Ruta y el Barrio. La Experiencia de las Organizaciones Piqueteras*, Buenos Aires: Biblos, 2003.

COUNTER-REVOLUTION AGAINST
A COUNTER-REVOLUTION:
EASTERN EUROPE TODAY

G.M. TAMÁS

In Hungary, a socialist-liberal coalition led by the young and gifted Ferenc Gyurcsány, a billionaire businessman and a former secretary of the Communist Youth League before 1989, was returned to office in 2006 after an election campaign based on left-populist promises which, in a secret speech to his parliamentary party, Mr Gyurcsány himself announced to have been a bunch of deliberate lies. After the speech had been leaked, riots erupted in Budapest, and the headquarters of state television – the symbol of mendacity – was torched. On October 23, 2006, the fiftieth anniversary of the Hungarian revolution of 1956, the police, who had been so signally defeated in the riots a few days before, visited retribution on the protesters, beating up rioters, passers-by, already immobilized prisoners and whoever else was in their way. (The liberal intelligentsia, to its eternal shame, took the side of police terror.)

Protests continued for months, deteriorating rapidly, dominated by the symbolism of the Arrow-Cross, the Hungarian Nazis famous for their anti-Jewish terror in the encircled Budapest of 1944. The protests were adroitly mined by the parliamentary right, led by the former prime minister, Viktor Orbán. The government coalition proceeded with its radical austerity measures, immense tax increases, social and health expenditure cuts, closing down hospitals (the first deaths caused by the chaos in the health service have already occurred), schools and cultural institutions, cutting or stopping subsidies altogether, planning to privatize the hospitals, the railways, the electricity board and municipal services, liberalizing prices (e.g., those of medications), introducing fees for every visit to a (state) doctor, fees for university students, doubling the price of public transport, freezing wage and pension increases – all necessary to reduce public debt and trade deficit in order to meet the so-called 'convergency criteria' demanded by the European Union, mandatory for joining the eurozone. Credit-rating agencies such as Standard and Poor's, have more influence on government policy than the electorate.

All this is opposed by deafening *anti-communist* vociferation, xenophobic, anti-Semitic, anti-Western and anti-immigrant agitation (there are practically no immigrants in Hungary, but never mind, there may be at some point in the future if the rootless cosmopolitans now in office are not chased away). The polls show that the parliamentary centre-left may disappear; government supporters are openly threatened. There would be a referendum, initiated by the parliamentary right, on the most unpopular measures – certain to be another, unsurprising major defeat for the socialist-liberal government. Because of police abuses, the three major chiefs of the national police, the head of the secret service and the justice minister responsible had to resign in ignominy. Corruption is rife. Motorway and underground railway construction is in tatters. High-rise office blocks are unfinished or empty. Trust in public institutions is nil.

Thousands of motorcyclists, sporting imitation Wehrmacht helmets, huge Nazi and Arrow-Cross flags on their machines, with the official name of their association – *Goy Bikers* – proudly emblazoned on their leather jackets, are filling the main streets of central Budapest with their thunderous noise and billowing exhaust fumes. The country is rife with rallies demanding an unelected, non-party upper chamber, and a constitution ascribing sovereignty to the Holy Crown (instead of to the people).

What sense can we make of this outbreak of political lunacy? Unlike the revolutionary upheavals of 1953, 1956, 1968 and 1981 (respectively: East Berlin, Budapest, Prague, Gdańsk), the East European régime change of 1989 did not proclaim a purer and better socialism, workers' councils, self-management or even higher wages for proletarians. It was seen as a re-establishment of 'normalcy', historical continuity and a restoration of the triple shibboleth: parliamentary democracy, 'the market' and an unconditional allegiance to 'the West'.

As I have shown elsewhere,[1] this idea of continuity was a mirage. No such system existed in Eastern Europe before, but only a backward agricultural society based on ramshackle latifundia, an authoritarian political order led mostly by the military caste drawn from the impoverished gentry, prone to *coups d'état*, and a public and intellectual life dominated by bitter opponents of a perceived hostile 'West'. Elements of modernity, such as they were, were introduced subsequently by Leninist planners and modernizers who, exacting an extremely high price in blood, suffering, scarcity, tyranny and censorship, were able to impose mobility, urbanization, secularization, indus-trialization, literacy, numeracy, hygiene, infrastructure, nuclear family, work discipline and the rest.

These were the foundations on which the new market capitalism and plu-ralist democracy were built: not a rediscovery of a spurious liberal past, but its introduction by decree for the first time. It was an extremely popular decree for that portion of the population (of which I, too, was an enthusiastic and active member) which participated in the marches, rallies, meetings – not to speak of the shenanigans and skulduggery unavoidable even in utopian poli-tics – and which seemed at the time to have been 'the people', but which was at best 5 per cent of the actual, empirical *dēmos*. Still, to us, stepping into the light from our sombre dissident conventicles of a few dozen people, a hun-dred thousand people appeared as 'the masses'. This minority, since dispersed, possessed a political attitude and a world-view that was a combination of 1848 and 1968: a joyful democratic nationalism and constitutional liberalism mingled with a distaste for authority, repression (cultural and sexual), disci-pline and puritanism.

These transient ideological phenomena which seemed so profound, in-teresting and solid to us at the time, reflected a state of affairs that nearly all observers had been very slow to understand and even slower to describe comprehensively.[2] Neither the leftish bent of most dissident criticism of 'real socialism', nor the sixty-eightish, libertarian feel of 1989 was ever explained satisfactorily. Even the most glaringly obvious historical comparisons were not made. What I find most curious is that the coincidence in time of the crisis of the welfare state – East and West – did not awaken any interest. Historical and political imagination was paralyzed by the unthinking accept-ance of the claim that Soviet bloc régimes must have been (in some elusive sense) 'socialist' since this is what they have declared themselves to be; and, in a more important sense, this was why they were relentlessly fought by the great Western powers of various hues.

Here, a few precisions should be made. I don't think there can be any doubt as to 'real socialism' having been state capitalism of a peculiar sort.[3] It was a system with commodity production, wage labour, social division of labour, real subsumption of labour to capital, the imperative of accumulation, class rule, exploitation, oppression, enforced conformity, hierarchy and ine-quality, unpaid housework and an absolute ban on workers' protest (all strikes illegal), not to speak of a general interdiction of political expression. The only remaining problem is, of course, the lack of 'market co-ordination' and its replacement by government planning. The term 'private property' is misleading here, since if the essence of its significance is the separation of proletarians from the means of production, it also refers to state property, even if we should not try to minimize the considerable differences between the two. If property is control (and legally it is control) then 'state property' is private property in this sense: nobody can pretend that in Soviet-type régimes the workers controlled production, distribution, investment and consumption.

Nor can there be any doubt that post-Stalin state capitalism in the Soviet bloc and in Yugoslavia (roughly 1956-1989) attempted to create a kind of authoritarian welfare state with problems very similar to, and immanent in, any welfare state in the West, be it of the social democratic, Christian Democrat or Gaullist (or, for that matter, New Deal) variety. (I shall neglect features of welfarist state capitalism in Fascist and Nazi régimes, however apposite.)

The social purpose of any welfare state – including post-Stalinist 'real socialism', with the Gulag closed down – was (we can safely use the past tense here) the attempt to bolster consumption through counter-cyclical demand management, to include and co-opt the rebellious working class through affordable housing, transportation, education and health care, to create a *dopolavoro* (a Mussolinian idea already much admired by New Dealers, but of course equally prevalent in the Stalinist Russia of the 1930s) replete with paid holidays, mass tourism, cheap popular entertainment, moderately priced sartorial fashions, and The Motor Car. *The Merry Kids*, a 1930s Soviet musical featuring Young Pioneers (the greatest Russian box-office hit ever), with its unbearable happiness, is undistinguishable from Hollywood or the Third Reich UFA studios' deliriously smiley output, if perhaps with less stress on sauciness and girls' legs.

At the same time, in 'socialist' Eastern Europe there were a few features more reminiscent of South East Asian corporate welfare methods – company holiday camps and company-owned holiday hotels, usually free for the employees, managed by the trade unions (access to them was basically a right for all citizens), free crèches and kindergartens for the workforce's offspring – and some features inherited from European social democracy, but generalized and made mandatory, such as well-stocked lending libraries and cut-price bookshops in every enterprise, affordable good books, theatre and cinema tickets (moreover, books and tickets ordered through your trade union were to be had at half of that already non-competitive price), positive discrimination in favour of working-class youngsters in admission to higher education, job security, cheap basic food, cheap alcohol, cheap tobacco, cheap and plentiful public transport, easy access to amateur and spectator sports. The absence of conspicuous wealth, let alone ostentatious luxury, of the ruling class, together with ever-recurrent shortages and a very reduced consumer choice, sexual puritanism, lengthy terms of military service, the cult of hard work ('popular mechanics' and space flight cults for the young) and a relentless propaganda emphasizing the plebeian and 'collectivist' characteristics of the régime where everybody was supposed to know what to do with a tool-chest, a hoe or a pitchfork – all promoted an atmosphere of equality.

An atmosphere, a mood, yes, but also a reality of incomparably greater equality than today. Under 'real socialism' nation-states oppressed ethnic minorities – outside Soviet Russia, especially *after* Stalin's fall – offering assimilation instead (training films for Hungarian social workers and local council officials in the early 1960s show forcible baths, haircuts and delousings for nomadic Roma families, operated by police and military hospital personnel, amid scenes of infernal humiliation and artificial for-camera grins), suggesting 'unity' and 'harmony' and an end to age-old cultural conflicts. The transfer of peasant populations to industrial townships, unlike in the nineteenth century, had been relatively well organized: until the 1970s, when resources had begun to run out, they were moved into high-rise council estates, and immediately offered the whole set of comprehensive and egalitarian social services including health and culture – there are countries, such as Romania or the former Czechoslovakia, where the majority of the urban population still lives in disintegrating 'communist'-era blocks of flats.

There is no doubt that these societies were intolerably authoritarian, oppressive and repressed, but we are beginning to see how well-integrated, cohesive, pacified, crime-free and institutionalized they were; a petty-bourgeois dream, but a dream nevertheless. Also, 'vertical': that is, upward social mobility was fast and comprehensive and, since we speak of initially backward, peasant societies, the change (from village to town, from back-breaking physical work in the fields to technological work in the factory, from hunger, filth and misery to modest cafeteria meals, hot water and indoor plumbing) was breathtaking. And the cultural change was dramatic. The route from illiteracy and the inability to read a clockface to Brecht and Bartók was astonishingly short. (By the way, it is instructive to see how institutionally embedded cultural needs can be – how half a continent stopped reading serious literature and listening to classical music in a couple of years once the social and ideological circumstances ceased to make such activities both handy and meaningful: *Doch die Verhältnisse, sie sind nicht so* – 'the circumstances are never just so'.)[4]

When, after the régime change of 1989 (in which the present writer played a rather public rôle, and about which his feelings are retrospectively quite ambivalent), the concomitant onslaught on 'state property' through privatization at world market prices, asset-stripping, outsourcing, management buy-outs (companies subsequently bought up by multinationals and closed down to minimize competition and to create new captive consumer markets), caused unheard-of price rises, plummeting real wages and living standards, and massive unemployment. Market liberalization meant that hitherto protected, cushioned, technologically backward local industries could not withstand the intense competition in retail markets which has led to the collapse of local commerce, unable to resist dumping and similar techniques. Almost half of all jobs have been lost. The very real rejoicing over pluralistic political competition and hugely increased freedom of expression was dampened by immiseration and lack of security, accompanied by the ever-increasing dominion of commercial popular culture, advertising, tabloids and trash. What had been conceived of at first as colourful proved merely gaudy, and as it became more and more shopsoiled its novel charm has waned.

All this was regarded by the unhappy East European populations as unmitigated and incomprehensible catastrophe. The political groups on the ground who possessed a little critical sense had been those which fought the former régime and continued to fight its ghost for a long time to come, and pushed the post-World War II liberal agenda – freedom of expression, constitutionalism, abortion rights, gay rights, anti-racism, anti-clericalism, anti-nationalism – certainly causes worth fighting for but bewildering to the popular classes, who were otherwise engaged – without any attention to the onset of widespread poverty, social and cultural chaos. These groups combined the 'human rights' discourse of the liberal left with the 'free to choose' rhetoric of the neoconservative right (they still do, after 18 years) and thought of privatization as the break-up of the almighty state, which – armed with the weapon of redistribution – appeared to be the enemy to beat, saw the 'dependency culture' as the ideological adversary, preventing the subjects of the *Sozialstaat* from becoming freedom-loving, upright, autonomous citizens. I remember – I was a member of the Hungarian parliament from 1990 to 1994 – that we discussed the question of the republican coat of arms (with or without the Holy Crown; the party of 'with' won) for five months, but there was no significant debate on unemployment while two million jobs went up into the air in a small country of ten million.

The task of a welfarist rearguard action went to any political force now considered to be beyond the pale. In countries where there was official discrimination against functionaries of the 'communist' *apparat* and where the members of the former ruling party had to stick together for self-protection and healing wounded pride, as in East Germany and the Czech Republic, this was incumbent upon the so-called 'post-communist left'; and for the rest, the task was usually taken up by extreme nationalist and 'Christian' parties. Since there was a certain continuity of personnel between the ruling 'communist' parties' pro-market, reformist wing (and their expert advisers in universities, research institutes and state banks) who, being at the right place at the right time, profited handsomely from privatizations, there was a superficial plausibility to the popular theory according to which 'nothing has changed'; it was just a conspiracy to prolong the rule of a discredited ruling class. The truth of the matter is, of course, that the changes have been so gigantic that only a fraction of the *nomenklatura* was able to recycle itself into capitalist wheeler-dealers. The ultimate winner was nobody local, but the multinational corporations, the American-led military alliance and the EU bureaucracy.

Nevertheless, there is a grain of truth in this popular theory, namely the suspicion that the contrast between planned state capitalism (a.k.a. 'real socialism') and liberal market capitalism may not be as great as was solemnly proclaimed in 1989. Popular theories formulated as paranoid urban legends, however understandable, cannot (and should not) replace analysis. But they do have political significance, especially as many successor parties to former 'communist' organizations are now touting the neoconservative gospel (the term 'neoliberal' is something of a misnomer: today's ultracapitalists and market fundamentalists are no liberals by any stretch of the imagination) and are dismantling the last remnants of the welfare state. Hence the strange identification in some countries of Eastern Europe of 'communists' with 'capitalists' – after all, it is frequently former 'communists' who are doing this to us, it is always the same people on top, the democratic transformation was a fraud, this is all a Judeo-Bolshevist cabal and so on.

Now the identification of socialism and capitalism is well known to have been a Nazi cliché – both are racially alien – but 'the circumstances are never just so'; they could not be more different. After all, communists and social democrats in the 1920s and 1930s were united and adamant in their false consciousness concerning their integral opposition to capitalism and tyranny. False consciousness does not preclude sincerity. The ex-communist parties at the beginning of the twenty-first century are opposed not only to socialism but to the most elementary working-class interests: this is nothing new and it is also not limited to Eastern Europe. (When speaking of Eastern Europe, I always include the European part of the former Soviet Union, following the good example of General de Gaulle.) After all, the Italian Communist Party and its leader, Enrico Berlinguer, called for austerity measures and insisted on the proletarian duty to acquiesce in them two years before Mrs Thatcher's accession to power.[5] (The right wing of the former PCI, the DS, is now proposing a *merger* with its enemy of sixty years, the Christian Democrats…)

Therefore the cliché, while it has not become any truer, represents fair and just historical revenge.

This is why and how the neoconservative counter-revolution is countered by forms of resistance couched in the terms of the pre-war nationalist and militarist right, often intermingled with open fascist rhetoric and symbols and, in the case of the former Soviet Union, extreme eclecticism trying to synthesize Stalinism and fascism. (The Communist Party of the Russian Federation, the main opposition force in Russia, is inspired by the loony ideologues of the White Guards who represented the political 'brains trust' of the general staff of Admiral Kolchak and Baron Wrangel.) There is a great variety of political solutions. After the defeat of the 'neoliberal' or neoconservative régime of ex-communist President Kwaśniewski in Poland, the ultra-Catholic Kaczyński twin brothers' act, however ridiculous it may have appeared at first, is quite successful and is consolidating itself by combining extreme social conservatism, anti-gays, anti-women, anti-minorities, anti-Russian, anti-German, anti-Semitic and, above all, anti-communist paranoia, with monetarist orthodoxy, pro-Bush military zeal, persecution of everybody on the left (they have stopped the pensions of the few surviving veterans of the International Brigades in the Spanish civil war in the 1930s), censorship and savage ethnicist propaganda. Forty-one Polish MPs, members of the majority in the Diet, proposed a bill for the election of Jesus Christ as honorary president of Poland (some would amend this to honorary *king*). The speaker threw it out on a technicality, they did not dare to put it to a vote: it might have won.

In Slovakia, the government of the left social democrat, Robert Fico, is an alliance of his own party with the nationalists of Vladimír Mečiar and the quasi-fascist National Party led by the notorious alcoholic blowhard, Ján Slota. Mr Fico had the effrontery to increase pensions, cut public transport prices, stop the dismantling of state-managed, essentially free health care and public education. It is an immensely popular government, made even more so by its sharp anti-Czech and anti-Hungarian nationalism combined with pro-Russian leanings. Add to this the seeming inability of the Czech Republic, Romania and Serbia to put together a working parliamentary majority; the anti-Russian madness gripping the Baltic statelets together with very real, apartheid-style discrimination against their ethnic Russian minorities; the persecution and segregation of the Roma minorities everywhere (said the president of Romania of a journalist from whom he personally wrestled and stole, well, confiscated, her mobile phone: 'I won't talk to this stinking Gipsy girl'); the total collapse of ethnic enclaves 'statified' by the august 'international community' – Bosnia, Kosovo, Montenegro, Macedonia,

Moldova/Transnistria, and the Stalinist *intermundium* of Belarus; the expulsion of ex-Yugoslav residents from Slovenia: and you have a picture of the 'new democracies', the brave soldiers of the 'coalition of the willing', Mr Rumsfeld's and Mr Cheney's 'new Europe'.

Liberal commentators speak of an insurgency against modernity. This is utter nonsense. The neoconservative (or neoliberal) counter-revolution has attacked the nation and especially the lower middle classes on two fronts.

First, it has ignored the fact that social welfare institutions are the backbone of national identity, the only remaining principle of cohesion in a traditionless capitalism. It is not only the loss of livelihood, but the perceived loss of dignity, the loss of the sense of being looked after, protected, and thus respected by the community represented by the state which is at stake. Upward mobility was the greatest triumph of planned welfare states, internalized as dynamic equality. The loss of class status (this latter characteristically symbolized in East-Central Europe by a university degree: even a starving *Herr Doktor* is a gentleman), the feeling that the descendants of tradespeople, civil servants, teachers and physicians may have to do physical work, *again*, or flee somewhere as illegal migrants, to be *déclassé*, is an intolerable threat. This insurgency is the revolt of the middle classes against loss of nation and loss of caste.

Second, identifying with the bulwarks and battlements of the welfare state *created by the communists* is ideologically impossible for the middle classes. It would be a tremendous loss of face, since 'communism' symbolizes defeat and the past, and the petty bourgeoisie is nothing if not modernist and driven by the myth of achievement, self-improvement and the rest. They cannot openly defend the institutions that gave them their dignity in the first place, which have made peasants into bureaucrats and intellectuals, since this would be to acknowledge the shameful agrarian past and the equally shameful 'communist' legacy. Thus, by representing the neoconservative (or neoliberal) destruction as the work of communists, shame can be avoided and the defence of pre-1989 institutional arrangements made acceptable. Also, former communist party or communist youth secretaries cannot say that they never belonged to that institutional order and they have nothing to be thankful for its blessings; they have to declare that the dismantling of that order is the correction of a mistake. So they appear fallible and opportunistic, not the harbingers of a new era, liberty or whatever.

So the new counter-revolutionaries can be fashioned as being of both the left and the right, and the impeccably anti-communist foes of the 'communist' privatizers, monetarists, supply-siders and globalizers. They can defend the Bolshevik-created welfare state without giving an inch to Bolsheviks who went from the International to the Multinational, since both can be opposed by the idea of militant ethnicity, something quite different from classical nationalism, the latter built upon the legal and political equality of all citizens, regardless of creed and race within an independent and sovereign nation-state.

Since this outbreak of political lunacy in Eastern Europe is as much a defensive reaction to neoconservative or neoliberal globalization and neo-imperialism as the anti-capitalist version of the new social movements in the West, we need to consider briefly the question of parallels between the two. The former's struggles are *largely symbolic*: compare, e.g., the protests against the G8 summit meeting at Heiligendamm, taking place as I write. Let us suppose for a moment that the protesters were to 'win' and manage to chase away the assorted heads of state and other great panjandrums from Mecklenburg-Vorpommern – what would happen? They would return to their respective seats of government, with a few bruises, perhaps – end of story. There are no specific demands (*'make capitalism history'* is not one); therefore the protesters are not meeting 'bourgeois politics' at the level where it is designed and implemented – and the few really specific demands (in fact, requests) voiced by a moderate wing are confined to the framework of bourgeois politics and therefore not revolutionary (for example, those concerning carbon emissions, migrant labour, intellectual property rights, etc.), so ultimately compatible with bourgeois (mainstream liberal) politics even if they have few prospects of immediate success. Violence erupts because the protesters are opposed to the 'system' but the system is not invested in this arbitrary congeries of nation-state bosses, who are not exercising their true, that is, legal power in this setting. What is threatened (unlike in the case of communist or socialist revolutions) is not a régime change, but chaos. Chaos cannot be met by repression (although it can be suppressed and 'cleaned up' by police and Bundeswehr), since only counter-power can be repressed, and protest as such is not power. Repression itself can be made, on the other hand, into chaos. Power does not encounter counter-power, unlike in the case of classical – especially European – revolutions.

Yet it is also important to recognize that the *Zeitgeist* of protest among young Western Europeans is very different from young East Europeans. For however they may imitate the formers' Palestinian scarves and bandannas, their hoods and masks, their stone-throwing and the rebel cool they have watched enviously on television, what distinguishes the latter is that they combine all this with extreme authoritarianism, racism and so on. The young middle-class protesters and the militants of Catholic, ethnicist, xenophobic-populist parties in Eastern Europe fear above all loss of status, becoming *déclassé*, something familiar from the young hard right in Central and Eastern Europe in the 1920s and 1930s but also from what we know about some of the motivations of student protest in the 1960s. With their demand for order, hierarchy, national unity, a definite end to everything they consider *deviant* behaviour – alarmingly reminiscent of *fatwa*s issued by al-Azhar and the Vatican – they, however opposed in principle to *haute finance* and rootlessly cosmopolitan globalization, unwittingly serve the present order which has nothing to fear from ethnic hatred, militarism, homophobia and a nostalgia for stiffly established order. Whatever their mistakes, the new social movements in the West and in the South are not guilty of anything like that.

Meanwhile, even more than in the West, the working class is silent. There are hardly any strikes. This battle is fought between transnational capital and its native agents and the local, ethnic middle classes and the ethnicist and clericalist intelligentsia. An authentic left has not surfaced.

Yet.

NOTES

1   'Un capitalisme pur et simple', *La Nouvelle Alternative*, vol. 19 no. 60-61, March–June 2004, pp. 13-40; 'Ein ganz normaler Kapitalismus', *Grundrisse: zeitschrift für linke theorie & debatte* 22, Summer 2007, pp. 9-23.

2   Cf. G.. M. Tamás, 'Socialism, Capitalism and Modernity', in Larry Diamon and Marc F. Plattner, eds., *Capitalism, Socialism and Democracy Revisited*, Baltimore and London: Johns Hopkins University Press, 1993, pp. 54-68; 'The Legacy of Dissent: Irony, Ambiguity, Duplicity', in Vladimir Tismaneanu, ed., The Revolutions of of 1989, London and New York: Routledge, 1999, pp. 181-197 (the first version appeared in the *Times Literary Supplement*, May 14, 1993); 'Paradoxes of 1989', *East European Politics and Societies*, vol. 13, no. 2 (Spring 1999), pp. 353-358; 'Victory Defeated', in Larry Diamond and Marc F. Plattner, eds. *Democracy After Communism*, Baltimore and London,: John Hopkins University Press, 2002, pp. 126-131.

3   An excellent survey of 'state capitalism' theories can be found in Mike Haynes, 'Marxism and the Russian Question in the Wake of the Soviet Collapse' (formally a review of books by Michael Cox, ed.; Paresh Chattopadhyay; and Neil Fernandez), *Historical Materialism*, 10.4 (2002), pp. 317-62. See also my 'Un capitalisme pur et simple', *loc. cit.*, and cf. Stephen A. Resnick and Richard D. Wolff, *Class Theory and History: Capitalism and Communism in the USSR*, New York and London: Routledge, 2002, compare Paresh Chattopadhyay's review, *Historical Materialism*, 14.1 (2006), pp. 249-270.

4   Bertolt Brecht, 'Die Dreigroschenoper', *Stücke*, I, Berlin: Aufbau-Verlag, 1975, p. 76. ('The circumstances are never just so'.)

5   See Ernest Mandel, *From Stalinism to Eurocommunism*, London: New Left Books, 1978, pp. 125-49. The opportunist turn towards straightforward bourgeois politics in the PCI explains the early rise and large influence of the Italian far left, cf. Steve Wright, *Storming Heaven: Class Composition and Struggle in Italian Autonomist Marxism*, London: Pluto, 2002.

RESISTANCE TO NEOLIBERALISM IN FRANCE

RAGHU KRISHNAN AND ADRIEN THOMAS

All eyes are once again on France in the wake of hard-Right candidate Nicolas Sarkozy's victory in the 2007 presidential elections. Mainstream media and academic commentators, especially in the Anglo-American sphere, have heralded the Sarkozy victory as a tremendous opportunity to carry out the neoliberal reforms we are told the country requires if it is to emerge from the years of conflict and stagnation that these same commentators decry with alarm and indignation. They fervently hope that president Sarkozy will stay the course of free-market reform, whatever opposition he encounters from 'over-protected' and 'conservative' sectors of the population.[1]

However, while the results of the presidential and legislative elections have further tilted the relationship of forces against those millions of men, women, students and youth who have taken to the streets in recent years against neoliberal reforms, it would be premature to declare the definitive triumph of neoliberalism in France. Sarkozy faces two major difficulties. The first is the breadth of the resistance to neoliberalism in France, and the eroded political legitimacy of the neoliberal project on a global scale. In the first part of our essay we explore the strengths and weaknesses of resistance to neoliberalism in France – focusing on the cycle of anti-liberal struggles and critical thinking that began with the massive strike and protest movement of late 1995, and the striking resilience of anti-neoliberal resistance since that time. The second difficulty Sarkozy faces is the particular character of his victory. Precisely in order to reckon with the depth of anti-neoliberal feeling in France, Sarkozy's neoliberal fervour often takes a back seat to neoconservative and populist appeals to xenophobic and authoritarian sentiments. Indeed, his victory depended quite heavily on a strategy aimed at obscuring socio-economic questions and capturing the electorate of Jean-Marie Le Pen's neofascist Front National. Though very much a part of the right-wing political establishment going back many years, and tied into the country's most powerful industrial and media interests, Sarkozy has also succeeded in portraying himself as an outsider poised to rescue France from crisis and various real or imagined internal and external threats.

To be sure, it is very worrying that such a figure should occupy the Elysée Palace and have a parliamentary majority at his disposal. But it is not clear that he will have a much freer hand than his predecessors to attack the various key pillars of the French welfare state that remain standing, even if badly battered after a quarter century of neoliberal reforms under both the Left and Right: strong public pensions, healthcare and education, and relatively stable long-term employment contracts with comparatively generous benefits for a large majority of workers. These institutions are as cherished by many of the retirees and workers swayed by Sarkozy's straight-talking, populist 'law and order' posturing, as they are by many of the millions of working and middle-class people who voted for Socialist Party candidate Ségolène Royal.

Quite clearly, the success of the Sarkozy enterprise depends on his ability to continue polarizing the country around the questions of 'law and order', 'national identity' and 'moral decay' that he raised with surprising virulence in the latter days of the presidential campaign. A key episode in Sarkozy's rise to power was the November 2005 confrontation in the *banlieues* (urban periphery) of the country's main urban centres – the largest social disturbance in the country since May 1968. In hindsight, it is tempting to see the entire episode as a surreal pantomime deliberately provoked by Sarkozy, when he was the Interior Minister, to outflank his rival for the presidency within the ruling party – and Chirac's preferred successor – prime minister Dominique de Villepin. But it is also important to consider the underlying reasons for the uprising in the poorest *banlieues*: the depth of anger and frustration brought on by more than twenty years of neoliberalism under Left and Right, on the one hand; and on the other, the accumulated failures of the Left in countering the Right and far-Right's attempts to ethnicize and criminalize socio-economic questions. With this in mind, we devote the second part of our essay to the condition of the poorest *banlieues* and the disproportionate number of non-white youth of immigrant origin who live there.

THE FAILED 'NORMALIZATION' OF FRANCE

In 2005-2006 France was shaken by three major episodes of resistance to neoliberalism: the No vote to the European Constitution in May 2005, the riots in the French *banlieues* in October-November 2005 and the student-led movement in February-April 2006 against the CPE labour-law reform (*Contrat Première Embauche*). The backdrop to these events was the enduring and mounting socio-economic difficulties faced by broad sectors of the population, signalling the slow demise of the 'French social model'. This model was built up during the *trente glorieuses*, the 30 years of post-war economic growth and rising living standards that followed the post-Second World War socio-economic and political compromise between Gaullists and Communists. While this model was much more related to reconstructing and planning a capitalist social order than paving a 'French Road to Socialism', and was at times contested by social movements (most spectacularly in May 1968), it nevertheless offered forms of social stability to the working class and a path to integration for immigrants. For the last 25 years, the country's political and economic elites have sought to dismantle this model through the social and political 'normalization' of France and its alignment with the Euro-Atlantic mainstream, but they have repeatedly faced strong resistance from broad layers of the population.

Especially since the 1980s, European integration has come to be seen by centre-left and centre-right modernizers alike as a way out of a 'French exception' whose origins are described as stretching back to the Jacobins. In this widely-held view, the French 'malady' stems from the poisonous relationship between an omnipotent state and a disorganized civil society prone to irrational outbursts of potentially violent collective action.[2] Another feature of the 'French exception' is said to reside in the 'archaic' antagonism between the political Left and Right, seen as an obstacle to efficient technocratic governance. French elites have promoted and regularly hailed the demise of this supposed exception in a world seen as increasingly conforming to the Anglo-American model.[3] They celebrated the end of both Gaullism and Communism, the main features of this French exceptionalism, as a sure sign the stage was finally set for such a 'normalization' of the country, hand in hand with the accelerating process of European integration. However, the referendum on the European constitution, a document presented as the crowning achievement of European integration, ironically provided an occasion for the popular rejection of a neoliberal Europe, with the vote turning into a referendum on neoliberalism. During debates on the European Constitution, the word *libéral* became definitively established as a political insult in France with the No campaign from the left being waged under the slogan *Non à l'Europe libérale* (No to liberal Europe).

The project for a EU constitution aimed to enshrine the main tenets of neoliberal economic policy. Its rejection by 55 per cent of voters was achieved against all odds. The major political parties and the media vociferously supported the treaty, whereas the coalition in favour of the 'No' formed a heterogeneous grouping with limited representation in parliament and in the mainstream political sphere. The referendum outcome highlighted the breadth of the gap between the population and the political elite. Leaders and activists from the social movements, the Communist Party (PCF) and the mainly Trotskyist far-Left organizations led the No campaign, joined by minority currents from the Socialist and Green parties (the largest trade union, the formerly Communist-oriented CGT, also came out in favour of the No, but did not actively campaign due to internal divisions). Since far-Right and marginal figures of the centre-Right also came out in favour of the No, biased media reports depicted No voters as driven by xenophobic resentment. But the dynamic of the grass-roots campaign against the treaty, as well as the opinion polls, showed that among the No voters social considerations (fear of heightened unemployment and of further outsourcing, lack of social guarantees) prevailed over nationalist concerns (immigration, and the proposed accession of Turkey to the European Union).

The rejection of the European Constitution was seen as a disaster by French elites, who interpreted it as an explosion of xenophobia and national isolationism on the part of the backward masses. A few days after the referendum the conservative historian René Remond declared on public radio, 'I am tempted to say that it's as bad as Munich'. As in other countries, the European Union had come to be regarded by elites as an undertaking whose greatest advantage was that it was insulated from popular demands. European integration had been initiated primarily by conservative Christian Democrats, for whom fascism had largely been the product of the base instincts of the masses. After fascism, the Second World War and the social upheavals of the post-war years, these founding fathers saw an elite-centred European unification as a way to let rational and dispassionate political decision-making by the knowledgeable prevail over national self-interest and unpleasant annoyances such as the class struggles in the different member states.

In the context of the Cold War and Franco-German post-war reconciliation, European integration was seen by many progressive forces in France as playing an essentially protective role; in more recent times, however, the European unification process has come to be seen as a threatening, destructive battering ram for the neoliberal order. In no other European country is there such widespread scepticism about the free-market economy, as evidenced both in opinion polls[4] and in the number and strength of social protests against neoliberalism in recent years.[5] On the other hand, France is one of the developed countries where financialization and liberalization of controls on foreign investment have gone furthest. After having been protected until the 1980s from international competition by a benevolent state and stable alliances between the main capitalists, French industry has entered the age of globalization. The progress of neoliberalism has been accompanied by the financialization of the French economy. Whereas in 1985, foreign investors controlled only 10 per cent of the firms listed on the Paris stock exchange, by 2000 the proportion had risen to 44 per cent – even higher than in Great Britain (30 per cent) or the United States (less than 20 per cent).[6] The resilience of anti-free market sentiments and social movements, on the one hand, and the rapid transition to Anglo-American-style shareholder capitalism, on the other, have deepened the contradictions of French society.

The financialization of the French economy has gone hand in hand with the stagnation or regression of wages, the adoption of new labor management strategies and an extension of market relations through the privatization of public services.[7] But the most devastating effect on the balance of forces between labour and capital has come from the constantly high level of unemployment (around 10 per cent over the last two decades) and the expansion of precarious working conditions (part-time jobs, short-term contracts). The reduction in support payments to the unemployed, along with measures designed to further deregulate the labour market on the workfare model, has led not only to the stigmatization of the unemployed and social-welfare recipients, but also to a destabilization of employment in the core sectors of the economy. The fear of unemployment and its attendant personal and social consequences has had a chilling effect across the breadth of society, a fear regularly reinforced by threats of offshoring which allow employers to roll back wages and increase working time without any financial compensation (as in the case of the electronics manufacturer Bosch which in 2004 threatened to shift a car parts factory from Vénissieux, near Lyons, to the Czech Republic).

Mobilizations and struggles against the growing precariousness of employment and social welfare encounter numerous difficulties. The unemployed are isolated and without strong unifying organizations, while wage-earners with precarious jobs are not shielded from employer pressures given the great weakness of trade unions in the private industrial and service sectors where these types of jobs are most numerous. The unions have also had tremendous difficulty waging general campaigns and struggles on the issue of precariousness. The defeat of the 2003 movement against the pension reform illustrated the difficulties French trade unions have in uniting public and private-sector workers. Although the public sector, and especially schoolteachers, mobilized quite massively, even the major industrial segments of the private sector saw only very limited strike activity.[8] The 2003 conflict, as well as the defeat without much of a fight in 2004 over a reform of the public healthcare system, showed that French trade-unionism cannot be sustained on the basis of its strength in a few areas of the shrinking public sector.[9] All this puts the very essence of trade-unionism – its ability to nurture solidarity and act collectively – under threat.

In such a context, it is significant that it was mainly a student-led mobilization in 2006 that produced a setback for the neoliberal project of labour-market deregulation in the form of the successful struggle against the CPE labour-market reform which aimed to create a new category of precarious employment by making it easier to lay off young workers. Over a period of three months, with the support of student organizations and trade unions, young people and their parents took to the streets against the CPE. During the working week, post-secondary and high school students occupied universities and schools, held general assemblies and protested in the streets. Their parents and other wage earners, called into action by the unions, joined them in huge demonstrations on the weekends and in several *journées d'action* – protest days with partial nationwide strikes, culminating in countrywide protests involving three million people on April 4, 2006.[10]

Although the riots in the Latin Quarter of Paris received tremendous attention from the international media, they were not the most important dimension of the conflict on the CPE. Far more important than the symbolic re-enactments of May '68 around the Sorbonne were the links made between students and trade unionists, and the amazing geographical spread and self-organization of the movement. Indeed, the most vibrant and enduring initiatives were not necessarily taking place in Paris, but in smaller cities and towns. The protests finally forced the initially inflexible government of Dominique de Villepin to yield and repeal the CPE – although the law had already been adopted by parliament. In the end, even employer organizations called on the government to give in. The government's stubbornness had become counter-productive, threatening the viability of future deregulation initiatives.

NEOLIBERALISM'S DEAD ENDS

France's entry into the age of deregulated capitalism has meant the parallel demise of 'social Gaullism' and of the social-democratic Keynesian project. 'Social Gaullism' was founded on the idea of overcoming class conflict by means of a personal relationship between a people and its leader, and through the limited involvement of wage-earners in company decision-making – topped off by a strong state presence in infrastructure projects. The difficulties of the centre-right in establishing a stable post-Gaullist identity stem from its inability to push through a neoliberal reform agenda, given the enduring attachment to state regulation of the economy. The about-faces of former president Jacques Chirac illustrate these difficulties. He ran his 1995 campaign with the promise of healing the *fracture sociale*, but once elected was eager to prove his allegiance to the neoliberal model by initiating a reform of the public healthcare system and several public-sector pension plans – sparking the 'winter of discontent' of November–December 1995, during which the country was paralyzed by a railway strike.[11] It remains to be seen if Sarkozy will be better able to impose his neoliberal agenda.

One of the outcomes of the 1995 rejection of Chirac's frontal attack on the welfare state was the Socialist Party's (Parti Socialiste, PS) victory in the 1997 legislative elections. However, the PS failed to fulfill expectations of at least a partial reversal of neoliberal policies. Not only was the PS unwilling to reverse the retrograde measures of the defeated right-wing government, but from 1997 to 2002, under prime minister Lionel Jospin, it actually proved itself to be a worthy successor to the right wing in its dismantling of the welfare state. It pursued an agenda of privatization and deregulation of public services and tax cuts, and accepted the idea of raising the retirement age. As a result, the party widened the gap between itself and the working-class electorate. While the PS managed to make headway among highly-paid white-collar workers, especially in the trendy city centres of Paris and Lyons, it did not succeed in creating a broader class alliance.

The gap between the French socialists and the working class has reached a point where in the run-up to the 2002 presidential election the former Socialist prime minister Pierre Mauroy felt compelled to warn his comrades: 'You know, "worker" isn't a four-letter word!' The distance between the PS membership and the working class is also a sociological one. Party members are increasingly drawn from the middle classes, and even primarily the upper middle classes.[12] Working-class disaffection from the PS is spectacular: in 2007, only 25 per cent of the workers who participated in the election voted for Ségolène Royal in the first voting round, against 20 per cent who voted for the neofascist Jean-Marie Le Pen, and 20 per cent for Sarkozy.[13]

Nearly three decades ago, Margaret Thatcher and Ronald Reagan were able to present neoliberalism as a form of utopia. But this is not possible for Mr Sarkozy. Nowadays, unbridled capitalism provokes fear and resentment – not enthusiasm and support. Even when neoliberalism was rolled out in France in the mid-1980s there were no promises of a better world. Rather, it was seen as a temporary adjustment to the economic crisis and to changes in the economy that were beyond the country's control. Austerity policies were meant to give way relatively soon to renewed stability and security. But today it is clear that neoliberal reforms have not led to the establishment of a new, stable order. Instead, one neoliberal reform merely paves the way for the next, without any improvement on the employment front. The inability to build a historic bloc in favour of neoliberalism results from its failure to offer forms of social stability to broad layers of the population.

Growing economic distress, combined with the dismantling of workplace collectives and of traditional industrial workplaces, has brought about a fragmentation of the working class and an erosion of class solidarities and consciousness.[14] In a context where individual success is celebrated and 'losers' are derided, social Darwinism has gained ground to such a degree that some sectors of the working class have come to look favourably upon those promoting the exclusion of immigrants and their children from employment, social benefits, and the country itself. Spewers of anti-immigrant vitriol, the neo-fascist Front National – the federation of neo-Nazis, fundamentalist Catholics and embittered and nostalgic remnants of France's colonial empire led by Jean-Marie Le Pen – has thrived on these sentiments since its first electoral successes in 1983. It has been in the vanguard of those who want the issue of immigration to push questions of socio-economic well-being into the background, a process that has been described as the *Lepénisation des esprits*.

THE REVOLT IN THE *BANLIEUES*

The 2005 uprising in the *banlieues* was a powerful illustration of the social and political processes of resistance and fragmentation at work in contemporary French society. Late in the afternoon of October 27, 2005 in the Paris suburb of Clichy-sous-Bois, two teenage children of Malian (Bouna Traoré, age 15) and Turkish-Tunisian (Zyed Benna, age 17) immigrant parents died of electrocution while hiding from police in an electrical substation.[15] Their deaths sparked a three-week period of rioting and confrontations with the police that spread to the *banlieues* of a number of French cities. It was the most significant episode of confrontation with police and security forces since the events of May 1968.

Conflicts in the *banlieues* are not new. The first contemporary instance was in the periphery of Lyons in the early 1980s, and they have become more frequent since the mid-1990s. They follow a predictable pattern, in which an incident involving the mistreatment or death of a youth at the hands of the police ignites a wider conflict between young people and the police and acts of vandalism to cars, shops and public buildings. The human cost of the conflicts is generally minimal, usually limited to injuries to both the youth and the police directly involved in the running street battles. Though similar in all other respects, the November 2005 events were striking because they strayed from this pattern by lasting longer and being more widespread.[16]

It is important to focus on the immediate and specifically political cause of the *banlieue* explosion. In hindsight, it is clear that the events were a key chapter in Mr Sarkozy's ultimately successful quest for the presidency. Immediately following his return to the Ministry of the Interior earlier in the year (in the cabinet reshuffle that followed the government's humiliating defeat in the EU constitutional referendum), Sarkozy pursued a very deliberate strategy of insulting and provoking residents of the poorer *banlieues* in the country. After the death of the two teenagers, and as the riots continued, Sarkozy and his entourage within the ruling party continued to make false and inflammatory claims about the deceased teenagers and refused to acknowledge any police responsibility for the deaths or apologize for police excesses committed in response to the riots – such as the tear-gas canister hurled at a community mosque, and the racist and sexist insults hurled at women fleeing the gas-filled mosque.[17] The Interior Minister, his entourage in the ruling UMP party, and police spokespeople variously blamed criminal gangs, foreigners, far-Left and Islamic 'extremists', and even 'polygamists', for the riots.

A leaked November 23 internal report from the French intelligence service (DCRG) rejected claims of involvement by Islamists, criminal gangs and the far-Left. The Islamists kept a low profile and in some instances sought to calm things down, whereas the far-Left was entirely caught off guard by the uprising, and criminal gangs generally require calm and stability to conduct their affairs. The DCRG report describes the riots as a 'form of unorganized urban insurrection… a popular revolt of the housing estates, with neither a leader nor a programme, involving young people with a strong feeling of identity based not solely on ethnic or geographic origin but also on their social condition of people excluded from French society'.[18] When, on November 8, the government decided to resurrect a colonial law of 1955 to declare a state of emergency, the number of incidents had already peaked and started to decline; the state of emergency was renewed for a further three months on November 15, even though disturbances had been tapering off for some time.[19] Clearly, there was a political dynamic at play in government circles that went well beyond the specific requirements of restoring calm and order to the affected neighbourhoods.[20]

The uprising in the French *banlieues* has often been presented as yet another example of the failure of the French social model and compared – unfavourably – to the situation in certain American inner-city ghettos. This is quite misleading, and it is necessary to probe more deeply into the causes of the *banlieue* revolt and its implications. Sarkozy's cynical manoeuvering notwithstanding, the tragic deaths in Clichy-sous-Bois would not have provoked such a response had the poorest *banlieues* not been at the confluence of three deep crises: a socio-economic crisis, a post-colonial crisis and a crisis of political representation.

As far as the socio-economic crisis is concerned, there is no getting around the repercussions of the neoliberal restructuring on the poorest of the peripheral urban areas. In this respect, France is no different from other Western countries that undertook massive restructuring of their economies in the wake of the economic crisis of the 1970s. In the working-class areas of the *banlieues* this meant the fragmentation of an entire social universe based on full employment, rising living standards and expanding forms of social protection. Combined with deregulated housing policies from the mid-late 1970s onwards, involving a shift from support for social-housing projects to incentives for private ownership, this accelerated the flight from these areas by the white-collar and skilled workers who had long been the primary social force in the PCF-controlled municipalities.[21] Increasingly, the bastions of the PCF and the confident working classes it represented were becoming sites of social segregation for the working poor and the unemployed churned out by a leaner and meaner social dispensation.[22] Not only was there heightened competition for a reduced number of increasingly precarious unskilled and semi-skilled industrial jobs, but the flipside of the steep increase in enrolment in secondary and post-secondary education from the 1970s onwards was a growing disdain for these types of jobs. A working-class hero was no longer something to be.

Most of the places affected by the events of November 2005 have been classified as Sensitive Urban Zones (ZUS) since 1996. The ZUS designation – applied to 751 areas inhabited by 4.7 million people, or eight per cent of the entire population – was an extension of the urban-planning initiatives taken by the Socialists in the early 1990s in response to riots in the Lyons and Paris *banlieues*, to address the deteriorating situation in these working-class zones. The unemployment rate in the ZUS is two to three times higher than the national average. The incidence of low-wage, precarious work and underemployment is also much higher. Dramatically high school drop-out rates and youth unemployment rates – regularly surpassing 30 and 40 per cent – are even more significant when one considers that families in a ZUS are generally larger and under-25s often account for upwards of 50 per cent of the total population in these areas. Housing in the ZUS is insufficient, overcrowded and often dilapidated. Finally, rates of petty criminal activity (vandalism, burglary, fights, drug dealing) are high too.[23]

The government response has generally been to treat these problems as stemming from insufficient 'social mixing' and poor urban planning. They have focused efforts on luring the socially more 'desirable' categories of the population into these declining neighbourhoods and providing a wide range of tax cuts and incentives to businesses that invest in the ZUS, which are often situated on or near strategic transportation arteries. The methods involved include demolishing some of the older housing estates, keeping social housing to a minimum and bringing in public-private partnerships to build more attractive (and often private) housing. The aim is to subject the poorest areas of the *banlieues* to the same treatment applied in the 1980s and 1990s to deteriorated housing stock in the city centres – replaced by gentrified residential neighbourhoods, expensive office property and cozy tourist hideaways. While such an approach may shuffle around and mask the problems of these areas – and enrich a few developers and real-estate speculators – it cannot resolve them. Worse, with social and racial 're-balancing' set out as an explicit objective, it tends to further stigmatize and atomize the precarious and marginalized layers of the population whom such policies are supposed to assist.[24]

And here we come to the post-colonial crisis. Compounding and perpetuating the problems of the poorest *banlieues* is the discrimination faced by the youth from these areas, especially the non-white children and grandchildren of North African and sub-Saharan African immigrants. The effects of the economic restructuring of the mid-late 1970s onwards were particularly harsh on the unskilled North African labourers who, by the mid-late 1970s, were just beginning to see some of the fruits of their labours and sacrifices, thanks to the struggles waged in the post-1968 period and the declining stigmatization of their status as (former) colonial subjects.[25] This in turn had a knock-on effect on the children of these immigrants – the repercussions of the economic crisis on their families and their status in the new zones of social segregation now deprived them of many of the opportunities for social advancement that they and their parents had previously expected.[26]

These youths face discrimination in every aspect of their lives. In the school system, they face streaming, stigmatization for their difficulties with the French language, harsher disciplinary measures and greater intrusion into private and family affairs from school authorities.[27] In the job market, qualified applicants are less likely to be hired than their non-immigrant counterparts.[28] And, as comes up over and over again in the accounts of the youths themselves, the police and special security forces (CRS, BAC) subject them to regular harassment and verbal and physical abuse.[29]

It would be wrong to conclude from this, however, that the poor *banlieues* are ghettos or racialized slums of the kind one finds in the United States. As Tyler Stovall writes, most scholars have observed that these areas have nowhere near the level of racial homogeneity one often finds in African American ghettos.[30] In fact, they continue to house large white, working-class populations, who live alongside the families of immigrants from North Africa, sub-Saharan Africa and, increasingly, East and South Asia. Stovall also explains:

> These areas also lag far behind their American counterparts in their access to firearms, not to mention the frequency of violent death. The level of disinvestment and public abandonment of American slum neighbourhoods has no parallel in a France which retains a certain commitment to the interventionist state.[31]

Indeed, when one considers the treatment of North African migrant workers in the 1950s and 1960s, one can actually speak of a process of de-ghettoization in the 1970s and 1980s. From this period onwards, these workers and their families began to gain admission into the mainstream of working-class life – for example by being granted far greater access to normal public housing. This represented a real break from the preceding period, during which most North African workers first lived in abject shantytowns only to be subsequently transferred into the notorious Sonacotra hostels. Established in 1956, in splendid isolation from shops, services, transportation and other residential neighbourhoods, these hostels were a direct extension of colonial policy. While living conditions were harsh, it appears that the draconian rules imposed by hostel directors – a majority of whom were retired army officers who had served in the Algerian War – were even more humiliating.[32]

MISSED OPPORTUNITY IN THE EIGHTIES

The shift from the margins to the mainstream of French society was accelerated by the expansion of public education and by the rising expectations and confidence of the children of these immigrant workers – which blossomed into a full-blown mass movement for equality in the early-mid 1980s. The great tragedy is that this social progress and political assertiveness coincided with the deepening of the social and political crisis of their working-class surroundings – creating an especially fraught context for the encounter between the rising, militant sectors of youth of post-colonial immigrant origin, on the one hand, and the declining and distraught sectors of the native working class that remained in the poor *banlieues*, on the other. The outcome is what Olivier Masclet refers to as a *rendez-vous manqué* (missed opportunity) – the Left's failure to seize the opportunity presented by the emergence of a generation of politicized post-colonial youth in the early-mid 1980s. This failure further weakened the Left in working-class areas and created enormous frustration and despair among the youth themselves.

On the national stage the failure took shape in a different way. Between 1983 and 1985 the new assertiveness of the children of North African migrant workers on the local level translated into a series of mass marches that criss-crossed the country with the primary objectives of demanding equality for the children of North African immigrants, and creating an autonomous organizational framework for pursuing this goal. The movement emerged in the *banlieues* of Lyons following the 1981 disturbances there and gained steam nationally precisely at the moment (1983) when the Socialist government elected in 1981 was making its neoliberal turn and the Front National was beginning to rise in the polls and made its first electoral breakthrough in the city of Dreux. It is not surprising, then, that the movement became a hostage to forces well beyond its control. The governing Socialists seized on the popularity of the movement to revive their own fortunes by building a broader, abstract form of 'feel good' anti-racism focused on rallying a broad range of forces against the FN. In the process, the post-colonial youth at the origin of the movement were co-opted or sidelined, and the initial radical dynamic was undercut by the emergence of SOS Racisme, very much a creature of the governing PS and its youth organizations.[33] This experience on the national stage was mirrored locally in the working-class *banlieues* by the PCF's growing fear of being associated too closely with these radicalizing immigrant youth, lest this fuel local support for the FN. As a result, virtually an entire generation of politicized children of post-colonial immigrants was effectively shut out of the political sphere.

As the 1980s drew to a close, events on the national and international stage gave rise to an often hysterical debate about the Republic, secularism and Islam, out of all proportion to the marginal public role of religious feeling – leave alone fundamentalist belief and activity – among post-colonial immigrant communities in the *banlieues*. The backdrop for the impassioned national debate touched off in September 1989 by the *affaire du foulard* (involving the suspension of three schoolgirls for wearing the Muslim headscarf) was a France understandably scandalized by the Ayatollah Khomeini's *fatwa* earlier in the year against British writer Salman Rushdie; and shaken by the collapse of the Berlin Wall, which signalled the end of the post-War division of Europe – and France's special place within that world.

Developments in the years that followed only further inflamed the debate about France's Muslim population, the largest in Europe: the October 1990 riots in the Lyons *banlieue* of Vaulx-en-Velin; the French (Socialist) government's support for the first Iraq War in 1991; the bloody civil war in Algeria and related terrorist incidents in France in the mid-1990s; the further degeneration of the conflict in Israel and the Occupied Territories; the September 11, 2001 attacks and the US-led 'war on terror' that followed; and chapter two of the '*affaire du foulard*' in 2003.

This led to a major shift in the wider public perception of the *Beur* (Parisian *banlieue* slang for the children of Arab immigrants) and *Black* sons and daughters of post-colonial immigrants. By the early-mid 1980s, they had acquired the positive (if somewhat paternalistic) public image of charming and dynamic *potes* (buddies), bulwarks against fascism and veritable reservoirs of youthful dynamism for an ageing nation. However, over the two decades that followed, they would come to be seen as criminal deviants, symbols of an insufficiently stern Republic's inability to integrate its youth, as well as a potential fifth column for Islamic extremism. In a context of economic crisis, the Left's turn to neoliberalism, and the ideological disarray accompanying the stagnation and subsequent collapse of the Soviet bloc, broad sections of Left and progressive opinion would find solace in a rigid and ahistorical version of 'republican values'. This approach has had little to do with the real situation on the ground, and has become a substitute for seriously addressing the problems confronting post-colonial youth, and the broader crisis these problems betoken.

In summary, from the 1970s onwards we actually find increased ethnic mixing and growing social and physical proximity between the post-colonial population and the established (or 'native') working class – and not the widening gap between black and white one finds during the same period in the United States. It is in a specific context of economic crisis, geopolitical tension and Left disorientation and failure that one ultimately sees a rise in support for authoritarian and xenophobic politics among the native working class in these traditionally Left areas.[34] What this suggests is that while 'post-colonialism' may be a useful analytical category, one cannot trace a straight causal line between France's colonial past and the present-day treatment of French youth of North African and sub-Saharan African origin. Certainly, France has had tremendous difficulty coming to terms with its colonial past.[35] This is centrally important for understanding the present impasse in dealing with the role of the post-colonial population and Islam in the country.

However, a full understanding of this injustice requires that one give equal attention to recent factors – and much older ones. We have examined the factors at play over the past quarter century. The historical factors are beyond the scope of this essay. Suffice it to say that the foundational revolutionary events of 1789-1794 have bequeathed a very specific approach to matters involving foreigners and foreignness. A particular feature of French political life since the Revolution has been the polarization that has re-asserted itself at key junctures in the country's history. This polarization has been political – between Left and Right; and social – between propertied sectors and the working classes. On the one hand, this polarization has been a mechanism for incorporating millions of immigrant workers and their descendants into the nation over the past century – largely through participation in the labour movement, the Left and the fight against fascism. On the other hand, the rejection of origins (social, ethnic, regional, religious, racial or otherwise) that was part and parcel of the radically anti-aristocratic, egalitarian content of the Revolution soon became intertwined with the setting-down of fixed frontiers to be defended against the many invaders that besieged the nascent Republic. This has tended to create a blind spot on the Left – especially in periods of popular retreat such as the present, when the social and political lines of division become blurred. In such periods, the Left – including its most radical sectors – often seems unwilling to engage seriously and specifically with enduring systematic ethnic and racial discrimination, for fear of shattering the original republican framework of Left and popular advance.[36]

Taken together with the other forms of socio-economic and political dislocation we have examined, this has left much of the post-colonial population in a political and social no-man's land – further divorcing the Left from working-class realities and giving greater margin for manoeuvre to the Right. Overcoming this state of affairs presents a complicated challenge to the Left. On the one hand, it must sustain and nurture the antagonistic relationship between Left and Right, and between the working class and propertied elites. In general, this is the life blood of any project for radical change; in France, it has been a pre-condition for the very survival of a viable Left. On the other hand, the Left cannot adopt a siege mentality (as most currents did during the second '*affaire du foulard*' in 2003) in relation to those sectors of the population who now find themselves incompletely – or differently – incorporated into the accumulated gains of the French social model and republican project.[37]

A very positive effect of the 2005 uprising in the *banlieues* was to spark an important debate on the radical Left about the nature and origins of the difficulties faced by those living in the urban periphery – and on the strategic implications this has for the work of Left rebuilding and renewal that must now take place. This debate has shown that particular attention will have to be paid to the specific problems faced by the post-colonial population in these areas and the way the Left incorporates these issues – and the non-white youth most directly affected by them – into its strategy, campaigns and organizations.[38]

One thing is clear: those seeking to turn back the neoconservative tide cannot afford another *rendez-vous manqué* in the *banlieues*.

CONCLUSION: THE CRISIS OF POLITICAL REPRESENTATION

This brings us to the crisis of political representation – and to our conclusion. The re-emergence of a xenophobic and authoritarian bloc in the mainstream of French affairs is a relatively recent development. Fundamentally, one can associate this criminalization and ethnicization of socio-economic questions with the neoliberal turn in economic policy – initiated in 1983 under a Socialist government and president and pursued by every Left and Right government since – and with the rise of the neofascist Front National; all taking place in a context of economic restructuring and persistent high unemployment, a declining trade-union and Left presence at the workplace and in working-class neighbourhoods, and overall disaffection from the formations of both the mainstream Left and Right.

There has been considerable hope that the period of resistance and remobilization opened up by the spectacular social movement of late 1995 would in relatively short order resolve the crisis of political representation for the forces of the anti-neoliberal and anti-capitalist Left. Many on the European and international Left have rightly seen France as standing at the forefront of resistance to neoliberalism – shoulder to shoulder with the resurgence of radical forces in a number of Latin American countries. Following the successful activist-Left campaign against the European Constitution, and the victorious struggle against the CPE labour reform, it even seemed to some that a break with the neoliberal model might be possible in the short term.

However, the election of Nicolas Sarkozy has delivered a serious setback to such a perspective. The present situation provides grounds for both fear and guarded optimism. The juxtaposition of two separate polling results captures this quite well. Following the three-week uprising in the poorer *banlieues* of the country's main cities in November 2005, 70 per cent of respondents said they approved of the way in which Sarkozy as Interior Minister had handled the crisis; yet just four months later, 70 per cent of respondents said they sympathized with the massive and victorious student-led protest movement against the CPE labour-law reform.[39]

On the one hand, then, there appears to be considerable support for an authoritarian and racializing response to the tensions engendered by record levels of unemployment, precariousness and deteriorating infrastructure in poor neighbourhoods – the results of the decline of France's post-war model of social and economic development and 25 years of neoliberal counter-reform. Yet, at the same time, and in spite of this long period of setbacks for working people, broad sections of the population are prepared to support and participate in periodic mass campaigns of resistance against attacks on the gains of almost a century of working-class struggles.

President Sarkozy has a consistent right-wing political agenda – one that seeks to defeat this mass resistance by exploiting the enormous margin for manoeuvre provided by fears and prejudices about and within the *banlieues* and by attacking the social movements, the Left and the non-white population on many fronts. For defensive struggles to grow into a counter-offensive against neoliberalism and its representatives, one key requirement is that the high levels of mobilization must finally find some form of political representation. The fragmented forces of the social movements and the equally fragmented forces of the anti-neoliberal and anti-capitalist Left require a common framework that will enable them to unite their efforts. But the division of the radical Left in the recent elections is but the latest example of how elusive an objective this has been so far. It is fair to wonder if France, though somewhat further ahead than most of the rest of the world in this respect, must also go through a long period of rebuilding and renewal of the Left and social movements before the specific matter of political representation can be resolved – and hopes of a breakthrough against neoliberalism can materialize. Yet while the short-term forecast may be gloomy, France's remarkable capacity for resistance has most certainly not spoken its final word.

NOTES

1   'France's Presidential Election: Sarkozy's Moment and, Mercifully, a Fresh Start for France', *The Economist*, 10 May 2007. Also see Timothy Smith, 'The Socialists are the Real Conservatives in France', *The Globe and Mail* (Toronto), 5 May 2007.

2   For example: Pierre Birnbaum, *Logique de l'Etat*, Paris: Fayard, 1982; Michel Winock, *La fièvre hexagonale. Les grandes crises politiques de 1871 à 1968*, Paris: Calmann-Lévy, 1981; Samuel Barnes and Max Kaase, *Political Action: Mass Participation in Five Western Democracies*, London: Sage, 1979.

3   In 1988, on the eve of the bicentennial of the French Revolution, the French historian François Furet declared 'the end of the French exception' and the emergence of a 'Republic of the centre' thanks to presidents Valéry Giscard d'Estaing and François Mitterand. François Furet, Jacques Julliard and Pierre Rosanvallon, *La République du centre*, Paris: Calmann-Lévy, 1988. In 1995,

Furet gleefully declared: 'From now on we are condemned to live in the world in which we live'. Furey, *Le Passé d'une illusion*, Paris: Calmann-Lévy, 1995.

4   An international survey found that only 36 per cent of the French considered the 'free-market economy' the best system on which to base the future of the world, whereas 65 per cent of Germans and 66 per cent of British citizens did so (GlobeScan, June–August 2005).

5   See Isabelle Sommier, *Le renouveau des mouvements contestataires à l'heure de la mondialisation*, Paris: Flammarion, 2003.

6   See Laurent Mauduit, *Jacques le Petit*, Paris: Stock, 2005, p. 162.

7   Especially on the new flexible work organization, see Luc Boltanski and Eve Chiapello, *The New Spirit of Capitalism*, London: Verso, 2006.

8   See Jean-Marie Pernot, *Syndicats: lendemains de crise?*, Paris: Gallimard, 2005, pp. 23–68. The overall rate of unionization is 8 per cent and less than 5 per cent in the private sector.

9   Even the supposed strength of French unionism in some parts of the public sector may be more of an illusion, as was shown by the relatively smooth privatization of the energy sector in 2004. See Adrien Thomas, 'En apesanteur. La CGT face à la privatisation d'EDF et Gaz de France', *Variations*, 3, 2006, pp. 63–72.

10   On the anti-CPE movement, see Stathis Kouvelakis, 'From Revolt to the Alternative', 12 May 2006, available from http://www.europe-solidaire.org. For a detailed defence of the movement against its many detractors in the neo-liberal press, see David R. Howell and John Schmitt, 'Employment Regulation and French Unemployment: Were the French Students Right After All?', April 2006, available from http://www.cepr.net.

11   Daniel Singer, 'The French Winter of Discontent', *Monthly Review*, 49, July–August 1997; Raghu Krishnan, 'December 1995: The first revolt against Globalization', *Monthly Review*, 48, May 1996.

12   Rémi Lefebvre and Frédéric Sawicki, *La société des socialistes. Le PS aujourd'hui*, Paris: Editions du Croquant, 2006.

13   CSA-CISCO poll, 22 April 2007.

14   The stark example of the automobile industry, previously the industrial core of Fordism, is examined in: Stéphane Beaud and Michel Pialoux, *Retour sur la condition ouvrière. Enquête aux usines Peugeot de Sochaux-Montbelliard*, Paris: Fayard, 1999.

15   A third teenager, Muhittin Altun, survived the electrocution. The three teens were returning home from a soccer match in a neighbouring town when they encountered another group of youths being chased by police following a robbery. Not carrying their identity cards, having spotted one of the policemen preparing his flash-ball gun, and resenting the repeated ID checks they had endured in the past, the three youths decided to run for cover. Rejecting Interior minister Sarkozy's repeated denials of any police responsibility, an inquiry from the Inspector General of Police Services (IGS) concluded that a policeman had indeed seen the youths climb into the substation and notified his superiors but that both he and his superiors chose not to help the teens.

16   Laurent Mucchielli and Abderrahim Aït-Omar, 'Les émeutes de novembre 2005: les raisons de la colère', in Véronique Le Goaziou and Laurent Mucchielli, eds., *Quand les banlieues brûlent… Retour sur les émeutes de novembre 2005*, Paris: La Découverte, 2006.

17   'Une grenade lancée à l'heure de la prière', *L'Humanité*, 2 November 2005.

18   Quoted in 'Le rapport explosif des Renseignements généraux', *Le Parisien*, 7 December 2005.

19   Stéphane Berger and Jérôme Leguay, 'Chronologie' in Collective, *Une révolte en toute logique. Des banlieues en colère,* Sainte Colombe: L'Archipel des pirates, 2006.

20   Nasser Demiati, 'Nicolas Sarkozy, ministre de l'Intérieur et pompier-pyromane', in Goaziou and Mucchielli, eds., *Quand les banlieues brûlent.*

21   Olivier Masclet, *La Gauche et les cités: enquête sur un rendez-vous manqué*, Paris: La Dispute, 2003. Our overall understanding of the crisis in the *banlieues* owes a great deal to this fascinating look at the evolution of a housing complex in the Gennevilliers suburb of Paris.

22   Loïc Wacquant, 'La marginalité urbaine au nouveau millénaire', *Contretemps*, 13 May 2005.

23   These figures are all drawn from Laurent Mucchielli, 'Les émeutes de novembre 2005: les raisons de la colère', in Goaziou and Mucchielli, eds., *Quand les banlieues brûlent.*

24   Patrick Simon and Jean-Pierre Lévy, 'Questions sociologiques et politiques sur la "mixité sociale"', *Contretemps*, 13 May 2005.

25   Laure Pitti, 'Différenciations ethniques et luttes ouvrières à Renault-Billancourt', *Contretemps*, 16 May 2006.

26   Laurent Mucchielli, 'Immigration et délinquance: fantasmes et réalités', in Nacira Guénif-Souilamas, ed., *La république mise à nu par son immigration*, Paris: La Fabrique, 2006.

27   Laurent Ott, 'Pourquoi ont-ils brûlé les écoles?', in Goaziou and Mucchielli, eds., *Quand les banlieues brûlent.*

28   The International Labour Organization (ILO) recently released the results of a study involving 350 'testers' responding to 2,440 job ads. The study revealed that in 67 to 80 per cent of cases employers selected candidates from the 'majority' population over citizens of North African and 'Black African' origin with similar credentials and experience, see E. Cediey and F. Foroni, 'Les Discriminations à raison de 'l'origine' dans les embauches en France', Genève: Bureau international du Travail, 2006.

29   'S'il y a des personnes qui arrivent à accepter ça, moi je n'accepte pas', in Collective, *Une révolte en toute logique.*

30   Cinematic depictions of these areas also reflect this multi-ethnic, multi-racial reality. See for example Mathieu Kassovitz, *La Haine* (1995) and Abdel Kechiche, *Games of Love and Chance* (2003).

31   Tyler Stovall, 'From Red Belt to Black Belt: Race, Class and Urban Marginality in Twentieth-Century Paris', in Sue Peabody and Tyler Stovall, eds., *The Color of Liberty – Histories of Race in France*, Durham: Duke University Press, 2003.

32   Mireille Ginésy-Galano, *Les immigrés hors la cité – Le système d'encadrement dans les foyers (1973-1982)*, Paris: L'Harmattan, 1984.

33   Saïd Bouamama, 'De la visibilisation à la suspicion: la fabrique républicaine d'une politisation', in Nacira Guénif-Souilamas, ed., *La république mise à nu par son immigration*, Paris: La Fabrique, 2006.

34   Loïc Wacquant, 'Ghetto, banlieues, État: réaffirmer la primauté du politique', *Nouveaux regards*, 33, April-June 2006. Initially the preserve of traditional right-wing sectors exasperated by the victory of the Socialists in the early 1980s, and then of small-business sectors worried for their future, the FN made its first breakthrough in traditional Left, working-class areas in the 1995 elections. See Nonna Mayer, *Ces Français qui votent Le Pen*, Paris: Flammarion, 2002.

35   This was illustrated most recently by the February 2005 parliamentary passage of a measure obliging schools to 'recognize the positive role' of French colonialism – and by the presidential repeal of the same measure one year later! Michael Haneke's disturbing film *Caché* (2005) deals with repressed memories of the country's colonial past and their link to the post-colonial present.

36   See Gérard Noiriel's pioneering work, *The French Melting Pot – Immigration, Citizenship and National Identity*, Minneapolis: University of Minnesota Press, 1996. See also Sophie Wahnich, *Impossible citoyen, l'étranger dans le discours de la Révolution française*, Paris: Albin Michel, 1997.

37   For an interesting point of view on French republicanism and the Left, see Denis Sieffert, *Comment peut-on être (vraiment) républicain?*, Paris: La Découverte, 2006.

38   For an overview of the questions involved in this debate, see Didier Fassin and Eric Fassin, eds., *De la question sociale à la question raciale? Représenter la société française*, Paris: La Découverte, 2006; and Karim Bourtel and Dominique Vidal, *Le mal-être arabe*, Marseille: Agone, 2005.

39   The idea of juxtaposing the two polls comes from Dominique Mezzi, 'Une guerre de mouvement gagnée par la droite dure', 15 May 2007, available from http://www.europe-solidaire.org.

HARVEST OF EMPIRE: IMMIGRANT WORKERS' STRUGGLES IN THE USA

KIM MOODY

On May 1, 1886 hundreds of thousands of workers, many of them immigrants, struck across the USA for the eight-hour day, thereby setting the stage for what would become International Workers' Day almost everywhere in the world – except, ironically, in North America.[1] One hundred and twenty years later on May 1, 2006, millions of immigrant workers struck and demonstrated for the right to work without harassment in the United States. It was called 'A Day Without Immigrants', and many of the nation's worst paying jobs would go unperformed for all or part of the day. If the estimates of five or six million participants are right, then perhaps as many as a quarter of the country's 21 million foreign-born workers took action of some sort. Unlike May 1, 1886, unions did not call this action and played only a supportive role in it. Along with a series of ad hoc coalitions that called each of the demonstrations leading up to May 1 in March and April, the organizational backbone for May 1 was a network of some 600 advocacy and community organizations with strong backing from the Catholic Church.[2] The turnout was all the more impressive because the organizers in different cities had different approaches. Some called for a boycott or stay-at-home, but others, like Cardinal Roger Mahony of Los Angeles, warned potential demonstrators not to risk their jobs.[3] Still, they turned out by the tens and hundreds of thousands in cities across the country.

Unions played a supporting role in these events. In Los Angeles, for example, they put up more than $80,000 and handled much of the logistics. Service Employees International Union (SEIU) and American Federation of State, County and Municipal Employees (AFSCME) leaders acted as liaison to the immigrant organizations and the Teamsters provided two 18-wheelers to lead off the march.[4] Labour support was aided by a dramatic change of policy by the AFL-CIO in 2000 when they embraced the call for an amnesty for undocumented workers. This in turn had been preceded by a demonstration of 15,000 in Washington, DC called by the National Coalition for Dignity and Amnesty. Indeed, this Coalition had been holding demonstrations on May 1 since 1999.[5] The growing interaction between immigrant groups and unions reached a new level when several unions went on to play a key role in the 2003 'Immigrant Workers' Freedom Ride', a caravan that crossed the country and ended in a mass demonstration in New York. This high visibility event helped to build confidence about going public with the issue of immigrants' rights.[6]

The actions on May 1, 2006 also revealed the often overlooked strategic position that immigrant workers have in many industries. The Mexican and Central American waterfront truckers in the nation's largest port, Los Angeles/Long Beach, brought 90 per cent of that port's activities to a standstill on May 1. The meat and poultry processing industry reported that 50 per cent of its operations across the country had been halted. The American Nursery and Landscaping Association said that 90 per cent of its workers struck, as did a similar percentage of workers in garden supply warehouses. Construction was also heavily hit in many areas as immigrant workers, like the California drywall hangers, walked out for the day.[7] Thus May 1, 2006 showed not only the willingness and ability of immigrant workers to act on their own despite the high risk of job loss or even deportation, but also the strength of the immigrant workforce in significant parts of the US economy.

HARVEST OF EMPIRE

In the United States, where the immigrant population had declined in the 1950s and remained stagnant in the 1960s, the foreign-born population rose from 9.7 million in 1970 to 34.2 million in 2004, 21 million of whom were not yet citizens.[8] By 2004, the employed foreign-born workforce had risen to over 20 million, composing 14.5 per cent of those employed in the US. Of these, 12 million were not citizens.[9] By 2004 there were 11.6 million legal permanent resident immigrants (those with 'green cards') in the US. Of these 3.1 million were of Mexican origin, by far the largest group. The next largest groups were from the Philippines and India with half-a-million each; followed by China, the Dominican Republic, and Vietnam, each at about 400,000.[10] In addition, according to estimates by the Department of Homeland Security, which has replaced the Immigration and Naturalization Service in tracking and regulating immigration since 2002, there were 10.5 million 'unauthorized' or undocumented immigrants in the US as of January 2005. Over 80 per cent of these undocumented immigrants had arrived since 1990.[11] Some, however, put this 'unauthorized' immigration as high as 20 million by 2007.[12]

The list of major countries of origin is suggestive of the most basic causes of such growth in immigration in recent years. With the exception of India, all of these countries have established trails of immigration that go back to US economic and/or military involvement in these nations. Mexico, China, Cuba and the Philippines go back to the initial period of US empire-building just over a hundred years ago, but also reflect, with the exception of Cuba, the deep contemporary involvement of US business in these areas. Korea, of course, entered the US orbit during the Korean War in the early 1950s. Vietnam and the Dominican Republic trace back to US military interventions, albeit on a very different scale, in the 1960s. El Salvador, Korea, and Cuba with 300,000 each, are all sites of US intervention within the last half century. In the cases of Mexico, the Dominican Republic and El Salvador, the correlation between the impact of globalization, US foreign policy, and accelerated emigration from those countries to the US is all too clear.

Like the Caribbean, Central America became part of the US 'backyard' after the Spanish-American War. By the 1920s, US business had more invested in all of Latin America, mostly in Central America and the Caribbean, than in Europe. It was mainly of US military intervention in this region that it could be said that 'there was never a day from 1919 to 1933 when American marines did not intervene in or occupy the sovereign territory of another country'.[13] After the Second World War this practice was resumed with interventions in the Western Hemisphere, sometimes covert, in Guatemala (1954), Cuba (1960), Brazil (1964), the Dominican Republic (1965), Chile (1973), Grenada (1983), and Panama (1989).[14] In all but one case, Cuba, they were directed against elected officials or governments.

It wasn't just military intervention, overt or covert, that pushed millions of Latin Americans from their homelands. It was that other favourite policy of Corporate America and virtually every administration of the last half century or more – free trade. 'Free Trade', as a policy, isn't just about trade, it's about opening all nations to investment by the big corporations. Because many nations developed their domestic industry by protecting it from imports and foreign ownership, free trade required that these nations abandon that development strategy. An opening was first found by US capital through the development of free trade zones (FTZs), in which government labour and safety regulations were largely suspended and corporations given a free hand. Next came the border development program in northern Mexico, with its *maquiladora* plants, in principle similar to a FTZ. In 1985, the Reagan Administration negotiated the Caribbean Basin Initiative, which opened countries in the region to this type of investment. By 1992, there were 200 FTZs in Mexico and the Caribbean, housing more than 3,000 plants employing 735,000 workers. All of this was only a rehearsal for NAFTA, which did more of the same.[15]

This, however, was only one side of 'free trade'. The other was investment by the banks in New York, London, etc, in the Third World. In Latin America this meant, above all, the New York City banks – Wall Street. When oil money poured into these banks in the early and mid-1970s they promoted low-interest loans to Third World countries. But then inflation and high interest rates took hold and by the early 1980s, countries throughout Latin America were increasingly unable to pay even the annual interest. What became known as the Debt Crisis became the lever by which the US and other industrial powers, with the help of the International Monetary Fund, not only ended barriers to their investment, but literally forced the redesign of many Third World economies.

Mexico was the prime example, and as a result of the neoliberal restructuring of the Mexican economy, average real wages dropped by 67 per cent from 1982 to 1991 and those of Mexico's slightly better-paid industrial workers by 48 per cent. Before NAFTA was implemented four dollars a day became the wage along the Mexican border.[16] Foreign investment in agribusiness and plantation farming, another side of 'free trade', also served to drive millions off the land in Mexico (as well as across Central America and the Caribbean) with no hope of work in their own lands. So, Mexican legal immigration into the US rose from 640,294 in the 1970s to 1,655,843 in the 1980s, 3,541,700 in the 1990s, and 876,823 from 2001 through 2005.[17]

ECONOMIC IMPACT

The economic importance of immigrant labour to the US economy is beyond doubt. Former Secretary of Labor Ray Marshall recently wrote:

> Immigrants are particularly important to the US economy, accounting for over half of the workforce growth during the 1990s and 86 per cent of the increase in employment between 2000 and 2005. Because there will be no net increase in the number of prime-working-age natives (aged 25 to 54) for the next 20 years, the strength of the American economy could depend heavily on how the nation relates immigration to economic and social policy.[18]

Immigrant workers in the official economy are more heavily concentrated in services, construction, transportation and factory work than native-born workers and on average they make 76 per cent of what the latter make.[19] Millions work on the edges of recorded employment and in the growing informal economy for much less. So it is likely that wage levels in these industries were lower than if there had been a severe labour shortage pushing up the wages of native-born workers. While there is no way to measure this, the cost savings in industries such as food processing, consumer services and construction probably lowered the relative cost of living to some degree and rendered some industries more globally competitive than might otherwise have been the case. As in the last great wave of immigration from 1870 through 1920, the recent wave has no doubt contributed to the accumulation process within the US.

The question is raised, then, did this immigration have a negative impact on the wages of employed native-born workers? In any overall sense, the answer has to be no because the timing is wrong. Real weekly wages of production and non-supervisory workers began their descent in 1973, well before the major upswing in immigration numbers that occurred in the 1980s and 1990s. The causes of that fall in wages were the recession of 1974–75, the 'stagflation' that followed into the 1980s, and the wage concessions that began nationally with the 1979 Chrysler bailout and spread throughout industry from the early 1980s onward. Furthermore, if there was to be an overall negative impact on wages, one would expect it to come in the wake of the enormous increase of immigration from the mid-1980s through the 1990s and beyond. This would presumably raise unemployment and depress wages. But, in fact, real weekly wages rose after 1995 through 2003. After that they did fall somewhat but then rose to a new high in early 2007.[20] The pattern follows the contours of the economy rather than that of immigration. It is possible, nonetheless, that the huge proportion of immigrant workers in the growth of the workforce after 2000 had the statistical effect of flattening the overall average wage level even if it did not impact the wages of already employed workers.

Competition for jobs between immigrants and natives is blunted by the 'ethnic niche' or 'queue' phenomenon.[21] That is, immigrant and other low-wage workers are entering jobs abandoned by other groups, often as a result of industrial or occupational restructuring, so that 'significant African American labour market niches in New York, Los Angeles, Miami, San Francisco, and Chicago in 1970 and 1990 showed an overall pattern of succession, as opposed to competition between African Americans and Immigrants… there is no direct evidence to show competition between African American and immigrant workers'.[22]

It would be naïve, however, to deny that there is some level of competition between newer immigrant groups and other working-class people. Like jobs, space in cities is finite and the transition from one group to another in a given neighbourhood is full of friction. An organizer for the worker center Carolina Alliance for Fair Employment (CAFÉ) said of his mainly African American members, 'What I kept hearing was that Hispanics are taking over the neighborhood'. While he stated that they exaggerated, there was a problem of friction.[23] While employment levels are more flexible, there can be friction here too. Yet what appears to be the case is that there is a strong tendency today, as there was over a hundred years ago, for the various ethnic immigrant groups to concentrate in particular occupations or industries in a given geographic region where jobs were being or had been abandoned by native-born workers. So in Los Angeles, for example, building maintenance workers are heavily Mexican and Central American, as are dry wall installers, and truckers on the waterfront. In New York, Latino immigrants are found in greengrocer stores and restaurant kitchens, but also in construction, while Indians and Pakistanis are found driving cabs, Chinese and Latino women in garment sweat shops in New York and Los Angeles, etc. In these cases, there is little evidence of competition with other groups of workers.

IMMIGRANT WORKERS AND TRADE UNIONS

According to the Migration Policy Institute's estimate, 1.8 million foreign-born workers belonged to unions in 2003, up from 1.4 million in 1996, increasing as a proportion of union membership from 8.9 per cent to 11.5 per cent in that period. The rapid increase in the proportion of foreign-born union members was due in part to the decline in membership among native-born workers.[24] Ruth Milkman has shown that 'recent immigrants (those arriving in 1990 or later) are the least likely to be unionized, whereas those who have been in the United States the longest (arriving before 1980) have unionization levels roughly double those of newcomers, and in California over four times as great'. She goes on to say, 'In fact, for the nation's most settled immigrants, union membership is as likely – and for most sub-groups more likely – as for native workers'.[25] In other words, as time goes on and immigrants become more accustomed to their new home, establish documented status, or become citizens, they are as or more likely to join or organize a union than native-born Americans. The outpouring of millions of immigrant workers on May 1, 2006 was certainly a signal that they will fight for a better life even in the face of repression and possible job-loss. These signs are extremely important as they can lay the basis for current and future organizing. Although US unions have a history of anti-foreign attitudes and practices, that has begun to change. In addition, immigrants are already attempting to organize in a variety of ways. The question is, are the strategies and structures of today's unions fit for the job? Are they even looking at some of the immigrant groups with the most potential bargaining power?

If the carefully planned and centrally directed 1990 Justice with Janitors strike was one of the first strikes by non-agricultural immigrant workers to capture public attention, the 1992 strikes by some 4,000 drywall hangers in Southern California pointed to something new. That strike was initiated and sustained by the immigrant workers themselves. While they would receive support from the Carpenters and eventually join that union, the immigrant construction workers organized and led the strike on their own terms, closing down the residential construction industry in much of southern California for five months. This was a piece of the residential construction industry that had gone non-union, like that in the rest of the country. In 1992, striking on their own, these drywallers would bring back the union – a union that had given up organizing this industry years before and was at first reluctant to bring the drywallers under contract. The organization of the strike initially came from immigrants from the town of El Maguey, Mexico, several hundred of whom worked in the industry. This pattern would be repeated in countless other strikes and organizing drives.[26]

The uniting of workers from the same place in new communities and in the same work had re-established links long broken for many native-born workers. The connection of common origin, shared neighbourhood or community, and work provides a source of strength for immigrant organization in many cases. It had been a factor in the 1990s Justice for Janitors campaign.[27] It also helps explain much of the self-organization that has taken place among immigrant workers. This was seen, for instance, in southern California where waterfront trucking, like building services and construction, had gone through a major restructuring in which Teamster members had been replaced by independent owner-operators in declining conditions in the 1980s. Once again, Latino immigrants filled the void. In 1988 and again in 1993, the Latino truckers had struck with only informal organization. Though further organization was largely initiated by the workers themselves, Communications Workers of America Local 9400 offered to help. As owner-operators and independent contractors, the truckers had no statutory rights to unionize or strike. Together, however, they planned a complex strategy that involved the creation of an 'employer' and, in 1996, a strike. Unlike the drywallers strike, the truckers efforts failed, largely due to the massive efforts of the truck contractors and extensive legal barriers, but the potential of self-organization had shown itself once again.[28] The fight of the waterfront truckers, however, didn't end in the 1990s. In 2004 and 2005 they would strike again over government harassment and fuel prices. Then on May 1, 2006, the 'Day Without Immigrants', they struck along with millions of others, once again closing the port of Los Angeles/Long Beach.[29]

This transformation from formerly unionized workers to owners or drivers who leased their equipment was common to other areas of transportation as well. Across the country in New York, both the taxi and 'Black Car' or limousine services had been reorganized so that the fleet drivers ceased to be employees and became independent contractors who now had to lease their cars. In both cases, the immigrant drivers who filled these new contracted positions organized themselves to resist the near-poverty earnings they made and the long hours they worked to make them. Taxi drivers who had been employees earning a percentage of 'the meter' until the 1970s now had to lease their cab and pay for their own fuel. They literally spent the first few hours of each day working off their daily lease-fee. Most of the drivers were now Indian or Pakistani. In 1998, they transformed an older ethnically-based group into the New York Taxi Workers Alliance open to all yellow cab drivers. In May 1998, the new organization surprised the city when virtually all 24,000 working cab drivers struck for 24 hours. Although as independent contractors they have no collective bargaining rights, they have functioned as a union ever since with about 5,000 actual members. They scored an enormous victory in 2004 when they negotiated a fare increase with the city, with 70 per cent of the increase going to the drivers.[30]

The city's 12,000 'Black Car' drivers worked for fleets that serve corporate customers who want the elegant cars for their executives and clients. But, like the taxi drivers, they were independent contractors who had to lease these cars. After paying their lease fees and other expenses they make between $4.00 and $6.00 an hour. Most are South Asians, but there are also East Asians and Central Americans. In 1995, they began organizing themselves. In this case, through an acquaintance they approached District 15 of the International Association of Machinists which allowed the drivers to organize and lead their own local, Machinists' Lodge 340. In an unusual turn of events that does not seem to have been picked up by other unions, the Machinists won a National Labor Relations Board case in 1997 which declared the drivers employees. In 1999, Lodge 340 won its first contract with one of the major companies. Resistance from employers was intense and, because many drivers were Muslims, so was harassment by the Federal government after 9/11. Nevertheless, by 2005, Lodge 340 had 1,000 dues-paying members. The effort to organize the whole industry continues.[31]

Unfortunately, unions are not always this attentive to those who try to organize themselves. When the mostly Mexican workers in New York's green-grocery stores began to organize themselves in the 1990s, they were at first helped by UNITE Local 169. In a jurisdictional dispute, however, they were passed on to United Food and Commercial Workers (UFCW) Local 1500 which, by most accounts, was not particularly attentive to the needs of these immigrant workers. A similar case occurred with UFCW Local 338 in New York with African grocery store delivery workers who had also organized themselves before approaching the union.[32]

The phenomenon of common origin, community and work doesn't only occur in big cities. The example of the Guatemalan workers at the Case Farms poultry plant in Morganton, North Carolina shows that it can work in a semi-rural area as well. These workers, Mayas from the same areas of Guatemala, composed the majority of the 500 workers in this plant. As in most poultry plants, the conditions were horrible and unsafe and in 1993 these workers staged a brief strike. The Laborers' International Union would help them through another strike in 1995 and on to union recognition. What was clear, however, was that the union found an organized group of workers. As one union representative put it, 'We didn't organize anybody. There was a union there before the union got there.' Unfortunately, neither the workers nor the Laborers' Union were able to force a first contract on the company. Rather than simply abandoning the Case workers, the Laborers agreed to fund the formation of a worker center that would address the problems of the many Central American workers in that part of North Carolina.[33]

If it is true that union organizing among immigrants is often enabled by the overlap of place of national or ethic origin, shared neighbourhood or community, as well as common work, it should come as no surprise that much of the organizing that goes on among immigrants is community-based. This includes a very broad range of organizations providing services, advocacy, legal rights, education, political mobilization and policy development. As we saw above, hundreds of such organizations were involved in the massive mobilization of May 1, 2006. Many of these organizations serve or 'do for' immigrants and are run by middle-class professionals focusing on broad issues of immigrant rights or social welfare. What concerns us here are those organizations that organize immigrant workers with a focus on their work.

WORKER CENTERS

Worker centers differ from other community-based organizations in that they focus mainly, though not exclusively, on workplace issues. Most of them engage in a combination of service-delivery, advocacy, leadership training and organizing. All four functions tend to focus on issues related to work: pay and failure to pay, health and safety, immigration status, various employment rights. It is the organizing function and leadership development, however, that give worker centers the potential to play an important role in the development of unionization and a broader social and political movement. As community-based organizations they are geographically bound. Most of the workplaces or jobs in which their members are employed are within or near the communities. In some cases, like those of day labourers or farm workers where the work itself may be distant, the center focuses on sites where workers obtain jobs (street corners, contractors, or agencies). In almost all cases it is the employer-employee relationship, the reality of exploitation, that gives the worker center its significance.[34]

The worker center phenomenon grows out of many of the changes in work itself that have taken place in the last thirty or so years, some of which were described earlier. Subcontracting, sweatshops, the fast-expanding food service and hospitality industries, relocated/de-unionized industries, new retailers giant and small, and the growth of 'off-the-books' work in the informal economy. All of these sources of employment have in common low wages, poor benefits, and workers of colour. Increasingly the latter are also immigrants. By 2005 there were by one count 137 workers centers, 122 of which dealt specifically with immigrant workers. In terms of the regions of origin of those immigrant workers who participate in worker centers about 40 per cent come from Mexico and Central America, another 18 per cent from South America, 15 per cent each from East Asia and the Caribbean, 8 per cent from Africa, 3 per cent from Europe, and 1 per cent from the rest of Asia.[35] In terms of their region of settlement in the US, worker centers reflect concentrations of immigration: 41 are in the Northeast; 36 on the West Coast; 34 in the South; 17 in the East North Central region; and the rest scattered around the West. Almost 80 per cent of the workers involved are immigrants. The relatively large number in the South tells us something about the geographic distribution of reorganized and subcontracted industries such as food processing and automobile parts production.

The rise of worker centers has followed the rhythm of both work reorganization and of immigration and has come in three waves. The first group began in the late 1970s and early 1980s initiated by politically-minded activists with some connection to union organization. One of the first was the Chinese Staff and Workers Association (CSWA) in New York City's Chinatown. CSWA was born out of a 1978 drive by Hotel Employees and Restaurant Employees Union (HERE) Local 69 to organize the city's Chinese restaurants. Workers joined Local 69 but became disillusioned with the neglect they experienced. In 1979, those at Chinatown's huge Silver Palace voted to form their own union with the support of what became the CSWA. Others soon followed suit. CSWA organizers linked the independent unions to the community and went on to help workers not in unions as well and to deal with other neighbourhood issues such as housing. One of their organizers explained their view of organizing: 'By organize, we don't just mean joining the union. We see the union as a means to organize something greater... We organize where we live and work'.[36]

A number of other worker centers were formed around this time. La Mujer Obrera (the Woman Worker) in El Paso, Texas grew out of a garment workers strike at Farah Clothing. Formed in 1981, it focused on women in the small garment shops on the border after the big outfits like Farah folded up or moved across the border and the unions left the area. Not all of these women workers are immigrants. Many are citizens whose families have been there for decades or more, in areas overlapping the Rio Grande (or Rio Bravo on the Mexican side) that forms the border. The Black Workers for Justice, based in Rocky Mount, North Carolina, came out of a fight against discrimination at K-MART. This is an African American organization in an industrializing area of the South's 'Black Belt'. It brought together workers from many of the plants in and around Rocky Mount on a community-wide basis.[37] Black Workers for Justice, CSWA and La Mujer Obera set the pattern of community-based worker organization for most of those that came after. Another organization that began as part of the first wave was the Committee Against Anti-Asian Violence (CAAV) in New York City formed in the 1980s to defend Asian women in particular. In addition to that work, the CAAV would spin-off at least two other organizations that would form part of the third wave of worker centers: the Lease Driver Coalition that became the New York Taxi Workers Alliance discussed above, and the Domestic Workers Union.[38]

The second wave came from the late 1980s through the mid-1990s. Many of these were driven by the wave of immigration from Central America as people fled the wars, death squads and counter-revolutions that were largely the result of US foreign policy in the region.[39] One of the earliest second wave worker centers was the Workplace Project based on suburban Long Island, New York. Founded in 1992, the Workplace Project was a spin-off of a Central American Immigrant service organization. The Workplace Project organized among those working in this suburban area's restaurant, construction, landscaping and house-keeping jobs. Many of these workers were un-documented and were being paid well below the minimum wage. Often they worked as day labourers, gathering on street corners to be picked up by potential employers. The Project began by taking legal cases to gain unpaid wages, a common problem for immigrants. But the Project's founder, Jennifer Gordon, realized this was not increasing the power or security of the workers. So, the Project hired Omar Henriquez, a Salvadoran, to help the workers organize to press their claims collectively, learning from CSWA and La Mujer Obrera. In particular, day labourers who gathered on certain street corners organized and demanded a common wage and succeeded in increasing their earnings significantly.[40]

Another second wave worker center is Make The Road By Walking located in Brooklyn's Bushwick neighbourhood, one of New York's poorest. With new waves of immigrants in the 1980s and 1990s, Bushwick became a predominately Latino area. Make The Road is a multi-issue organization dealing with housing, education, community development and even Gay and Lesbian issues as well as workplace problems.[41] The heart of its organizing program is Tabajadores en Acción, which focuses on local garment sweatshops and the area's retail stores which employ mostly immigrants at notoriously low wages. Like other workers centers, one of its main activities is recovering unpaid wages. In one year, they recovered $200,000 in back wages.[42] At one store, MiniMax, as organizer Deborah Axt explained: 'We won $65,000 in back wages. More importantly, though, was that the women were organizing to change the conditions of the workers who are there now. We were able to win paid sick days, an FMLA [Family Medical Leave Act] kind of coverage, and public posting of legal and workplace rights'.[43] Make The Road also worked with the Retail, Wholesale and Department Store Union to successfully organize a small athletic shoe chain, Footco, winning their first contract in January 2006.[44]

The third wave of worker centers came after 2000, and more of these were connected to unions than in the past.[45] One example is the Restaurant Opportunities Center (ROC) set up in the wake of 9/11 by workers from the Windows on the World restaurant in the World Trade Center. Under pressure from displaced workers, HERE Local 100, to which the workers belonged, asked former workers to set up the ROC as a self-help effort in 2002. Soon, however, it became an organizing project willing to work with those in restaurants the union hadn't approached in the past. Like other worker centers it helped non-union workers win back pay, paid days off, lunch breaks and other improvements. ROC has its own Board composed mostly of immigrant workers, but still maintains a relationship with HERE Local 100, which acts as ROC's fiscal sponsor.[46] In part, ROC sustained itself by acting as a catering cooperative, but in 2005 it set up its own full service restaurant, 'Colors'. Another third wave organization is the Domestic Workers Union based primarily in Brooklyn among a very broad base of immigrant groups. In 2003, the DWU succeeded in winning a Domestic Workers Bill of Rights from the New York City Council, requiring agencies to spell out terms and condition of employment and the actual employer to sign an agreement to those terms.[47]

No account of worker centers would be complete without reference to the Coalition of Immokolee Workers (CIW) founded in 1995. CIW differs from most worker centers in that it is rural and based mostly on farm labour, though workers from other low-wage industries also belong. Immokolee is a dirt poor town in the midst of Florida's tomato fields. CIW members come mostly from Mexico, Guatemala and Haiti. Although it is not affiliated with either the United Farm Workers or the Farm Labor Organizing Committee and does not regard itself as a union, it has used the same tactic as those unions to make its major gains: the boycott. In fact, CIW has used a number of tactics in its efforts to get Taco Bell, purchaser of most of the tomatoes they pick, to pay a penny more per pound – enough to double their wages. They have organized three strikes in the area, held a 30-day hunger strike in 2003, and marched 240 miles across Florida to make their point. Some of these actions produced wage increases. It was, however, the boycott that finally won the amazing victory of several hundred farm workers over Taco Bell and its parent, fast food giant Yum Brands, which also owns Kentucky Fried Chicken, Pizza Hut, Long John Silver's and A&W. Like the UFW and FLOC boycotts before it, the CIW's Taco Bell boycott got widespread support from other organizations, including Jobs with Justice, church groups and unions. Student 'Boot the Bell' campaigns got Taco Bell kicked off of 22 campuses by the time of the victory.

Key to the CIW's going national with their campaign was the network of other worker centers around the country. This reminds us that worker centers are becoming a nation-wide force. What CIW won with this support would affect more than their own members. Yum agreed to double the percentage of the tomatoes' price going to the workers by a 'pass-through' increase in what it pays. Taco Bell agreed to buy only from growers who agree to the 'pass-through'. An enforceable code of conduct for fast food industry suppliers, with the CIW as a monitoring organization, was also part of the agreement. With the victory of the Immokolee workers and others that came before like the Asian Women's Immigrant Association's victory of Jessica McClinock in the 1990s, worker centers have staked a claim as part of the American labour movement.[48]

STRENGTHS AND WEAKNESSES OF WORKER CENTERS

Worker centers are an important addition to working-class organization in the US, but like the unions they have their limits and structural problems. First, they are small. Most of those that are membership groups have 500 or fewer members. Perhaps more important is the matter of social power. Steve Jenkins, who was an organizer for Make the Road, argued that shared injustice does not necessarily mean shared social power. Unlike unions, the centers cannot stop production. They can exercise social power through rent strikes or civil disobedience, but their power over workplace issues, which is a major focus and purpose, is limited to appealing to governmental units or agencies and other elite institutions. Whether lobbying city hall for housing improvements or going to the courts or state agencies for back pay, there is a strong tendency for the workers to be dependent on professionals – organizers, lawyers, etc. Most of these centers are also dependent on foundation grants, which means dependency on the priorities of foundation officials and boards, and on those who are best at writing grant proposals. Thus, community-based groups tend to be dependent on staffers who are frequently, though not exclusively, drawn from the educated middle class.

Viewed only in the terms in which worker centers and similar community-based groups define themselves and act today, these limits are real. But it is possible that in a period of more general social upsurge they can become a source of broader mobilization. The power of the poor, as most past upheavals show, lies in three areas: the disruption of business as usual; organization into and/or alliance with other working class organizations, notably unions; and in political action by virtue of numbers. The first, analyzed by Piven and Cloward, is the traditional recourse of the poor whether in the form of urban disorder, concerted civil disobedience, rent strikes, even mass workplace strikes. The 1960s provided many examples of this.[49] The second, unionization or alliances with unions, is trickier. There is a history of tension between many workers centers and unions they have tried to work with. As one ROC leader put it in terms of the HERE, the union 'seems to have trouble letting go'.[50] Unions as bureaucratic institutions don't like sharing power with risky or unfamiliar groups. Yet there are also many examples of cooperation between the two. And while many unions prefer to ignore low-wage workers, many of the recent gains have in fact been among low-wage workers with no central workplace, such as home health care workers in New York as well as in California. Once again, the context is crucial and periods of more general resistance and upsurge offer greater possibilities, as do changes in union practices and perspectives. Jenkins, despite his criticisms, also notes:

Workers centers are an oasis of support and useful services for workers facing inhumane working conditions and have few other resources available to them. Many are playing a central role in developing linkages between progressive unions and community-based organizing efforts that have the potential to strengthen both organizing arenas. It is possible that this will open up new strategies for organizing workers that improve upon traditional union-organizing models by broadening workplace struggles to involve the working class communities.[51]

A good example of just that was the successful campaign to organize four big meatpacking plants in Omaha, Nebraska. The meatpacking industry had been drastically reorganized, the unions broken, and its new plants filled by recent immigrants from Mexico and Central America. It was the Omaha Together One Community (OTOC), a faith-based community organization affiliated with the Alinsky-inspired Industrial Areas Foundation, that first took notice of the plight of the packinghouse workers. In 1999 they held a mass demonstration of 1,200 people to protest these conditions. The OTOC, as a worker center, could spread the word and protest, but by itself it lacked the power to change things. Eventually, they decided that a union was needed and a joint plan with the Food and Commercial Workers union to organize 4,000 workers was announced in June 2000. With OTOC mobilizing the community as well as recruiting workers, the campaign was a success. This was a huge boost for the UFCW and a demonstration that this sort of alliance can bear fruit. There were, however, problems once the union began negotiating the contract. Basically, as we have seen before, the union officials didn't really listen to the workers. The contract they negotiated neglected many of the workers' most heart-felt workplace issues, or the question of immigration status.[52] There is a gap between the culture of most unions and many worker centers that needs to be addressed. In particular, union officials and staff need to see worker centers as part of the same movement, but with unique functions.

Perhaps the UFCW leaders have learned something from this. In 2003, they set up a worker center in North Carolina as part of their long-term effort to organize the 5,500-worker Smithfield hog-processing plant in Tar Heel, North Carolina. About 60 per cent of the workforce are Latino immigrants and the UFCW has made a long term commitment. Drawing on community leaders and activists, the union called a May 1, 2006 rally and 5,000 people from many plants and communities showed up. Most plants had to shut down production for the day. In June, rallies were held in seven cities around the country. Here is where the union, the worker center, other community-based groups, and the national upsurge of immigrant workers came together.[53]

The organization of the May 1, 2006 'Day Without Immigrants' reflected this strength. 'The Great American Boycott', as it was also called, was done largely city-by-city, town-by-town by local coalitions of worker centers, advocacy and grassroots organizations, with the Catholic Church also playing a key role in many places and unions in some. Even 'The' Church was divided between the hierarchy who cautioned against strikes and consumer boycotts and the parish priests in the immigrant communities who were caught up in the spirit of resistance. To be sure, the calendarized coalitions (March 10, March 25, April 9, May 1) that called the national actions and brought 600 organizations together to meet just before May 1 were galvanized in part by the Republican-dominated Congress, whose Border Protection, Antiterrorism, and Illegal Immigration Control Act of 2005 was a massive threat to all immigrants. The outpouring of May Day killed that bill.[54]

Success, however, soon brought new problems. For one thing, the Department of Homeland Security's Immigration and Customs Enforcement Agency (ICE) waged a fierce crackdown on undocumented workers. For another, the movement lost the single focus of 2006. With softer bills appearing even before the newly elected Democratic Congress convened, the movement began to divide over support for new legislation. WE ARE AMERICA, led by the SEIU, UNITE-HERE, and several liberal advocacy groups, supported the Kennedy-McCain bill with its guest-worker provisions. The National Alliance for Immigrant Rights (NAIR), formed in August 2006 by mostly grassroots organizations, opposes any guest worker program or repressive immigration enforcement. Along with older rights groups such as the Network for Immigrant and Refugee Rights, it will continue to fight for the legalization of all immigrants.[55] Lacking a national focus and organizational push, the turnout on May 1, 2007 was much smaller. The biggest turnout was in Chicago where estimates ran from 150,000 by police to 250,000 by the organizers. Los Angeles saw two separate demonstrations draw 100,000 each, while in New York two feeder marches brought an estimated 20,000 to Union Square. Altogether, the LA-based Immigrant Solidarity Network estimated that about half a million people in more than 100 cities and towns across the US demonstrated on that day.[56] Had this been the first such demonstration, it might well have been seen as a remarkable turnout, but it was put in the shadow of the brilliant success of the 2006 May Day mobilization.

Nevertheless, it is clear that immigrant workers will play a major role in the revitalization of organized labour in the US. In August 2006, the AFL–CIO took a significant step toward greater unity of trade unions and worker centers when they reached an agreement with the National Day Laborer Organizing Network, a nation-wide network of community-based day labour organizations, that would allow workers centers to affiliate with state and local labour councils. In late 2006, the New York Taxi Workers Alliance announced that it would affiliate with that city's Central Labor Council. These moves follow on other local efforts at cooperation between unions and workers centers, such as those described above and that between the Korean Immigrant Workers Alliance and building trades' Ironworkers Local 416 in Los Angeles in order to bring more immigrants into the union.[57] These recent developments represent a new direction in the way at least some of organized labour in the US sees itself

On the other hand, it is important that the worker centers be understood in the context of a broader *labour movement* of which they are one piece. Like unions trying new ways to organize and still not making huge breakthroughs, they need to be seen for their potential as much as for their current achievements and limitations. They are a potential training ground for groups of workers who are finding their own leaders and voicing their own demands and concerns. One measure of their potential is their survival rate as organizations. In a political atmosphere where most of the mass social movements have faded, unions have lost members and power, and politics has largely been unfavourable to working-class people in general and immigrants in particular, even the oldest of the worker centers have survived and thrived, while new ones have arisen to challenge this atmosphere.

NOTES

1   The demonstration in Chicago spilled over into support for locked-out workers at a major farm-implements factory, followed by pitched battles between picketers and scabs, the shooting of two workers by police, and a subsequent protest rally in Haymarket Square – where policemen fired indiscriminately at the crowd after a bomb was tossed into the police ranks. Eight anarchist leaders were arrested, tried and sentenced to death (three were later pardoned). These events triggered international protests, and in 1889 the first congress of the new socialist parties associated with the Second International called on workers everywhere to join in an annual one-day strike on May 1st – not so much to demand specific reforms as an annual demonstration of labour solidarity and working-class power. May Day was both a product of, and an element in, the rapid growth of new mass working-class parties of Europe – which soon forced official recognition by employers and governments of this 'workers' holiday'.

But the American Federation of Labor, chastened by the 'red scare' that followed the Haymarket events, went along with those who opposed May Day observances. Instead, in 1894, the AFL embraced President Grover Cleveland's decree that the first Monday of September would be the annual 'Labor Day' – and Canada soon followed suit.

2   *New York Times*, 12 April 2006, http://www.nytimes.com.

3   *New York Times*, 2 May 2006, http://www.nytimes.com; Brian Grow, 'May Day: The Fight Behind the Protest', *Business Week online*, 28 April 2006, http://www.businessweek.com.

4   *Los Angeles Times*, 3 May 2006, http://www.latimes.com.

5   *Labor Notes*, #253, April 2000, pp. 1, 14 and #273, December 2001, pp. 15, 16.

6   Immanuel Ness, *Immigrants, Unions, and the New U.S. Labor Market*, Philadelphia: Temple University Press, 2005, p. 43.

7   *Labor Notes*, #332, November 2006, p. 13.

8   The 1965 Hart-Cellars Act ended the highly discriminatory national quota system and opened the door, within limits, to Third World immigration, particularly for those with sought-after skills or relatives in the US.

9   Bureau of Labor Statistics (BLS), *News*, 'Labor Force Characteristics of Foreign-Born Workers in 2004', USDL 05-834, 12 May 2005, Table 1, http://www.bls.gov/cps; U.S. Department of Commerce, *Statistical Abstract of the United States 2006*, Washington, DC: U.S. Department of Commerce, 2006, pp. 44, 45, 46.

10 *Statistical Abstract of the United States 2006*, p. 45; Bureau of Labor Statistics, 'Foreign-Born Workers: Labor Force Characteristics in 2005', *News*, USDL 06-640, 14 April 2006, Table 4, http://www.bls.gov.

11 U.S. Department of Homeland Security, 'Estimates of the Unauthorized Immigrant Population Residing in the United States: January 2005', *Population Estimates*, Office of Immigration Statistics, August 2006, p. 5.

12 Ray Marshall, 'Getting Immigration Reform Right', *EPI Briefing Paper*, Washington, DC: Economic Policy Institute, 15 March 2007, p. 1.

13 Sidney Lens, *The Forging of the American Empire*, New York: Thomas Y. Crowell Company, 1971, pp. 269-71; Juan Gonzales, *Harvest of Empire: A History of Latinos in America*, New York: Penguin Books, 2000, pp. 58-60.

14 Beth Sims, *Workers of the World Undermined: American Labor's Role in U.S. Foreign Policy*, Boston: South End Press, 1992, p. 6; Gonzales, *Harvest of Empire*, p. 77.

15 Kim Moody and Mary McGinn, *Unions and Free Trade: Solidarity vs. Competition*, Detroit: Labor Notes, 1992, pp. 1-11; Gonzales, *Harvest of Empire*, pp. 228-29.

16 Kim Moody, 'NAFTA and the Corporate Redesign of North America', *Latin American Perspectives*, 22(1), Winter 1995, p. 102; Gonzales, *Harvest of Empire*, p. 239.

17 INS, *1997 Statistical Yearbook*, p. 26; DHS, *Yearbook*, Table 3, http://www.uscis.gov.

18 Marshall, 'Getting Immigration', p. 1.

19 BLS, 'Foreign-Born Workers', 2006, Tables 4 & 5, http://www.bls.gov.

20 *Statistical Abstract*, 2001, p. 386; Council of Economic Advisers, *Economic Report of the President 2005*, Washington, DC: US Government Printing Office, p. 266; BLS, 'Real Earnings in February 2007', *News*, USDL 07-0377, 16 March 2007,

p. 1; Labor Research Association, 'Real Wages on the Downswing Again', 23 March 2001, http://www.workinglife.org/.

21　Roger Waldinger, *Still the Promised City? African-Americans and New Immigrants in Postindustrial New York*, Cambridge, MA: Harvard University Press, 1996, pp. 94–136.

22　Janice Fine, *Worker Centers: Organizing Communities at the Edge of the Dream*, Ithaca: Cornell University Press, 2006, p. 69.

23　Ibid., p. 67.

24　Migration Policy Institute, 'Immigrant Union Members: Numbers and Trends', *Immigration Facts*, 7, May 2004, p. 4.

25　Ruth Milkman, ed., *Organizing Immigrants: The Challenge for Unions in Contemporary California*, Ithaca: Cornell University Press, 2000, p. 13.

26　Ruth Milkman and Kent Wong, 'Organizing the Wicked City: The 1992 Southern California Drywall Strike', in Milkman, ed., *Organizing Immigrants*, Ithaca: ILR Press, 2000, pp. 169–88.

27　Ibid., p. 111.

28　Ibid., pp. 122–26.

29　*Labor Notes*, #327, June 2006, pp. 1, 6.

30　Biju Mathew, *Taxi! Cabs and Capitalism in New York City*, New York: The New Press, 2005, pp. 1–7, 68–69, 196–97.

31　Ness, *Immigrants, Unions,* pp. 150–61.

32　Ibid., pp. 58–129.

33　Leon Fink, *The Maya of Morganton: Work and Community in the Nuevo New South*, Chapel Hill: University of North Carolina Press, 2003, pp. 2–6, 54–78, 96–97.

34　Fine, *Worker Centers,* pp. 2–3, 11–14.

35　Ibid., pp. 7–21.

36　Vanessa Tait, *Poor Workers Unions: Rebuilding Labor From Below*, Cambridge: South End Press, 2005, pp. 165–69, 173–74; Fine, *Worker Centers,* p. 9.

37　Tait, *Poor Workers Unions,* pp. 188–92; Fine, *Worker Centers,* p. 9.

38　Fine, *Worker Centers,* pp. 137–38, 174.

39　Ibid., pp. 10–11.

40　Tait, *Poor Workers Unions,* pp. 178–81.

41　Make The Road By Walking, 'Building Power in Brooklyn & Beyond', *2005 Annual Report*, Brooklyn, NY, 2005, www.maketheroad.org.

42　Steve Jenkins, 'Organizing, Advocacy, and Member Power', *Working USA: The Journal of Labor and Society*, 6(2), Fall 2002, pp. 65–8.

43　Jane Slaughter, *A Troublemaker's Handbook 2*, Detroit: Labor Notes, 2005, pp. 262–63.

44　Make The Road By Walking, *2005 Annual Report*, p. 12.

45　Fine, *Worker Centers*, p. 11.

46　Saru Jayaraman, 'In the Wake of 9/11: New York Restaurant Workers Explore New Strategies', August 2004, http://www.labornotes.org; Fine, *Worker Centers,* p. 17.

47　Fine, *Worker Centers*, pp. 174–75.

48　*Labor Notes*, #289, April 2003, p. 5; #313, April 2005, pp. 1, 14; Slaughter, *A Troublemaker's Handbook 2*, pp. 148–52; Fine, *Worker Centers*, pp. 104–7.

49   Frances Fox Piven and Richard Cloward, *Poor People's Movements: Why They Succeed, How They Fail*, New York: Vintage Books, 1979.

50   Jayaraman, 'In the Wake of 9/11', August 2003, http://www.labornotes.com.

51   Jenkins, 'Organizing, Advocacy', p. 72.

52   Fine, *Worker Centers*, pp. 120-25; Slaughter, *A Troublemaker's Handbook 2*, pp. 251-54.

53   *Labor Notes*, #329, August 2006, pp. 10-11.

54   Nativo V. Lopez, 'Strategy and Tactics for Immigrants' Rights in 2007', *Against The Current*, 127, March/April 2007, pp. 4-9.

55   Ibid., p. 9.

56   Immigrant Solidarity Network, 'Coverage of May Day 2007', *Immigrant News Briefs*, 10(12), 6 May 2007, http://www.immigrantsolidarity.org.

57   *Labor Notes*, #334, January 2007, pp. 1, 14.

NEOLIBERALISM AND THE LEFT: A SYMPOSIUM

Marxian and Keynesian Critiques of Neoliberalism: Alfredo Saad-filho

Roots of Neoliberalism: Elmar Altvater

Neoliberalism and the Discontented: Gregory Albo

MARXIAN AND KEYNESIAN CRITIQUES
OF NEOLIBERALISM

ALFREDO SAAD-FILHO

Neoliberalism has lost much of its political legitimacy and nearly all its popular appeal during the last decade. Apologias of privatization, fiscal restraint, high interest rates, capital account liberalization, trade union-bashing and other policies overtly associated with the neoliberal reforms are in retreat. After sailing triumphantly to world domination in the eighties and nineties, neoliberalism has become a political liability. Its strident rhetoric has grown tired, and no longer brings votes – quite the contrary; neoliberal platforms must now be disguised. The political shrivelling of neoliberalism has been especially evident since the East Asian crises and the collapse of the dot.com bubble. The corruption scandals that came to light under Bush II have helped to unmask the regressive nature of the neoliberal project and its organic links with the reconstitution of US imperialism. The political retreat of neoliberalism is startlingly evident in any reputable bookshop: the number of titles purporting to defend the neoliberal reforms has declined precipitously both in quality and in market appeal, while a large number of critical works have become available to growing numbers of readers.[1]

In spite of these political defeats, neoliberalism continues to be not only the dominant economic policy, but also the dominant modality of social and economic reproduction in most countries. It could easily be argued that the economic grip of neoliberalism is becoming stronger even as its political legitimacy wanes. This disconnect is examined below, through a specific angle: the sources, significance and political implications of the Keynesian and Marxist critiques of neoliberalism. These are important questions for readers of the *Register* for two reasons. First, and quite obviously, Marxist theory loses much of its relevance if it is disconnected from political action. Clarification of the differences between Marxian and rival interpretations of neoliberalism can help to strengthen the former and enhance its political relevance and mass appeal. Second, the argument developed below suggests that neoliberalism is a resilient system of accumulation which will neither collapse spontaneously, nor be dislodged simply through the workings of the electoral process. Mass action remains the essential lever for social transformation in the age of neoliberalism. However, neoliberalism has transformed the modalities of reproduction of the working class and the scope for independent working-class action. New forms of political participation need to be found, and new modes of organization developed, in order to challenge its dominance.

KEYNESIANISM AND NEOLIBERALISM

In neoclassical economic theory and in neoliberal rhetoric, capitalist ('market') economies spontaneously gravitate towards full employment and the most efficient use of resources, unless the adjustment path is blocked by market imperfections. These imperfections can include misguided government policies, trade union activity, peculiarities of the industrial structure or technology, and a whole host of 'distortions' which, ultimately, separate the real world from the mirage conjured up by the apologists of unbridled capitalism.

One of the most significant intellectual achievements of John Maynard Keynes was his alternative conceptualization of the capitalist macroeconomy. For Keynes, the aggregate level of output and employment is limited by aggregate demand (subject to capacity limits). If demand is insufficient, for example because of adverse profit expectations on the part of the investors, or because the state fails to adopt sufficiently proactive fiscal and monetary policies, firms will reduce production and employment. This could trigger a recession from which the economy may not emerge spontaneously. Conversely, if aggregate demand is excessive, output will eventually hit capacity limits, leading to inflation and balance of payments deficits.

Keynes developed this fundamental insight in the midst of the Great Depression. It led him to believe that, in an advanced capitalist economy, the level of activity could stabilize at any level of unemployment. If there is no spontaneous tendency towards full employment, the economy can find itself lumbered with high unemployment indefinitely, at great economic and social cost. This may also lead to political instability. Keynes's reasoning offers a sharp break with the logic and the policy implications of neoclassical economics. It suggests that government intervention is essential to stabilize the economy at the desired level of unemployment, which should not be too high (to avoid needless deprivation) or too low (because of the possibility of inflation). Keynes believes that the government can secure full employment and low inflation simultaneously if it fine-tunes aggregate demand using fiscal, monetary and incomes policy instruments (for example, adjusting the level and structure of taxation and government spending, fiddling with interest rates, regulating industrial relations, and so on).

Inspired by Keynes, economists developed an impressive technical and institutional apparatus that enabled the Western economies to avoid a repetition of the Great Depression. Relative economic – and, therefore, social and political – stability has been a lasting triumph of Keynesianism. Keynesians claim that their preferred policies were largely responsible for the postwar 'golden age', when most capitalist countries experienced high growth rates, near-full employment, rising income levels and unprecedented levels of social integration. But Keynesianism has been in retreat since at least the mid-seventies. The neoliberal transformations in the US, the UK and elsewhere have reversed significant aspects of the Keynesian consensus, for example, through the large-scale privatization of productive state assets, reduced tolerance for trade union activity, and the reintegration/subordination of the working class through policies of high unemployment, low economic growth, concentration of assets and income, and the partial rollback of the welfare state. The Keynesian consensus is long gone. Contemporary capitalism has shifted, instead, towards specific modalities of economic, social and political reproduction associated with neoliberalism.

Keynesian economists typically account for the retreat of Keynesianism in terms of two key processes.[2] First, the success of Keynesian management during the postwar era was so complete that it seemed that the problems of income distribution and mass unemployment in the advanced economies had been resolved once and for all. With the disappearance of the most obvious symptoms of poverty and inequality, and the seemingly irreversible stabilization of capitalism, many people became convinced that Keynesian policies, institutions and economic management were no longer needed. Second, Keynesianism was deeply divided between relatively conservative US Keynesians and relatively left-wing British post-Keynesians. The latter were traditionally based at the University of Cambridge, where Keynes, Sraffa, Joan Robinson and their disciples once taught. The Cambridge Faculty of Economics is today viciously neoclassical. It is easier for a camel to stray into the White House than for a non-mainstream economist to be hired at Cambridge. These divisions among Keynesians hinged, to a large extent, on their differing theories of income distribution. US Keynesians were generally committed to the neoclassical theory of distribution based on the marginal product of labour (which was accepted by Keynes himself) which implied that the existing distribution of income in a competitive economy is fundamentally fair – governments need only tinker with distribution at the margins, and real wage flexibility can raise the level of employment. These policy conclusions were rejected by British post-Keynesians, for whom the distribution of income depends primarily on institutional variables and power relations. US Keynesians also focused much more narrowly on short-run economic management, in which a stable environment is important to foster business confidence, while UK Keynesians tended to focus on long-term dynamic stabilization and the amelioration of entrenched inequalities. The theoretical conflicts among Keynesians contributed to their growing paralysis and, ultimately, made it impossible for a clear Keynesian ideology to emerge and compete against the neoliberal rhetoric which became increasingly popular in the late sixties and seventies.

The internal disagreements among Keynesians became especially problematic when the world economy entered into a long downturn in the early seventies, which Keynesians could neither explain nor address adequately. In the end, their school of thought dissolved into confusion. Only five years separate Richard Nixon's 1971 statement that 'we are all Keynesians now' from Jim Callaghan's pathetic admission at the Labour Party Conference during the 1976 IMF crisis that 'We used to think that you could spend your way out of a recession and increase employment by cutting taxes and boosting government spending. I tell you in all candour that that option no longer exists'.

The retreat of Keynesianism opened the way to the neoliberal reforms, which Keynesians have always insisted can only lead to a significant rise in unemployment, a shift of the distribution of income and power towards business, and greater economic volatility. A Keynesian policy would instead increase state economic intervention to rebalance the distribution of income and social power, provide public goods and services in greater abundance and promote systemic competitiveness and diffuse new technologies to secure higher saving and investment rates and stabilize aggregate demand.

A MARXIAN ALTERNATIVE

The Keynesian analysis of neoliberalism outlined in the previous section includes important insights and several appropriate policy proposals. However, it does not go far enough, or deep enough. For these reasons, it offers misleading hopes, three of which are examined here: the level of analysis, the problem of agency, and the role of the state and the scope for alternative economic policies.

1. Level of Analysis

The Keynesian account of the decline of the 'golden age' and the rise of neoliberalism outlined in the previous section is too abstract and indeterminate because it fails to contextualize the transformations in capitalist production and in economic and state institutions taking place between the mid-forties and the late seventies. Instead, the analysis focuses on horizontal distributive conflicts between rival social groups and between states. These conflicts include disputes between the US, Western Europe and Japan, and between governments and the private sector, between finance and industry, and between industrial capital and the workers. These conflicts are normally not explained in detail; they are usually merely described as disputes over shares of the national (or, in the case of states, global) income. This is insufficient because it bypasses completely the conditions of work and the distribution of power on the shopfloor and in society. In summary, Keynesian analyses tend to describe conflicts *around* the process of accumulation, while obscuring or ignoring completely conflicts *about* the nature of capitalist accumulation.[3]

Consequently, little explanation is offered of the crisis of profitability in the sixties and seventies, except that wages were too high. There is no significant attempt to incorporate into the analysis the anti-systemic social struggles taking place in the rich countries, or the socialist and anti-imperialist struggles in the poor countries. And there is not even token recognition of the erosion of the political legitimacy of the capital relation in the sixties and seventies. Consequently, Keynesian analyses fail completely to realize that neoliberalism was a project of *recomposition* of the hegemony of capital under new conditions of accumulation.

Keynesians take the extraction of surplus value for granted: the cake must grow so everyone can have more. The rest is just a matter of detail: it is who gets more icing and how the crumbs are scattered, which can be discussed in a civilized manner whether in parliament, or in bilateral negotiations or through a social accord brokered by a 'neutral' state. Fundamentally, everyone can become happier at the same time. The need for social discipline in order to preserve the conditions for the production and accumulation of surplus value, and the necessity of legitimacy and social order for economic stabilization is completely obviated in Keynesian analyses.

What is missing in Keynesian analysis is a methodologically structured account of the nature of capitalist accumulation, and an explanation of its intrinsic instability. This is *not* because the future is unknown, or because of distributive conflicts in the sphere of exchange (both of which are transhistorical phenomena), but because of *radical uncertainty* in the sphere of production, which is created by conflicts over the extraction of surplus value under specific modalities of capitalist accumulation. Keynesians generally fail to explain why and how their preferred policies interacted with the process of accumulation between the forties and the seventies, how their interaction released forces that would render Keynesianism itself obsolete, and leave the field open to the advance of neoliberalism.

2. Agency

The second problem concerns agency. In Keynesian analyses of the economy the main determinant of collective action is narrow economic interest, whether it is located at the level of the individual or an interest group. These competing interests play against each other in an institutional context in which the state is both separated from society and the market, and intrinsically neutral, even if it can be temporarily captured by specific interest groups (including, for example, the rival neoliberal and Keynesian camps). This supports the Keynesian commitment to the transformative power of democracy, as the best way to remove the grip of neoliberalism and restore the conditions for stable growth and development.

But neoliberalism is not merely a set of economic and social policies, which can be easily replaced by an alternative set through the democratic process. Neoliberalism – just like the Keynesianism which it replaced – has a specific material basis.[4] Neoliberalism combines an accumulation strategy, a mode of social and economic reproduction and a mode of exploitation and social domination based on the systematic use of state power to impose, under the ideological veil of non-intervention, a hegemonic project of recomposition of the rule of capital in all areas of social life. This project is guided by the current imperatives of the international reproduction of capital, which are represented most clearly by financial market interests and the global interests of US capital.

Under neoliberalism, domestic politics has become tightly constrained by the need to insulate the process of accumulation (the 'market') from popular demands, especially the imperative to control labour in order to secure international competitiveness. This has reduced drastically the scope for social policy, and led to higher unemployment and job insecurity in most countries. It has also created an income-concentrating dynamics of accumulation that can be limited, but not reversed, by marginal Keynesian interventions.

When viewed from this angle, the notorious inability of the neoliberal reforms to support high levels of investment or high GDP growth rates is really irrelevant. In any case, neoliberalism *has* been able to support much higher standards of consumption for the top strata of the population, due to its concentrating dynamics and its promotion of consumer debt. The Keynesian claim that the neoliberal reforms have increased the returns of financial capital at the expense of industry is also a red herring. For the purpose of the neoliberal reforms is not to promote growth, reduce inflation or even to increase the portfolio choices of the financial institutions. The *aim* of the neoliberal reforms is to subordinate local working classes and domestic accumulation to international imperatives, promote the microeconomic integration of circuits of capital, mediated by finance, and expand the scope for financial system control of the three main sources of capital in the economy: state finance, the domestic savings pool, and the linkages between domestic and foreign capital.

The transfer of the main levers of accumulation to international capital, mediated by tightly integrated US-led financial institutions, and regulated by US-controlled international financial organizations, has consolidated the material basis of neoliberalism globally. The prominence of finance expresses the subsumption of sectoral capitalist interests by the interests of capital as a whole. In policy terms, it ensures that accumulation is no longer regulated by contingent sectoral coalitions, especially in the poor countries, but by the capitalist *class*.

Specifically, there can be no presumption that there is an 'antagonic' relationship between production and finance under neoliberalism, and no expectation that industrial capital will 'rebel' against finance and push for the restoration of Keynesianism. Industrial capital has a stake in the neoliberal model, and it is structurally committed to its reproduction. The internationalization of the circuits of capital, and financial market control of state funding, have made investment and the realization of profits dependent on world market conditions and the interests of international capital. This would make any attempt to decouple from the neoliberal compact very costly indeed – this is an unattractive business proposition.

3. The Role of the State and the Scope for Economic Policy

The third problem concerns the role of the state and the scope for economic policy. In Keynesian analyses the state is disembedded from society, and a Keynesian government could rise above the sectional interests that have hijacked the state under neoliberalism in order to implement policies that are both more egalitarian, and more in tune with the interests of productive capital rather than finance.

This proposition is politically appealing but it is analytically flawed. If the state is disembedded from society, why should it select policies that maximize the rate of accumulation or employment generation, or avoid financial crises? In principle, anything goes; all that the progressive camp needs to do is get their electoral act together. But the state, and the institutions comprised within it, are shaped by technology and ideology, and by class relations, conflicts, and material interests. Under these complex circumstances, it is hopelessly naïve to expect that the social basis of the state can be transformed via the electoral process alone. Since neoliberalism has developed its own material basis, it cannot be undone simply through the electoral process.

The Keynesian prescription thus fails to realize that, given the strength of the material basis of neoliberalism, progressive policies will tend to consolidate and fine-tune the current order, rather than undermine it. For example, open regionalism and liberal interventionism limit the scope for activist industrial and trade policies, membership of the IMF and the World Bank rule out the imposition of controls over finance and the balance of payments, and support for the WTO curtails the possibility of internalization of systems of provision, which is essential for macroeconomic stability and long-term sustainable growth. Since neoliberalism is the contemporary form of capitalism, stable accumulation has become synonymous with accumulation *under* neoliberalism. Any fundamental change to the dominant system of accumulation is *always* destabilizing. Such fundamental change is necessary – but it is going to be neither smooth nor costless.

CONCLUSION

A Marxist examination of the material basis of neoliberalism throws light on several limitations of Keynesianism. Two of these limitations are especially significant. First, Keynesians often argue that macroeconomic instability and frequent financial and balance of payments crises show that neoliberalism is fundamentally flawed. This is correct in exactly the same sense that, in the abstract, economic crises show that capitalism is a flawed mode of production. However, just as crises offer the opportunity to restore balance in capitalist accumulation, crises play a constructive – and even a *constitutive* – role under neoliberalism. They help to impose policy discipline on governments, and they compel both capitalists and workers to behave in ways that support the reproduction of neoliberalism. Perversely, economic and financial crises show that the system *works*, and they help to make it work more smoothly in the long-term. Second, it is widely known that most governments promising to introduce alternative policies have failed. These failures clearly show that transcending neoliberalism is difficult and costly. At a deeper level, they also show that moving away from, or beyond, neoliberalism is not primarily a subjective problem of selecting the 'correct' industrial, financial or monetary policies.

Transcending neoliberalism will involve both economic and political transformations that can be addressed only through the construction of an *alternative system of accumulation*. This project will require dismantling systematically the material basis of neoliberalism through a set of radically redistributive and democratic economic policy initiatives. These policies will support a decisive shift to less unequal distributions of income, wealth and power, as a fundamental condition for democracy. These policy measures cannot be simply entrusted to government initiatives. They must be driven by a politically re-articulated working class, as one of the main levers for its own economic recomposition. The problem is that this virtuous circle cannot be wished into being. It requires the development of new structures of political representation corresponding to the mode of existence of the working class under neoliberalism, and supporting the development of new modalities of reproduction for this class. These achievements cannot be resolved theoretically or through purely conceptual analysis: they are political problems, to be addressed strategically in the process of struggle for the emergence of a new working-class movement for the age of neoliberalism.

NOTES

1   See, for example, D. Harvey, *The New Imperialism*, Oxford: Oxford University Press, 2005; D. Harvey, *A Brief History of Neoliberalism*, Oxford: Oxford University Press, 2005; D. Harvey, *Spaces of Global Capitalism: Towards a Theory of Uneven Geographical Development*, London: Verso, 2006; K.S. Jomo, ed., *Globalization under Hegemony: The Changing World Economy*, Oxford: Oxford University Press, 2006; K.S. Jomo and B. Fine, ed., *The New Development Economics after the Washington Consensus*, Oxford: Oxford University Press, 2006; R. Kiely, *Empire in the Age of Globalisation: US Hegemony and Neoliberal Disorder*, London: Pluto Press, 2005; R. Kiely, *The New Political Economy of Development: Globalization, Imperialism, Hegemony*, London: Palgrave, 2006; and J. Stiglitz, *Globalization and Its Discontents*, Harmondsworth: Penguin, 2003.

2   See, for example, T. Palley, *Keynesianism: What it is and why it still matters*, 2005, available from http://www.thomaspalley.com.

3   For additional details, see A. Saad-Filho, 'Monetary Policy in the Neoliberal Transition: A Political Economy Review of Keynesianism, Monetarism and Inflation Targeting', in R. Albritton, B. Jessop and R. Westra, eds., *Political Economy of the Present and Possible Global Futures*, London: Anthem Press, 2007.

4   See A. Saad-Filho, 'Introduction' in Saad-Filho, ed., *Anti-Capitalism: A Marxist Introduction,* London: Pluto Press, 2003; and A. Saad-Filho and D. Johnston, 'Introduction' in Saad-Filho and Johnston, eds., *Neoliberalism: A Critical Reader*, London, Pluto Press, 2005.

THE ROOTS OF NEOLIBERALISM

ELMAR ALTVATER

The modern version of liberalism began under Thatcher and Reagan, who provided the political basis for Milton Friedman's triumphant declaration of the 'neoliberal counter-revolution' following the crisis of the Keynesian state in the West, the dismantling of the 'planning state' in the South, and the collapse of the planned economies of the East. However, the roots of neoliberalism go back much further than the past thirty-five years. Some of the most striking ingredients of neoliberal theoretical approaches can be traced back to the origins of liberal thinking in the early 18th century, to Adam Smith, David Hume, Bernard de Mandeville, etc. In the 'fable of the bees' Mandeville even tried to show that private vices turn into public virtues, and that competition in free markets also produces social equilibrium (later formulated mathematically by Leon Walras, Vilfredo Pareto and in the vast literature on their 'optima'). Long before Fukuyama's famous statement about 'the end of history', after the demise of 'actually existing' socialism, Antoine-Augustin Cournot was saying much the same thing when he argued that since such 'optima' are the outcome of economic processes there is no need to change the political order and its ruling principles.

Some trace twentieth century neoliberalism back to a conference which took place in 1938 in Paris, where Friedrich August Freiherr von Hayek and Walter Eucken, among others, presented the free market ('freie Verkehrswirtschaft') as the only real alternative to the centrally managed markets ('Zentralverwaltungs-wirtschaften') of Soviet Russia and Nazi Germany. All planning systems follow the 'road to serfdom' – the title of Hayek's very influential book published at the end of the Second World War. Their assault on socialist and capitalist planning presaged in this respect Hannah Arendt's theory of totalitarianism, published a few years later in 1951.

Thirty years later still, a new twist was famously given to this by Reagan's ambassador to the United Nations, Jeane Kirkpatrick, who in trying to formulate the fundamental principles of US foreign policy drew a distinction between totalitarian and authoritarian regimes. A totalitarian regime was any one with a planned economy and widespread public or state property, even if it was manifestly less dictatorial and oppressive in political terms than what she called merely 'authoritarian regimes', which sustained and protected private property in a capitalist market economy. Fidel Castro's Cuba was 'totalitarian'; Chile under Pinochet was merely 'authoritarian'.

In fact, however, the central idea behind this distinction had already been developed by the Freiburg School of 'Ordo-Liberalism', particularly by Walter Eucken, in the 1930s. In his view the fundamental principles of a social order are: private property rights; the unregulated formation of prices on free markets; free decision-making by the autonomous (vis-à-vis the state and trade unions) managers of enterprises; sovereign consumers; the absence of monopolies; and monetary stability. Only when these fundamental economic principles ('Grundprinzipien') are realized will the political order be a 'free' one. Since modern societies are characterized by a so-called 'interdependence of orders', no free and democratic political order can be said to exist, according to Euken, unless it sustains a free market economy and an efficient private property regime.

After the Second World War such ideas still were influential, not least with Germany's first minister of economic affairs, Ludwig Erhard and his secretary, Alfred Müller-Armack. But as was clear from the fact that Erhard was also a disciple of the early 'third way' theorist Franz Oppenheimer, and the fact that Müller-Armnack coined the term 'Soziale Marktwirschaft' (social market economy), a consistent economic policy based on neoliberal ideology could not then be as extreme as it was to become after the neoliberal counter-revolution in the 1970s. It is indeed worth recalling that even this decade began with Richard Nixon declaring that 'we all are Keynesians' now. Keynesianism had indeed become the hegemonic concept in both economic theory and policy under the post-war umbrella of an international monetary system of fixed exchange rates and restrictions on the convertibility of currencies. Relatively small international capital flows allowed considerable autonomy for national governments and central banks which influenced fiscal and interest rate policy with an eye to balancing the priorities of economic growth, full employment, price stability and balance of payment equilibrium. The first quarter century after the Second World War was thus a period in which it made sense for Andrew Shonfield to translate the title of his famous 1965 book *Modern Capitalism* (on the highly developed market economies of the USA, Great Britain, France, Germany and Italy) as *Geplanter Kapitalismus* (planned capitalism) for the 1968 German edition.

Yet neoliberal ideas had actually been spreading across the Western world even during the Keynesian 'golden age' of capitalism, during which there was a modernization of simple-minded earlier liberal (what might now be seen as 'paleoliberal') ideas. 'Establish a free order of competition and its outcome will be the best for the people' was the simple expression of the promise that market competition was the means of transforming the self-interest of individuals into a social welfare optimum for the collective good. Such ideas were spread with the aid of highly sophisticated methods, heavily funded by businesses and wealthy individuals. The foundation of the Mont Pélerin Society as an international venue for neoliberals, and of national organizations such as the 'Aktionsgemeinschaft Soziale Marktwirtschaft' in Germany, preceded by decades the setting up in 1983 of the European Round Table of industrialists to coordinate neoliberal lobbying in the EU. This was accomplished by intensifying the cooperation between well-endowed national policy foundations sponsored and financed by big business in the US and in Europe in order to produce harmonized manifestos for the propagation of free market policies against the welfare- and interventionist-state. But in terms of its influence over political decision-makers more globally, it was of utmost importance that neoliberalism also became hegemonic in international institutions such as the IMF, the World Bank, the GATT (later the WTO), staffed by the students of neoliberal economists at American elite universities, who also showed up as government-consultants (and even as NGO activists) in third world countries to help apply dose after dose of structural adjustment, following the rules of the Washington consensus.

The strategy of establishing a world-wide ideological hegemony for neoliberalism, however, could not have succeeded without the deep changes that occurred in the world economy in the 1970s. First of all, the Keynesian carapace of economic policy literally broke into pieces with the end of the Bretton Woods system of fixed exchange rates, followed by the flotation of exchange rates in globalized financial markets. After that the formation of the crucial prices of the world economy – the exchange rate and the interest rate – was no longer left up to state agencies and officials but was rather in the hands of international banks, speculative investment funds and transnational corporations. This was one of the first acts of privatization which swept over the entire world in the following years. The new private actors immediately used their new freedom to invent new financial instruments to increase their profits and to force countries lagging behind in financial market deregulation to give up their 'financial repression'. Thus it happened that financial markets came to exert their own repression on one society after another. Not to worry – in the words of Margaret Thatcher: 'There is no such thing as society'.

But neoliberalism's spread was also enhanced by another dramatic change, and this time by no means left to private bodies, in how another crucial price in the world economy was determined. Only a few months after the final breakdown of the Bretton Woods system in October 1973, the dramatic change in the way oil prices were formed – i.e. by the formation of OPEC – triggered radical repercussions in the relationship between the industrialized world and the 'Third World'. Liberalized financial markets helped recycle the so-called 'petrodollars' accumulated by the OPEC countries into oil-importing Third World countries. The enormous debts they now accumulated soon landed them in the debt crisis of the 1980s. The priority of servicing their debts, imposed by the IMF and World Bank, was an early expression of what Stephen Gill would later appropriately call 'disciplinary neoliberalism'. Paradoxically, therefore, just as the Bretton Woods system broke down, the Bretton Woods institutions became more powerful than ever. They moved from protecting a system of fixed exchange rates to protecting the flow of capital in the interests of rich private lenders, multinational corporations and financial institutions.

The 'crisis of governability' proclaimed by Samuel Huntington and the Trilateral Commission amidst the inflationary pressures and fiscal crises that attended the crisis of Keynesianism led, moreover, to the formation at Rambouillet in 1975 of the G6 (later the G7 and today the G8). The annual summits of the leading capitalist leaders were a very visible sign of what Carl Schmitt would have called the changing 'pluriverse' of nation states, characterized by the emergence of new informal modes of global political regulation – what by the 1990s would come to be called 'global governance' – which stressed their collective responsiveness to 'market signals' rather than coordinated Keynesian-style policy-making. The internationalization of the state changed the form of the nation state as well as the system of international relations.

But it was the end of full employment and the emergence of a new reserve army of unemployed across the world that was the most important change brought about in the 1970s. Unemployment in the industrialized countries became structural, and now became the fate of large masses of workers there. In the Third World, however, a new form of labour was discovered in the 'informal economy'. Workers who were not formally employed in any way comparable to workers in industrialized countries could by the same token not be considered 'formally unemployed'. Labelled 'informal' workers (initially by the ILO at the beginning of the 1970s in East Africa), the category of informal labour has since experienced an astonishing career. Thirty-five years later nearly 90 per cent of workers in Africa, nearly 60 per cent in Latin

America, and even up to 30 per cent in the OECD-countries are categorized as informal. The new 'precariat' of informal labour has become 'normal'; formal labour is now a reality for only a relatively small minority of workers in the world.

These changes marked the passage from the 'golden age' of post-war Keynesianism to a neoliberal era defined in terms of pressures to increase the competitiveness of local sites of production (and 'workfare') in competitive global spaces. Nothing less was involved in this transformation than a radical rupture of many of the key forms which had earlier regulated economic development, social life and policy concepts. Neoliberal ideology thus stepped into the open space left by the crisis of the post-war economic and social model of the Keynesian welfare state. It was against this background that Milton Friedman could speak in terms of the neoliberal 'counterrevolution' against Keynesianism, with 'monetarism' as his own favourite alternative economic policy concept.

The neoliberal dogma can be summarized in the following way: its basic assumption is that the private sector is fundamentally stable. If instability or even crisis tendencies occur, this can only be due to political actors and institutions taking irresponsible actions that violate the laws of the market. Inflation or a devaluation of the currency is caused by such actions and has nothing to do with real economic processes. Therefore an independent central bank must commit itself to preventing inflation and nothing else as its sole priority (even controlling the quantity of money in circulation proved a chimera). In the long run fiscal policy has no influence on the growth rate and employment and therefore it should serve monetary stability alone, and not the policy target of full employment. Unemployment is the result of an inefficient allocation of labour and economically unjustified wage levels pushed up by oligopolistic unions.

The final obstacle to the full victory of neoliberalism in the world was removed at the end of the 1980s in the course of the 'velvet revolutions' in Central and Eastern Europe, and with the crumbling of the Soviet Union into a series of new states. It was Margaret Thatcher who again coined the most famous slogan of neoliberalism's final victory: 'There is no alternative'. No alternative to what? To a neoliberal world order. The theoretically more ambitious and demanding expression of the political triumph of neoliberalism was Fukayama's 'the end of history'. Neoliberalism was by this point also well on the way to becoming dominant as an ideology in the social sciences, and in the political domain of social democracy; it was also adopted by the green movements and parties – sometimes only partly, but often fully. Representatives of all of these act as the spokespersons of corporations, of foundations or lobby-associations. They are the conscious-unconscious incarnation of neoliberal hegemony.

Neoliberalism is a very optimistic ideology because it also follows the supposition that humankind finds solutions for all its problems. Yet the result of neoliberalism has been by no means convincing. The political practice of neoliberalism in following a simple set of rules, all of which point to more competition in the global capitalist space, requires that the impact of democratic politics be reduced while states enforce the market power of powerful private capitalist agencies. Unemployment has increased in nearly all countries. The distribution of income and wealth has become more unequal in most countries and in the world as a whole. The Gini-coefficient of global distribution of income as of 2005 was 0.892, i.e. about 10 per cent of the world population disposes of 90 per cent of global wealth, whereas 90 per cent of the world population dispose of only 10 per cent of the wealth. Economic development is everywhere crisis-ridden. From the debt crises of the 1980s to the financial crises of the 1990s, the liberalization of financial markets destabilized one society after another. The world rule of the disembedded market proved extremely destructive for the social fabric – thereby paradoxically reinforcing the crackpot validity of Margaret Thatcher's perverse claim that 'there is no such thing as society'.

The notion that the solution to all problems can be found through markets is supposed to apply even to environmental problems, because markets are – as von Hayek so often repeated – held to be the best available method of making discoveries and thus of making technical and organizational innovations. A good example of this kind of neoliberal hegemony is the success in promoting the concept of emissions trading as the most effective (and as some say, only) instrument for mitigating CO_2 emissions. The establishment of a market in atmospheric pollution rights is broadly accepted by mainstream academia, the political class, business and finance, and even by green parties, NGOs and trade unions. Only a few left academics and political movements doubt the ecological sense of emissions trading. Business and finance see profit opportunities in new fields of investment, new deals on a new market, through calculating the costs of emissions rights which never have to be paid by the companies, a licence for riskless profit making.

But why do green party representatives and concerned ecologists support this? In some cases it is pure naiveté; in most cases, however, it is an emanation of a belief-system that sees the market alone as the adequate problem-solver. Yet markets only work when some crucial prerequisites are fulfilled: the establishment of private property rights and the subsequent commodification of all goods, whether formerly private or public. Global financial markets are required to circulate the highly unconventional commodities of securitized 'pollution rights'. This complex of preconditions is a further powerful vehicle of privatization, liberalization and financial globalization. Thus the constructed double character of atmospheric pollution – of real CO_2 emissions into the air, and of paper emissions traded on markets – perfectly fits the neoliberal ideal world. At the end of the day the atmosphere, an undeniable global common, is increasingly privatized, because the right to use it as a dumping-site for CO_2 emissions has been legally established by the state or by international institutions. Liberal markets for the trading of new commodities (pollution certificates) have been created and financial investors can crowd into this new politically created area in order to offer innovative and profitable financial instruments and to absorb part of the world's excess liquidity. Emissions trading, designed for the reduction of CO_2 emissions, is transformed into a new vehicle of financial speculation. Neoliberalism does not only know that 'there is no such thing as society'; it also knows there is no such thing as nature. It only takes notice of it when it is securitized for trading in markets.

Neoliberalism's disdain for both society and nature is a consequence of the conception of the world as made up of *homines oeconomice* whose rationality operates in a spaceless and timeless world, lacking the coordinates of nature. These artificial creatures are comparable to the *homunculus* in the 'Faust' of Goethe, while the capitalist 'annihilation of time by space and of space by time', as Marx called it in the *Grundrisse*, finds its fullest and most enthusiastic expression in a neoliberal belief-system that cares nothing for the specificities of time or history, space or territories. Only thanks to this reduction was it possible to develop and then apply a menu like that of the 'Washington consensus' to all countries at all times – countries which have just two characteristics in common: they are highly indebted and they have to follow the rules of global financial markets.

Because societies and nature are not taken into account, the application of the neoliberal agenda can be as ruthless as necessary in order to meet the requirements of financial capital. Shareholders want high returns on their investment, in the range of 20 per cent and more. Interest rates and rates of return on investment are pushed upwards in the global competition of financial places whose returns in the last instance can only be obtained by overexploiting labour and nature. This is why the promise of the paleoliberals of yesteryear, and of the neoliberals today, that the wealth of nations will increase by widening and deepening the international division of labour through establishing free markets everywhere and in everything, becomes more and more hollow. The real experience of billions of people is that neoliberalism is a predatory order, harmful for people who depend on their labour and destructive for local and global ecosystems. Moreover, neoliberalism threatens peace in the world. For the appropriation of surpluses also relies on using coercion, including military force, to sustain the economic mechanisms for the expropriation of the world's masses. Neoliberals and neoconservatives converged in the first decade of the 21st century to produce the aggressive politico-economic project of the Bush–Cheney-type.

However, this is not so different from the paleoliberal notions of Adam Smith who, while he was an ardent advocate of free trade, was also a supporter of the protectionistic Navigation Act, of diplomatic relations conducted on the basis of aristocratic noblesse oblige among the 'civilized' nations, and of their military suppression of 'barbarians'. But the consequences of supporting those who follow the bourgeois mission of integrating the whole earth into the capitalist value-chain, and repressing those who try to defend their class-interest in decent work and life, and in the survival of nature, were soon felt when people rose up against the bourgeois project in the 19th and 20th centuries. And like their paleoliberal ancestors, neoliberalism's 21st century advocates will surely sooner or later reap the whirlwind of protest against what they have sown.

NEOLIBERALISM AND THE DISCONTENTED

GREGORY ALBO

When neoliberalism made its debut as a political project at the end of the 1970s, it was taken for granted in most quarters of the Left that it was neither politically nor economically sustainable. The emerging New Right regimes of Ronald Reagan, Margaret Thatcher, Helmut Kohl and Brian Mulroney could intensify class conflict and spread the ideology of market populism, it was suggested, but they would leave no enduring institutional or political legacy. The monetarist and free market policies trumpeted by these governments – and incorporated into the policy arsenal of the international financial institutions – could only magnify the economic problems that had ended the postwar boom. The increasing complexity of post-Fordist technologies and organization demanded far greater institutional capacities than capitalist markets and firms could supply on their own. Growing civil society movements were, moreover, beginning to forge a political accord with traditional working-class unions and parties: a new egalitarian politics was being fashioned for the 'new times' to accommodate previously oppressed social identities.

The political question of the day was, as Eric Hobsbawm was one of the foremost in arguing, the voting and programmatic agenda of such a 'rational left'. The prospect of a 'popular front' government, built on a coalition of disciplined unions, new social movements, and social democratic parties supported by communists, would serve as the foundation from which to bridge the neoliberal interlude. In 1986, two decades ago, Hobsbawm, speaking with respect to Britain, had already concluded that the neoliberals' performance was 'utterly discredited, in the minds of most people, the privatizing "free market" ideology of the suburban crusaders who dressed up the right of the rich to get richer among the ruins as a way of solving the world's and Britain's problems. They have had their chance and we can see what happened'.[1]

The expectation of Hobsbawm's 'rational left' was that once the New Right governments were defeated and social democratic parties returned to power, a progressive reform agenda would re-assert itself. The failure of this strategy has, perhaps, been one of the most painful political lessons that neoliberalism delivered. The social democratic governments that came to power in the 1990s – from Blair and Schröder in Britain and Germany to Mbeki and Lula in South Africa and Brazil – proved just as forceful in advancing neoliberalism globally. Neoliberalism was consolidated as the ideological framework guiding public policy, and it defined the terrain of 'legitimate' politics under their stewardship as much as under the presidency of Bill Clinton in the US. This is what in fact happened: a more aggressive Western imperialism extended its capacities for military and economic intervention across the globe; new zones of accumulation, notably China and Eastern Europe, were incorporated into the global circuits of capital; tax cuts and social austerity continued to be extended in the face of mounting social inequalities and collapsing public infrastructure; and by the end of the millennium centre-right political movements were back in office in much of the advanced capitalist world.

It was Gramsci who noted that in a crisis the 'ruling class, which has numerous trained cadres, changes men and programmes and, with greater speed than is achieved by the subordinate classes, reabsorbs the control that was slipping from its grasp. Perhaps it may make sacrifices, and expose itself to an uncertain future by demagogic promises; but it retains power, re-inforces it for the time being, and uses it to crush its adversary and disperse his leading cadres'.[2] Neoliberalism has entailed just such changes of cadres and programmes, demagogic promises and exercises of power. It continues to register an astonishing political resilience in the centres of political and economic power; it has become institutionalized in the apparatuses of the state; it forms the economic calculus of financial and industrial capitalists; and it has also become internalized in the behavioural norms and strategic responses of unions and civil society organizations. The programme of neo-liberalism may well be discredited and the numbers of discontented growing. But, as far as the balance of political power is concerned, this has not yet shifted in a way that allows anyone – least of all political militants – to speak honestly about a period 'after neoliberalism'.

THE NEOLIBERAL STATE

The flawed political readings of neoliberalism have their source in persistent conceptual errors. A standard charge on the Left remains that neoliberalism is simply 'bad policy', especially in attempting to achieve a minimal state at the 'wrong scale' as capital, markets, information and technology have all surpassed the capabilities of national states. A contrasting view has insisted that neoliberalism is still first and foremost a strategic response by capitalist forces that can break workers' resistance but cannot resolve a capitalist crisis that continues to unfold. Neither position is very helpful in explaining the durability of neoliberalism, nor in offering strategic insight into the impasse of the Left. Voluntarism and fatalism are equally useless for political thinking.

Neoliberalism needs, first of all, to be understood as a ruling-class political programme to respond to challenges from the Left. It is important to recall that the initial political initiative in response to the crisis of the 1970s was seized by the Left. It came in the form of an array of strategies for reflation, redistribution and socialization: the Meidner Plan in Sweden, the civil rights mobilization for the Humphrey-Hawkins Full Employment Bill in the US, the left-nationalist turn in Canada, the Bennite Left in Britain, Euro-communism, and revolutionary and nationalist upheavals across the South.[3] Neoliberalism was the policy of those who recognized that these movements and cadres needed to be crushed.

In the postwar period, neoliberal thinking, in the works of Hayek, Friedman, and Buchanan, had been a relentless voice of dissent to Keynesianism and the welfare state, which they saw as the 'road to serfdom'. Their views on trade, monetary policy, and taxation were always given space in policy debates, particularly in Anglo-American institutions. Neoliberalism as a political practice began as policies calling for greater monetary discipline and freer markets to constrain some of the ascendant demands from the Left. The New Right governments of the 1980s, in their agenda of 'passive revolution' to overturn working-class advances, widened the political framework to include virtually all spheres of state activity. The continued economic slowdown through the 1980s, coupled with mounting social inequalities and the internationalization of capitalist social relations, generalized a situation of 'competitive austerity'. Neoliberal policies of wage compression, cuts in social programmes and export-led growth in liberalized markets were adopted in one country after another, whatever party was in power.[4] Neoliberalism was no longer limited to a set of ideas promulgated by revanchist intellectuals or a political strategy of 'market populist' parties of the New Right. By the 1990s it became a far broader project of regulating social life through market imperatives, and incorporated within it the Third Way strategies of 'progressive competitiveness' that accepted the parameters imposed by the current distribution of income and assets, and by world markets. Neoliberalism had become the political form in which political and social relations are reproduced at the local as well as the national level of the state, and across the international state system.

Second, neoliberalism needs to be located in crucial transformations in the general circuit of capital by the late 20th century. A notable feature has been the uneven pace and spatial distribution of new accumulation: the European and Japanese zones of postwar equalization have slowed relative to the reassertion of American capitalism and the rapid growth of East Asia and some of the Gulf oil states; while Latin America, Africa and Eastern Europe have fallen behind, or even had phases of 'disaccumulation'.

This uneven development reflects unrelenting asymmetries in the value flows in the world market under neoliberalism. This is seen in the tendency of the current account deficit in the US to rise remorselessly from the early 1980s onwards, with the offsetting surpluses accumulating in East Asia and the Gulf overflowing the treasuries of their central banks; international financial transactions and debt levels massively outstripping the expansion in trade and new production; the growth of service industries – not only financial services, but also 'producer services' (such as advertising, call centres, computer and data processing, personnel supply, consulting, security, legal, accounting, etc.) – relative to manufacturing and processing sectors; and a general trend to increasing concentrations of capital controlled by new forms of financial capital, centred in key global urban centres. Neoliberalism, in other words, has produced a dominant pattern of finance-led extroverted growth, increasingly dependent upon the world market – US debt loads and the Chinese market transition being the central bulwarks sustaining global accumulation – for the realization of new value.[5]

Third, new ruling class alliances – varying according to whether we are dealing with a social formation at the centre of the global system, or at its periphery – have been formed within this changed configuration of the world market. The postwar period was anchored in an alliance between industrial and commodity capital, with financial capital managing credit and investment flows. This alliance acted as a 'national bourgeoisie' in protecting the domestic economy as its sphere of accumulation, and keeping foreign (and imperialist) capital within confined parameters. This alliance is no more.

Neoliberalism has given rise to a new form of hegemony by finance capital over the power bloc. The deepening separation between the legal ownership of corporations via shareholding, and real economic possession by their corporate managers, who control the disposition of their capital assets, has allowed new corporate organizational structures to emerge. New financial agents, such as hedge funds and private equity groups, and traditional financial actors such as banks, brokerage houses, and trusts, have acquired leverage over industrial capital. In turn, industrial capital has obtained the organizational capacity to diversify into a range of its own financial activities. These new corporate forms have fostered the reorganization of industrial and commodity capital into international production networks. With the internationalization of capital, foreign capital now plays a central role in supplying funds, technology, and management across the spectrum of the sectors of capital accumulation in most countries. This has a fundamental political meaning: foreign capital is no longer a marginal element, or something imposed from outside on national capitalist classes. Neoliberalism constitutes 'interior bourgeoisies' as integral components of domestic power blocs. Under neoliberalism the political-economic foundation for Hobsbawm's 'rational left' has vanished.[6]

A fourth dimension of the neoliberal project is the way state economic intervention in the circuits of capital has been transformed.[7] This is not a question of delimiting the space of the state relative to that of the market; it involves a reorganization of the way state policies relate to the valorization of capital, and to class struggles. In the field of macroeconomic management, restrictive budgetary and debt management policies in the state sector have been coupled with inflation-targeting by independent central banks. These policies have tended to produce a deflationary bias, which has partly been offset by credit expansion and asset inflation in the private sector. Industrial and commercial policies and apparatuses have also been reordered to aid international competitiveness and sponsor the internationalization of capital. Indeed, both macroeconomic and industrial policies are premised on liberalized capital and trade flows and exchange rates which themselves were, in good part, the result of neoliberal state policies.

The consequences of these policies include: tying production more and more to commercial exchange values; expanding the capacity of capital to use regulatory arbitrage to seek tax and environmental concessions at the expense of other social objectives and protections; and reinforcing the use of subsidies and workplace concessions to maintain investment by firms. All these measures reduce democratic capacities and bolster capitalist control over the use of the social surplus – both inter-temporally, between present consumption and future investment, and inter-sectorally, between the public and private sectors in the composition of output.

A fifth and very important way of understanding neoliberalism in practice is as a distinct institutional framework for governance and administration internal to the state. The advanced capitalist state is so deeply embedded in the reproduction of capital that the neoliberal ideology of a 'laissez-faire' minimal state is a fantastical proposition. The change that has actually occurred has often been described as a 'hollowing-out of the state', as welfare and redistributive functions are 'downloaded' to local governments and a range of policies to support the internationalization of capital and protect private property rights are 'uploaded' to international state agencies and multinational blocs such as the EU and NAFTA. 'Hollowing out' is, however, a quite misleading image. It especially misses the authoritarian hardening of the central state and the reorganization of its administrative apparatus.

The exercise of political power is increasingly concentrated in the central state apparatuses relative to democratic actors such as parties, unions and civic organizations. This can be especially seen in the decline of legislative bodies relative to the exercise of unilateral and unaccountable executive power. The hardening of state power is evident with respect to war-making and national security powers, and it also now extends to a host of administrative measures around treaties, contracts and appointments. The departments of the state have also been re-ordered to strengthen the central state's role in advancing neoliberal policies: those dealing with budgetary controls and economic internationalization have been strengthened; branches of the state dealing with labour and social justice have been marginalized. The military, security policing and prison branches of the state have also tended to grow in relative power; they increasingly define state behaviour with respect not only to international relations, but also to civil protest. A parallel neoliberal administrative measure has been to insulate agencies dealing with economic matters from democratic accountability by increasing their operational autonomy. This strategy has especially been deployed to secure the 'independence' of central banks, regulatory agencies and economic development bodies. A similar effect is produced by the adoption of administrative modes of deregulation, privatization and marketization.[8]

Sixth, and last, neoliberal economic interventions have also enforced new relations of exploitation between capital and labour, particularly through changes in the law regulating labour markets. This has underpinned the distributional patterns that are commonly called 'social polarization'. Annual wage increases are kept below the combined rates of inflation and productivity, thereby shifting an increased share of net income to profits; higher levels of labour reserves, longer hours of work, the racialization of labour market access and the growth of informal and precarious work mean increased inequalities within working classes; sharp cuts in welfare transfers fall especially hard on women and migrants; credit is increasingly relied upon for current and future living standards; and privatization and user fees limit equal access to public services, and extend people's dependence on the market in all aspects of daily life.

CONTESTING NEOLIBERALISM

Over the period of neoliberalism, the Left has suffered major historical defeats. This has generally been defined, for both good and ill, in terms of the end of authoritarian communism and the realignment of social democracy toward increasing accommodation of the market and existing distributional relations. But the structural transformations associated with neoliberalism have also altered the organizational foundations for Left political alternatives: the changes in the nature of employment towards more networked pro- duction processes and fragmented service provision; the increasing interna- tional circulation of capital; the reorganization of the state; and the internal differentiation and stratification of the working class. These developments have affected working-class capacities in terms of workplace organization, political leadership, and ideological inventiveness. Neoliberalism's greatest political achievement, it needs to be stressed, does not lie with privatization, globalization or financialization, but in the way ruling classes have adapted neoliberalism so as to wage 'class struggle from above' to defeat, isolate, indi- vidualize and disorganize the Left and the working-class movement.

Locating the political terrain for contesting neoliberalism has been enor- mously difficult and complex. One response has been to search for an anti- neoliberal project in specific alternate policies (thereby narrowing even fur- ther the horizons of a 'rational left' popular front strategy like Hobsbawm's in the 1980s). In this vein, Robin Blackburn's penetrating analysis of the commodification of pensions ends with the modest call for 'responsible accumulation'. A similar pragmatism lay behind Roberto Unger's enumera- tion of all the alternative democratic and institutional arrangements that are possible within contemporary capitalism. And most of the innumerable cri- tiques of neoliberal globalization end with liberal calls for the democratiza- tion of global governance.[9] But such exercises in economic logic and politi- cal judiciousness have failed to create greater policy and institutional space for the Left.

The anti-globalization movement has gathered together the discontented against neoliberalism in many corners of the world, in major demonstrations and in the World Social Forum and its offshoots. The movement has been theorized as an anti-neoliberal project 'from below': a leader-less move- ment requiring neither party nor programme, neither disciplined cadres nor political line. The organizational disarray of the Left is, in effect, represented as one of its primary sources of renewal. Michael Hardt and Antonio Negri foresee a 'multitude' escaping the present political space of neoliberalism, and the new logic of power of decentred 'empire', to forge in the present an alternate world order. John Holloway has turned the inability to contest political power on its head to theorize how to 'change the world without taking power'. And Naomi Klein rebuts those critics of the anti-globalization movement who call for organizational depth as infringing on emergent 'possibilities'. 'Maybe', she writes, 'out of the chaotic network of hubs and spokes, something else will emerge: not a blueprint for some utopian new world, but a plan to protect the possibility of many worlds – "a world", as the Zapatistas say, "with many worlds in it". Maybe instead of meeting the proponents of neoliberalism head on, this movement of movements will surround them from all directions'.[10]

Neoliberalism has, however, managed to stand its ground. As a consequence, Left politics under neoliberalism has oscillated between, on the one hand, short-term political calculation to avoid further social erosion, and, on the other, a politics of predicting imminent economic crisis if not total socio-economic chaos that in fact reflects the disarray of Left forces and organizational weakness. Yet this is precisely why the socialist Left must be actively engaged, above all, in fostering the formation of new political agencies.

One necessary aspect of such an engagement is class reformation through the revitalization of unions, and the linking of unions to workers in new sectors – those struggling for gender and racial equality, and the marginalized, people outside 'normal' work processes. It is also necessary to experiment in organizational convergence between the remnants of the independent Left, civic organizations, and the sections within social democracy that remained committed to a transformative project. Such a reformation needs to be grounded in the building up of the educational, communicative and cultural resources – the political and human capacities – necessary for a 'new socialism' for the 21st century.[11] And concrete anti-neoliberal alliances will need to be forged in struggle to defeat particular initiatives and make inroads against neoliberalism, so as to make such a process of re-formation 'organic'.

Neoliberalism has consistently generated political flashpoints that have blunted its appeal and forced a recalibration of the global ambitions of the ruling classes. The imbalances of world trade, the contradictions of military occupation, the social inequalities of income and work, the inefficiencies and monopolies of privatized public assets, the abject failure of carbon trading and other pollution markets to address the global ecological crisis – all these have spawned often inspiring kinds of social and political struggle against neoliberalism. But unless the Left develops viable new collective and democratic organizational capacities, the barbarism that is global neoliberalism will indeed continue to yield its daily horrors in every part of the earth.

NOTES

1   Eric Hobsbawm, *Politics for a Rational Left*, London: Verso, 1989, p. 177.
2   Antonio Gramsci, *Selections from the Prison Notebooks*, New York: International Publishers, 1971, pp. 210-11.
3   Donald Sassoon, *One Hundred Years of Socialism*, New York: New Press, 1996; Daniel Singer, *Whose Millennium? Theirs or Ours?*, New York: Monthly Review Press, 1999.
4   David Harvey, *A Brief History of Neoliberalism*, Oxford: Oxford University Press, 2005.
5   Gerard Dumenil and Dominque Levy, *Capital Resurgent: Roots of the Neoliberal Revolution*, Cambridge: Harvard University Press, 2004; Leo Panitch and Sam Gindin, 'Finance and American Empire', in *Socialist Register 2005*.
6   William Carroll, *Corporate Power in a Globalizing World*, Oxford: Oxford University Press, 2004.
7   Alfredo Saad-Filho and Deborah Johnson, eds., *Neoliberalism: A Critical Reader*, London: Pluto, 2005; Ray Kiely, *The New Political Economy of Development*, New York: Palgrave, 2007.
8   Colin Leys, *Market-Driven Politics: Neoliberal Democracy and the Public Interest*, London: Verso, 2001.
9   Robin Blackburn, *Banking on Death*, London: Verso, 2003; Roberto Unger, *Democracy Realized: The Progressive Alternative*, London: Verso, 1999; Daniele Archibugi, ed., *Debating Cosmopolitics*, London: Verso, 2003.
10 Michael Hardt and Antonio Negri, *Multitude: War and Democracy in the Age of Empire*, New York: Penguin, 2004; John Holloway, *Change the World Without Taking Power*, London: Pluto, 2005; Naomi Klein, 'Farewell to the "End of History": Organization and Vision in Anti-Corporate Movements', in *Socialist Register 2002*, p. 13.
11 Michael Lebowitz, *Build It Now: Socialism for the 21st Century*, New York: Monthly Review Press, 2006.

Socialist Register – Published Annually Since 1964

Leo Panitch and Colins Leys – Editors
with Barbara Harriss-White, Elmar Altvater and Grego Albo
2007: COMING TO TERMS WITH NATURE

Can capitalism come to terms with the environment? Can market forces and technology overcome the 'limits to growth' and yet preserve the biosphere? What is the nature of oil politics today? Can capitalism do without nuclear power, or make it safe? What is the significance of the impasse over the Kyoto protocol?

Contents: Brenda Longfellow: Weather Report - Images from the Climate Crisis; Neil Smith: Nature as Accumulation Strategy; Elmar Altvater: The Social and Natural Environment of Fossil Capitalism; Daniel Buck: The Ecological Question - Can Capitalism Prevail?; Barbara Harriss-White & Elinor Harriss: Unsustainable Capitalism - the Politics of Renewable Energy in the UK; Jamie Peck: Neoliberal Hurricane - who framed New Orleans?; Minqi Li & Dale Wen: China - Hyper-development and Environmental Crisis; Henry Bernstein & Philip Woodhouse: Africa - Eco-populist Utopias and (micro-) capitalist realities; Philip McMichael: Feeding the World - Agriculture, Development and Ecology; Erik Swyngedouw: Water, Money and Power; Achim Brunnengraber: The Political Economy of the Kyoto Protocol; Heather Rogers: Garbage Capitalism's Green Commerce; Costas Panayotakis: Working More, Selling More, Consuming More - capitalism's 'third contradiction'; Joan Martinez-Alier: Social Metabolism and Environmental Conflicts; Michael Lowy: Eco-socialism and Democratic Planning; Frieder Otto Wolf: Party-building for Eco-Socialists - Lessons from the failed project of the German greens; Greg Albo: The Limits of Eco-localism - Scale, Strategy, Socialism.

384 pp. 234 x 156 mm.

0850365775 hbk £35.00   0850365783 pbk £14.95

Canada: Fernwood Publishing; USA: Monthly Review Press; UK and Rest of World: Merlin Press

Leo Panitch and Colin Leys – Editors
2006: TELLING THE TRUTH

How does power shape ideas and ideologies today? Who controls the information on which public discussion rests? How is power used to exclude critical thought in politics, the media, universities, state policy-making? Has neo-liberal globalisation introduced a new era of state duplicity, corporate manipulation of truth and intellectual conformity? Are we entering a new age of unreason?

Contents: Colin Leys: The cynical state; Atilio Boron: The truth about capitalist democracy; Doug Henwood: The 'business community'; Frances Fox Piven & Barbara Ehrenreich: The truth about welfare reform; Loic Wacquant: The 'scholarly myths' of the new law and order doxa; Robert W. McChesney: Telling the truth at a moment of truth: US news media and the invasion and occupation of Iraq; David Miller: Propaganda-managed democracy: the UK and the lessons of Iraq; Ben Fine & Elisa van Waeyenberge: Correcting Stiglitz - From information to power in the world of development; Sanjay Reddy: Counting the poor: the truth about world poverty statistics; Michael Kustow: Playing with the Truth: the politics of theatre; John Sambonmatsu: Postmodernism and the corruption of the academic intelligentsia; G.M. Tamás: Telling the truth about the working class; Terry Eagleton: Telling the truth.

304 pp. 234 x 156 mm.

0850365597 hbk £35.00   **0850365600 pbk £14.95**
Canada: Fernwood Publishing; USA: Monthly Review Press; UK and Rest of World: Merlin Press

Leo Panitch and Colin Leys – Editors
2005: THE EMPIRE RELOADED

How does the new American empire work? Who runs it? How stable is it?
What is the new American Empire's impact throughout the world?
What is its influence on gender relations? On the media? On popular culture?

Contents: Stephen Gill: The Contradictions of American Supremacy; Varda Burstyn: The New Imperial Order Foretold; Leo Panitch & Sam Gindin: Finance and American Empire; Chris Rude: The Role of Financial Discipline in Imperial Strategy; Scott Forsyth: Hollywood Reloaded: The Film as Imperial Commodity; Harriet Friedman: Feeding the Empire: Agriculture, Livelihood and the Crisis of the Global Food Regime; Vivek Chibber: Reviving the Developmental State? The Myth of the 'National Bourgeoisie'; Gerard Greenfield: Bandung redux: Imperialism and Anti-Globalization Nationalisms in Southeast Asia; Yuezhi Zhao: China and Global Capitalism: the Cultural Dimension; Patrick Bond: US Empire and South African Subimperialism; Doug Stokes: US Counterinsurgency in Colombia; Paul Cammack: 'Signs of the Times': Capitalism, Competitiveness, and the New Faces of Empire in Latin America; Boris Kagarlitsky: The Russian State in the Age of American Empire; John Grahl: The European Union and American Power; Dorothee Bohle: The EU and Eastern Europe: Failing the Test as a Better World Power; Frank Deppe: Habermas' Manifesto for a European Renaissance: A Critique; Tony Benn & Colin Leys: Bush and Blair: Iraq and the American Viceroy

343 pp. 234 x 156 mm.

0850365465 hbk £35.00   **0850365473 pbk £14.95**
Canada: Fernwood Publishing; USA: Monthly Review Press; UK and Rest of World: Merlin Press

Leo Panitch and Colin Leys – Editors
2004: THE NEW IMPERIAL CHALLENGE

"As Rosa Luxemburg observed, it is 'often hard to determine, within the tangle of violence and contests for power, the stern laws of economic process.' This is what Panitch, Gindin, Harvey, Gowan, and their colleagues on the Marxist left are trying to do …. For this, whatevever our other differences, the rest of us owe them much gratitude" George Scialabba, *Dissent*, Spring 2004

What does imperialism mean in the new century?
Do we need new concepts to understand it?
Who benefits, who suffers? Where? Why?

Contents: Leo Panitch & Sam Gindin: Global Capitalism and American Empire; Aijaz Ahmad: Imperialism of Our Time; David Harvey: The 'New' Imperialism - Accumulation by Dispossession; Greg Albo: The Old and New Economics of Imperialism; Noam Chomsky: Truths and Myths about the Invasion of Iraq; Amy Bartholomew & Jennifer Breakspear: Human Rights as Swords of Empire; Paul Rogers: The US Military Posture - 'A Uniquely Benign Imperialism'?; Michael T. Klare: Blood for Oil - The Bush-Cheney Energy Strategy; John Bellamy Foster & Brett Clark: Ecological Imperialism - The Curse of Capitalism; Tina Wallace: NGO Dilemmas - Trojan Horses for Global Neoliberalism?; John Saul: Globalization, Imperialism, Development - False Binaries and Radical Resolutions; Emad Aysha: The Limits and Contradictions of 'Americanization'; Bob Sutcliffe: Crossing Borders in the New Imperialism.

290 pp. 234 x 156 mm.

0850365341 hbk £30.00   **085036535X pbk £14.95**
Canada: Fernwood Publishing; USA: Monthly Review Press; UK and Rest of World: Merlin Press

Leo Panitch and Colin Leys – Editors
2003: FIGHTING IDENTITIES – Race, Religion And Ethno-Nationalism

"these contributions... show a left able to avoid both economic reductionism and post-modern identity-fetishism in confronting and understanding a world of mounting anxiety, instability and violence." Stephen Marks, *Tribune*.

Contents: Peter Gowan: The American Campaign for Global Sovereignty; Aziz Al-Azmeh: Postmodern Obscurantism and 'the Muslim Question'; Avishai Ehrlich: Palestine, Global Politics and Israeli Judaism; Susan Woodward: The Political Economy of Ethno-Nationalism in Yugoslavia; Georgi Derluguian: How Soviet Bureaucracy Produced Nationalism and what came of it in Azerbaijan; Pratyush Chandra: Linguistic-Communal Politics and Class Conflict in India; Mahmood Mamdani: Making Sense of Political Violence in Postcolonial Africa;

Hugh Roberts: The Algerian Catastrophe: Lessons for the Left; Stephen Castles: The International Politics of Forced Migration; Hans-Georg Betz: Xenophobia, Identity Politics and Exclusionary Populism in Western Europe; Jörg Flecker: The European Right and Working Life- From ordinary miseries to political disasters; Huw Beynon & Lou Kushnick: Cool Britannia or Cruel Britannia? Racism and New Labour; Bill Fletcher Jr. & Fernando Gapasin: The Politics of Labour and Race in the USA; Amory Starr: Is the North American Anti-Globalization Movement Racist? Critical reflections; Stephanie Ross: Is This What Democracy Looks Like? -The politics of the anti-globalization movement in North America; Sergio Baierle: The Porto Alegre Thermidor: Brazil's 'Participatory Budget' at the crossroads; Nancy Leys Stepan: Science and Race: Before and after the Genome Project; John S. Saul: Identifying Class, Classifying Difference

396 pp, 234 x 156 mm.

0850365074 hbk £29.95   **0850365082 pbk £16.95**
Canada: Fernwood Publishing; USA: Monthly Review Press; UK and Rest of World: Merlin Press

Leo Panitch and Colin Leys – Editors
2002: A WORLD OF CONTRADICTIONS

Timely and critical analysis of what big businesses and their governments want, and of the problems they create.

Contents: Naomi Klein: Farewell To 'The End Of History': Organization And Vision In Anti-Corporate Movements; André Drainville: Québec City 2001 and The Making Of Transnational Subjects; Gérard Duménil & Dominique Lévy: The Nature and Contradictions of Neoliberalism; Elmar Altvater: The Growth Obsession; David Harvey The Art Of Rent: Globalization, Monopoly and The Commodification of Culture; Graham Murdock & Peter Golding: Digital Possibilities, Market Realities: The Contradictions of Communications Convergence; Reg Whitaker: The Dark Side of Life: Globalization and International Crime; Guglielmo Carchedi: Imperialism, Dollarization and The Euro; Susanne Soederberg: The New International Financial Architecture: Imposed Leadership and 'Emerging Markets'; Paul Cammack: Making Poverty Work; Marta Russell & Ravi Malhotra: Capitalism and Disability; Michael Kidron: The Injured Self; David Miller: Media Power and Class Power: Overplaying Ideology; Pablo Gonzalez Casanova: Negotiated Contradictions; Ellen Wood: Contradictions: Only in Capitalism?

293 pp, 234 x 156 mm.

0850365023 hbk £30.00   **0850365015 pbk £16.95**
Canada: Fernwood Publishing; USA: Monthly Review Press; UK and Rest of World: Merlin Press

Previous volumes:

Leo Panitch and Colin Leys – Editors
2001: WORKING CLASSES, GLOBAL REALITIES

Socialist Register 2001 examines the concept and the reality of class as it effects workers at the beginning of the 21st Century.

"an excellent collection". Bill Fletcher, *Against The Current*

Contents: Leo Panitch & Colin Leys with Greg Albo & David Coates: Preface; Ursula Huws: The Making of a Cybertariat? Virtual Work in a Real World ; Henry Bernstein: 'The Peasantry' in Global Capitalism: Who, Where and Why?; Beverly J. Silver and Giovanni Arrighi: Workers North and South; Andrew Ross: No-Collar Labour in America's 'New Economy'; Barbara Harriss-White & Nandini Gooptu: Mapping India's World of Unorganized Labour; Patrick Bond, Darlene Miller & Greg Ruiters: The Southern African Working Class: Production, Reproduction and Politics; Steve Jefferys: Western European Trade Unionism at 2000; David Mandel: 'Why is there no revolt?' The Russian Working Class and Labour Movement; Haideh Moghissi & Saeed Rahnema: The Working Class and the Islamic State in Iran ; Huw Beynon & Jorge Ramalho: Democracy and the Organization of Class Struggle in Brazil; Gerard Greenfield: Organizing, Protest and Working Class Self-Activity: Reflections on East Asia; Rohini Hensman: Organizing Against the Odds: Women in India's Informal Sector; Eric Mann: 'A race struggle, a class struggle, a women's struggle all at once': Organizing on the Buses of L.A.; Justin Paulson: Peasant Struggles and International Solidarity: the Case of Chiapas; Judith Adler Hellman: Virtual Chiapas: A Reply to Paulson ; Peter Kwong: The Politics of Labour Migration: Chinese Workers in New York; Brigitte Young: The 'Mistress' and the Maid' in the Globalized Economy; Rosemary Warskett: Feminism's Challenge to Unions in the North: Possibilities and Contradictions; Sam Gindin: Turning Points and Starting Points: Brenner, Left Turbulence and Class Politics; Leo Panitch: Reflections on Strategy for Labour.

403 pp. 232 x 155 mm.

0 85036 491 4 hbk £30.00   **0 85036 490 6 pbk £16.95**

Canada: Fernwood Publishing; USA: Monthly Review Press; UK and Rest of World: Merlin Press

Leo Panitch and Colin Leys – Editors
2000: NECESSARY AND UNNECESSARY UTOPIAS

What is Utopia? An economy that provides everyone's needs? A society which empowers all people? A healthy, peaceful and supportive environment ? Better worlds are both necessary and possible. "This excursion to utopia is full of surprise, inspiration and challenge". Peter Waterman

Contents: Preface; Transcending Pessimism: Rekindling Socialist Imagination: Leo Panitch & Sam Gindin; Minimum Utopia: Ten Theses: Norman Geras; Utopia and its Opposites: Terry Eagleton; On the Necessity of Conceiving the Utopian in a Feminist Fashion: Frigga Haug; Socialized Markets; not Market Socialism: Diane Elson; The Chimera of the Third Way: Alan Zuege; Other Pleasures: The Attractions of Post-consumerism: Kate Soper; Utopian Families: Johanna Brenner; Outbreaks of Democracy: Ricardo Blaug; Real and Virtual Chiapas: Magic Realism and the Left: Judith Adler Hellman; The Centrality of Agriculture: History; Ecology And Feasible Socialism: Colin Duncan; Democratise or Perish: The Health Sciences as a Path for Social Change: Julian Tudor Hart; The Dystopia of our Times: Genetic Technology and Other Afflictions: Varda Burstyn; Warrior Nightmares: Reactionary Populism at the Millennium: Carl Boggs; The Real Meaning of the War Over Kosovo: Peter Gowan.

301 pp. 232 x 155 mm.

0850364884 hbk £30.00   **0 850364876 pbk £14.95**
Canada: Fernwood Publishing; USA: Monthly Review Press; UK and Rest of World: Merlin Press

All Merlin Press titles can be ordered via our web site: www.merlinpress.
co.uk

In case of difficulty obtaining Merlin Press titles outside the UK, please contact
the following:

Australia:
Merlin Press Agent and stockholder:
Eleanor Brasch Enterprises. PO Box 586, Artamon NSW 2064 Email:
brasch2@aol.com

Canada:
Publisher:
Fernwood Publishing, 32 Oceanvista Lane, Site 2A, Box 5, Black Point, NS B0J
1B0
Tel: +1 902 857 1388: Fax: +1 902 857 1328 Email: errol@fernpub.ca

South Africa:
Merlin Press Agent:
Blue Weaver Marketing
PO Box 30370, Tokai, Cape Town 7966, South Africa
Tel. 21 701-4477 Fax. 21 701-7302 Email: orders@blueweaver.co.za

USA:
Merlin Press Agent and stockholder: Independent Publishers Group, 814 North
Franklin Street, Chicago, IL 60610.
Tel: +1 312 337 0747 Fax: +1 312 337 5985 frontdesk@ipgbook.com

Publisher:
Monthly Review Press, 122 West 27th Street, New York, NY 10001
Tel: +1 212 691 2555 promo@monthlyreview.org